COMPARATIVE IN
& EMPLOYMENT RELATIONS

COMPARATIVE INDUSTRIAL & EMPLOYMENT RELATIONS

edited by

Joris Van Ruysseveldt,
Rien Huiskamp &
Jacques van Hoof

OU *in association with the*
Open University of the Netherlands

S SAGE Publications
London • Thousand Oaks • New Delhi

First published 1995

SAGE Publications Ltd
6 Bonhill Street
London EC2A 4PU

SAGE Publications Inc
2455 Teller Road
Thousand Oaks, California 91320

SAGE Publications India Pvt Ltd
32, M-Block Market
Greater Kailash - I
New Delhi 110 048

British Library Cataloguing in Publication data

A catalogue record for this book is available
from the British Library

ISBN 0 8039 7966 5
ISBN 0 8039 7967 3 pbk

Library of Congress catalog card number 95-69793

Typeset by Photoprint, Torquay, Devon
Printed in Great Britain by Redwood Books, Trowbridge,
Wiltshire

Contents

Acknowledgements

A book like the present one, which explores a wide variety of topics in the field of employment and industrial relations, and which does so from a comparative perspective, can only be the product of teamwork. I would like to thank the various authors for their persistence and patience in the face of repeated requests for revision of their texts. This book originated from a Dutch Open University distant teaching course on Industrial Relations in Europe. Several people were involved in producing a translated and extensively revised version of this course. I particularly wish to thank Arndt Sorge for praising the original Dutch edition of this book and for encouraging us to have it translated into English. My colleagues Jos Claessen, Jasper von Grumbkow and Frits Kluytmans provided valuable assistance in the form of funding, comments and moral support. I would also like to thank those students who gave the first draft of the manuscript a trial reading for their critical and useful remarks.

I would further like to express my thanks and admiration to Cecilia Willems-Gretton, who translated the chapters written in Dutch. Annette Bouwels, John Schobre, Jet Quadekker and Albert Kampermann dealt skilfully with the preparation, layout and word-processing of the manuscript and provided logistical support. I have been most impressed by the punctuality, attention to detail and conscientiousness shown by Sage while transforming our manuscript into a book. These qualities and the friendliness and helpfulness of Sage's staff have made our cooperation extremely pleasant. I would especially like to thank Stephen Barr, Nicola Harris and the freelance copyeditor, Elaine Leek.

Joris Van Ruysseveldt
Lummen

Notes on the contributors

Ben Dankbaar studied Social Science and Economics at the University of Amsterdam and received his PhD from the University of Limburg with a dissertation entitled 'Economic crisis and institutional change: the crisis of Fordism from the perspective of the automobile industry'. From 1976 to 1982 he served as Lecturer for the Economic Seminar of the Faculty of Social Sciences at the University of Amsterdam. In 1982 he moved to Berlin and worked for the Wissenschaftszentrum Berlin für Sozialforschung and the VDI-Technologiezentrum. Since then he has worked at MERIT (Maastricht Economic Research Institute on Innovation and Technology), where he heads the Technology, Work and Organization research unit.

Jacques van Hoof is Professor of Industrial Sociology at the Dutch Open University and Professor of Empirical Sociology at the University of Leyden. Many of his publications deal with such labour market and industrial relations problems as unemployment, education and training, working time reduction, and paid and unpaid work. His present research focuses on relating these topics to wider issues of social stratification in a post-industrial society. His recent publications include a book on the transformation of industrial relations in Central and Eastern Europe (*Westbound?* together with H. Slomp and K. Verrips).

Rien (M.J.) Huiskamp studied Economic Sociology at the Free University of Amsterdam. In 1971 he was appointed Lecturer at the University of Amsterdam; he has also been Visiting Fellow at the London School of Economics and at the Industrial Relations Research Unit, Warwick University. As Senior Lecturer he published a study on shop stewards in the British engineering industry 1830–1975 (PhD, 1976). He worked for several years in personnel management and in the early 1980s joined the Dutch Social Economic Council as a staff member. In the early 1990s he established Huiskamp Research and Consultancy. He is also part-time tutor at the Dutch Open University. His present research interests focus on the re-engineering of collective bargaining, human resource management, and teamwork.

Willem de Lange is head of the Personnel Management and Quality of Work unit at the IVA, where he has worked since October 1991. He studied Economics at Tilburg University and received his degree in 1978. Between 1977 and 1991 he worked at Tilburg University, first as a member of the academic staff of the Organizational Science Department (Faculty of

Economics), and from 1989 to 1991 as Senior University Lecturer for the Personnel Studies Department (Social Sciences Faculty). In 1989 he received his PhD for the dissertation 'De configuratie van arbeid – Vormgeven aan arbeidstijden, bedrijfstijden en arbeidstijdpatronen'. His current activities focus on research and consultancy in the areas of personnel management, work periods and break periods/working time patterns and the quality of working life.

David Marsden studied French and Russian at the Sorbonne University (Paris) and Philosophy, Politics and Economics in Oxford and Leeds. He received his Doctorat d'Etat from the University of Aix-Marseille with a critique of the economic analysis of labour markets ('Marchés du travail: limites sociales des nouvelles théories/The end of economic man? Custom and competition in labour markets'). He is currently Reader in Industrial Relations at the London School of Economics. His current research interests are the impact of industrial relations and management practices on unemployment; pay structures and management practices; comparative labour markets and industrial relations in Western Europe.

Albert Mok is Professor of Business Policy at the University of Antwerp (Belgium) and Wageningen Agricultural University (the Netherlands). He has published articles and books on general sociology, occupations and professions, labour market segmentation, management culture and service work.

Joris Van Ruysseveldt is Assistant Professor at the Open University of the Netherlands. He studied Sociology of Labour and Organization at the University of Louvain in Belgium and is preparing his dissertation on recent developments in industrial relations and personnel policy in Belgium. He has served as editor/co-editor for the following publications: *Kwaliteit van de arbeid* (1989), *Oosteuropese arbeidsverhoudingen* (1993), *International HRM* (1995) and *Industrial Relations in Europe* (1996). His own writings focus on industrial relations and personnel policy in the context of technological and organizational innovation, European industrial relations, international HRM and the quality of working life.

Arndt Sorge specializes in the organization and management of industrial enterprises, vocational education and training, and personnel policy and industrial relations. He studied Economics and Sociology at the Universities of Freiburg and Cologne, Germany. Since 1972 he has held academic posts in Germany, England, France and the Netherlands. His books include *Informationstechnik und Arbeit im sozialen Prozess* (1985) and *Comparative Factory Organization* (with Malcolm Warner) (1986). Since the end of 1992 he has served as Professor of Industrial and Organization Sociology at Humboldt University, Berlin.

Kea Tijdens is Senior Lecturer for the Faculty of Economics at the

University of Amsterdam (the Netherlands). She has published articles and books on the impact of information technology on clerical workers, personnel composition in banks, occupations segregation and the gender gap in banking.

Jelle Visser is Associate Professor of Sociology at the University of Amsterdam. He has taught at and received fellowships from the European University Institute in Florence, the University of Mannheim, the University of Wisconsin, Stanford University and Nuffield College (Oxford). He has written about European industrial relations, trade unions, labour participation, working time and the transnational organization. His books include *European Trade Unions in Figures* (1989), *In Search of Inclusive Unions* (1994) and (with Bert Klandermans) *De vakbeweging na de welvaartsstaat* (1994).

Frans van Waarden is Professor of Organization and Policy for the General Social Sciences Department at the University of Utrecht. He studied Sociology in Toronto and Leyden and worked for the Universities of Leyden and Constance. His writings focus on industrial relations, co-determination, the history of technology, the cotton industry, industrial policy, unemployment, interest groups and corporatism, employers' associations and the relationship between government and business. His publications include *Fabriekslevens* (1987, co-author), *Het geheim van Twente* (1987, about employers' associations in the cotton industry), *Organisatiemacht van belangenverenigingen* (1989, co-author), *Organizing Business for War: Industrial Policy and Corporatism During the Second World War* (1991, joint editor) and *Culture of Unemployment* (1993, co-author). He is presently working on a study comparing the policy styles of public servants in their dealings with interest groups.

PART 1

INTRODUCTION

---

1 Growing cross-national diversity or diversity *tout court*? An introduction to comparative industrial and employment relations

Joris Van Ruysseveldt

---

1 Employment relations and industrial relations

Employees are only willing to perform and employers only willing to utilize labour under certain specific conditions reflecting a wide variety of issues: wages and other employment terms and conditions, working hours, job autonomy, opportunities for promotion, and employee participation in company policy-making. These issues emerge in the continuous exchange between the two parties involved in the employment relationship. They do not regulate every aspect of the employment relationship, however; there is also consultation and negotiation between the organizations which represent their interests, namely the trade unions and employers' associations. After all, no modern society has ever accepted a purely individual-istic determination of the employment relationship (see Hartog and Theeuwes, 1993: 422). Indeed, modern societies have developed a whole range of *labour market institutions*, ranging from social custom and moral codes to labour law and collective agreements, that is, the outcome of collective bargaining at an aggregate level which lies above the private level between employer and employee.

The Fordist type of employment relationship and beyond

Between the two world wars, and in particular immediately following the Second World War, most Western capitalist economies developed institu-tions *to govern the employment relationship*. These institutions did not develop at the same pace and in the same way in every country. In general, however, a process of *collectivization and institutionalization* of the employment relationship got under way. Employment terms and con-ditions were increasingly subject to a form of collective regulation involving the trade unions, usually at the industry or national level, but in some cases at the company level as well. The process of collectivization was accompanied by increasing *standardization* of employment terms. Between the Second World War and the 1980s, the terms of employment within industries and companies converged more and more. Variation, for example based on job category, professional status, company size or region, was tolerated, but only within strict sectoral or nationally agreed parameters.

It was under the relatively favourable economic conditions of continuous growth and quasi-full employment that what are considered to be modern labour standards began to evolve. By labour standards we mean more or less generally accepted and enforceable norms which stipulate the con-ditions under which work is to be performed. Gradually the *Fordist* type of employment relationship came to dominate the labour market. This rather stable employment relationship is characterized – at least as far as European countries are concerned – by a permanent, full-time job, wage increases based on experience and training, additional bonuses for incon-veniences and unfavourable working conditions, regular working hours and a collectively arranged working week, paid holidays, the general right to collective representation when establishing employment terms and a certain degree of (indirect) participation in specific areas of company policy. The Fordist employment relationship is not only linked to post-war industrial relations, but also to the type of production organization which prevailed during that period – the Taylorist organization. As mass producers of standardized, price-competitive goods, these organizations supplied what were often protected domestic markets that had not yet been saturated. They were generally highly mechanized and had an extreme horizontal and vertical division of labour. The goal of such organizations was to become as efficient as possible by calculating and controlling production, labour and worker behaviour as much as possible. This meant the *centralization* of management and the *bureaucratization* of the organization, that is, the detailed demarcation of jobs and competencies, close supervision of work, elaboration of hierarchical lines of authority and the development of a personnel policy which aimed to rationalize employee relations. Although in theory it was easy to replace unskilled and semi-skilled production workers within Taylorist production processes, companies were put under pressure by quasi-full employment and union strength to extend to all employee groups their policy of binding employees to the company by means of durable employment relationships. This *internalization* of the labour market led to greater job security and the prospect of a more or less predetermined career with increasingly attractive employment conditions and job opportunities.

From the mid-1970s on, however, both industrial relations and employment relationships underwent a fundamental change. Again, such changes have not affected every country in an equal and comparable fashion. In general, we can say that pressure has been brought to bear on the dominant Fordist employment relationship and related labour standards. For example there has been a striking, although initially modest rise in the number of temporary and/or part-time jobs and of different types of flexible work. This phenomenon was initially called *atypical employment*. However, the number of jobs which deviate from the 'normal' Fordist employment relationship pattern has grown so dramatically in the past decade that we are justified in asking whether this atypical employment is indeed so very atypical. Job security has probably been put under the greatest pressure in recent years. First, most companies were involved in far-reaching reorganizations. In general, economic restructuring was not only accompanied by the internal relocation of personnel but also by mass redundancies. Secondly, jobs that offer a reasonable degree of security to newcomers in organizations have become a rare commodity. Confronted with uncertainty in the market and with the high costs of dismissals, employers prefer to hire younger employees on a temporary basis. Only the high performers among the newcomers can count on more or less stable jobs and attractive career prospects in the company. Thirdly, many companies are introducing lean production, concentrating on core activities and hiving off unprofitable and non-core activities to subcontractors and specialist suppliers. Consequently, the internal job market tends to be reduced to the core employees. Employment at subcontractors and suppliers – often small or medium-sized enterprises with no trade union representation on the shop floor – is generally less stable and offers less favourable employment terms and working conditions. Finally, even the security enjoyed by core employees in the internal labour market has become something other than the near 'lifetime employment' of decades past. Evidence can be found in the concept of 'employability', the new management watchword. 'Employability' means that while the employee cannot expect a guarantee of lifetime employment, his or her employer will help maintain that employee's market value, for example by providing opportunities to retrain or to update knowledge. Security no longer depends on a job or an organization, but on the employee's competences and willingness to learn and adapt to changes in the organization and the market. Core employees, incidentally, pay a heavy price for their position within the organization; in the present circumstances of persistent high unemployment, they are under constant pressure to improve their performance.

Growing heterogeneity on the demand and supply side of labour markets

In general, companies now face fierce competition, and this in turn affects the employment relationship, which is increasingly subject to the logic of the market. Competition between companies has gradually filtered through to affect the labour exchange. This becomes obvious when we look at changes in the area of wages. There is serious pressure to develop more flexible wage systems which tolerate greater variation. Wages should vary much more depending on productivity or the added value that employees bring to their work. The idea is that fluctuations in wages should correspond to fluctuations in productivity. This leads, among other things, to the decentralization of wage bargaining and consequently to an increasing wage gap between companies. There is also growing support for the idea of lowering or even abolishing the minimum wage, which is being blamed for high unemployment among unskilled, less productive workers. Even within companies, there is a tendency to link wages more directly to individual or group performance. Evidence can be found in 'payment-by-results' schemes (PBR), in which a portion of an employee's wage is variable and depends on achieving certain targets related to output, productivity, product quality, material or machine utilization, customer satisfaction and so on. PBR schemes encourage employees to carry out more thorough preventive maintenance, avoid production stops, constantly monitor product quality and so on. There is also greater variety and more flexible arrangements with respect to working time. Although jobs with more or less fixed working hours (9 to 5, five days a week) and a fixed number of hours a week (generally between 35 and 40) still predominate, in recent years there has been a major increase in the number of working time arrangements tailored specifically to meet a company's or employee's needs. In addition to the spread of part-time jobs, the number of flexible working arrangements has also increased sharply. Such arrangements allow better coordination between the deployment of labour and the company's requirements. The number of hours worked daily, weekly or monthly varies depending on the production capacity required. Again, the indication is that the employment relationship is increasingly subject to market forces.

Recent years have seen more flexible, less uniform and more diverse employment relationships. Between the two extremes of stable employment relationships on the one hand and (post-Fordist?) flexible employment relationships on the other lies a growing range of options. Behind this increasing diversity, complex processes are at work which are giving rise to an increasing degree of heterogeneity in labour markets, both on the demand side (companies) and on the supply side (workforce).

The economic restructuring of recent decades together with social and demographic changes have had a tremendous impact on the *labour market*. The share of total employment accounted for by industry has dropped (de-industrialization), while employment in private and public services has risen. Nowadays there are fewer unskilled or semi-skilled industrial workers and more skilled, white-collar service or knowledge workers. The social composition of the workforce has also changed drastically, thanks in particular to a rise in the overall level of education, the *feminization* of the labour market (that is, the rising number of women participating in the formal economy) and the increasingly multi-ethnic nature of European society. Finally, the workforce has become much more heterogeneous as a consequence of cultural trends such as individualization. Today's employees are more inclined to articulate specific individual preferences and choices regarding their terms of employment; for example, they may want to arrange working hours around their family and social life. The labour movement was ill-prepared to deal with the increasingly hetero-geneous nature of the labour market. Its focus was traditionally on represent-ing the collective interests of a large, relatively homogeneous segment of the workforce, in particular male manual workers employed in manufac-turing. Increasing heterogeneity is forcing unions to search for innovative solutions to classic problems such as interest aggregation and articulation.

The demand side of the labour market has also seen a growing measure of heterogeneity. That is a result of the different ways in which companies – even those operating within the same industry – respond to developments in the market and in product technology. Changes in the market are becoming less predictable. The far-flung markets for standardized mass products are becoming saturated, slowly but surely. Moreover, individual-ization has made consumer tastes more varied, so that consumer demand has become fragmented. Finally, the barriers thrown up to protect domestic markets are gradually being dismantled by the progressive liberalization of the world economy. More than ever before, companies are competing on global markets. These events have landed managements in a situation of uncertainty, and they can no longer turn to 'one-best-way' solutions to their problems. Managements are being forced to make strategic choices with respect to market, competition, production and personnel policy. Between the uncertainty of management and the man-agement of this uncertainty (see Streeck, 1987) lies a wide variety of possible strategies and policy interventions, with distinct consequences for the structure of the organization and its personnel. Modern production technology has further expanded the number of alternatives. Micro-electronic information technology does not have as decisive an impact on the structure of the organization as did its predecessor, electro-mechanical technology (see Streeck, 1992b). Micro-electronic circuitry can support radically different patterns of work organization. Vastly increased capacities to process and transmit information allow for centralization of control and differentiation of tasks far beyond what was possible only a decade ago. At the same time, they also enable organizations to delegate decisions to flexible subunits with integrated, overlapping functions, so as to respond better to more complex and specific demands from their environment.

Strategic choices under uncertain conditions

From the viewpoint of personnel and organizational policy, the principal choice which management faces is that between competitiveness based on low prices/low costs and competitiveness based on production criteria such as quality, customer-specific production, product differentiation and innovation.

Low price/low cost-based competition presupposes at least one of the following two measures: a downward adjustment of labour costs (for example in the form of efficiency measures, redundancies or lower wages) and/or a sensitive improvement in performance and a more intensive deployment of labour (for example by increasing the work pace or by introducing new working methods and technology). In both instances, productivity rises. The most successful approach is to reduce labour costs and improve performance at the same time. Managements in Western capitalist economies which decide to pursue this competitive strategy will unavoidably find themselves facing some difficulties.

First, wages in modern economies tend to demonstrate downward inflexibility, a consequence of the institutionalized system of wage determination. In most European countries, companies can only succeed in introducing a downward adjustment in wages if they withdraw from collective wage bargaining systems and decide to act autonomously and unilaterally in setting the terms of employment for their employees. If a number of (larger) companies decide to do so, that would be the end not only of multi-employer bargaining but also of the practice of taking wages out of competition through collective bargaining. A second problem inherent to the low price/low cost strategy is that lower wages and higher productivity are generally thought to be mutually exclusive. It is almost impossible to lower wages and improve performance at the same time without creating social unrest. Sooner or later, employees who are forced to work harder will seize upon the rise in productivity and the subsequent increase in profit margins as a reason to demand wage rises. If management gives in to these demands, chances are that it will also gradually cut back on staff: small scale, gradual redundancies to compensate for wage rises of the remaining employees. This strategy may have a few undesirable, or at any rate irksome and in the long run intolerable side effects: the workload will increase, unemployment will rise, social security expenditure will increase substantially and the difference between 'insider' wages and 'outsider' benefits will increase.

Theoretically it should be possible for Western producers to avoid the problems associated with a low price/low cost-oriented strategy by moving certain parts of the production process to countries which offer employees lower wages, with a lower level of social protection and with less powerful trade unions (the so-called relocation strategy). And indeed, in the past few decades labour-intensive production processes and activities have been relocated, leading to an international division of labour. We should note, however, that in many cases relocation is not prompted by low wages so much as by the opportunity to conquer fast-growing local markets. After all, not only are wages lower in developing countries than in modern capitalist economies, but so is productivity. Indeed, there is a good chance that unit labour costs may be lower in a given Western country than in a given low-wage country.

An alternative to low-price competitiveness is the so-called innovation or niche strategy, in which companies supply market segments which are less concerned with price and more concerned with quality, customer-specific production, a broad product range, short, reliable turnaround times and so on. This high wage/high skill/high productivity strategy has far-reaching implications for the structure of the organization, the composition of the existing staff and for personnel policy. The Taylorist production organization is not equipped to handle this type of competitive strategy, nor does it have the resources to supply a constantly changing market. Taylorist organizations must undergo a drastic transformation. A functionally integrated and decentralized organization is required, together with highly educated, multi-skilled employees who have non-specific, broad cognitive and social competences. It will be obvious that employment relationships in this innovative type of production organization are subject to an entirely different dynamic than those within Taylorist production organizations.

2 Analytical perspective

The available analytical and theoretical frameworks do not in our opinion succeed in providing a satisfactory analysis of the changes in employment and industrial relations. The analytical perspective presented in the present book distinguishes it from a host of other studies and handbooks in the field of comparative industrial relations.

The 'classic' analytical frameworks are a reflection of the times in which they were conceived: a time when employment in industry accounted for a greater share of overall employment than it does today; when a strong labour movement could depend on the support of a more or less homogeneous rank-and-file consisting of male industrial workers, and on a government which believed that the labour movement could play a part in supporting macro-economic change; when the labour market was populated by a relatively homogeneous workforce; when 'national' companies were more stable and bureaucratized because they supplied more or less predictable, protected domestic markets which had not yet reached the saturation point; and when the national government, more than is the case today, still enjoyed full sovereignty in the field of national socioeconomic and fiscal policy. As mentioned before, the 1980s were a decade of change – change in organizations, in labour markets and in industrial relations. This means that we must reconsider thoroughly the existing analytical frameworks. It is particularly important to recall that there has been a fundamental shift in the position of the various different actors. The unfavourable economic climate of the 1970s and 1980s, the saturation of markets, the progressive liberalization of world trade and the removal of protective tariffs in certain markets all led to companies in advanced capitalist economies throwing all their effort during the past decade into improving their competitive position. They were backed by governments which had placed a premium on improving the competitive position of domestic trade and industry. This relative shift from macro-economic demand management to supply-side economic policies, and from institutionalized practices to management strategies, has had important consequences for the terms of employment. That is why it is no longer possible to analyse employment relationships as if they are relatively insulated from changes in markets and within organizations. Viewed from this perspective, many 'classic' industrial relations studies may devote too much attention to the formal, collective relations between the 'two sides of industry' – that is, the trade unions and employers' associations – and the state agencies. Mainstream authors in continental Europe put too much emphasis on 'collective relations' and not enough on work and employment terms and conditions. In our opinion, the institutions which undertake to regulate employment relations should be linked to the context in which work is performed and to the factors which influence this context.

When analysing the employment relationship, we should not only consider all the relevant factors, but also all the relevant actors. The criticism levelled at industrial relations studies and handbooks – that they give too much attention and weight to the collective actors and to industrial relations – is equally true of more recent studies and approaches, which only seem to focus on the actions (strategic or otherwise) of one specific party: management. It is true that the institutional ties have become 'looser' in recent years and that interest organizations have less influence than they used to, but that does not mean that the collective regulation of the employment relationship has disappeared altogether. While fierce competition has increased the pressure on management to improve company performance on an ongoing basis, management today has more room for manoeuvre when it comes to introducing innovative strategies in the field of personnel and organization. And indeed, in a number of instances management has actually taken advantage of its expanded scope. One piece of evidence can be found in such social and organizational innovations as human resources management, teamwork, total quality control, lean production techniques, kaizen, business re-engineering and so on (concepts which are not as widely and successfully diffused in practice as in the literature). None of this is meant to imply that recent changes in employment relations can be traced back solely to these management strategies, nor that analysis should shift from a concern with industrial relations to the flexible deployment and utilization of labour under the management prerogative. In our opinion, the employment relationship always involves a whole range of participants, all of whom should be taken into account in a balanced analysis. In the first instance there are the individual employer and employee who enter into the exchange. In addition, however, there are the collective actors such as interest organizations, the works councils, the trade union representatives on the shop floor, the autonomous workgroups, and the quality circles. All these participants have specific needs, goals, values and interests; they all have the ability to take action based on strategic choices.

The limits of the existing analytical frameworks have inspired us to develop a more balanced analytical framework for the present book. Here the *employment relationship* serves as the main concept, as the focus of analysis. This 'employment relationship' refers to the *conditions* under which an employer decides to hire labour and under which the employee decides to sell his manpower to the employer. These conditions are the result of a continuous exchange and are related to different aspects of the deployment of labour, for example wages and other employment terms, working hours and the working week, job security and career prospects, safety at the workplace, and job autonomy and control. We have taken the developments in employment relations as our central object of research. Such developments can only be understood when viewed in context, that is, from the perspective of the organizations in which labour is deployed, the markets in which these organizations operate, the institutions which regulate certain aspects of employment relations and the interest organizations which operate within this institutional framework. The employment relationship is the *result* of economic, social and technological developments, and of the way in which the various actors respond to such developments. It can also be viewed as a mirror which reflects interrelated changes in markets, organizations and institutions.

A comparative approach

Among continental EU member states, the most important terms of employment of at least two-thirds of the workforce are laid down in collective bargaining agreements; in Great Britain that applies to only 47 per cent of the workforce, in Japan to 25 per cent and in the United States to only 18 per cent (Traxler, 1994). There are considerable differences between European countries with respect to the importance of labour market institutions and the role they play in determining the terms of employment. Both the scope of collective action and the way in which workers and employers mobilize themselves to take collective action vary significantly from one country to the next (see Hartog and Theeuwes, 1993: 422).

Do institutions matter? Do interest organizations matter? These questions have lost none of their urgency in recent years. The globalization of markets, global competition, improved communication and transport technology and the development of trade blocs and supranational political institutions such as the European Union have made the need for cross-national comparative research even more pressing. Frequently such research gives priority to considerations: how are different countries performing and to which institutionalized practices can we attribute superior performance? At the socioeconomic level, the main question is how such institutions as nationwide or sectoral collective bargaining, extension practices, co-determination rights and so on contribute to a country's economic and social performance (for instance in terms of profits, GDP growth, employment growth and labour market participation rates, labour-market mobility, distribution of wealth, diffusion of new technology, social peace).

Although these practical questions are valid, we are much more interested in the scholarly significance of cross-national comparative research. We have not limited our work to the study of national differences in industrial relations. These differences are the subject of another book (*Industrial Relations in Europe*, Sage, 1996), edited by Jelle Visser and Joris Van Ruysseveldt. In the present book, our particular interest is the answer to the question: in what respect do institutions matter? More specifically, what are the consequences of labour market institutions for the terms and conditions under which work is performed? National differences in the areas of wages, working hours and flexible time arrangements, and organizational and qualification structures in companies, are all related to the system of industrial relations and the collective bargaining structure specific to a particular country.

3   Outline of the book

The present book takes as its subject the changes which have affected the employment relationship in recent years. We have narrowed our focus to the larger European countries and to three specific dimensions of the employment relationship: wages, working hours and qualifications (competences). These dimensions are placed within the context of changes which have affected the market, production technology, organizations and institutional relations. In addition, attention is given to institutions and interest organizations, once again against the background of important economic, technological and social changes.

Part 1 deals with important theoretical perspectives on industrial and employment relations and elaborates on the analytical framework applied in this book.

Interest organizations and industrial relations in a changing Europe

Part 2 deals with the interest organizations of employees and employers. In general, these organizations have had a long and often turbulent history. They have had to fight to gain legal and factual recognition from third parties and the government as the legitimate representatives of such interests. Employers' associations and trade unions have had a major impact on the economic and political history of their countries, and this history is in turn reflected in the identity and structure of these organizations. In recent years interest organizations have come under increasing pressure. Membership is falling, partly as a consequence of individualization and the general rise in the level of education, but also because there is growing scepticism about the utility of collective forms of regulation. They have also been affected by the loss of national sovereignty due to globalization, and by the fact that governments plagued by debt and uncontrollable budget deficits have less and less room for manoeuvre. Interest organizations are furthermore under attack from a more ideological viewpoint. Belief in their ability to make a constructive contribution to economic growth and social progress is fading away. Increasingly they are being held responsible (at least in part) for high (minimum) wages and the attendant high level of unemployment, for (excessively) short and inflexible working hours, for rigid job structures and for unnecessary delays in introducing technological, social and organizational innovation. In short, in the present-day context of far-reaching economic restructuring, interest organizations have, in the eyes of some, become part of the problem. Others, however, view them as part of the solution to socioeconomic problems. As we will see in Part 2, the contribution which interest organizations can make to socioeconomic development depends in part on their own organizational structure and resources.

The study of interest organizations should contribute on the one hand to a better understanding of the developments affecting industrial and employment relations. On the other hand, interest organizations are an 'independent' object of cross-national comparative research. Why and how do employees and employers organize? What are the problems and what solutions have been found? What resources and structures do interest organizations have at their disposal and how have they acquired them over the course of their social and political history? How have they recruited, retained and mobilized their members to undertake collective action? In what way have the members succeeded in influencing the strategies, programmes and interventions of their interest organizations? The cross-national comparative analyses set out in Chapters 3 and 4 show that both trade unions and employers' associations are complex organizations which juggle contradictory organizational requirements, because they must deal simultaneously with their own members and with other interest organiz-ations and state agencies. As interest organizations, their success depends on the degree to which they succeed in actually furthering the interests as perceived by their members. As participants in socioeconomic decision-making and as one of the parties which regulates the labour market, they are forced to make compromises. Hence, the credibility of interest organizations as bargaining partners depends on the degree to which they can compel their members to comply with the stipulations of a collective agreement. It is not surprising that external clout and internal democracy are often at odds within such organizations.

In Chapter 5 we will look at how the position and role of government in industrial relations varies between European countries. In the 1980s, the government seemed to be withdrawing, apparently intent on creating more room for free markets and for self-regulation by the market participants. This is a one-sided evaluation, however. It is probably better to say that governments redefined their roles and objectives. They have continued to intervene, but this time with a view to improving the competitiveness of their economies, for instance by cutting back on social expenditure in order to create a leaner welfare state, or by enforcing wage moderation in order to restore exports and fight unemployment. Industrial and employment relations have without a doubt felt the effect of the redefinition of government policy. Nevertheless, we should not underestimate the role of government in industrial relations. As legislator it regulates important substantive aspects of the employment relationship. It pursues a socio-economic policy, either in consultation with labour and management or alone. It determines to a large extent the rules of the game for industrial relations. It is even the biggest employer, and in this capacity it determines the terms of employment for a large section of the working population. Finally, the government provides important collective goods such as education, health care and infrastructure, without which a modern economy cannot function.

Institutional and organizational change

Part 3 focuses on the most important industrial relations institutions and processes. Chapter 6 discusses collective bargaining agreements, and Chapter 7 the various bodies, both voluntary and statutory, which provide a platform for employee participation in company policy-making. We will continue to look at differences between European countries as regards the importance of these institutions and how they function, as well as the changes which have become apparent in the past few years. Like many other aspects, collective bargaining structures have also felt the pinch of global competition. To retain or expand their share of the market, managements are at times forced to intervene drastically in the structure and technology of production, in the organization and working methods applied, and in areas of personnel policy. Company-specific solutions are being sought for company-specific problems. Whenever such solutions have repercussions for the terms of employment of at least a portion of the workforce, it is often the case that the chosen strategies are incompatible with provisions set out in the collective bargaining agreement. There is tension between the collective regulation of the employment relationship and the actual processes which are set in motion on the shop floor. This leads in a limited number of cases to deregulation, specifically the rejection of collective forms of regulation, and in extreme instances to a radical policy of union avoidance. In a number of other cases, a process of de-centralization gets under way; the regulation of the employment relationship no longer takes place at national or sectoral level, but rather at company or plant level. In general, in most countries collective bargaining structures have become more complex and flexible; the regulation of the employment relationship takes place at various more or less mutually coordinated levels, leaving more room for company-specific or even individual arrangements. The question is to what extent institutional innovations have been or are being introduced, and whether such innovations will make it possible for the parties to respond effectively to the processes of economic restructuring.

Wages, working time and qualifications

In Part 4 we look at changes in three dimensions of the employment relationship. Chapter 8 offers an analysis of wage differences, not only between countries but also between sectors and job categories within countries. The chapter also discusses why wage differentials have increased since the 1980s in most European countries. In Chapter 9 we discuss national differences in working time arrangements, a volatile subject in the field of industrial relations in recent decades – recall, for example, the strongly articulated demand for a collective reduction in working hours as a means to create new jobs. In the mid-1980s a shift became evident in most West European countries from collective working time reduction to more flexible working time arrangements and extended operating hours. The reason for this shift is that management had 'discovered' time as a manipulable factor of production. In many countries, flexible working time arrangements are an outcome of collective bargaining. On the other hand the importance of individual agreements between employer and employee on this issue has increased as well.

Chapter 10 explores a third dimension of the employment relationship, that is, the competences required to perform a job. The qualitative aspects of the employment relationship are seldom the object of collective regulation. Nevertheless, cross-national comparative studies have shown that there is a relationship between the organizational structure of companies and the educational and industrial institutions which typify a particular country. The societal effect approach proposes that differences in the way companies are organized are related not only to technological and economic factors (contingencies), but also to social and institutional factors (societal effect).

New technologies, organizational change and employment relations

Finally, in Part 5, we take a dynamic view of the relationship between markets, organizations, employment and industrial relations. A comparison of different countries in Chapter 11 once again reveals that the way in which companies respond to developments in the markets they supply and the repercussions that these responses have for the organization and qualification structure are influenced by the industrial relations system specific to that country. We may conclude, then, that institutions do matter and that they should continue to be the object of study.

In Chapters 12 and 13 we look at the interrelations between developments in markets and technology, organizations and industrial relations in three important industrial sectors: the automobile industry, the banking industry and the retail trade. Our observation remains the same: competition has placed common pressure on enterprises in the same industry to improve performance. Economic rivalry impels enterprises to compare their methods and accomplishments and to imitate those practices which lead to improved performance. Innovations in personnel and organizational policy often have an impact on industrial and employment relations. However, there is no direct relationship such that each intensification of competition has immediate and direct consequences for industrial and employment relations. Competitive pressure does not therefore necessarily lead to convergence, or to the evolution of comparable labour market institutions. On the one hand, institutions are an important influence on the way companies respond to competitive pressure. On the other hand, the goal of enterprises is not to transform industrial and employment relations, but to remain competitive. If that goal can be achieved within the parameters of existing institutions, they are not likely to be altered.

4   Convergence or fragmentation?

It was not the intention of the editors of this book to provide an all-inclusive description and analysis of developments in the field of industrial and employment relations in Europe. It is becoming more and more problematic to describe such developments with overused terms and concepts such as decentralization and flexibility. Reality is growing subtler and more complex, and developments are often ambiguous or paradoxical. Then again, developments in industrial relations and those in employment relations often lead to very different results.

We expect that the future will bring only greater diversity in employment terms and industrial relations, not only between countries and sectors but also between companies and occupations. The question for the future, then, is not so much whether we will see 'growing or declining cross-national diversity', but whether we will see growing 'diversity *tout court*', that is to say at all levels and in all sectors of the economy. Instead of the convergence of country-specific systems of industrial relations towards a common (European) model, the years ahead may instead reveal the disappearance of national models and the development of more fragmented labour markets with increasingly important 'new' actors (such as works councils or quality circles), and the development of institutions closely allied to specific parts of these fragmented labour markets. Diversity is increasing; alongside classic institutions for the regulation of the employment relationship – more specifically collective bargaining above the level of the company – other, 'new' forms are emerging: consultations at company level (whether or not within the context of statutory bodies), individual bargaining between employer and employee, or unilateral decision-making by employers as a consequence of the gradual restoration of management prerogatives. Whether the process of de-collectivization and fragmentation continues and becomes dominant will depend among other things on government policy. Do European governments consider deregulation and flexibilization of the labour market as the only effective instruments to combat the persistently high rate of unemployment? Or are they setting a new course leading to new, economy-wide institutions focusing, for example, on the redistribution of labour or on a structural reduction in labour costs along with the preservation of modern labour standards?

It is our hope that the analytical framework presented in this book will make a significant contribution to the analysis of future developments in industrial and employment relations.

2 Regulating the employment relationship: an analytical framework

Rien Huiskamp

1 Introduction

Our goal in this chapter is to develop a closer understanding of the dynamics of organizational and institutional relationships. To achieve this goal, we will apply a perspective which deviates from that used in classic analyses: we will focus not so much on the system or subsystem of industrial relations in relation to other subsystems, but rather on the direct relationship between employer and employee within the company: the employment relationship (ER).

The chapter will give a detailed definition of the concept of the employment relationship and describe the consequences of this innovative perspective for industrial relations analysis.

2 The employment relationship: definition and analysis

The term 'employment relationship' can be traced in the English-language literature to such authors as Fox (1974), Barbash (1984), Williamson (1985) and Watson (1987), who treated the employment relationship explicitly as distinct from the system of industrial relations. Box 2.1 summarizes Barbash's analysis of the employment relationship by way of example.

> ## Box 2.1 *Barbash's analysis of the employment relationship*
>
> One of the few authors in the field of industrial relations to concentrate on the employment relationship is Barbash. In his approach the employment relationship replaces the system of industrial relations as the object of analysis. Barbash believes that the interaction at work between employer and employee is largely aimed at regulating the employment relationship.
>
> Figure 2.1 summarizes the most important elements of Barbash's analysis. The following points are central to the figure. First, there is the degree to which the behaviour of management and employees/trade unions is determined by market forces. This is in contrast to many other analyses of industrial relations, in which the connection between market forces and the behaviour of the actors is not so direct. In Barbash's view, management behaviour is determined by fluctuations in the product market, whereas the behaviour of the employees is heavily influenced by the labour market. The product market stimulates management to attempt to achieve cost discipline. Constant pressure on prices on the product market results in the need to use labour as efficiently as possible and to keep the cost of labour as low as possible. Management sees labour in the first instance as a good or commodity, but one which is nevertheless furnished by people. Management purchases the presence of people and their willingness to work, which must then be converted into effort. The result is a large number of systems geared to controlling employee behaviour. The second main element in Barbash's analysis is that the behaviour of the actors is guided by an intention, by a social principle. For management, that principle is cost efficiency as dictated by the product market. In Barbash's view, the labour market situation determines to what extent employees will accept the relationship imposed by the employer between the price of labour and the effort which is to be made in return. Employees and trade unions are therefore a countervailing force, providing a balance against management's constant efforts to control costs. They not only negotiate over the price of labour, they also focus on the effort which is required during the labour process. Employees and trade unions emphasize equity as a social principle, as opposed to management's cost efficiency. Management in turn resists the limitations which employees impose on the attempt to achieve efficiency.

In Barbash's view, the employment relationship is given shape:

- within the limitations imposed by the product and labour markets;
- in the exchange between the price of labour (wages) and performance;
- in a permanent system of negotiations, since a formal employment contract cannot be expected to define the relationship between price and performance in detail, and because cost control must be repeatedly emphasized and achieved.

Formulated in this fashion, the employment relationship covers a field much wider than does the individual employment contract between

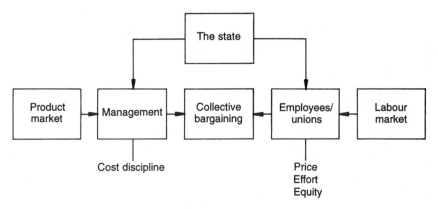

Figure 2.1   *Barbash's analysis of the employment relationship*

employer and employee. Only part of this relationship is written down in an employment contract. Watson (1987) distinguishes between explicit and implicit employment contracts. Employer and employee enter into a relationship and become parties to a written agreement. The formal employment contract only covers certain rights and obligations on such matters as wages and working hours. However, employees place their skills at the disposal of the employer and surrender part of their autonomy and decision-making capacity; the employer, in turn, expects them to defer to his decision-making authority. In return he offers them a measure of job satisfaction and status, and may create expectations concerning career opportunities. Many of these aims and expectations are not laid down in the formal employment contract, nor can they be. They form an implicit contract between the employer and the employee.

Each time an employer and employee wish to enter into a work relationship, an exchange takes place. The employer is only prepared to hire labour under certain conditions; by the same token, the employee is only willing to apply his or her labour in the production process under certain conditions. In rare cases, the employer and employee will immediately agree on these conditions. Most of the time, however, there is a need to negotiate: both parties make promises and offers, use their position of power to obtain the best possible conditions and ultimately reach agreement or decide not to enter into an exchange after all.

The term employment relationship refers to the conditions under which the employer decides to hire labour and the employee decides to sell his manpower to the employer. These conditions are related to the specific characteristics which distinguish exchange on the labour market from that which occurs on other markets in terms of:

- the nature of the exchange;
- the position (of power) of the parties to the exchange;

- the regulation of the exchange.

We will discuss each of these points below in the same order.

3   The nature of the exchange

The employment relationship covers every aspect of labour, either explicitly or implicitly. In addition to wages, the employer offers an individual way of dealing with people and the quality of the work to be done. Is the work mind-numbingly monotonous or varied? Is the employee allowed a measure of responsibility? Is the work clean and safe? The answer to these questions determines what the employer has to offer. The employee also has a major input. First of all, there is the employee's educational background, training, experience and specialist know-how. In addition, the employee contributes enthusiasm and involvement in his or her work. And we should not forget to mention the amount of time that he or she intends to spend on the job.

The exchange in the employment relationship may therefore involve many different aspects. Some of them will give rise to explicit negotiations. Others will only become bargaining issues at a later stage – for example when they become problematical.

Our analysis now requires us to distinguish three substantive dimensions in the employment relationship. The relationship is based on an exchange between work and non-work hours, required and available qualifications, and wages and performance. Time, qualifications and wages are the three central dimensions of the employment relationship (see Figure 2.2). We will discuss the three dimensions in greater detail below.

Time/work pace

The nature and level of inter-firm competition changed in the 1980s. In addition to the price of a product or service, quality, flexibility and innovation became more and more important as competitive advantages. The increasing level of competition also added speed to this list. Examples

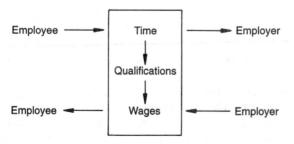

Figure 2.2   *The three dimensions of the employment relationship*

are: the shorter product life cycle, the rapid commercialization of R&D efforts and the shorter delivery times. Businesses became entranced with just-in-time delivery, cutting back on processing times, extending operating hours and increasing turnaround times by means of flexible automation. Higher demands are now being placed on workers, not only because of the introduction of new technologies, but also because more intense use is being made of the working time available.

Elchardus has drawn a distinction between time as spent performing an activity, a task, and time as related to an external point of reference, such as a clock or calendar. In the first instance, the sequence is from activity to time, time becoming significant because of the activity. From the beginning of the Industrial Revolution, it was the task as measured from an external reference point which gained significance in the eyes of management. Tasks were timed by stopwatch right down to the second. The amount of time it took to perform a task was a consequence of the underlying activities required to produce a product.

In a system which applies a far-reaching division of labour, and in which the work cycle is just a few seconds long, the employee is not really focusing on the content of his task, but on the time it takes to perform it. The sequence mentioned previously is turned on its head: the activity takes its significance from the fact that it must be performed within a prescribed period of time. Management views individuals as units of time, made concrete in a series of activities and objects, including products. Marx too commented that the value of labour is expressed in time (Elchardus, 1990). In industrial society, time is increasingly becoming another means of production.

For the employee, working time is most important in relation to work pace. An acceptable work pace might be described as the pace which can be borne by a person performing a specific task during a specific period of time and from which that person can recuperate fully afterwards. The workload imposed by a particular task is closely tied to the amount of time available to perform it. Manipulating the work pace and the time available to do the work allows the person involved to perform better (make fewer mistakes) and control his or her own efforts more effectively.

We see, then, that time influences performance in a number of different ways, for example the total duration of a task, the amount of time to be worked in a working day (and the distribution of time over the various tasks), and recuperation time, meaning the time during which a person is not called upon to do work or at least to do less work, so that he or she can recover from earlier efforts.

Working hours have recently become an important bargaining issue between management and employees, as employers attempt to institute shorter processing times and extend operating hours. The unions, on the other hand, are focused on issues such as working time reduction and work intensification.

Required and available qualifications

By qualifications we mean the knowledge, skills and psychosocial abilities which are required to perform certain tasks. We can make a distinction between required and available qualifications, which an employee possesses at a certain point in time. The concept of qualification plays a crucial role in retaining or expanding the work capacity which the employee makes available to the employer.

Businesses can only extend competition to include factors such as quality and innovative capacity if they make use of versatile, well-trained employees. That is why process control becomes so important – controlling and monitoring production or services from the moment the order is placed until the product or service reaches the customer. Employees are called upon to feel responsible for the entire primary process of the company, not only the operational tasks but quality assurance, work preparation and internal logistics as well. In many companies management is asking its personnel to get more involved in regulating and supervising processes. Whereas previously employees only dealt with matters beyond their own routine tasks if problems arose, now employers are asking them to apply problem-solving skills in unexpected circumstances. Employees, who once prided themselves on being quick and dexterous in performing practical tasks, now find that the ability to observe sharply and respond quickly are growing more important. Working according to instructions handed down by superiors or according to fixed procedures is being replaced by self-initiative, a sense of responsibility and creativity. The external control exercised by the boss is being replaced by self-control. Tasks are so varied and at the same time so specialist that guidance by someone at supervisory level is becoming increasingly difficult. The larger measure of self-control is derived from the willingness to bear responsibility and cooperate with others. The growing emphasis on regulatory tasks means that work will increasingly consist of observing visual and/or aural data on a continuous basis and taking decisions based on comparisons with other data and standards. This indicates a shift from operational knowledge to cognitive-abstract knowledge, for example understanding the organization and the capacity to analyse and solve problems. In addition, there is also a shift from skills which have been acquired through training and which become almost automatic (sensory-motor control) to conceptual problem-solving.

The qualifications required are subject to the following changes.

- Employees must now have an operational knowledge of not just one, but multiple specialist areas, either technical or administrative.
- Cognitive-abstract qualifications, for example an understanding of the organization and the ability to analyse and solve problems in unexpected situations, are becoming more significant.
- Socio-normative qualifications are becoming more important as well, with an accompanying shift from 'classic' to 'modern' social norms:

from accuracy, punctuality and loyalty to creativity, customer-orientation, responsibility and cooperation; the 'modern' socio-normative qualifications should guarantee that employees are capable of integrating the various tasks which they perform, both on their own and with others.

They also imply that the personality of the employee is becoming increasingly important in the qualification process. Having a specific educational background as a selection requirement is a significant factor not only in determining whether someone can do a particular job, but also as an indication of whether he or she can be called on to do other jobs as well.

Wages and performance

Baldamus sees the relationship between wages and performance as the core of the employment relationship, expressed in his theory as the 'wage-effort bargain' (Baldamus, 1961). Because the relationship between employer and employee is not entirely delineated, it allows scope for continuous bargaining over the wages to be exchanged for a certain effort. It also makes it possible to adjust performance when the wage in question cannot be negotiated. The literature can provide many excellent analyses of 'gold bricking'. The relationship between wages and performance is often formalized as a system of appraisal and compensation. Changes in the organizational structure have also placed the relationship between wages and effort in a new light. It is not the actual, prescribed activities which determine the compensation level, but the qualifications and potential of the employee. Neither does the simple link between performance and output suffice any longer. In many production processes, the employee has very little to say about the quantity of the output. We will explain this in further detail with a few examples (see Box 2.2).

The three plants featured here have developed different solutions for the application of job evaluation and compensation schemes:

- replacing appraisal based on daily tasks by skills appraisal and level of training;
- replacing individual job descriptions by group task descriptions;
- replacing individual job evaluation schemes by performance pay schemes.

In some companies we will find a mixture of different solutions.

In summary, the employment relationship is in fact the exchange between time, qualification and wages which takes place between employer and employee during the labour process. Within each component, moreover, the pressure of change within the organization has generated dynamic relationships between working and recuperation time, required and available qualifications, and wages and performance.

Box 2.2   *Changes in compensation strategies*

At **TWR Inc.**'s plant in the United States (Kochan et al., 1989: 96), there are 150 employees producing cables by working in workgroups which vary in their degree of autonomy. All of the production work is divided into nine levels. All activities and skills are represented by points. The difference between these levels is expressed in a series of points (10 points between each level), and the system is a 'pay for knowledge' system. Each employee entering the firm can reach level 1 within 30 days. An employee remains on a level for four months before he can move on to the next one. This time limit has been built into the system because production was beginning to suffer from the number of employees being trained for the next level. Everyone may in principle move up to the very highest level. The step to the next level consists of two parts: first, learning a new task, and secondly, reaching a degree of skill in carrying out the task. Group members are involved in appraising whether an employee has met the requirements of the next level up. Since some group members are better than others in training their colleagues, a separate 'trainer's classification' has been introduced with a wage scale that exceeds that at level 9. In 1983, 70 per cent of the employees had reached level 9 and the rest (30 per cent) were spread out over levels 5 to 8.

At **Volkswagen** individual job evaluations were done away with because management saw it as an obstacle to the introduction of technological and organizational change (Brumlop, 1986). Employees feared demotions. A new method was discovered in the development of an *Arbeitssystem*, a task cluster in which similar jobs are combined. The various clusters have requirements as to training and qualifications. Wages are determined on the basis of the training courses completed and the qualifications achieved, and not on the work performed on a particular day or week. The unions agreed under the terms of a collective bargaining agreement that the employer may order every employee to perform each task within a task cluster. The 28 job categories have now been replaced by 12 wage levels. The limits of the *Arbeitssystem* and the performance of the employees are monitored by the *Betriebsrat* (works council). In a few production situations there are dissimilar activities grouped into one task cluster, for example operational work, quality control, minor maintenance work, etc. In such cases the *Arbeitssystem* approaches the concept of an autonomous working group.

At the **Nissan UK** plant, all tasks and activities are condensed into 15 job descriptions (Wickens, 1987). For example, all technicians, controllers and departmental heads are grouped into one category. All production workers are classified as Production Staff, all maintenance workers as Maintenance Staff. Job descriptions within these categories have been eliminated. Moving up the wage ladder within a category depends on the performance of the individual employee on such points as: know-how, number of tasks mastered, flexibility, cooperation with colleagues in the working group. There are 14 appraisal factors in all. In fact, what used to be an extensive job evaluation system has been replaced by an extensive performance evaluation system.

4 The position of the parties in the employment relationship

Two aspects of the position of the parties in the employment relationship will be emphasized here. In the first place, we will consider how this relationship is situated between the market and the organization. In the second place, we will look at the employment relationship as an asymmetrical power relationship.

Between market and organization

Barbash emphasized that the behaviour of the parties in the employment relationship is affected by developments in the market (see Box 2.1). For employees, the labour market is most important; for employers the product market also plays a major role.

This behaviour is not, however, determined by the market alone. Once the parties have signed an employment contract, the employee is subject to the employer's decision-making authority and a member of the employer's organization. This is a crucial element in the employment relationship. The employee must perform a number of tasks resulting from the division of labour which the employer has introduced in the organization, and the employee must perform these tasks according to the employer's guidelines. For employers, getting employees to act the way they want them to act means developing control systems. For example, compensation systems can be structured in such a fashion that pay is linked to performance or, more indirectly, to the achievement of organizational goals. Wages can also be linked to the number of years of employment, in other words to loyalty to the employer. Valuable employees can be bound more securely to the company in a number of different ways, for example by providing them with company-specific training, by promising attractive career prospects, by allocating company-specific advantages such as profit sharing, supplementary insurance, a company car etc.

The employment relationship is linked on the one hand to the division of labour within the company and to the control system which governs behaviour, and on the other hand to the position of employers and employees in the market, specifically the labour market. Figure 2.3 represents this relationship. The employment relationship is situated between the market and the organization.

In some instances the market-like aspects of the employment relationship dominate. That might be the case whenever an employee is taken on temporarily, to perform a specific job. In the most extreme case, the employment relationship is played out entirely outside the company, for example when the employer decides to contract out work to small independent businesses or subcontractors. It is also possible that the organization-like side of the exchange will gain the upper hand. That is the

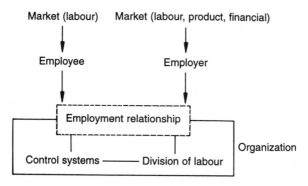

Figure 2.3   *The employment relationship between market and organization*

case when the employment relationship involves a permanent, full-time job. The employment relationship is enveloped by the company and institutionalized in the internal labour market.

Williamson (1985) wondered at what point a loose relationship between two market parties, regulated only by contract, turns into a permanent organizational relationship. His model can also be applied to the relationship between employer and employee in the labour market (see Box 2.3).

One important lesson we can learn from Williamson's analysis is that control systems vary depending on how heavily the employment relationship leans towards a market relationship or an organizational relationship. Watson (1987) distinguishes between diffuse and restrictive employment relationships. He has sketched a number of characteristics of these two types. In the restrictive employment relationship the implicit employment contract is highly specified; the employee is given detailed instructions and the relationship is based on mistrust. Cooperation is achieved by what Friedman called 'direct control'. In the diffuse employment relationship, the implicit employment contract is more general; the employee has a measure of discretion and autonomy and the relationship is based on mutual trust. Cooperation can be achieved by what Friedman called 'responsible autonomy'. In this way, Watson establishes a link between the nature of the employment relationship and the control systems used in an organization. An organization can, incidentally, have both types of employment relationship as well as control systems for different types of work:

- restrictive employment relationships for simple, manual tasks in parts of the organization with a strict division of labour and an extensive hierarchy of managers supporting a regime of 'direct control';
- diffuse employment relationships for more complex work in parts of the organization with a modest division of labour and a regime of 'responsible autonomy'.

Box 2.3   *Williamson's analysis of the employment relationship*

Williamson's (1985) question is: what is more efficient, completing a transaction (the exchange of price and performance) in a market or within an organization? Completing transactions within an organization means that the coercive power of the contract must be replaced by a whole range of control systems if performance is still to be regulated.

There is a price attached to setting up and maintaining control systems, and it should be taken into account when considering whether to convert a contractual relationship into an organizational one. The choice, then, is between a market relationship regulated by contract and an organizational relationship regulated by control systems.

According to Williamson, a contract in the labour market differs from a contract in other markets because the exchange involves a specific price which must be paid for an effort that has yet to be made. The actual content of the performance is much more difficult to determine ahead of time, and the effort is much harder to measure than in other transactions, for example the purchase and sale of a house in the real estate market.

Are employees replaceable or are their contributions unique? In Williamson's view, that depends most of all on the employee's qualifications. If the qualifications are specifically required to produce the product, then it goes without saying that the market relationship will be transformed into an organizational one, aimed at controlling the relationship between price and performance over time. If the qualification is not company-specific and the performance can be measured easily, there will be no impetus to convert the market relationship into an organizational one. This is the situation of the casual labourer, hired in from day to day.

The more company-specific the qualification is and the more difficult to measure performance, the more intricate the control structure will be, encompassing promotion ladders, compensation systems etc. In reality, the company is busy developing its own internal labour market.

This type of approach allows us to question what the transition from restrictive to diffuse might mean for the three dimensions of the employment exchange: time, qualifications and wages. If such a transition takes place, will it lead to requalification, to higher wages with more autonomy in determining the relationship between working time and recovery time, or to a more intense level of work (higher level of performance)? Can the employee take charge of his own performance, or will new control systems evolve to replace the supervisory hierarchy (for example career planning and group compensation)?

Asymmetry in exchange relationships

We can deduce from the foregoing that the employment relationship is also a power relationship. On the one hand there is the employee's desire to determine the conditions of the employment relationship and on the other hand the employer's desire to control behaviour. This can lead to conflict. Crucial is the fact that the relationship between employer and employee in the labour market is uneven, asymmetrical. Dependency on wages will always be more of a disadvantage to the employees than dependency on performance will be to the employer.

Giddens (1974: 104) proposed to replace the concept of ownership as a basis for the analysis of power relationships by the concept of market capacity. Ownership encompasses more – in classical Marxist terms – than the employer owning the means of production and the employee owning manpower. For example, one of an employee's most important character- istics is his or her qualifications. If a production worker gradually forfeits his qualifications or if they become increasingly company-specific, he will become more and more dependent on his employer. His market capacity will fall, and he will be restricted to the company's internal labour market. On the other hand, an employee who takes training courses to improve and increase qualifications which might be applied elsewhere is expanding her market capacity.

Nevertheless, an employer can more easily replace an employee than an employee can secure a new job and a new employer at the same wage level. At a certain point, the tightness of the labour market will restrict or extend the behaviour alternatives available to both parties.

The power aspect of the employment relationship not only applies to market factors, but also to organizations (see Box 2.4). Organizations of

---

Box 2.4   *Power in sociological exchange theories*

Basing themselves on sociological exchange theories, Pfeffer and Salancik (1978: 39–61; see also Lammers, 1989: 172–211) have analysed relationships between organizations in terms of dependence. The possession and distribution of resources is central to their theory. They propose that 'if an organization or coalition of organizations (party A) has resources at its disposal which are needed by another organization or coalition of organizations (party B), then A has power over B in so far as:

- the resources in question are more important to B than to A;
- B will have more trouble than A obtaining the same resources elsewhere;
- B is unlikely to find a substitute for the resource in question to satisfy its need.'

The key, then, is the degree to which the resource possessed by one party is irreplaceable to another, and the degree to which the latter party is able to obtain the resource or substitutes for it elsewhere.

Dependent relationships may be symmetrical or asymmetrical. A relationship is asymmetrical when organization A controls resources which are important to organization B, whereas B possesses no resources equally important to A. Asymmetry in relationships between organizations is a precondition for the exercise of power.

employers and employees depend on each other's resources. The employer, for example, may substitute labour by capital in order to make himself less dependent on the factor labour, and may join an employers' association to try to impose lower wages. Employees have managed to capture a position of power by joining together in collective interest organizations, and may withdraw their resource (labour) in strikes or production slow-downs.

Power implies that organizations can (and must) sanction one another. Without sanctions, there is no position of power. Sanctions can be both positive and negative. Positive sanctions are, for example, when employees agree to sign a collective agreement if wage concessions are rewarded by the employer, or when employers award pay rises for a well-rated performance. The parties can impose negative sanctions by denying their opponent certain things: for example refusing to negotiate with them or slowing down production.

5   Regulating the exchange

The exchange in the employment relationship takes place on a continuous basis. The relationship between wages and performance, time worked and recovery time, required and available qualifications is in a constant state of flux. For example, when technological innovations are introduced, the employer will demand that (a portion of) his permanent workforce be retrained. An employee who has been retrained will probably insist on a pay review. In exchange for accepting more flexible working hours, employees will want extra bonuses or recovery time to compensate for non-standard hours.

The employment relationship can also come under pressure due to fluctuations in the balance of power. Certain changes in the labour market can undermine the existing balance and force one of the parties to make new concessions. To ensure a measure of stability in the employment relationship, the parties have developed rules and regulations. The employment relationship is a regulated relationship – in other words, there are rules governing how the exchange should take place and what the substance of the exchange should be. For example, there are rules which must be observed when employees are being hired or fired. Employment contracts must comply with certain legal stipulations. And quite often working hours and minimum wages are subject to regulation as well.

Although such rules provide structure and continuity in the employment relationship, they themselves also change. The process of reinterpreting expectations and the rules governing the employment relationship is an almost permanent one.

The regulation of the employment relationship gives rise to a direct connection between the employment relationship and collective labour relations. Specific bodies have been created to monitor the process of regulation whereby representatives of both employer and employee organizations attempt to arrive at a mutual understanding concerning the rules governing the employment relationship. The question then is: who (bargaining partners) is bargaining, in which institutional setting (collective bargaining agreement, works council), at which level (company, corporation, industry) and on what issue (wages, working hours, jobs, qualifications etc.)? Why is one employer prepared to accept that certain aspects of the employment relationship will be settled through collective bargaining at the industry level, while the other does everything in his power to regulate the employment relationship within the company by signing a collective company agreement or by determining the company's rules and regulations unilaterally? In one company management is prepared to talk to an employee delegation about the implementation of new technologies, while in the other management takes decisions on this issue autonomously. In one company the board consults the trade union representatives, in another the works council and in still another its own hand-picked personnel representatives (for example quality circles or autonomous working groups). In one company the parties consult or bargain on every dimension of the employment relationship, in another only about wages.

At first glance, we can distinguish between two different levels: the internal and external regulation of the employment relationship. Internal regulation takes place within the company and with a specific employer. External regulation takes place at levels above the company: the region, industry or central level. The rules which are agreed apply to more than one employer. External regulation affects the actors involved within the framework of the collective bargaining or political decision-making which underlies labour law. Internal regulation affects the actors involved in works councils, quality circles, working groups, etc.

At second glance, the dividing line between internal and external regulation is often blurred. For example, even if the wage level is regulated by a collective bargaining agreement (external regulation), a performance pay system may be part of the company's internal regulations or may be part of the informal shop floor arrangement between foremen and workers on the amount of work to be performed. Formal working hours may be determined by an industry-level collective agreement, but it is management and the works council who draw up the actual work schedules.

To summarize, the employment relationship is subject to rules and regulations governing the three dimensions of the exchange: wages, time and qualification. Regulation takes place at multiple levels: the company (internal regulation) and the levels above the company (external regulation). Each dimension can be regulated at one of these levels or at multiple levels (see Box 2.5). There are certain connections between the levels, as we can see in the diagram presented in Figure 2.4.

Box 2.5   *Mixed regulation models*

We can think of other combinations in which the employment relationship consists of varying degrees of internal and external regulation.

1   It is possible that the conditions under which work must be performed are determined unilaterally by the employer (internal regulation only). The employee can only accept these conditions or find another job. This type of situation may arise, for example, in a small firm in a sector that is not covered by an industry-level agreement. Even so, the employer will have to comply with the minimum statutory rules. Unilateral, exclusively internal regulation of the employment relationship has to all intents and purposes been eliminated in modern industrial society.

2   An employer can confine himself to strictly upholding and applying the provisions set forth in the collective bargaining agreement and in legislation. This is external regulation to the exclusion of all else. We might see this situation, for example, in public services or in organizations which are highly dependent on government, for example universities or hospitals. There is often an excess of rules prescribed and imposed from above. The bureaucratization of the employment relationship may be somewhat frustrating for the contracting parties, because there is little or no scope for exchange or negotiation.

3   In most instances we see a balance of internal and external forms of regulation, in a broad range of combinations. For example, the emphasis may be on external regulation, with the employer complying strictly with collective agreement provisions, but nevertheless making supplementary agreements with his employees on such issues as holiday leave, supplementary insurance, overtime bonuses, and so on. On the other hand, the emphasis might be on internal regulation. The employer views the external agreements as an established fact, but wants to determine much of the employment relationship himself within this framework, either unilaterally or in consultation with the employee(s). Such consultation can take place in a number of different ways: directly with the employee or employees involved, or indirectly via the works council or trade union representatives.

In analysing the regulation of the employment relationship, then, it is crucial to take account of the interconnections and associations between the various levels and how they relate to the company's internal behavioural control systems mentioned previously.

The most striking thing about our framework is the extent to which the employment relationship can be determined outside the company, far away from the place where the work is actually being performed. Actors impose rules other than those directly involved in the exchange. The best example of external regulation is the industry-level agreement, but labour law and social legislation imposed by the government is also a form of external regulation. In this way, collective labour relations can acquire

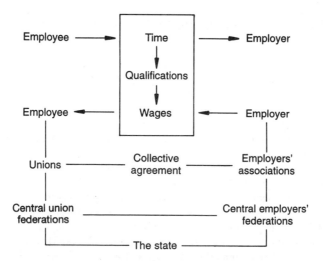

Figure 2.4   *Employment relationship and collective labour relations*

their own dynamic and may become completely divorced from the employment relationship. A great deal of tension may arise between the institutionalization of the employment relationship by collective regulation and the almost permanent process of interpreting and reinterpreting these rules within the company. Particularly interesting are the initiatives taken by actors which lead to changes in the employment relationship and to shifts between collective relationships and behavioural control systems, for example the increasing importance of human resource management at the expense of traditional forms of collective bargaining (see Box 2.6).

In their analysis, Kochan et al. emphasize the strategic choices which management can make as an important actor at the company level (Kochan et al., 1989). Changes in the position of the company brought on by external developments (competition, technical innovation) force management to reconsider the existing traditional institutions (such as collective bargaining) as a regulatory framework for the employment relationship. The 'strategic-choice' approach, proposed by Kochan et al., gives rise to a dynamic perspective by emphasizing the connection between market fluctuations and the strategic choices made by actors.

British researchers have questioned the extent to which policy with regard to industrial relations actually belongs to the core of management strategic decision-making (Purcell and Ahlstrand, 1989). After all, one might argue that the strategies applied by companies in the first place involve decisions concerning markets, product types and technology, with economic and technical considerations being paramount. The social aspects of management are derived from these considerations and only play a role in policy-making at a later date, when it becomes clear that the strategy cannot be pursued without adopting a well-considered social policy. In this respect, one might question whether decisions related to

---

Box 2.6   *Institutional change and management strategies*

In 1984 Kochan et al. published the results of a study on the relationship between management strategies, the position of the trade unions at company level, and the introduction of social innovations such as grievance procedures, employee participation and consultation bodies, profit sharing schemes and the application of new production and work concepts, for example autonomous working groups (Kochan et al., 1984).

In some countries trade unions have a harder time gaining recognition than in others. That applies not only within Europe, but even more so outside of Europe. In the United States, for example, employers are only obliged to recognize trade unions as bargaining partners if the trade union is voted in by a majority of the employees in a legally prescribed vote. Is management attempting to undermine the position of the trade unions by making use of the social innovations mentioned above? That seems to be the case in many companies, as Kochan et al. have shown. The chance that a trade union will lose a vote for recognition in a company increases with the introduction of social innovation by management. By establishing new companies and by introducing social innovation, management has the power to marginalize the trade unions. A large-scale shift is taking place from external regulation of the employment relationship (collective bargaining agreement with trade union) to internal regulation or unilateral regulation. In the latter instance, management shapes the employment relationship without the involvement of the employees or representative bodies.

---

personnel policy and labour relations do not frequently constitute operational decisions which follow in the wake of strategic ones, for example opening or shutting down plants, introducing a new product, technological innovation etc.

It is not only the strategies pursued by employers which should be considered, however, but also the strategies pursued by employees and trade unions. Employees and their representatives are not just the 'victims' of the employer's strategic choices. They can take action by anticipating or responding, propose countermeasures and develop strategies which will put limits on management in taking strategic decisions, or try to intervene in the substance of the policy. Nevertheless, Kochan et al. (1989) have observed that in recent decades it has been the employers who have taken the lead, while the employees and trade unions have been forced to take up a defensive position.

6   Intra- and inter-organizational relations

By placing the employment relationship within its own regulatory framework, we have established a link with collective labour relations. Our analysis would not be complete, however, if we extended it only to include the relations between employer and employee interest organizations. The relations between employees and trade unions and between employers and employers' associations, shown in Figure 2.4, also deserve our attention.

Recent years have seen the development of a number of new approaches to collective action within an organizational context and to the internal functioning of organizations of employers and employees. Why do people join organizations and under what conditions do they participate in collective action? One of the important concepts in considering these questions is that of the 'logic of collective action'. The economist Olson has developed an important approach in this respect.

Olson conducted two studies (1965, 1982) on the 'logic of collective action'. He concluded that the goals pursued by trade unions can be viewed as collective goods which they deliver to their members, or 'clients': for example, a pay rise negotiated in collective bargaining. The remarkable thing is that it makes little difference whether or not an individual employee is a member of a trade union or participates in collective action; either way, that employee receives the goods. The collective bargaining agreement signed by the trade union generally applies to non-members as well. In effect, the trade union movement functions as a collective service: even non-payers can benefit from its product, namely the collective bargaining agreement, free of charge. It is as if the sanitation department still collected one's (stinking) rubbish without one having to pay local taxes.

For employees who think this situation through rationally and who put their own interests above everything else, joining a trade union or a strike is not the most obvious choice. Because trade unions are not selective in providing their services – for example by offering them exclusively to paying members – they encourage 'free-rider' behaviour. The question then is: why would you want to join a trade union or run the risk of losing your job by supporting a strike when you can have all the advantages that membership or participation offers without signing up or taking part? Where is the logic in that?

In his study on 'Disorganized capitalism', Offe has attempted to formulate an answer to this question (Offe, 1985). He rejects the traditional Marxist view of capitalist society as a well-organized system. One of the many tensions in disorganized capitalism is that between the individual self-interest and a collective solidarity. In Offe's view, the individual perspective is beginning to overshadow the solidary 'logic of collective action', partly because of changes in the labour market. He cites, for example, the distinction between the employed and the unemployed, or between those who belong to the core of well-trained permanent employees and those who perform simple jobs in uncertain, flexible employment relationships. In his opinion, the nature of the employment relationship influences the degree to which employees become members of organizations and take part in collective action. Later, together with

Wiesenthal, he reasoned that there were two logics of collective action, closely derived from the split between capital and labour. According to them, employers have an easier time forming collective organizations than employees (Offe and Wiesenthal, 1979).

Crouch warns against oversimplifying the logic of collective action when analysing how the actors weigh up its advantages and disadvantages (Crouch, 1982). There are several degrees of rationality. The choices can be reduced neither to the dilemmas which individual actors face (Olson's analysis goes in this direction) nor to the class struggle between paid labour and those who own the means of production (as in Offe's analysis). The issue is the collective nature of behaviour and choices, in which the actors make rational calculations within certain constraints. Power also plays a major role in the process of weighing up the costs and benefits, defined as the ability of one party to exclude the other party from certain behaviour alternatives. The rational calculations, hence, are made within asymmetrical social relations.

A number of authors, particularly Streeck, have integrated the analysis of the 'logic of collective action' with the perspective on intra- and inter-organizational relations in the field of organizational sociology. The relationships between employee and trade union, and between employer and employers' association, coincide with the intra-organizational perspective, which focuses on relationships within organizations, for example between the leadership and its members. The analysis of the collective relationships between organizations is more in keeping with the inter-organizational perspective.

According to Lammers (1981), the basic premise of this perspective is the existence of mutual and partially dependent relationships between organizations. As odd as it may sound, the leaderships of the trade unions and employers' associations need each other when they face third parties, or even their own members. To gain recognition by relevant third parties and to continue to attract members, trade union officers and employers' association administrators must, for example, recognize each other as legitimate representatives, and as the effectual spokesperson for their members. Streeck (1992a) draws a connection between the externalization of interest organizations (seeking ties with one another and with third parties) and the intra-organizational processes within trade unions and employers' associations, for example translating heterogeneous into homogeneous interests, the process of internal discipline and mobilization processes (sse Box 2.7).

Organizations of employers and employees function as interfaces between their members (employer or trade union member) and the larger society. One crucial representative of that society is the state, the third party in the external regulation of the employment relationship. In order to come to terms with this representative, the leadership of a trade union or employers' association must have sufficient control of its own intra-organizational processes. It must, for example, be able to bring the

---

Box 2.7   *Interest heterogeneity and organizing capacity of interest organizations*

Together with other researchers, Streeck (1992a) conducted a detailed comparative study on the degree of interest heterogeneity and the organizing capacity of trade union and employers' associations in Europe. He found that as the degree of interest heterogeneity increased, the organizing capacity decreased. Streeck rejects Offe and Wiesenthal's theory that employers' associations have an easier time in this respect than do employee organizations.

The study shows that trade unions are broader, more 'encompassing' than employers' associations because their interest base is simpler. Trade unions organize interests which are principally derived from the labour market. Employers' associations must deal with their interests both in the labour market and in the product market in which they operate.

---

sometimes contradictory interests of its members under an acceptable, common banner and be able to mobilize its members to support the collective demands. As a representative organization, it translates the goals of its members into demands which the state can understand. By the same token, the bargaining process also requires it to interpret the demands of the opposition – for example the state – for its members.

On the one hand, then, the leadership of a trade union or employers' association has a representative function, in that it promotes the interests of its members. On the other hand, it must also be able to control its members and the way in which they articulate their demands. These two functions are often at odds with each other. Organizational leaders might even call in the assistance of another organization in order to be able to act more autonomously with respect to its own members. For example, employers may relinquish a portion of the wage sum to finance trade union activities, so that the union does not have to rely on its members as its sole source of funding. At the same time, this makes the leadership of the two organizations more dependent on each other, which in turn requires both to exercise even more internal control. This will ultimately have a major impact on the internal organizational structure of a union or employers' association.

Trade unions and employers' associations, then, are not only institutions, partners in a collective relationship, but also organizations with their own organizational problems in the areas of leadership, internal decision-making and member participation. With respect to trade unions, we have only to consider aspects such as participation by trade union members in union leadership and strategic decision-making, the allocation of tasks among paid and unpaid union officials, internal participation (union councils), the appointment of officials and decision-making on strikes or other forms of collective action. Employers' associations, in turn, are concerned with dividing tasks among administrators and secretariats, setting up rules for mutual support and internal sanctions, and ensuring coordination during collective negotiations.

In summary, organizational changes within companies have a direct impact on the employment relationship. New technologies and new forms of work organization directly affect the use of working hours, the qualification of workers and wage levels or wage systems, identified as the main items in the exchange between employers and employees. The analysis of the employment relationship, however, should not be restricted to the relationship between the parties involved in the exchange at the company level. Employers or employees are sometimes replaced by their respective interest organizations, which impose a framework within which the exchange of wages, working time and qualification is regulated to a greater or lesser extent.

In expanding our perspective, we have explicitly added an analysis of the relationship between the interest organizations (inter-organizational) and within these organizations between the leadership and the members (intra-organizational). Trade unions and employers' associations are not only the components of an institutional relationship, but also organizations in their own right. From the perspective of organizational science, the first element can be denoted as inter-organizational relations and the second as intra-organizational relations. The dynamic between labour market institutions and interest organizations can therefore be studied as the dynamic between inter- and intra-organizational relations.

PART 2

INTEREST ORGANIZATIONS AND INDUSTRIAL RELATIONS IN A CHANGING EUROPE

3 Trade unions from a comparative perspective

Jelle Visser

1 Trade unions as an object of study

Trade unions have evolved in three different ways from their beginning some 150–200 years ago. First, they are labour market institutions. As such, they can be found in every democratic and capitalist society in which labour is performed in exchange for a wage or salary and in which workers have the freedom of association. Secondly, they are part of a social movement aimed at emancipating the workers and improving their status. In Europe trade unions evolved before the advent of universal suffrage, and they played an important role in the struggle to extend political democracy to the 'lower' classes, a struggle which led them to forge alliances with political parties. Finally, trade unions are interest groups. In this final capacity, they put pressure on governments, parliaments and public administrators, and are comparable to other groups that defend special interests, for example business lobbies, environmental campaigners or consumer groups.

Trade unions are the object of study in a wide variety of disciplines. Economists study them above all as a labour market institution; they are interested in the impact of union action on wage determination, labour market supply and demand, unemployment, productivity, prosperity and income distribution. Historians and sociologists, on the other hand, are interested in trade unionism as a social movement. They study the contribution of the trade union to the process of democratization in society and organizations, the internal functioning of trade unions, the participation of members and industrial conflict. Political scientists, finally, concentrate on how the trade union functions as an interest group and on the relationship between trade unions and political parties.

The emphasis has shifted during the course of this century. In the early stages of the labour movement – when the freedom of association and the right to demonstrate were still contested, when joining a strike meant losing one's job or even going to jail, and when universal suffrage did not exist – the emphasis was naturally on the emancipatory role of the labour movement. After these and other rights and freedoms had been secured, the attention shifted to the corrective role of the movement, or rather its supervisory role in ensuring the preservation of such hard-won rights, and in defending the income, work, status and human dignity of the workers (van Zuthem, 1973).

Throughout their history, trade unions have become stronger as organizations and their position in society more legitimate. Their role, however, is still debated; at times they are the object of praise, and at times of censure. Any evaluation is always a temporary one. Thirty years ago trade unions in many countries were given a pat on the back for their work in helping to restore the post-war economy and for putting the 'public interest' first; nowadays they are chastised for standing in the way of economic reform and for defending the 'special interests' of insiders. In short, there are two sides to the trade union coin: sometimes they are the 'sword of justice', at other times the henchmen of the 'vested interests' (Flanders, 1970: 15).

The American economists Freeman and Medoff (1984) call these two sides *voice* and *monopoly*. In the latter capacity, the trade union is viewed as an evil monopoly which frustrates the working of the market because it undermines a nation's or an industry's competitive position and because it protects *insiders* (that is, those with stable jobs) to the detriment of *outsiders*, who cannot enter employment as a result. In addition, it is frequently said that the existence of the union as a bargaining agent is no longer defensible. Employees nowadays have more rights, are more mobile, more skilled and have no qualms about resisting domineering or unreasonable employers by going to court or by resigning (Hayek, 1971). Some argue that this applies only to highly skilled workers, but others point out that it is precisely those workers with the best protection – for example, employees in large companies or in the government service – who join trade unions, whereas one has to look long and hard to find groups with a weak labour market position (for example, ethnic minorities, employees in small companies, young people, part-time workers) among the trade unions' rank-and-file. To summarize: from the neo-liberal perspective, workers are now capable of standing up for themselves, and trade unions are only one among many interest groups that want to draw attention to their special interest. As a social movement their role (emancipation of the workers) has become redundant and as a labour market institution, bridging the power gap between employer and employee, the negative effects outweigh any benefits.

The positive side of trade unionism is that it gives employees a 'voice' – the right to participate in the employment relationship – without which they would have no other option but to *exit* if they did not like the situation in which they found themselves (Hirschman, 1970). But exiting is not a possibility for everyone and will depend on the state of and position in the labour market. Nor is it always desirable, since investment in training is lost. If exit rates are high, employers will not make the investment in training in the first place because they fear that others may reap what they have sown. The result often comes down to *sufferance*; employees reluctantly endure a situation of which they are critical because they have no other alternatives in the labour market and no rights within the company. Freeman and Medoff argue that exiting is often inefficient and that both the employee and the employer lose out. Sufferance, on the other hand, is always inefficient; after all, it is only by 'going slow', by following orders slavishly, by working according to the book, by carrying out minor acts of sabotage and by not getting involved that the employee can right the balance.

By offering employees the certainty that their voice will be heard when employment terms and conditions are undergoing change, trade unions are able to encourage employees to make an effort, to allow themselves to be trained, to agree to change (Streeck, 1992b). After years of negotiations, employers and employees have grown accustomed to one another and have built up a degree of trust in each other which can lower the transaction costs of negotiating change. That is not to say that there is a positive impact on productivity, technical progress and training regardless of the circumstances. Not every trade union does or can achieve the same outcome, nor do they want to.

In assessing the significance of trade unions, we usually consider the impact on the size and distribution of wages and employment, the operation of the labour market, economic growth and income distribution. Additionally, we can think of factors that affect the welfare of the workers:

working hours, work pace, the quality of working life, safety and hygiene, training and skill etc. Finally, we might want to evaluate the importance of trade unions for the emancipation of the working class and for the progress of democracy. In modern pluralist societies and organizations, unions derive their legitimacy not only from their contribution to economic progress and social security, but also from their role as an instrument and channel of employee participation. This objective requires that trade unions are representative and operate under democratic rules. Are trade unions representative of all employees? Do they also take account of future generations, or other interested parties that have yet to gain a voice or power? Can members exercise sufficient influence on trade union policy?

Trade unions now have to contend with various competitors. One of these is the works council which now exists in many European countries. In addition, there is legislation at both national and European levels guaranteeing workers certain minimum rights, for example procedures, waiting periods and compensation in case of dismissal; safety and hygiene in the workplace; equal treatment and equal pay for men and women; maximum number of working hours; and the right to receive information in large transnational European companies. In many national welfare states workers have the right to a minimum wage and to social security: to schemes governing unemployment and accident insurance which were originally set up by the trade unions, subsidized by the state, and then taken over and expanded to cover all workers or citizens, although nowadays there is a movement from social security back to insurance.

Trade unions also face new challenges. While the market for interest representation has become crowded, a decreasing proportion of employees actually join collective organizations and take part in industrial action. If we consider indicators such as union density and strike involvement and standardize both measures for the size of the employed labour force, a downward trend has emerged since the end of the 1970s (Shalev, 1992; Visser, 1991, 1992). On the other hand, the trade unions have consistently succeeded in getting members elected to works councils (Rogers and Streeck, 1994). The same is true of the number of employees covered by a collective bargaining agreement, at least in Europe, with the exception of Great Britain (OECD, 1994).[1]

Internationalization is probably the biggest challenge which unions face. Countries are becoming more and more interdependent politically and economically, both within Europe and across the globe, reducing the sovereignty of the national states and of national trade unions to determine economic and social policy. If they fail to coordinate their policy, centralize

---

[1] Throughout this book we use the term Great Britain to denote England, Wales and Scotland. Although Northern Ireland has much in common with Great Britain, some important elements of industrial relations are different. However, where the situation is similar or where statistics cover Northern Ireland as well, we refer to the UK.

decision-making and merge together to form collective transnational European organizations, Europe's trade unions will be condemned to pursue a policy of adaptation and retreat while competing against one another for scarce resources and jobs (Ebbinghaus and Visser, 1994; Ulman et al., 1993).

2 Origins and evolution

Exclusive or inclusive?

Throughout the industrialized world, printers, cigar-makers and carpenters were the first to unite in 'trade' unions. They had in common a long period of occupational training, which took place during working hours under the supervision of other workers who had already mastered their craft. The power of these craft unions lay in a form of social and organizational exclusiveness (Weber, 1925). The work only went to skilled craftsmen, and they controlled to whom they taught their skills. Restricting the number of craftsmen also raised the price of their work. The growth strategy pursued by these unions was directed inward. That is why Turner (1962) calls them 'closed' unions: they concentrated on their own group to the exclusion of all others, and only attempted to achieve a high level of union density within this group. Unskilled workers had to make do with another source of power: the power of numbers. 'Open' unions tended to spring up in plants and urban centres with large concentrations of workers, in firms and working environments where employees were closely supervised by their bosses with respect to work organization and work pace. The textiles industry, the steel industry, the iron industry and the electrotechnical industry are prime examples. Initially these unions succeeded in sectors where labour peace, safety and working conditions quickly became public issues and therefore the object of governmental concern: some examples are the coal mines, the railways, ports and energy plants. Open unions wielded the following weapons: they put pressure on the most vulnerable employers and they put political pressure on governments, public opinion and parliament. The more members they had, the smaller the chance that employers would undermine the effectiveness of a strike by hiring strikebreakers or 'scabs'. After all, anyone could take over unskilled work in a twinkling. That is why they did not concentrate on the workplace but blocked the factory gates instead. The external trade union (outside the company) became more important than the internal one (inside the company). Connections with other unions and alliances with political parties were more important and easier to achieve than constant vigilance on the shop floor.

Craft unions are closer to the liberal ideology of self-help. The emphasis is on economic, not political, power (Marks, 1989). This does not rule out radicalization during economic or political hard times. No union is immune to the consequences of technological or economic change. In the last quarter of the nineteenth century, the craft unions came under increasing pressure because a growing number of tasks were being taken over by machines, either partly or in full (mechanization), and because progress in literacy, better technical training and a growing tide of immigration had increased the pool of available skilled workers. Product markets were subject to serious fluctuations, especially the market for crafted goods. There was always the possibility that war or trade restrictions could eliminate foreign markets. From time to time, then, the craft unions faced widespread unemployment and plummeting wages among their members. They tried to counter these problems by joining together to insure themselves against risks and by accumulating benefit funds to see their members through the lean years. That required a strict separation between the rights and privileges of the members in good standing (that is, those who paid their dues) and the non-members; it was not uncommon that risks which were difficult to insure were stopped at the door by strict entry requirements. Some organizations had a travel fund from which they paid out benefits and gave letters of credence to members who were unable to find employment in the local or national market. That encouraged centralization, as the worker's credentials had to be accepted elsewhere (Webb and Webb, 1920 [1894]). The local trade union relinquished its autonomy in this fashion and the first steps were taken towards the formation of national trade unions. Just as wage standardization (that is, 'taking wages out of competition') contributed to the rise of national product markets (Commons, 1909), so too did the standardization of qualifications contribute to the rise of national labour markets (Ulman, 1955).

The organization of unskilled workers began in the urban and industrialized regions of Europe around 1890 (Hobsbawm, 1964). Craft unions were pushed aside or adapted by merging to form industrial unions, whose members came from every sector, trade and skill level. The industrial union model came to dominate the European Continent. In some European countries (Great Britain, Ireland, Denmark), craft unions continue to persist alongside general unions. This is a typical example of the historical imprint of organizations (Stinchcombe, 1964) and path dependency (North, 1991). The later the industrial revolution arrived, the more rapidly it evolved, and the more the workers' social struggle to gain better living and working conditions was accompanied by a political struggle to secure the freedom of association, the right to demonstrate and strike, and universal suffrage, the more likely were workers to form industrial unions immediately and craft unions to find they were pushed to the background. The earlier the industrial revolution arrived, and the sooner the elite among the workers won civil and political rights, the more likely were the craft unions to secure an established position. In those countries, unskilled workers in infant industries had little choice but to form their own unions. Because these organizations were unable to grow in an 'upward' direction, they grew 'sideways' to become general unions. In turn, the craft unions did likewise and allied themselves with unions in other crafts or professions. There was consequently no room for the industrial unions, except in cases where the relevant industrial sector had not yet been organized (agriculture, trade) or in cases where long-term physical proximity (shipping), mutual dependence and early government supervision (mining) made mutual association across occupations unavoidable.

The industrial–political model

The German labour movement surpassed the British labour movement in size on the eve of the First World War. In both countries the labour movement encompassed almost a quarter of all employees. Efforts in this same period to organize unskilled workers in the United States failed, partly because of a ruthless counteroffensive by employers and conservative politicians. The craft unions, united in the American Federation of Labour (AFL), rejected unskilled workers and African Americans. They took pride in their role of pure economic pressure group or negotiating machine (business union). And indeed, there is no record in American history of these unions being part of a social movement or alliance with socialist parties. It was not until the 1930s, under pressure of the recession and with different political composture (the New Deal), that a new generation of unions, united in the Congress of Industrial Organizations (CIO), succeeded in reaching black, unskilled and female workers, although only those who worked in the heavy consumer goods industry (mass production unionism) (Brody, 1980). In the 1950s, the AFL and CIO merged, but the proportion of union members began its slow decline, in part masked by membership gains among federal employees and teachers in the 1960s (Goldfield, 1987). The Japanese labour movement was insignificant until the Second World War. After Japan's war defeat, union ranks swelled and unions were powerful, but the end of the 1940s, when the socialist and communist inspired unions suffered major defeats, witnessed the end of an open and inclusive labour movement. Thereafter, the Japanese enterprise unions in the private sector of the economy restricted themselves to representing employees in large companies (Shimada, 1988).

In Europe, the period between 1900 and 1913 saw the rise of the *industrial–political trade union model* (Streeck, 1993). The Democratic Question and the Social Question together politicized and centralized trade unions and industrial relations systems. Industrial unions and their peak organizations were typically set up as the industrial arm of socialist, catholic and in one instance protestant political parties. Under socialist leadership, the labour movement devoted its efforts to securing universal suffrage, which would make it possible to influence the composition of the elected representative bodies and achieve through legislation what at that time seemed impossible to achieve at the negotiating table: the 8-hour working day, better working conditions, industrial accident insurance, a ban on child labour, paid holiday leave etc. The socialist labour movement believed that the key to economic power lay in the power of parliament. Catholic and protestant union leaders, on the other hand, influenced by the doctrines of their respective churches (subsidiarity and sovereignty within one's own circle), insisted on cooperation between employers and employees, and the mutual regulation of the economy and social insurance (corporatism), preferably without direct government intervention. Where syndicalists or anarchists dominated, the unions worked to become self-governing, to eliminate the state and to gain autonomy from political parties. They rejected the most important institutional innovation in the labour market, the collective bargaining agreement, because it implicitly accepted the capitalist wage labour system.

Political and ideological divisions in the European labour movement

The flip side of politicization is fragmentation (Sturmthal, 1953). Just as the first trade associations separated organizational power along professional and status lines, so too did the industrial–political union model confirm and reinforce the political and ideological divisions as they existed in European society around 1900 (Ebbinghaus, 1993; Visser, 1987). This paralleled the rise of cleavages in the party systems of Europe, which remained highly stable until the late 1960s and beyond (Lipset and Rokkan, 1967). With the exception of the unions in culturally and religiously homogeneous (Lutheran) Scandinavia, and British trade unionism, which had not grown out of a political party, every European trade union was divided into distinct political, religious or ideological categories. During and after the First World War, these divisions were further intensified by the battle over the international orientation of the workers' movement (communism).

Despite the fact that the original doctrines have been watered down and the organizational ties between trade unions and political parties have become looser (Taylor, 1989), the cleavages of 70 or more years ago are still in evidence in the present European labour movement (see Table 3.1). After 1945, during the Cold War, dissension between socialists and communists intensified and led to new rifts in France, Italy and elsewhere. There were efforts undertaken in the post-war period to unite socialist and Christian unions, but these only succeeded in the German and Austrian labour movements, both of which had been persecuted by years of fascism and war. Changes in the Catholic Church and socialist doctrines as well as the loosening of the ties between political parties and trade unions eventually cleared the way for a partly successful merger in the Netherlands, and efforts to arrive at increased cooperation in Italy.

Table 3.1   *Trade union structures in 1990*

Country	Structure	Confederations	Ideology/ orientation	Proportion members (%)	No. of member unions
Belgium	Blue-collar:	ACV	Catholic	52.0	21
	industry	ABVV	Social Democrat	39.1	12
	White-collar: general	ACLVB	Liberal	8.9	1
France	Industry/region	CGT	Communist	30.1	28
		CFDT	Socialist	21.5	24
		FO	Social Democrat	20.1	38
		CFTC	Catholic	4.6	
		CFE	Professionals	6.5	
		FEN	Education	7.8	
Germany	Industry	DGB	Social Democrat/ Christian	81.1	17
		DAG	Employees	6.5	0
		DBB	Civil servants	8.2	22
		CGB	Catholic	2.7	13
GB	Craft/general	TUC	Labour	89.0	78
Italy	Industry/region	CGIL	Communist/Social Democrat	51.0	17
		CISL	Catholic/Social Democrat	34.6	17
		UIL	Social Democrat	14.4	27
Netherlands	Industry	FNV	Social Democrat/ Catholic	62.4	16
		CNV	Christian	19.0	15
		MHP	Professionals	7.4	3
		ACV	Public sector/craft	6.6	26
Spain	Industry/region	UGT	Social Democrat	42.2	
		CC.OO	Communist	37.8	
		ELA	Regionalist	3.0	
		USO	Christian Democrat	3.0	
Sweden	Blue-collar:	LO	Social Democrat	57.9	24
	industry	TCO	Employees	33.8	21
	White-collar: industry	SACO	Professionals	7.7	18

3   Organization and administration

Trade unions and collective bargaining agreements

It is the task of every new trade union to turn a temporary movement into a permanent organization. If it is to become more than a group of campaigners who retreat at the first economic setback, the union must acquire resources that make long-term membership attractive and even necessary. Craft unions did that by exercising a strong measure of social control and by providing mutual insurance through contributions, premiums and benefits. But this method only worked for a small group of workers and under favourable labour market conditions. The development of a bargaining relationship with employers became the most common path to a sustainable organization. Once a trade union is able to make an employer believe that there is benefit in negotiating with a reliable, long-term partner, then it has solved half of its organizational problem. The employer must be convinced that the alternative (strikes, unrest, unmotivated employees) will be more expensive. The other half of the problem is to convince employees to remain members and take action if asked. If employees are unwilling to become members and undertake action, the union cannot secure its place at the bargaining table. The problem of mobilizing members will be discussed shortly.

For a bargaining relationship to develop, the parties must be aware that they can frustrate each other's purposes. Employers are interested in the productivity and commitment of their personnel, and prefer not to have to deal with labour unrest and employees who interfere with management. The trade unions are interested in better employment terms and job security for employees, preferably with a bigger membership and more dues income. To sustain the bargaining relationship, it is essential that the connection between the union and its rank-and-file is based on membership, and not on one-time donations or on a performance-related reward (for example, each time the union negotiates a wage rise). A union must not break the promises it made at the negotiating table; it can sanction its members, but it cannot sanction contributors or customers. Presumably, members have voting rights and influence union policy. It is precisely this democratic legitimacy which gives trade unions their bargaining authority. A trade union without members, a possibility discussed by Rosanvallon (1988), would be a group of campaigners or a service centre, but not a party to a collective agreement.

Since the 1920s and 1930s, a growing number of employees have come to be covered by collective agreements. Initially such agreements did not cover much more than manual workers in industry and transport, but after 1945 unions also negotiated on behalf of workers in agriculture, commercial services, white-collar workers and even civil servants. The industry-wide agreement, which applies to all employers in a particular industry, has extended the unions' radius of action. Negotiating by industry has relieved the unions of the impossible task of organizing each company, however small. It furthermore satisfies the typical trade union ideal of employment security and equal treatment. For the employers, industry-wide negotiations have the advantage of being far removed from the workplace and hence from plant management. Another advantage is that wages are eliminated as an inter-firm competitive factor in the national product markets. Large companies and trade unions sometimes even agree to use the industry-wide agreement to rationalize the industry by eliminating small businesses. The diffusion of the collective agreement and the rise of a mutually dependent relationship between trade unions and employers have made unions viable (formal) organizations. The data on birth and death rates of trade unions are revealing. Once the collective agreement is firmly established in an industry or country, the average life expectancy of the unions increases, membership stabilizes and fewer new unions are founded. When we compare countries, it appears that the more legal protection the collective agreement has and the more centralized collective bargaining is, the smaller the fluctuation in organization and membership (Visser, 1987).

Organization, internal democracy and participation

Trade unions not only have two sides to them externally, but internally as well. They must be able to mobilize employees and get them to take part in collective action, that is, become members, do volunteer work, attend meetings, vote in works council elections, take on official functions, go on strike and demonstrate. On the other hand, they must be viewed as a reliable bargaining partner who guarantees continuity and industrial peace. The trade union, then, is both an association of members and a bargaining partner and must frequently satisfy contradictory demands. It has taken on the role of intermediary within an increasingly tighter network of other organizations, which include both employers and other unions, confederations, international organizations and public institutions (Streeck and Schmitter, 1985). To mobilize consensus, the unions need a form of participative democracy; bargaining, on the other hand, requires quick decision-making by administrators who have a broad mandate from their members. Trade unions often meet the requirements of external decisiveness and internal participation by organizing various forms of quasi-participation (see Child et al., 1972).

The issue of trade union democracy is an old one which has been the subject of much debate. Trade unions seem to be subject to the iron law of oligarchy, with the few governing the many (Michels, 1925 [1911]), in the sense that their officials have claimed an increasing measure of power and are almost impossible to remove from office. Lipset et al. (1956) offered a solution by taking parliamentary democracy as an example: the unions should institutionalize an internal two-party system leading to real competition for union office and requiring officials to be accountable to the members. According to Martin (1968) it would be sufficient if unions allowed internal factions and if union officials were chosen in regularly scheduled elections. Edelstein and Warner (1978) proposed introducing procedural rules which would increase the chance of effectively removing incumbent union officials from office. Limits to the terms of office and secret ballots, as now required by law in Great Britain, were also recommended. Almost a century ago, Sydney and Beatrice Webb (1913 [1897]) suggested restricting terms of office for union officials and holding referendums among the membership on any important decisions (collective bargaining agreements, strikes, amendments to the union charter, mergers). This has indeed become the case in many countries with respect to strikes, mainly because of the major interests involved and to pre-empt any claims for damages or penalties; referendums on collective bargaining demands and proposals are also on the increase. Leadership ballots have remained the exception, however.

Many unions have divided their authority between a legislative body (a convention of elected representatives and an elected council which exercises control between conventions), an executive committee (which handles day-to-day business) and an appeals tribunal (which monitors the union charter and rule book). Nowadays unions of any importance have an executive committee consisting of full-time union officers; only small unions with few resources and craft unions still have lay officers at the highest executive level. Full-time officers are employed and paid by the union. The chief officials are usually elected at the union convention, mainly through cooptation by the current executive committee. There are generally no other serious opponents. On the Continent officials share power, whereas in Great Britain the union's general secretary has much more authority (and is elected by secret ballot by the entire membership). Carew (1976) found that in many unions on the Continent, full-time officials, as a voting minority, dominated union conferences and membership councils. Full-time officials at the lower levels (region, district, industrial sector, occupation, special groups etc.) are appointed by and accountable to the executive committee.

The number of full-time officials and their status differs sharply from country to country. In his comparative study, Carew (1976) found the highest official-to-member ratios in Sweden, Germany, the Netherlands and Belgium; officials also had more staff available to them here than in other countries, and their status was higher. Relatively speaking there are fewer full-time officials in British unions, which can be explained in part by the tradition of craft unionism and shop stewards, as well as by the much higher level of competition between unions, which keeps the membership dues lower than in other countries. The same problem troubles French, Spanish and Italian unions, although the situation in Italy has improved greatly over the past 20 years. Unions in these countries also make frequent use of arrangements in which employers grant union officials leave of absence from work, a practice which is particularly widespread in the public sector. While the British labour movement has a relatively large number of voluntary and few full-time officials, in Germany and the Netherlands the opposite is true (Carew, 1976; Rogers and Streeck, 1994; Visser, 1987, 1991). In Sweden, manual workers' unions alone have 150,000 elected union representatives. According to Kjellberg, one out of every eight members of a manual workers' union and one out of every five members of a white-collar union is active as a representative at the company level (Kjellberg, 1992: 123). Given the high level of union density in Sweden (83 per cent), this implies a very tightly woven network. In Great Britain the number of shop stewards is estimated at 300,000.

According to a representative survey distributed in 1990, 71 per cent of all establishments with more than 50 employees had at least one trade union representative; six years earlier that figure was 82 per cent. When calculated across the board for all companies, the number of plants or companies with a representative fell from 54 per cent in 1984 to 38 per cent in 1990 (Millward and Stevens, 1992: 110). The average number of members per representative is somewhere in the neighbourhood of 20 in Great Britain (lower for smaller and higher for larger companies; lower in the private sector and higher in the public sector) (1992: 116). In Italy there are about 200,000 *delegati*, which amounts to 1 for every 30 employed members. In accordance with a 1993 agreement between the three recognized union confederations and the employers, every company must organize formal elections for a new collective trade union body within the company. This is similar to Belgium, where the trade unions have had recognized union representation (*syndicale afvaardiging*) in the company since 1947, when they reached an agreement with employers which was later backed by legislation. The *syndicale afvaardiging* is considered more significant than the statutory works council in Belgium, although in many companies it is difficult to tell the difference between the two. Only union members qualify for seats on the works council, though all employees are eligible to vote.

French trade unions gained the official right to set up trade union offices in (larger) companies in 1969; further rights were granted in 1982. In addition, France has had a system of employee representation since 1936, to which the works council was added in 1945. Furthermore, a law came into force in 1982 obligating employers and trade unions to draw up a joint code of regulation governing employee participation. The total number of representative posts in France is estimated at 300,000, but a lack of candidates and overlapping mandates means that the actual number of representatives is smaller. The extremely low union density rate (10 per cent or less; in industry probably only 5 per cent) means that there is very little separating the rank-and-file from the representatives or lay union officials (Rosanvallon, 1988). Fierce infighting among unions and a traditional emphasis on political influence have impaired the influence of French unions at the company level.

In Spain, companies with 50 or more employees are legally required to set up a works council. Seventy per cent of companies appear to comply with this obligation. The number of representatives is estimated at well over 200,000; most of them are trade union members. Like the French, the Spanish labour movement must contend with an extremely low union density rate and meagre financial, organizational and staff resources.

In Germany and the Netherlands the majority of lower-level lay officials can be found on works councils, which are required by law in both countries and which have a variety of rights and powers. In Germany companies with as few as six employees are obligated to have a *Betriebsrat*; three-quarters of all companies (covering 90 per cent of all German employees) comply with the law. In total there are close to 200,000 works council members (leaving out the five new German states created from the former DDR). As many as nine out of ten are not union members. In addition, there are some 40,000–50,000 *Vertrauensleute* who maintain contacts on behalf of the unions but who are not works council members.

Dutch law stipulates that companies and plants with 35 or more employees must have an *ondernemingsraad*. About 70 per cent of companies, covering a slightly higher percentage of employees, comply. In total there are well over 50,000 works council members in the private sector, and about 70 per cent of them are union members. In addition, there is a *bedrijfskadergroep* (union group) in one out of every three companies, but this body is not very important and in general it plays second fiddle to the works council. In Germany, the works council can be considered an extension of the union, although the law restricts its capacity for union action (it cannot call a strike or negotiate wages, for example) and prescribes certain duties and tasks (it must represent all the personnel, including non-union members, and treat certain information from management as confidential). In the Netherlands the unions have been less capable of capturing the *ondernemingsraad*, partly because of the debilitating consequences of inter-union competition.

Flanders (1954: 47–48) once wrote with respect to the British labour movement that there was probably no other institution in the country which had allowed so many people to help their fellow man through volunteer work and gain practical experience in democratic management. It is difficult to say whether the same is true for other countries. It can be said, however, that the unions have played and continue to play an important role, although legislation on the works council probably made this role more indirect. The shift from direct to indirect democracy is undeniable. The generally low attendance at meetings is compensated by the massive participation in referendums and works council elections. In countries where such elections are held once every two, three or four years (Germany, the Netherlands, Belgium, France, Spain and now Italy), the average voter turnout lies somewhere between 65 and 90 per cent. Together with the hundreds of thousands who serve as representatives, without much compensation in terms of time, training, remuneration and power, it is not the least among the union movement's accomplishments.

Horizontal and vertical integration

Each union must try to create 'unity out of diversity' – that is, bring together people with different backgrounds and interests. This is also known as the task of horizontal integration. At the same time, each union must put 'unity above diversity' – that is, provide leadership, vertical integration, or in other words bind all levels of the organization, from top to bottom, to a chosen policy. This can be called the task of vertical integration. The problem with both forms of integration increases as the union becomes larger and more diverse. For example, because of their internal heterogeneity (different occupational groups, large and small companies), industrial unions face a more difficult task than craft unions. The task of a confederation is less easy than that of its affiliates, and the international and European labour movement are facing the most serious integration problems of all (Ebbinghaus and Visser, 1994).

The national trade unions are usually unitary organizations; in other words, their territorial and functional units are subdivisions which may choose their own leaders but not determine their own budgets or policies. The legal personality is vested in the national organization, represented by the executive council. Confederations, on the other hand, are organizations of organizations, that is, federations of unions. The same is true of the international and the European labour movement – indeed, the ETUC (European Trade Union Confederation) is an organization consisting of organizations (46 confederations from 21 countries and 16 international trade secretariats) of organizations (some 800 national trade unions). There are few examples of transnational trade unions; North American unions sometimes organize in both Canada and the United States, and British craft unions have members in the Republic of Ireland; in the European Union there is a transnational union for civil servants deployed at the EU institutions and Europe-wide unions for engine drivers and commercial airline pilots.

Unions traditionally united their members by rallying them round strategic groups – the skilled craftsman, the male manual worker in industry with a wife, two children and a full-time job etc. This (horizontal) integration model was naturally subject to constant criticism, and from time to time 'special' subdivisions arose for white-collar employees, women, young people, benefits recipients etc. By making the functional categories subordinate to the territorial ones, however, the logic of uniting members round a central or 'average' figure could be retained. The unions continued to draw up their package of demands based on this figure, but the sharp increase in labour market diversity, both on the supply and the demand side, is making unity through standardization more difficult and is forcing unions towards decentralization, to ease problems of internal organization. This does not make the task of union leadership – putting 'unity above diversity' – any easier. Streeck (1982) claims that unions can compensate for the loss of control through internal decentralization by building up their ties with the works council. The union can 'borrow' control over its decentral negotiators from the law; after all, works council members are not allowed to strike and are obligated to represent the entire workforce.

The integration problem is even more substantial for the confederations; they cover a larger diversity of interests and serve as an umbrella for independent affiliates. A confederation that brings together a large number of unions, all of which have conflicting organizational principles and policy preferences (for example, in the UK) cannot help but be weak.

If the affiliated unions are well matched in terms of size and power but serve diverse interests, the confederation will be subject to diverging pressures and become weaker – as have the German, Swedish and Dutch confederations. In the past 10–20 years, rivalry between private sector unions on the one hand (which are concerned with the consequences of international competition), and public sector unions on the other (which are more interested in levels of government spending and domestic expenditure) has crippled confederations to some degree and explains the failure of various social pacts and nationally concerted agreements in the 1970s (Visser, 1987).

This type of problem is naturally even more serious in the European labour movement, particularly because it is attempting to expand its representativeness long before it has the authority to act. The ETUC's problem is not only that trade unions in each of the 21 countries it represents have a different organizational structure, a different power base and a different form of involvement in social and economic policy, but also that these organizations have acquired strong national identities because of the successful national integration of the labour movement in the past. That is why international cooperation has become even more difficult and more improbable than it was on the eve of the First World War, the fatal moment when the international labour movement chose the path of nationalism.

Although the growing economic and political interdependence is driving unions in the direction of internationalization, they will not all move at the same pace or even in the same direction, given the variation in national problems, different levels of integration and varying opportunities in the national arena. Neither does Brussels act as a magnet: employers are not to become a social partner at the European level, and the European Union has not yet acquired enough authority with respect to industrial relations and social policy to force or tempt them to do so (Ebbinghaus and Visser, 1994). The magnetism that Brussels lacks was present in the history of many European nation-states. According to de Swaan (1989: 180), the process of centralizing unions and employers' associations is very similar to the dynamism of state formation: it is an example of a configuration in which opponents force each other to develop higher levels of integration. State intervention took this one step further and forced employers and workers to consolidate their interests and articulate them at a central level. The history of Dutch industrial relations shows that these processes are not irreversible. If the government retreats and employers support a process of de-collectivization and decentralization of industrial relations, the spiral may reverse.

The centre of power in the labour movement is wherever collective bargaining takes place (Clegg, 1976). If collective bargaining agreements are signed company by company, trade unions tend to be decentralized as well. Industry-wide bargaining, on the other hand, requires executive control at the union centre. If confederations are to participate in central consultations concerning income policy and wage determination, they must have a bargaining mandate and must be able to exercise authority over their affiliated member organizations. Confederations are seldom, if ever, parties to collective agreements. The central accords or framework agreements sometimes arrived at in Sweden, the Netherlands, Belgium, France, Italy and Spain set out instructions, conditions, guidelines, recommendations or suggestions for negotiators at the industry or company level. In Germany and Great Britain, the confederations have no mandate from their member organizations. Central coordination is becoming increasingly difficult because employers keep pushing for decentralization, the government tends to withdraw and the unions are increasingly divided among themselves.

To summarize, we can say that it becomes easier for the labour movement in a given country to create 'unity out of diversity' if the confederations and unions are closely linked, if there is little divergence between confederations and their member unions over organizational principles and policy objectives, and if all important unions are members of a confederation (Visser, 1987). Sweden and Germany have the highest score on the index of horizontal integration; France, the Netherlands and Great Britain score much lower; and Italy and possibly Spain and Belgium fall somewhere in between. Putting 'unity above diversity' is easiest when the central organizations have a bargaining mandate, consult regularly with government and employers, and have a large staff, considerable resources and a centralized strike fund from which to draw strength. Sweden scores higher on vertical integration than Germany, and Great Britain has an isolated position in last place. The other confederations are situated between these two extremes, with the Belgian and Dutch confederations ahead of the German, and the Italian ahead of the Spanish and French (Visser, 1987). Every confederation is now undergoing a process of decentralization (Baglioni and Crouch, 1990) resulting from the decline of political exchange. They are apparently on their way to becoming relatively weak federations holding together a few large but divided union cartels in the public and private sectors.

4 Power and mobilization of members

Three sources of power

The power of trade unions depends on various internal and external factors. We can distinguish between organizational power (how many internal sources of power can unions mobilize?), institutional power (which external sources of support can unions depend on?) and economic power (which market forces play into the hands of unions?).

In organizational terms the potential power of the trade union is greatest when it

1   can mobilize a large, stable, paying and well-trained membership;
2   has managed to unite operational, technical and supervisory personnel, indirect and direct production workers into one organization;
3   has succeeded in escaping the organizational fragmentation of the craft unions;
4   has avoided political or ideological divisions or has been able to neutralize such divisions through close cooperation;
5   works closely with several political parties without becoming dependent on just one or a few of these parties;
6   has an extensive external organization with branches at the company level and central control of funds and decision-making.

Points (2) to (5) were discussed in the previous sections; in this section we will look at the first aspect, the mobilization of members.

The institutional power of the unions is related to their ties with other organizations, for example, employers' associations and public institutions, through consultation, negotiation and representation. This institutional power is greatest where unions have been granted a 'semi-public status' (Offe, 1981) and where the government explicitly supports a policy of self-regulation between employers and employees. Unions which are too dependent on politics and government, or which do not enjoy constitutional or legal protection, may run into problems. The *Tarifautonomie* of the German constitution, with its attendant idea that the law should encourage a balance of power between unions and employers' associations, presumably offers a greater measure of stability and protection against momentary political moods.

Finally, trade unions cannot run any further than their legs can carry them. A union that represents employees who are in demand and who possess scarce skills is much more powerful than a union whose membership includes many unskilled and unemployed workers. Unions of skilled workers usually have a relatively large measure of economic power, as do air-traffic controllers, airline pilots and computer specialists today, except for those whose power was stripped by politics – as in the case of the air-traffic controllers in the early 1980s, for example, when President Reagan brought in military personnel to replace them when they went on strike. Trade unions generally lose economic power in periods of recession and high unemployment. Employers are often stuck with excess capacity and are therefore less impressed by the threat of strikes. Membership declines during a recession because the jobless turn in their membership cards (unless the union is involved in distributing unemployment benefits or in finding new jobs, as is the case in Belgium, Denmark, Finland, Iceland and Sweden). The unions can survive hard times if they are well organized and have institutional protection. Employers and politicians will be more cautious in that case; they will avoid adding insult to injury. They might rather view the situation from a long-term perspective.

Unions can try to change market outcomes, but they cannot ignore market forces. If they want to influence market forces, they must be sure to cover the same territory as the market does. If the product or labour market expands beyond its borders because of internationalization, then the trade unions must keep pace; in other words, they must set up transnational organizations, or at the very least coordinate their activities with trade unions in other countries. If they fail to do so, they will go into decline. The process of deterioration may be delayed by political alliances, market imperfections and national sensitivities. In the past the same logic led from local to national trade unions.

Membership and union density rate

The collective mobilization of employees over the past 100 years can be illustrated as a long, rising line with growing divergences between the various countries and a clear dip after 1980 (see Figure 3.1). The rising line has had its interruptions – for example, immediately after the First World War employees who had joined the union movement in droves suddenly resigned en masse. The problem was that many unions were ill-equipped to handle the massive numbers of members, finding it impossible to live up to their high expectations (in part because of the post-war crisis as the war economy came to an end). They therefore suffered defeat after defeat. Only a minority of workers were covered under the terms of a collective

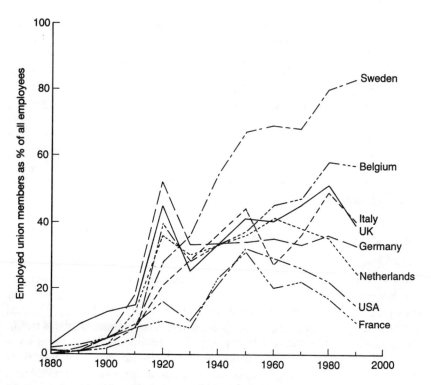

Figure 3.1   Membership rates, 1890–1990

bargaining agreement, and the industry-wide agreement was still rare. In Italy and Germany, moreover, this period also saw the advent of a serious political crisis which ended in the rise and triumph of fascism. In the 1930s a number of countries tried to fight the crisis by adopting the industry-wide agreement as a market 'floor' preventing sharp declines in pay. In the long run this generated an increase in membership and greater economic and membership stability (Sweden, Great Britain, the Netherlands, Belgium, and after 1945 Germany). The institutionalization of the labour movement and its involvement in social and economic policy also served as stabilizing factors, although in the 1950s and 1960s the growth of unionism stagnated. The difference between membership rates in Italy and France, where the Cold War split the labour movement internally, stifled the resistance of the employers, and marginalized the unions, is quite clear in Figure 3.1. In the 1970s, white-collar and public sector employees tried to catch up, partly as a protest against the levelling effect of price inflation. The labour movement also benefited from the rapid expansion of the welfare state, especially in the education, culture and health care sectors.

The data given in Figure 3.1 give rise to two important analytical questions. First, how can we explain the pattern that emerged in that period? Was it the product of economic business cycles, or did political and institutional factors weigh more heavily? The answer to this question is also important for assessing the most recent period, after 1980. Is this just a deep but temporary trough comparable to the 1920s, or are we witnessing a reversal of trends, signalling an end to fifty years of union growth and stability? Secondly, how do we explain the increasing divergence between countries? Can institutional and political factors alone account for the differences, or do economic factors also play a role? What role does trade union policy play? The answers to these questions are important for assessing the future: is the European labour movement irrevocably heading in the same direction as the American labour movement? Is the case of France unique? We will return to these questions shortly. First, however, we must say something about the social profile of union membership and about the differences within countries, that is, between specific categories of employees.

The social profile of the labour movement

Table 3.2 presents data on the changing composition of the trade unions. A number of trends emerge. In 1920, the majority of union members worked in industry. This continued to be the case in 1950, but by 1990 it was only just true of Germany. In the Netherlands, France and Sweden, only a third of union members are employed in industry. That means that the trend-setting unions in the metal industry, which were long ago absorbed by the industrial unions in such countries as the Netherlands, have lost their commanding leadership positions in the confederations and in industrial relations in general. The union movement is no longer a (manual) workers'

Table 3.2 *Composition of union membershp in 1920 and 1990 (category share expressed as a percentage of total membership)*

| | Industry | | Market sector | | | | | | | |
| | | | Blue-collar workers | | White-collar employees | | Public sector | | Women | |
Country	1920	1990	1920	1990	1920	1990	1920	1990	1920	1990
Belgium	70	45								
France	50	35	66	33	7	12	26	55		28
Germany	66	57	68	49	17	18	16	33		25
GB	67	38	71	41	8	20	21	39	15	38
Italy		42		46		21		33		33
Netherlands	50	36	61	34	8	16	31	50	8	19
Sweden	57	37	73	36	4	23	23	42	8	50

movement, not in any country. Public sector and private service sector unions together now represent the majority, and they have taken over the leadership role in many countries. It is interesting to note that the public sector is particularly well represented in countries with a low union density rate, such as France and the Netherlands. With reference to female members, the figures we present were drawn from the unions' own historical statistics and archives and are unfortunately quite incomplete. It seems that women members were rare in 1920 – women were subject to restrictions not only in the labour market but in the labour movement as well. Data from 1950 and 1960 (not presented here) show that the situation had not changed very much in this respect (Visser, 1989). A small cultural revolution took place in Scandinavia and the English-speaking countries in the 1970s and 1980s, with women joining the labour movement in droves thanks to the feminization of the public health care, culture and education sectors and the growing number of women entering commercial professions. Today, half of all union members in Sweden are female. Women account for overall net membership growth since 1980 in all of the countries shown (there are no figures available for Belgium).

Unfortunately there are no comparative data available on changes in age group, educational level and company size. The data which we do have show that union members have become older; in part, this can be explained by demographic trends. Younger birth cohorts became smaller after the 1960s. Moreover, thanks to increased educational opportunities, young people tend to stay in school longer, and enter the labour market at a later age. They also seem less inclined to join unions and retain their membership in them. The educational level of the average member has increased along with that of the average worker, and there is generally little difference between organized skilled workers and organized unskilled workers. There are differences, however, between employees with technical or vocational training and those with a general education – the first category tends to be more unionized. There is a significant size effect

Table 3.3 *Union density rate around 1990 (working members as a percentage of employees)*

Country	Market sector	Public sector	Industry	Trade, hotel restaurant and catering industry	Financial sector	Men	Women
Belgium			95	36	23		
France	8	26	5			13	7
Germany	30	45	48	15	17	47	22
GB	37	47	41	14	25	44	33
Italy	32	54	47	19	22		
Netherlands	19	44	25	7	12	34	15
Sweden	81	84	100	49	72	82	85

related to union density rates, with workers in large firms being more unionized than workers in small firms (alhtough there are exceptions, for example Italy).

The differences between countries are confirmed by the data presented in Table 3.3. With the exception of Sweden, women are clearly less likely to be union members, particularly in Germany, France and the Netherlands. Figures for the Netherlands show that the low union density rate of women there is related to the fact that they are more likely to work in temporary or part-time jobs. The service sectors (trade and restaurant/ hotel, and financial services) clearly have a lower union density rate than industry or the building trade (not shown here). The transport sector (also not shown), especially traditional sectors such as ports, shipping and the railways and the post office, are highly organized. Finally, the public sector has a much higher union density rate than the commercial sector. Explanations can be found in the sector structure (large or small companies, regional concentration); in the balance of power (industry-wide or company agreements, or both, or neither); in the presence of works councils and union representation in enterprises; in the economic position of the sector within the international division of labour; in the social profile and mutual social ties between employees; and in the organizational tradition and policy of the trade unions.

The data on the social profile of the trade unions indicate which employees they represent. These figures may be helpful in interpreting and explaining the internal tensions and policies of the union movement. For example, in almost every country, union membership in agriculture, the building trade and the public service sector – sectors dependent on national or European government policy – is larger than union membership in industry, trade and commercial services – sectors which are forced to compete internationally. What effect does this have on policy? Is this why the traditional alliance between unions and social-democratic parties (which also have fewer workers now among their voters, members or officials) has been subject to much tension of late? Is the rising female membership responsible for the unions' greater willingness to accept flexible working time arrangements and to turn their attention to the quality of working life? Or is it the other way around?

The figures in Tables 3.2 and 3.3 have been calculated for employed union members. But the number of members who do not work – either because they are unemployed, retired, in early retirement, sick or disabled – has grown rapidly in each country. This category presently represents about 10 per cent of union membership in France and Great Britain, 10–20 per cent in Germany, Sweden and the Netherlands, 30 per cent in Belgium and 40 per cent in Italy. Among the reasons for the increase are: an ageing membership (fewer young people become members), an increase in unemployment or compensatory benefits (disablement benefits), early retirement schemes, and the general rise in life expectancy. Sometimes people retain their membership out of habit or loyalty, but there are unions that provide services and facilities for retired and unemployed members. For example, Swedish and Belgian unions are involved in administrating unemployment benefits and in addition provide a wide range of individual services to members. In Italy the union helps to assess and administer pension claims. Unlike the North American labour movement, trade unions in Europe – which were originally rooted in politics – employ a more 'inclusive' or 'class' concept of membership: workers who lack a position of power in the company or in the labour market take a share of the power of those who do. The organization of these groups is a matter of great concern to the trade unions, especially now that the confederations are losing authority and the unions are focusing their attention on the company. In many countries the confederations have taken up the task of representing these groups, but with very limited success. Some observers have argued for separate unions for the unemployed, the retired or benefit recipients, or indeed for women, so that the problems which these groups face are given a voice in the general union movement and especially with regard to the political agenda. Others fear that if the unemployed, long-term sick or disabled leave the unions of which they have been members, these unions will forget about them and focus all their attention on members in employment. In historical terms, little has been achieved in setting up separate organizations for the unemployed, for example – they do not really get through to their target group and are not able to achieve much on their behalf. Indeed, many of such organizations died an early death (Garraty, 1978; Pollard, 1969). There are many early examples of separate unions for female employees, but only one (in Denmark) has survived until the present day (see Cook et al., 1983).

Why join a trade union?

The most obvious answer to this question is that unions have something to offer: better employment terms and working conditions, job security, protection, a feeling of self-respect. The problem with this answer is that you actually do not have to be a member yourself to get many of these things. It is enough that other people have joined; after all, most of the 'products' that the unions have to offer (for example better employment terms, security, protection against the power of the employer) are 'collective goods': it is impossible or difficult to exclude people who have not paid their share from enjoying the benefits. This is known as the *free rider* problem (Olson, 1965) – people benefit at no charge from what others have done.

The paradox of collective action is that if everyone acted according to this logic, there would be no collective action and consequently no trade union. Nevertheless, there are trade unions (and similar organizations) and many cost-conscious and rational people do become members. How can we explain this?

Olson argues that organizations such as trade unions can prevent free riding by offering individual services to members and by imposing sanctions on non-members. Such measures presuppose that the union already exists and has a relatively secure position. If that is the case, then services provided exclusively to members may be the answer, especially if these services cover issues in which the trade unions are experts – for example, legal and moral assistance and advice in the workplace, vocational training, job mediation. Danish trade unions, for instance, provide vocational training and job mediation to their members (Scheuer, 1992: 181). Comparative research has shown that trade unions that supply part of unemployment insurance or have taken on some of the administrative tasks have a much higher union density rate. Rothstein (1991) estimates that countries which have retained this system have at least a 20 per cent higher union density rate *vis-à-vis* countries where the government has completely taken over the administration of unemployment benefits. Not only are the unemployed in Sweden, Belgium etc. more likely to be organized than the employed, but the threat of unemployment means that many working people become or remain members as a precaution. Trade unions also try to recruit or retain members by providing other services linked to membership. For example, American and British trade unions offer their members credit cards and discounts. Belgian trade unions help members fill in tax forms and advise them on housing problems (Vilrokx and van Leemput, 1992: 370). For a long time German trade unions were active in the housing and mortgage market, and suffered many financial losses. As the final example indicates, these activities are not always a success: other organizations are just as good or better and the effect on the recruitment and retention of members is questionable.

The closed shop is becoming increasingly rare, even in Anglo-Saxon countries, where the practice of compelling workers to contribute to the costs of collective action had been more widespread than elsewhere. In most countries the practice is unlawful, as on the Continent, because it does not fit in well with the constitutional freedom of association and has the same disadvantages as the truck system: when there is no choice, the quality of both the organization and the product will decline. If the intention is to reward trade unions for their public services, then the same can be achieved by means of subsidies (by the tax payer) or a tax on wage costs that non-members must pay as well. If the intention is to bind all employees, including non-members, under the terms of a collective agreement, then a statutory works council that oversees compliance is a suitable functional equivalent of the closed shop.

Centralization and decentralization

There are strong indications that both centralization and decentralization encourage union membership. This seems paradoxical but perhaps it is not so. Membership can be seen as a step with two hurdles (Green, 1992; Visser, 1993): there are people who do not join because there is no trade union in their environment, and there are people who do not join even though there is a trade union. If there is a trade union at hand, three things may happen.

1 People do not agree with the trade union and do not see how they will benefit either collectively or personally from becoming a member.
2 People believe that they will benefit but decide to become free riders.
3 People become members.

The latter possibility will depend on both the collective and the personal benefits of membership, the cost of membership and the cost associated with not being a member. With respect to the latter, a very pro-union atmosphere and social control in the workplace can increase the costs of non-membership considerably.

If there is no (internal) trade union, the individual employee faces another problem: the choice is no longer between joining or not joining a union, but between investing or not investing in founding a union (within the company). According to the *mobilization theory* employees will only decide to make this investment if they are convinced that the goal (having a union in the company) matters to them personally, that their own participation is essential for success, that enough of their fellow employees will join and that they have a chance of succeeding if they work together. Outside help, preparation, motivation, coordination and social control within the group are very important. This approach differs from Olson's reasoning in so far as the participation of others strengthens rather than diminishes the willingness to join (Hardin, 1982; Klandermans, 1984; Marwell and Oliver, 1993).

Highly decentralized systems of industrial relations, where unions negotiate on a company-by-company basis, give rise to the second problem. In the United States, and now in Great Britain as well, most companies and plants do not recognize or have a trade union. Where trade unions are recognized and present, most of the employees do join, although naturally enough there are also free riders. One out of three

Americans treasures union membership but works in a company where unions are not recognized and a majority vote in favour of bringing in a union is unlikely (Kochan, 1988). In Great Britain, the union density and bargaining coverage rate have both declined, while the industry-wide agreement has almost disappeared. In 62 per cent of all establishments there is no longer a trade union representative present. Comparable figures can perhaps be found in France and Spain, but in Sweden, Belgium, Italy, Germany and the Netherlands (at least in industry and thanks to the works council, which makes trade union recognition much easier) trade union coverage is wider, though there are many workplaces (particularly in the Netherlands) with only a few union members (see Klandermans and Visser, 1995). Millward and Stevens (1992) claim that the growing number of establishments without union members was the most striking development in British industrial relations in the 1980s. The split between union and non-union companies is leading to the type of competition that is so harmful to the American union movement (Blanchflower and Freeman, 1990). To recruit members, unions in the United States have to prove themselves by forcing employers to concede higher wages and better employment terms. Employers, for their part, face higher costs in the union sector and must compete with other employers who do not have the same costs. There is an incentive to resist the unions or shift new investments to the non-union sector. It appears that unions cannot win this game. American unions represent a shrinking group of employees in old industrial sectors and companies. There have been efforts to break out of this destructive game and search for cooperative solutions with employers, but these have been isolated and unsuccessful attempts.

Centralized systems have fewer problems of competition between union and non-union companies, thanks to the industry-wide agreement and the legal extension of collective agreements to cover an entire industry. Trade union recognition generally takes place at the national level or is arranged by law (works council), and employers do not have the same freedom to oppose the unions. The original idea was that negotiations at the industry level would neutralize the company or plant as an arena for struggle between employers and employees. It therefore limits the employers' need to oppose the union. That is why several comparative IR scholars have observed a positive relationship between centralization and union density rates (Blanchflower and Freeman, 1990; ILO, 1993; Visser, 1991, 1993; Western, 1993). Blanchflower and Freeman (1990) and Visser (1986) also claim that there is a positive relationship with an increase in union density in the past. Centralized collective bargaining extends the reach of the trade union but it also increases the distance to employees on the shop floor. Free rider behaviour becomes easier. That is why Clegg (1976) has emphasized the importance of the coverage and the depth of collective bargaining: is the industry-wide agreement translated into rights on the shop floor, into trade union representation and grievance procedures in the plant? It appears that trade unions with distinct representation within the company were better able to recruit and retain members during the 1980s (Hancké, 1993). This actually coincides with Olson's idea of splitting latent groups into small, recognizable units in which coordination and social control is possible. Unions which are organized both centrally and decentrally and which have succeeded in coordinating the two levels effectively appear to have the highest union density rates (Crouch, 1993a; Kjellberg, 1983, 1992). The Swedish and Belgian labour movements are closest to this combination, whereas in Germany, at least in industry, the works council has become so much an extension of the union that we can speak of an articulated system here (Thelen, 1991; Turner, 1991). Great Britain lacks the advantages of centralization, while the Netherlands lacks those of decentralization – as discussed earlier, the works council cannot play the same role here as it does in Germany. Italy has had a bi-polar system for a long time (somewhat comparable to the British system in the 1960s and 1970s); the trade union is present both at the central and decentral levels, but coordination is problematic and is attended by many conflicts. Inflationary pressures are considerable and employers doubt the usefulness of central agreements. While this has led in Great Britain to the decline of centralized organization and negotiations, the Italian unions are making tremendous efforts to arrive at a form of controlled decentralization within even stricter central guidelines. The renewed cooperation between the three recognized confederations may be helpful. In France, it is inter-union rivalry that makes coordination difficult. In the 1980s decentralized negotiations were encouraged through legislation which appeared to be inspired by the desire to marginalize the communist unions and by the need to counter employers more effectively. The ultimate effect on the unions was negative. The meagre achievements of the divided French trade unions are even more obvious now that they are being forced to prove themselves in the workplace (Segrestin, 1990). In Spain, where the trade unions only gained statutory recognition in 1977, the unions had trouble gaining a foothold vis-à-vis the works councils (in the bigger companies) and political parties (for which they initially served as junior partners), while they were unable to gain any access to many smaller companies. Owing to the intractable unemployment problem and the legacy of a rigid labour market, the Spanish labour movement is facing difficult choices with little political compensation.

5   Trade unionism in the future

The end of a success story?

There is a growing awareness that the labour movement has reached a turning point in its development. In a certain sense that is the consequence of the success which it was able to achieve in the past century. Thanks in part to the labour movement, employees have acquired rights which restrict the 'variable' use of their labour power. The 'civil war concerning working hours' (Karl Marx) was won by the trade unions, with assistance from churches and other supporters – although not for good, as we know now, and not for everyone. There are many areas in which social rights (minimum wage, dismissal rules, equal treatment) supersede or alternate the forces of the market.

A century of trade unionism began with the winning of civil and political rights. The arrival and expansion of collective bargaining made the trade union into an institution, a party without which today's labour markets in Europe would be very different. Crisis, unemployment, fascism and war led to the further national integration of the labour movement, partly because the unions were involved in co-managing general social and economic policies and social insurance systems.

The model of industrial relations which prevailed in Northwest Europe after 1945 was based on the ideal of strong and centralized trade unions and employers' associations and a government which guided or helped, but did not dictate (see Crouch, 1993b; Streeck, 1993; Visser, 1990). The union movement gained recognition and became part of the national welfare and productivity coalition. Employers had a free hand in managing companies but endorsed the objectives of the social market economy. The state accepted responsibility for sustaining full employment and the social care and security of its citizens. This constellation is seen as one of the building blocks of the longest period of economic growth and prosperity in Western Europe. And it all came about under an international security and monetary regime guaranteed and dominated by the United States. The tidal wave of actions and protests that surprised unions, employers and governments alike all across Europe between 1968 and 1973 (Crouch and Pizzorno, 1978) made the weak spot painfully obvious. Little had changed within the company. The redundancy schemes had improved, but workers were not involved in decisions on mergers, closures and dismissals. Employers and trade unions took such decisions for them.

The post-war compromise was due for an overhaul. The days of the centrally controlled wage policy were numbered, and there were arguments on all sides in favour of free wage bargaining. Trade unions began to revolt against their own confederations and union members against union executives. Employers saw similar tensions between large and small companies. Solutions were sought in increasing the level of employee participation in both unions and companies. In this same period, Germany and Sweden saw the first great projects focusing on the 'humanization' of the workplace and the improvement in the quality of working life. The international monetary and energy crises at the start of the 1970s, however, exposed the enormous vulnerability of the economies of Europe. While employees and trade unions exercised increasing pressure, external developments restricted the leeway of employers and governments. By intensifying cooperation with central organizations of employers and employees, governments attempted to control developments better, but were forced to accept concessions in order to arrive at increasingly vague agreements with union confederations and central employers' associations, while they in turn could count on less and less of a mandate from their rank-and-file.

There was another turning point around 1980, brought on in part by the sharp increase in unemployment, the election of President Reagan in the United States and of Prime Minister Thatcher in Great Britain. The role of the state and of public policy was called into question, and so was the role of the trade union. Mrs Thatcher began her policy of the 'rejection of compromise' (Crouch, 1990b), meaning that she intended to reduce the trade union to a mere interest group of minor importance. Her colleagues in the European Union did not follow her example, but they did admire her (albeit secretly). In any event, the predictable British veto in Brussels made it possible for them to put on a good show (Lange, 1992). Another industrial relations and economic policy agenda had emerged.

The themes in the 1980s were globalization, decentralization, flexible production and human resources management (Baglioni and Crouch, 1990; Kochan et al., 1989; Piore and Sabel, 1984). Under pressure from international markets, employers became convinced that they had to find cheaper and differentiated solutions rather than uniform or standard ones, that closer, more direct coordination with the market was needed and that customer service and quality were important competitive factors. The emphasis in industrial relations shifted from the national to the company level, and from the political to the industrial arena. The internal union became more and more important, but the major labour market problems (high and increasing level of unemployment, company shutdowns, restructuring and even the disappearance of entire sectors of industry) demanded a great deal in the way of staff, resources and attention and made radical change difficult. Trade unions which had traditionally built their organizations on political support and had little or no presence in the company came off the worst.

New challenges

The most important challenge which the labour movement now faces is that of internationalization. The increasing measure of economic and political interdependence on a world scale and in Europe has changed the rules of the game. The national model of industrial relations which proved so successful between 1880 and 1980, and which made so much of the economic and social progress of European employees possible, is now in a deep crisis. Japan and the United States took leave of the inclusive European model some two decades ago. The question is whether Europe will be able to retain the basic elements of this model, and this calls into question the entire philosophy and role of the trade unions. It is impossible to answer here whether unionism will be as important in the twenty-first century as it was in the twentieth in each of the three dimensions which we distinguished at the beginning of this chapter. What is certain is that the trade union must respond to three major challenges: the organization of solidarity across national borders; solidarity between the employed and the unemployed; and a new focus on work, training, occupation and the environment as the basis for a high-quality knowledge-intensive and environmentally sustainable economic growth strategy.

Within the framework of this chapter it is only possible to point out the organizational consequences of such a programme. International solidarity is not a luxury but a necessity to turn the current tide. Trade union leaders today can still choose between national and international options, but soon that choice will be gone. The road to transnational collective bargaining at the company and sector level is strewn with pitfalls and it is still a long and hard one. Nevertheless, it is a road that must be taken. Given that the European Union is only a quasi-state and does not possess any real authority in the field of industrial relations, and given that the EU lacks the ammunition to force or bluff European employers into the role of social partner, there is little prospect of centralizing industrial relations at the European level, even if the trade unions were able to overcome their internal differences. There would be a better chance of success if strong industrial unions were to attempt to coordinate activities horizontally at lower levels (company, region, industry) (Ebbinghaus and Visser, 1994).

In Scandinavia the unions have formed cartels with the intention of arriving at the organizational model of the German labour movement, except that they have retained a confederation which has much more authority than is the case in Germany. They also own a widespread network of 'voluntary' union delegates at company level. German unions are in the process of forming a few large union federations and reducing the tasks and authority of the peak association. This latter development also seems most likely in the Netherlands, partly because the process of uniting the various currents of the Dutch labour movement has stagnated. In Italy the labour movement has undertaken steps in that direction, but the outcome is uncertain. In Belgium the debate on the integration of manual and white-collar unions has stagnated again after a short burst of activity. In Great Britain the unions are trying to compensate for their loss of membership and financial resources through mergers which have made the structure of the British labour movement even more bewildering than it was before. A number of union blocs have arisen which will further erode the tasks and authority of the umbrella confederation, the TUC. In France and Spain, the labour movement is in deep trouble and there is little evidence of revitalization in the French case.

The picture, in short, is very mixed. Economies of scale are necessary, both because of the European dimension and because only the biggest unions can set up the expensive and intensive network of services required for members, works councils and company negotiations. The network is needed to recruit and retain members and representatives. Economies of scope are needed to make union presence in the company a reality.

Without this presence, the union lacks the internal flexibility and variation to respond on time to a demanding and changing environment.

Europe's accomplishments in the social arena can only be defended without protectionism if they are underwritten by a system of high-quality production and services. Unions must ask themselves how they might contribute to creating such a system. To justify their role in production, unions should return to their roots, the (internal) craft union, but without giving up what they have achieved through the industrial–political trade union model: inclusive representation and solidarity between the strong and the weak. In addition to encouraging the participation of people in work, organization and society, this is labour movement's *raison d'être*, and it will remain so into the next century.

4 Employers and employers' associations

Frans van Waarden

1 Introduction

Why are there employers' associations? The answer to this question is far from self-evident. Whereas employees are almost always represented (or must be represented) by a collective actor such as their trade union or works council, this is not necessarily the case with employers. In many countries and branches of trade and industry, individual employers negotiate with organizations of employees, and collective bargaining agreements are concluded for companies individually. Do employers have any need at all for organizations promoting their collective interests? The purpose of a collective organization is to create power. But do employers not have more power than their employees as it is? Why, then, would they join an organization of peers? After all, membership entails compliance with rules, regulations and outside agreements, and restrictions on the freedom to conduct a business. And if there was any reason for collectively organizing employers in the past, would that reason still be valid in the present era of individualization and decentralization of labour relations?

This chapter deals with employers' associations in Europe. We will first discuss the phenomenon of employers' associations as such and the problems that occur when employers decide to organize (section 2). Section 3 looks at why, despite these problems, such associations do exist and section 4 examines the types of associations that can be found. Secondly, we will look at the features of such associations (sections 5 to 9), and compare a large number of European employers' associations, both at the central and at the sectoral level. Section 10 lists some possible explanations for the variety of associations found in the different countries. More particularly, we will investigate parallels within countries between the structures of employers' associations and employee organizations (section 10) and collective bargaining systems (section 12). Finally, we will look at the impact of the recent decentralization trend in labour relations on the organization of employers (section 13).

2 Impediments to organizing employers

Employers have many individual sources of power at their disposal. These provide them with alternatives to collective action for defending their interests. Thanks to their power to dispose over capital and investments, and their control over production organizations, important for employment and economic growth, employers are able to influence the behaviour of employees, customers, suppliers, competitors and the government. Furthermore, in sectors with limited numbers of employers, the latter may rely on informal personal contacts. Finally, employers have what is known as 'structural power'. 'Capital is in a privileged position, which results from the fact that in a capitalist society the state depends on the flourishing of the accumulation process. Even before it begins to put explicit political pressure and demands upon the government, capital enjoys a position of indirect control over public affairs' (Offe and Wiesenthal, 1979: 85). Hence, employers' interests are supposedly secured by a structural bias in the political system. As employers have more of these alternative means of power at their disposal than employees and consumers, they will be less inclined to organize. Weber already pointed out that association (*Partei*) is an instrument used in particular by those who cannot derive power from status or class (Weber, 1925: 631 et seq.). Thus the 'power advantage' of employers becomes a disadvantage when it comes to getting organized.

There are many problems which employers must overcome when they want to organize. Their interests are much more heterogeneous than those of workers and consumers. This is first of all because employers operate on more markets. Whereas the interests of employees and consumers primarily lie on the labour market and product market, employers not only have to deal with these markets, but also with those for capital, raw materials and equipment. They derive interests from many more roles than do other social and economic actors.

Secondly, employers represent firms. Hence employers' associations are associations of organizations, whereas trade unions are organizations of individuals. The (prospective) members of employers' associations may well differ from each other on many more points than will individuals. To start with, firms harbour all the differences of the individuals who lead the organization. On top of that, firms have also their specific organizational characteristics and they can differ on these too, such as size, production method, sales markets, capital intensity, internal organization or the decision-making process. All these differences may result in different and, possibly, conflicting interests. This high interest heterogeneity is bound to complicate finding a common ground for organization.

A third obstacle impeding the organization of employers is the fact that they in particular are confronted with the well-known problems of collective action. Even if there is consensus on the interests and goals to be represented, it does not follow that individual employers should be willing to engage in collective action to attain these goals. This paradox of collective action has been framed into a general theory by political economist Mancur Olson (1965) and is also known as the 'prisoners' dilemma' or the 'free rider' problem. His line of reasoning is as follows.

Interest representation is typically directed at acquiring 'collective goods', that is, goods or services which must be collectively produced by a group and which can only be collectively consumed. The latter means that no relevant persons can be excluded from consumption. When the group has become so large that successful action is no longer conditional on the contribution of each individual member, some group members may be tempted not to contribute to the collective action. They expect the others to contribute, and to share in the benefits – no one can be excluded from consumption – but they will save on the costs of collective action. They may even gain extra benefits at the expense of those who are loyal, for instance, by taking over market shares in the case of a strike or a buyer boycott. Such disloyal members, also known as 'free riders', optimize their interests by maximizing benefits and minimizing sacrifices. This poses a problem in so far as every group member can make the same calculation. If one does not succumb to the temptation oneself, one may at least expect that there will be others who will do so. The fear of becoming a 'sucker' – one who makes his contribution only to benefit others – may eventually prompt the otherwise loyal members to refrain from supporting the collective cause. As a consequence, nothing will happen. Thus, rational individual choices will produce irrational collective results. This paradox of collective action is particularly a problem for employers. If there is one group which satisfies the premises of the theory regarding human action – rationality, motivation by self-interest, complete information about the choice alternatives and their consequences – it is the group of employers. More than any other economic group, they command the resources (finance, staff, expertise) to acquire information on choice alternatives and to make cost-benefit analyses of different choices. Their rationality is hence probably less 'bounded' than that of workers, who, because of the complexity of weighing the costs and benefits of trade union membership, usually choose tradition and become union members because their family and friends are members too (Crouch, 1982: 645–5). Moreover, employers are continuously exposed to competition, which forces them to seek their own interest in the most rational way in order to survive. This practice is further supported by norms in the business environment which sanction, legitimize and even positively approve of outwitting one's competitors. Thus, the temptation to free ride is much greater for employers than, for example, for workers.

3   Motives for establishing employers' associations

Notwithstanding all these obstacles, employers have organized and have done so in large numbers and in a great variety of interest associations. In the Netherlands alone, there were no less than 1,254 employers' associations in 1981. Out of a total of 217,468 businesses, this meant an average of one association for every 173 businesses. By contrast, there were 96 trade unions in that same year, which meant an average of one union for every 50,000 employees (van Waarden, 1991).

Employers' associations are certainly not a new phenomenon. They go back further in history than do trade unions. Long before the development of industrial capitalism and the ensuing conflict between capital and labour, there were employers' associations, namely the medieval artisan guilds. Although in many countries these were abolished during the French Revolution and the Napoleonic era, the new employers' associations that emerged at the end of the nineteenth century often saw themselves as a continuation of the earlier guilds, and they sometimes explicitly referred to them in their names.

Why were employers prepared, even under the individualistic norms and competitive pressure of capitalism, to sacrifice part of their entrepreneurial freedom in favour of cooperation with peers? In most cases, the immediate cause was an external threat. As the saying goes, a common enemy unites. Apparently, the individual sources of power were insufficient. Not surprisingly, then, the first to organize were the less powerful small and medium-sized businesses (in the Netherlands this began around 1870). The large industrial companies did not follow until a few decades later. The first and foremost threat was not the trade unions, as is often believed. Many employers' associations had already been formed before the first unions emerged. In fact, trade unions were sometimes a response to employers combining forces. Employers' associations were often formed as a reaction to unorganized threats on the labour market: industrial unrest, wildcat strikes, wage drift etc. By forming 'cartels' on the labour market, employers tried to curb competition, which incited or enhanced such labour unrest.

In the early days, there were other threats more important than those on the labour market, however. This becomes apparent when we read the constitutions of the first businesses' associations, which provided for the following: moderation and regulation of competition by agreements on pricing, wages, terms of delivery, advertising, exhibitions, product quality, market-entry restrictions; combating moonlighting; prevention of un-desired state intervention or, by contrast, the obtainment of desired state regulations; improvement of the image of employers; provision of collec-tive goods for the sector, such as vocational training or joint product promotion.

The influence of such external factors is also apparent from the cycles in the formation of Dutch businesses' associations, as shown by an analysis of the founding years of 1,841 nationally relevant employers' associations established between 1880 and 1960 (van Waarden, 1991). These cycles indicate a relationship between crises and interest organization. The num-ber of foundings increased in the years 1900, 1906–07, 1915–19, 1932–35, 1938 and 1945–52. These were all periods of 'crisis' for Dutch employers. Third parties – the church, trade unions and especially the state – also aided employers in overcoming the Olsonian problems of collective action. Various Dutch employers' associations were formed at the initiative of government agencies, such as the oldest employers' associations in the cotton industry (van Waarden, 1987a) and the docks (Teychiné Staken-burg, 1957). In other cases, employers organized in response to state offers to participate in formulating and implementing its policies. For example, during the First World War, many associations were created to assist the government in distribution measures, or to issue, on its behalf, certificates of origin as required by the combatant parties. In the 1930s, associations were established to assist in market ordering policies. Associations provided the vocational training needed to obtain an establishment permit, or they concluded cartel agreements which were subsequently declared generally binding by the government.

Over the years, the character of many employers' associations has changed. Originally, most of them were combat organizations. Their organizational structure was designed to fight strikes, wage drift, trade unions, state measures or suppliers' cartels. The purpose clauses in their articles show as much. They comprise many a page of detailed rules on how to organize a lockout or a buyer boycott, or how to operate anti-strike funds. However, as employers' associations built up more durable relations with opponents such as unions, suppliers and the government, their character changed. Increasingly they became partners in negotiations and consultations, or advisory organizations which assisted member employers in their negotiations with unions.

4 Types of employers' associations

Not all employers' associations are in fact employers' organizations in the strict sense of the word, as should be apparent from their constitutional goals. Only a minority promote the 'social' or labour market interests of entrepreneurs and serve as interlocutors for the trade unions. The majority confine themselves to representing the commercial, economic or technical interests of employers. Sometimes these associations are cartels in disguise. Furthermore, among the associations representing social interests, only a minority are pure and unadulterated employers' associations. The rest combine social representation with economic and technical interests. Thus, there are various types of employers' associations.

Besides classifying them by their professed task, associations can also be classified by their recruitment 'domain', that is, by the types of employers they wish to recruit. Thus there are highly specialized sectoral associations, like the Association for Animal Gutters, but also more comprehensive associations like the Dutch General Employers' Association (*Algemene Werkgevers Vereniging*), which organizes nearly the entire process industry. Furthermore, there are 'first order' organizations which have firms as members, as well as peak associations, which have other, sectoral, associations as their members. Finally, employers' associations may be classified according to the organizational models they represent. On the one hand, then, there are small loosely knit forms of cooperation, highly decentralized, with limited financial resources and no professional staff. At the other extreme are large representative, centralized and professionalized associations, which constitute considerable organizational power. Paradoxically, the formation and stabilization of powerful associational structures are enhanced precisely by those factors that also complicate the process of forming associations. In order to overcome the obstacles to collective action, a strong association is needed. The more powerful and effective an association is, the more attractive an alternative it will be to individual interest promotion and the better able to prevent employers from choosing the latter option. And the more indispensable it becomes to its members and the more powerful its sanctions, the more it will be able to discourage free-ridership.

5 The power of employers' associations

Similar to the trade unions, then, the *raison d'être* of employers' associations is hence the formation of economic and political power. What makes up this organizational power? Basically four variables: the cohesion of a (sectoral) system of employers' associations; the representativeness of the major associations in the system – dependent on their comprehensiveness and their density ratio; and their organizational capacity to control their members' behaviour.

A more cohesive associational system of employers – or trade unions for that matter – increases the power of the group as a whole. They close ranks against the opponent, who consequently has fewer opportunities to play different opponents off against one another and increase its own power by using divide-and-rule strategies. Cohesive and hence powerful associational systems can be less easily ignored by opponents. Both parties become more dependent on, or even 'condemned' to, each other. More cohesive associational systems may produce more frequent interaction between labour and capital, more need for negotiations, and in time more permanent and institutionalized labour relations.

The power of individual associations is first of all a matter of numbers. The larger the representativeness, the greater the power of an association, other factors remaining equal. Greater representativeness means in principle more mobilization power: more potential participants in strikes, lockouts, boycotts, or investment strikes. More important yet is that with a greater representativeness the importance of an association for its interlocutors increases. Opponents will be more likely to recognize such an association as partner in consultations or negotiations. State agencies will be more inclined to give such an association access – or even privileged access – to decision-making arenas. Representativeness depends in the first place on the comprehensiveness or inclusiveness of the member-recruitment domain: how many groups of businessmen, how many sectors and branches, does an individual business association purport to organize? Secondly, representativeness also depends of course on the share of potential members that have actually joined the association, that is, its density ratio.

Furthermore, the power of interest associations depends also on their capacity for self-discipline. More permanent relations between contract partners can only develop if they are not only representative and able to mobilize their members if necessary, but also able to control mobilization. The influence of unions will increase if they are not only able to organize a strike, but also end it when a compromise has been reached in negotiations. They should be able to prevent wildcat strikes and guarantee peace on the labour market. Otherwise they cannot offer that as a concession in negotiations. Employers' associations will be more influential the better they are able to get their members to engage in the organization, as well as the ending of lockouts, if the association so decides.

Associations should also have a certain freedom of action in order to aggregate the various – and sometimes conflicting – interests of their members and to reformulate them in the process if necessary to arrive at a more general group interest. In doing so, they must be able to take account of what is realistically possible, given the position and power of the other parties. In short, associations should be able to mitigate the demands of the rank-and-file. During negotiations too, some space for bargaining, for give and take, is desirable. An association should have the freedom to formulate compromises and the capacity to defend them *vis-à-vis* the members. Finally, the partners should be able to ensure and if necessary to enforce compliance with the agreements by their members.

Effective negotiations therefore require representative associations able to mobilize their members, but also capable of formulating and defending compromises and of enforcing compliance with agreements by the rank-and-file. External power, that is *vis-à-vis* opponents, presupposes internal power, that is, over the members. Whether organizations will be capable of these tasks depends on their organizational structure. The nature of the mutual relations is hence also dependent on the internal structure of the parties involved. They should not only be representative but also control organizations.

In this respect, the organizational problems encountered by trade unions and employers' associations differ. For unions, the greatest problem is to recruit members, that is, to maintain, or better still, to increase the density ratio. Control over members is usually less of a problem. Social control between workers facilitates this task, as solidarity tends to be an important norm. Workers usually have more problems with the financial costs of membership than with decisions by the organization. The reverse is the case for employers' associations. Most employers do not find membership expensive and easily join up, so that employers' associations generally have high density ratios. In many sectors this is up to 100 per cent. However, employers find it a much greater sacrifice to comply with the decisions and regulations of their associations, as these reduce their much cherished freedom of enterprise. Among employers, individualism rather than solidarity is the norm, with business people who outsmart their competitors being held in high esteem by their peers. Thus, employers' associations will have more difficulty acquiring organizational capacity than achieving high density ratios.

6 The organizational structure of employers' associations and the system of industrial relations

The pressure to create inclusive organizations and organizational capacity will often be brought to bear by the opponents, who have an interest in their negotiating partner having sufficient leeway to make concessions and sufficient authority to enforce compliance with the agreements reached. Centralized organization on the one side will encourage centralization on the other. In that respect, the organizational structures of employers and employees are interrelated.

There is furthermore also likely to be a relationship between the system of industrial relations and the organizational structures of employers' associations and trade unions. To start with the rather obvious, central, sectoral, or regional collective wage negotiations require contract partners of labour and capital at these aggregation levels. The size or comprehensiveness of the member-recruitment domain of the most important associations influences the level of negotiations. In turn, the level of negotiations will have strengthened the position of the associations at these levels or may have even spurred their creation. The existence of central peak associations is a precondition, but also a stimulus for central negotiations. On the other hand, such central negotiations give central organizations a more important function and may be able to increase their legitimacy and authority *vis-à-vis* their member-associations at lower levels of aggregation. In general, cohesive and comprehensive associational patterns increase the need for negotiation, step up the frequency of contacts between employers and employees, and may eventually lead to more institutionalized labour relations.

Cohesion of associational systems and comprehensiveness, high density ratios and capacity for self-discipline of individual associations make for more power, but also for greater responsibility. More cohesive associational systems or more comprehensive individual associations tend to follow more moderate policies. Thus organizational forms will also influence the substance of labour relations. There are at least three reasons why cohesive systems and comprehensive associations are so moderate. First of all, as such associations or associational systems are confronted with a wider variety of interest-input from their members, the common denominator of those interests – as it becomes apparent in policy – will be closer towards the political middle. For example, an employers' association which organizes both exporting engineering firms and department stores will have more difficulty advocating lower wages. Such a move could reduce the costs of exporting firms and hence increase their international competitive position; however, it could also mean less domestic buying power – at the expense of the department stores. Hence, such an organization is likely to adopt a more moderate wage policy. Secondly, more comprehensive associations have fewer opportunities to externalize the costs of their policies, that is, to shift the costs on to groups not organized by them, for the simple reason that there are fewer such groups. Hence they have to take external factors into account in their policies. Thirdly, as associations get bigger and more comprehensive, the macro-economic consequences of their policies will be greater. They are therefore more likely to come under pressure from others, such as the state, to behave responsibly. In this chapter we will further investigate the organizational power of employers' associations, that aspect of labour relations which has received the least attention in the literature. The focus will be on the four variables just introduced: cohesion, comprehensiveness, density ratio and organizational capacity. Power will be measured as a relative factor by comparing employers' associations in various democratic-capitalist countries. In the conclusion we will also dwell on the question of how we can account for national differences in the organizational power of employers' associations. The information presented has been taken largely from an international comparative study of employers' associations (see inter alia Schmitter and Streeck, 1981), covering 352 associations in nine countries, namely Canada, Germany, Great Britain, Italy, the Netherlands, Austria, Spain, Sweden and Switzerland. To add to and contrast these findings, other sources have been consulted to provide information on France and the United States.

7   Cohesion of the systems of general (peak) employers' associations

The degree of cohesion within a system of interest associations depends first of all on its degree of fragmentation or differentiation, that is the number and variety of associations found within a certain country or sector. Secondly, cohesion is also a function of the degree of coordination between these different associations. A good indicator for coordination is the existence of competition between the various associations found in the system. As long as associations compete with one another for members or for influence with interlocutors on behalf of the same interests, they apparently have not been able to reach agreement on the demarcation of their domains and competencies, a minimal form of coordination. Firms may of course be a member of different associations, but as long as they belong to different ones for different reasons – for example, for the representation of labour market or commercial interests – this does not imply competition. Competition therefore requires that associations vie for the same member categories and intend to represent similar interests. As long as they compete with each other for members and for influence over third parties, associations will have difficulty reaching a consensus about delineating their member recruitment domains and scope of authority. Any competition is a sign of 'weakness' in the system, since it may enable the other negotiating party to play the different associations off against one another.

The various general – that is, sector-unspecific – (peak) employers' associations in the various countries under investigation are listed in the Appendix. This list indicates that the associational systems are differentiated on the basis of various criteria. A first criterion is the task of the association. There are some associations which concern themselves solely with the social and labour market interests of the members. They are the pure employers' associations, indicated by the code 'EA' after their name. Then there are a larger number of so-called 'mixed' associations, which represent not only the labour market interests of business, but also their interests on other markets: products, raw materials, capital etc., in other words their social, economic, technical and commercial interests. They have the code 'M' in the box. Finally, the box also lists the most important general 'trade' associations, that is, associations which represent solely economic and commercial interests ('TA'). A few of them also perform some minor functions of employers' associations, such as lobbying the government on social legislation ('mostly TA'). However, these rarely concern themselves with trade unions and wage negotiations. Such associations are found in countries which do not have peak employers' associations (Canada, the United States, Great Britain). For lack of these, the peak trade associations assume some of their tasks.

A clear differentiation between employers' associations and trade associations is found in Germany (the *Bundesvereinigung der deutschen Arbeitgeberverbände* (BDA) for labour market, and the *Bundesverband der deutschen Industrie* (BDI) for economic interests), Sweden (SAF and SI) and Switzerland (the *Zentralverband schweizerischer Arbeitgeber Organisationen* (ZSAO) and the *Schweizerischer Handels- und Industrieverein Vorort*). Mixed general associations are found in France, Italy, Austria, the Netherlands, Spain and Great Britain, although the British CBI has so little to do with social interests that it is almost a trade association (Grant and Marsh, 1977). In the past the Netherlands also had separate social and economic associations. However, in 1968 they merged into the *Verbond van Nederlandse Ondernemers* (VNO). Only the catholic and protestant peak associations (see further) combined both interests in one association from the very start, as a matter of principle. Most national associational systems of employers are furthermore differentiated by firm size. In almost every country there are separate associations for small and medium-sized firms or handicraft firms. Often there are more than one, distinguished by compulsory or voluntary membership (the voluntary – small – German *Bund der Selbständigen* in addition to the compulsory *Zentralverband des deutschen Handwerks*), ideology (in France and the Netherlands the extremely conservative organizations CID–UNATI and KNO), religion (the Dutch NCOV in addition to the general KNOV), and political affiliation (Italy, see Box 4.1 below). In some countries there are also separate associations for large firms, such as the *Vereinigung Österreichischer Industrieller* (VOEI), which offers the larger firms a separate forum in addition to the *Bundeswirtschaftskammer*, dominated by small and medium-sized firms. Furthermore, the more informal and exclusive forums such as the Business Round Table (USA, 194 prominent entrepreneurs) and the Business Council on National Issues (Canada) are also *de facto* organizations of very large firms. In the federal states of Germany,

Switzerland, Italy, Canada and the USA, cantonal, provincial or *Länder* associations exist and are important. Wage agreements here are often negotiated at the regional level. The more important sectoral associations in these negotiations are therefore also regionally differentiated.

Countries with a sizeable state-owned section of the economy (Italy, Sweden) or with many important cooperative firms (the same two countries plus Austria) have separate employers' associations for these categories of firms. In Italy, for example, the Christian-Democratic governments forced state companies to leave Confindustria in the 1950s and form separate associations (ASAP and Intersind), allowing the government to pursue a model social policy in industry and break Confindustria's stronghold (Treu and Martinelli, 1984). Finally, France and the Netherlands still have separate Christian employers' associations.

The degree of competition is measured here as the size of the segment of the economy for which associations compete. In France and Italy competition exists mainly among associations for small and medium-sized firms and between these and the general associations CNPF and Confindustria for the smaller firms. Here overall competition is more moderate than in countries where two or more large associations compete for almost the whole industry, such as the CBI and the Institute of Directors in Britain, VNO and NCW in the Netherlands, and the NAM/CMA, the NCC/CCC and the Business Round Table/Business Council on National Issues in the USA and Canada respectively – countries whose patterns of employers' associations incidentally show great similarities.

Table 4.1 rank orders the various countries by the cohesion of the system of general employers' associations, on the basis of the variables 'differentiation' and 'competition' between associations. The differentiation score is the number of different dimensions on which businesses are organized separately. There is a maximum of five dimensions: function (social or economic interests), firm size, region, firm property structure (state firms, cooperatives) and religion or ideology. The scores for competition are based on an estimate made by researchers in the respective countries, who participated in the international OBI-project.

Table 4.1 shows that the cohesiveness of the pattern of general employers' associations is greatest in Austria, of which Marin has remarked that, 'a most important characteristic of the overall Austrian system lies in the simple fact that there is one, and just one, leading business representative' (1985: 96). The *Bundeswirtschaftskammer* is so important that competition from the other associations is of practically no significance. In addition to Austria, Sweden and Germany also have a rather cohesive system of general employers' associations. It is no accident that these are countries in which corporatist relations exist between the government and interest associations and among interest associations themselves. Cohesion, on the other hand, is low in the typically 'pluralist' countries of Great Britain, Canada and the United States.

Table 4.1 *Rank order of countries by cohesion of the pattern of general employers' associations*

Country	Differentiation (no. of dimensions on which separate associations)	Coordination (mutual competition)
Austria	2	Low
Germany	3	Low
Sweden	3	Low
Italy	3	Somewhat
France	2	Somewhat
Netherlands	3	Considerable
Switzerland	3	Considerable
GB	1	High
Canada	2	High
USA	3	High

For Spain there were insufficient data to enable placement on the scale.

8 Cohesion of the systems of sectoral employers' associations

In most countries the general employers' associations are only indirectly involved in wage negotiations, if at all. Only the Swedish SAF and Austrian BWK are direct contract partners. Elsewhere collective wage agreements are concluded only by sectoral associations. The general peak associations play only an indirect role. It might be that they conclude a central framework agreement with one or more trade union confederations, which is more in the way of a recommendation to the affiliated member-associations. They may play more of a role behind the scenes, in the sense that they provide a forum for coordination of labour market policies between sectors. However, the most important task of general employers' associations is usually the representation of business interests *vis-à-vis* the government, rather than in relation to trade unions. They try to influence general socioeconomic legislation and the labour market policies of the state.

Hence the systems of sectoral employers' associations are often at least as important as those of the general associations. Most of these systems are relatively strongly differentiated. The most important data are summarized in Table 4.2. It lists the number of employers' associations for some major industrial sectors (metalworking, chemical industry and construction) by country. The table also indicates whether there are special associations for certain regions, subsectors, firms of a certain size, political affiliation, religion or any other category. Box 4.1 further lists the major association in each country-sector system.

Table 4.2 *Number and differentiation among employers'*
associations representing labour market interests by country
and sector

Country and sector[1]	No. of employers' associations	Differentiation: separate associations for					
		Region	Product	Firm size	Political affiliation	Religion	Other criteria
D-Constr.	791	x	x	x	–	–	x
I-Constr.	294	x	–	x	x	–	x
E-Constr.	92	x	x	–	–	–	x
I-Metal	75	x	x	x	x	–	x
CAN-Constr.	46	x	x	–	–	–	x
D-Metal	45	x	x	–	–	–	–
I-Chemicals	33	x	x	x	–	–	x
NL-Constr.	31	x	x	x	–	x	x
GB-Metal	19	x	x	x	–	–	x
D-Chemicals	17	x	x	x	–	–	–
E-Chemicals	14	x	x	–	–	–	–
CH-Constr.	9	x	x	x	–	–	–
GB-Constr.	9	x	x	x	–	–	x
S-Constr.	4	x	x	x	–	–	x
S-Chemicals	3	–	x	–	–	–	x
S-Metal	3	–	x	x	–	–	x
NL-Metal	3	–	–	x	–	–	–
CH-Chemicals	3	x	x	x	–	–	x
GB-Chemicals	2	–	x	–	–	–	–
NL-Chemicals	2	–	x	–	–	–	–
A-Constr.	2	–	x	–	–	–	–
CH-Metal	1	–	–	–	–	–	–
A-Metal	1	–	–	–	–	–	–
A-Chemicals	1	–	–	–	–	–	–
CAN-Chemicals	None	–	–	–	–	–	–
CAN-Metal	None	–	–	–	–	–	–

[1]Chemicals = all associations which organize manufacturers of industrial chemicals and others;
Metal = all associations which organize the subsector for machine tools and others.

Abbreviations used in all tables in this chapter; A, Austria; CAN, Canada; CH, Switzerland;
D, Germany; E, Spain; GB, Great Britain; I, Italy; NL, Netherlands; S, Sweden.

Table 4.2 shows that large numbers of associations are only found in
sectors which are still to some extent handicraft-like, such as construction
and metalworking. These are sectors made up of large numbers of smaller
firms which are usually spread out over the country, especially construction. They consequently have many local and regional associations.
Furthermore, these sectors consist of a variety of trades or subsectors,
which have often formed associations of their own. By contrast, an industrialized sector dominated by large national and even multinational firms,
such as the chemical industry, is much more concentrated both territorially
and subsectorally, and therefore has fewer employers' associations.

Box 4.1   *The most important sectoral employers' associations*

Metalworking

Germany	Gesamtmetall	*Gesamtverband der Metallindustriellen Arbeitgeberverbände* [EA]
GB	EEF	Engineering Employers' Federation [EA]
Italy	Federmeccanica	*Federazione Sindicale dell'Industria Metalmeccanica Italiana* [EA]
Netherlands	FME	*Vereniging van de Nederlandse Metaalindustrie FME* [M]
Sweden	VF	*Verkstadsföreningen* [EA]
Switzerland	ASM	*Arbeitgeberverband schweizerischer Maschinen- und Metall-Industrieller* [EA]

Chemical industry

GB	CIA	Chemical Industries Association [M]
Italy	Asschimici	*Associazione Nazionale dell'Industria Chimica* [M]
Netherlands	AWV	*Algemene Werkgevers Vereniging* [EA]
Spain	FEIQUE	*Federación Empresarial de la Industria Quimica Espanola* [M]
Sweden	Ag-SAF	General Group of the SAF (independent section, which organizes eight different sectors, among them the chemical industry) [EA]
Switzerland	VBCI	*Verband Basler Chemischer Industrieller* [EA]

Construction

Canada	AECQ	*Association des Entrepreneurs en Construction du Québec* [EA]
Germany	HDB	*Hauptverband der Deutschen Bauindustrie* [M]
	ZDB	*Zentralverband des Deutschen Baugewerbes* [M]
GB	NFBTE	National Federation of Building Trade Employers [M]
Italy	ANCE	*Associazione Nazionale Construttori Edili* [M]
Netherlands	AVBB	*Algemeen Verbond Bouwbedrijf* [M]
Sweden	BF	*Byggförbundet*, Employers' Federation in Construction [EA]
Switzerland	SBV	*Schweizer Baumeister Verband* [M]

Table 4.2 also shows, however, that the variable 'sector' alone cannot explain the differences in associational patterns. The differences between countries are too large for that. The size of the country seems at first sight to play a role. The smaller countries – Austria, Sweden, Switzerland and the Netherlands – clearly have fewer employers' associations per sector than the larger countries of Germany, Italy, Spain and Canada (only construction for the latter). Given the fact that most associations in these countries are regional ones, it is to be expected that there will be more of them as the area or the population is larger. Nevertheless, this cannot explain the difference between Germany on the one hand and Canada and Great Britain on the other. Important also are the different political, legal and economic institutions in these countries, as they have been formed over many years.

The large number of associations in construction and metalworking in Germany and Italy reflect the guild tradition in these countries, in Germany also embedded in law. All 791 associations in the German construction trade have a regional domain. Of these, 766 are local *Innungen* (guilds) for various building trades. Although they are voluntary in character, they have a status in public law. They have the legal duty to operate training shops and are officially authorized to conduct wage negotiations for the handicraft sector. They exist alongside, but are closely related to, the regional non-sector specific *Handwerkskammern*, also associations under public law, but with compulsory membership. They are responsible for vocational training for business people, administer the examinations (the *Meisterprüfung*), award the *Befähigungsnachweis* without which one cannot practise a trade, and therefore regulate access to the market. They also regulate the market in other ways (see further Streeck, 1989). The *Handwerkskammern* are organized in the *Deutsche Handwerkskammertag*, the *Innungen* in the *Bundesvereinigung der Fachverbände des Deutschen Handwerks*. These two peak associations together form the *Zentralverband des deutschen Handwerks* (ZDH). The special legal status of the *Handwerk* interest associations is specific to Germany and arose from the old guild tradition, but it was only embedded in law in 1933 by the Nazis and has survived the post-war political reorganizations.

Austria and the Netherlands also have a guild tradition, but here the local handicraft organizations are not independent associations, but sections of larger national associations. They therefore do not show up in the data in Table 4.2. In the Netherlands they form part of the *Nederlands Verbond van Ondernemers in de Bouwnijverheid* (van Waarden, 1989a); in Austria they are sections of the BWK and have less autonomy than the *Innungen* and *Kammern* in Germany. The *Bundeswirtschaftskammer*, incidentally, is the only Austrian employers' association in metalworking and the chemical industry and one of two in construction. The very small number of employers' associations in Austria reflects the comprehensive nature of the BWK.

The presence of a federal state is more important than it would seem at first sight. In Germany this has contributed to the large number of *Handwerks* organizations, but it is still more clearly visible in the associational pattern of industrial firms. The domains of their regional associations often coincide with the *Länder* territories. Examples are the *Wirtschaftsvereinigung Bauindustrie Nordrhein-Westfalen*, the *Verband der Metallindustrie Baden-Württemberg* or the *Arbeitgeberverband der hessischen Metallindustrie*. These are important employers' associations in Germany, because they are the bargaining partners in wage negotiations, which are usually concluded at the *Länder* level. In Switzerland too the presence of a federal state is important for employers, but this is not as obvious in the sectoral associational patterns, because most regional employers' associations are not sector-specific. Exceptions are regionally concentrated industries, such as the chemical sector. Here the most important association is the *Verband Basler Chemischer Industrieller*, an association of the largest Swiss chemical firms like Ciba Geigy, Hoffmann-LaRoche and Sandoz, all with headquarters in Basle. We see then that the most important criterion of differentiation is region. Furthermore, various subsectors have their own association and there are often separate associations for small and for large firms. Political affiliation is still important only in Italy, while the Netherlands is the only country among the nine studied which still has sectoral associations on the basis of religion.

In Table 4.3 the various country-sector associational systems have been rank ordered by cohesion, on the basis of the criteria also used in Table 4.1. As far as sectors are concerned, the table shows that the chemical industry in particular shows a large degree of cohesion in associational systems. Seven of the eight chemical sectors score above average. This is of course because the sector has very few employers' associations (cf. Table 4.2), so that there is not much chance of competition. A low degree of cohesion on the other hand is found in the construction sectors. Seven of the nine sectors score below average. Most construction sectors have many associations, especially separate ones for industry and trade or for large and small firms. Because it is not always easy to separate these categories from each other, there is often considerable competition in areas where they border one another.

The variation within sectors is so great, however, that again the variable 'sector' cannot explain all of the variety. Relatively cohesive are the associational patterns in the (majority of) German-speaking countries, that is, Switzerland, Germany and Austria. In the latter, all employers' interests, even those at sector-level, come together and find expression in the BWK. On the other hand, differentiation and competition are high in Italy, Great Britain, Sweden and the Netherlands (except for chemicals). The major Dutch metalworking association FME, for example, faces fierce competition from the *Contactgroep van Werkgeversorganisaties in de Metaalnijverheid*, an association of small and medium-sized firms which

Table 4.3   *Rank order of country-sector systems of employers' associations by cohesion*

	Coordination (mutual competition)	Differentiation (no. of dimensions on which separate associations)
A-Metal	None	0
A-Constr.	None	0
A-Chemicals	None	0
NL-Chemicals	None	0
CH-Metal	None	0
GB-Chemicals	Low	1
CH-Chemicals	Low	1
D-Metal	Low	2
E-Chemicals	Low	2
S-Chemicals	Low	2
CH-Constr.	Low	3
D-Chemicals	Low	3
D-Constr.	Low	4
S-Metal	Average	3
E-Constr.	Average	3
CAN-Constr.	Average	3
S-Constr.	Average	4
NL-Metal	High	1
GB-Metal	High	3
I-Chemicals	High	4
I-Constr.	High	4
GB-Constr.	High	4
I-Metal	High	5
NL-Constr.	High	5

seceded from the FME's predecessor because they felt it was dominated by the large shipyards. In Sweden the dominant associations Ag-SAF, BF and VF, all affiliated to the SAF, face competition from associations which mainly, but not solely, organize firms with another ownership structure such as the KFO (cooperatives) and the SFO (state firms), as well as some branch-specific associations, for example in construction the SERAF and SVEMEK (Pestoff, 1983, 1984).

The organizational division of employers can really be a disadvantage, as various cases show. An example is construction in Great Britain. The dominant association is here is the National Federation of Building Trade Employers (NFBTE) (and the FCEC in civil engineering). It faces serious competition from the Federation of Master Builders (FMB), however, which generally organizes smaller firms. The NFBTE and FCEC used to have a monopoly in wage negotiations, owing to their reciprocal agreement on exclusive recognition with the major trade union, the Union of Construction, Allied Trades and Technicians (UCATT). The FMB has tried to break the NFBTE and FCEC's monopoly by introducing a similar division on the workers' side. It started separate negotiations with the excluded union, the Transport and General Workers' Union. To this end a separate forum was created in 1980, the Building and Allied Trade Joint Industrial Council. The result is that 'the industry now has two sets of negotiations, two wage rates, two arbitration procedures, two overtime calculators – and so on – a recipe for chaos even in an industry not facing recession' (Grant, 1983: 19–21).

9   Representativeness: comprehensiveness and density ratio of the dominant general employers' (peak) associations

The organizational power of employers is also dependent on the comprehensiveness and density ratio of the major peak associations, a factor also affecting the cohesion of the system as a whole to some extent. It does make a difference whether differentiation implies the existence of several smaller associations of about the same size, or whether it means one large and dominant association, flanked by some smaller and more specialized ones. In the latter case this dominant association will be able to unite almost all employers in the country and provide some cohesion in and of itself. Nevertheless, comprehensiveness cannot refer to the associational system as a whole, but is a property of individual associations.

Comprehensiveness could be measured in several ways. One could take sectors, for example. How many sectors does an association purport to represent? Only the industry? Or also parts of the service sector? How many? Does it include the financial sector? And what about state firms, such as the railroads? As it is not an easy matter to decide upon the sector-unit to be used, it might be simpler to use as an indicator the percentage of the total working population that an association wants to organize, either directly or through its affiliated associations.

Furthermore, a distinction can be made between broadness of the group organized (comprehensiveness by interest) and broadness of the tasks of the association. An association which intends to represent both the labour market as well as the product market interests of its members has a more comprehensive domain than an association which specializes in the labour market interests, that is, a pure employers' association. I have distinguished five categories in which associations can undertake tasks according to their constitutions: workers and trade unions, customers, suppliers, the state and the members themselves.

Density ratio is easier to measure. There is the standard criterion, also used for trade unions, namely the share of employers in the recruitment domain who are actually members. However, because employers' associations, unlike trade unions, organize organizations – business firms – or at least individuals who represent such an organization, the standard criterion might tell us less about the power of an association. It does matter whether the association organizes the larger or the smaller firms in its domain. That is why a better criterion is employment within the member firms – as an indication of the size and hence the resources of the firms – as a percentage of total employment in the domain.

In Table 4.4 the comprehensiveness and density ratio of the major employers' peak associations in the various countries are scored (and in addition the basic data on size, used to calculate density ratio, is presented). In column 9 of the table, the various associations have been rank ordered on the basis of these comprehensiveness and density ratio scores. Broadly representative general employers' associations are found in Austria (BWK), the Netherlands (VNO, NCW), Spain (CEOE), Sweden (SAF, SHIO), Canada (CMA) and Italy (Confindustria). The Swedish and Austrian associations owe their high score to their 100 per cent density ratios, among other factors. Membership is either formally (BWK, SHIO) or *de facto* (SAF) compulsory. The Swedish SAF (and SFO) have succeeded in making the association so important for employers that membership has become compulsory in practice. The only other association with compulsory membership is the German peak association of the artisan sector (*Handwerk*, ZDH). However, the latter scores low on comprehensiveness, owing to its specialization on *Handwerk*, giving it a lower overall score. The Austrian, Dutch and Spanish associations have the most comprehensive domains, both in terms of sectors of the economy covered and tasks. They all represent both labour market and product market interests that is, they are employers' associations as well as trade associations.

By contrast, the German and Swiss associations score low on representativeness, whereas the only British association for which data are available scores, as usual (see further), around the average. This is to a large extent due to their functional specialization in labour market interests of business. In addition they score low on interest comprehensiveness (except for the BDA) and on density ratio (except for the ZDH).

The table also indicates that there is not necessarily a relationship between cohesion of the system and comprehensiveness of the major associations. Although the dominant associations in the two most cohesive systems, Austria and Germany, do have a rather comprehensive domain (BWK 74 per cent; BDA 71 per cent) there are also two cases where no such relationship exists. The VNO, part of the rather uncohesive Dutch system, represents 78 per cent of the working population. It combines industry, commercial services and even parts of the public service sector. On the other hand, the SAF in the cohesive Swedish system organizes only 34 per cent of the working population. It is in the first place a representative of the industry, and only then of the private sector within the industry. State firms and cooperatives are separately organized. The SAF does organize some parts of the service sector (trade, transport) but banks and publishers for example are organized outside the SAF (Skogh, 1984: 149). The Italian Confindustria also has a low degree of comprehensiveness. It

Table 4.4 Representativeness: comprehensiveness and density ratio of the most important general employers' associations by country

Country/ association (1)	Comprehensiveness		Density ratio		Size (basic data)			Rank order
	By interest — Empl. in domain as % of working pop. (2)	By task — Index task-heterog.[1] (3)	As % (4)	Empl. members as % of working pop.[2] (5)	No. of member firms (6)	No. of member associations (7)	Employment members ('000) (8)	Aggregate rank order scores on columns 2–4 (9)
High score on representativeness								
A-BWK	74	0.75	100	74	235,500	–	1,877	9
NL-VNO	78	0.66	?	?	?	90	?	11.5
E-CEOE	81	0.65	?	?	–	159	?	12
NL-NCW	78	0.65	?	?	270	86	?	13.5
CAN-CMA	26	0.77	72	19	4,543	–	1,850	20
S-SAF	34	0.62	100	34	37,565	36	1,328	21
S-SHIO	12	0.65	100	12	41,517	46	450	22
I-Confindustria	29	0.73	71	21	–	205	3,000	22
GB-NFSESB	43	0.50	?	?	?	–	?	22.5
S-SFO	3	0.43	100	3	355	93	108	23
D-ZDH	15	0.63	100	15	–	42	3,434	23
D-BDA	68	0.49	80	57	–	291	12,800	24
CH-SGV	43	0.44	?	?	–	541	?	25
NL-KNOV	35	0.56	26	9	200	–	401	28
I-Intersind	4	0.44	91	3	269	–	471	33.5
Low score on representativeness								
Associations which could not be rank ordered (at least 2 unknown scores on the 3 relevant variables)								
I-Confapi	?	0.66	?	7	–	56	1,000	
CH-ZSAO	?	0.48	?	36	–	67	1,000	
GB-CBI	?	0.68	?	?	15,000	192	?	
CAN-CCC	?	0.69	?	?	3,000	600	?	
CAN-CFIB	?	0.50	?	?	55,000	–	?	

For an explanation of abbreviations see the Appendix at the end of the chapter.
[1] Index task-heterogeneity of the domain of the association (TASKHET): a Gibbs–Martin index, which calculates the diversification of the tasks – as listed in the

too is mainly a representative of industry. In Italy the service sector has its own peak association, Confcommercio.

10 Representativeness: comprehensiveness and density ratio of the dominant sectoral employers' associations

Table 4.5 presents data similar to that shown in Table 4.4, but now for the major sectoral employers' associations. On the basis of these scores the associations are rank ordered by comprehensiveness of the domain and density ratio in column 8 of the table.

Table 4.5 shows that the countries with most representative associations are, once again, Austria, the Netherlands and Sweden. Except for the Swedish construction association BF, all major sectoral associations in these countries score above average. The Austrian *Bundeswirtschaftskammer* tops them all, due to its compulsory membership, which produces a density ratio of 100 per cent, its coverage of the whole economy and its broad tasks. It represents both labour market and product market interests of business. All three Dutch associations are large, broadly representative and, except for the chemical association AWV, combine representing both labour market and product market interests. This AWV is among the few highly specialized employers' associations in our study. It organizes a large segment of the industry, however, that is, the processing industry: chemicals, food processing, paper etc. Countries whose associations score predominantly below average are Italy, Germany, Switzerland and Canada. British associations score in between. They are clustered around the average.

As far as sectors are concerned, the distinction between more and less representative associations is less clear. However, it seems that sectors dominated by large firms tend to have more representative associations than sectors composed of many small firms, which seems logical, given the greater propensity of larger firms to organize. Thus the majority of chemical industry associations score above average (four above, two below average), while the construction associations have a rather low representativeness (five below, three above average).

Those construction associations which score above average are found in countries (Germany, Switzerland, the Netherlands) which have special legal regimes for small handicraft firms. Such legal facilities (compulsory membership in Germany for a large number of trades, devolution of state tasks and statutory authority on associations) are likely to strengthen the position of the associations *vis-à-vis* the industry and may allow them to increase their density ratios and domain size. Construction associations in countries (Italy, Sweden) and subsectors (German HDB) which lack such a legal regime are the ones with the lowest density ratios.

Table 4.5 *Representativeness: comprehensiveness and density ratio of the major sectoral employers' association per country and for three sectors*

Country/sector/ association (1)	Comprehensiveness		Density ratio	Size (basic data)			Rank order
	By interest Index product-heterog.[1] (2)	By task Index task-heterog.[2] (3)	Empl. members as % empl. in domain (4)	No. of member firms (5)	No. of member associations (6)	Employment members ('000) (7)	Aggregate rank order scores on columns 2–4 (8)
High score on representativeness							
A-All: BWK	14	0.75	100	235,500	–	1,877	7.5
NL-Metal: FME	9	0.75	87	1,050	–	327	16
CH-Constr.: SBV	7	0.76	88	4,000	10	133	17
S-Metal: VF	5	0.72	98	2,272	–	323	24
I-Chemicals: Asschimici	8	0.66	?	800	–	?	24
NL-Constr. AVBB	3	0.76	93	–	10	200	25.5
S-Chemicals: Ag-SAF	9	0.62	?	1,681	–	127	26
NL-Chemicals: AWV	14	0.57	?	332	24	530	27.5
D-Constr. ZDB	7	0.64	90	–	31	743	28
GB-Chemicals: CIA	5	0.68	?	231	17	365	30
GB-Constr. NFBTE	3	0.72	?	11,000	11	376	31.5
I-Metal: Federmeccanica	6	0.49	100	–	100	1,000	32
GB-Metal: EEF	5	0.68	82	–	18	1,550	32.5
E-Chemicals: FEIQUE	8	0.61	75	–	21	116	33
CH-Metal: ASM	5	0.64	?	516	–	217	34
CAN-Constr.: AECQ	3	0.61	100	13,876	–	97	37
D-Constr. HDB	2	0.72	69	–	18	225	39.5
CH-Chemicals: VBCI	4	0.32	100	4	–	39	39.5
D-Metal: Gesamtmetall	6	0.57	73	–	13	2,924	40
I-Constr.: ANCE	5	0.65	28	–	89	289	40
S-Constr.: BF	2	0.69	63	1,722	–	84	42.5
Low score on representativeness							

[1]Index product-heterogeneity of the domain of the association (PRODHET): index of the number of different branches the association organizes. The sum of the scores on three variables: (a) INSECT: does the association organize the whole chemical, construction and metalworking industries as defined in the project, or only a smaller or larger part thereof; (b) OUTSECT: does it also organize branches (many or only a few, from four to two digit categories in the UN-industrial classification scheme) outside the sectors as defined? (c) UPDOWN: does the association also organize customers or suppliers of the sector (forward or backward integration) yes or no? Minimal value PRODHET 2, maximum 14.

The majority of metalworking associations also score below average (four below, two above). The overall low score seems to be due to the low score on task comprehensiveness (even though this specialization provides these associations with relatively high density ratios). Apparently the metalworking industry has a greater need for pure 'employers' associations', that is, associations specialized in labour relations. We find such in Italy, Switzerland, Canada and Germany. Again this is not surprising, given the fact that the workers in this industry are in most countries well-organized and strike readily, and that the industry has therefore become a leader in the annual wage negotiation rounds.

11 Organizational capacity for self-discipline in the most important general and sectoral employers' associations

Organizational capacity for self-discipline or authority and relative autonomy *vis-à-vis* members, characteristic of a control organization, makes certain demands on its organizational structure. Decision-making must be centralized to some extent, in order for the various particular member interests to be aggregated at a central level to more general group interests which can be pursued over a longer period. The executive board should have a certain authority over any sections present – often the representatives of more particular interests. The board has to be able to decide on binding rules – and hence the existence of such rules could be an indication of rule-binding capacity. Another one is the division of authority within the association. How great is the mandate of the executive board during wage negotiations? Does it have a monopoly on contacts with unions? Can it impose certain behaviour on members during strikes? Does it have a fund at its disposal to support members hit by a strike or do sections or member associations do so? Who decides on eligibility for support? To what extent do the central authorities control sections or member associations? Do the latter require approval of the central executive for certain policy measures or changes in their constitution? The association should furthermore be able to sanction its members. The ultimate sanction, expulsion, is only effective when the association has acquired a certain importance, if not indispensability, for the membership, or when membership has become *de facto* compulsory. One way an association can secure the loyalty of its members is to provide important services available exclusively to its members (so-called selective goods). Examples are insurance, an anti-strike fund, collective and inexpensive purchases of raw materials and machinery, statistical information, so-called firm comparisons (in which members provide the association with company results in exchange for a comparison of their results with the average in the branch), or individual advice regarding labour relations, taxes, price calculations, problems of succession etc.

Associations that succeed in acquiring a monopoly on the provision of certain services are in an even stronger position. That often requires the cooperation of interlocutors. Exclusive information, obtained from state agencies, can be passed on to members or be used to advise individual members. Membership can even become *de facto* compulsory if an association succeeds in securing the sole right to issue legally required export licences or product quality control certificates.

An association can also gain relative autonomy as it becomes less dependent on the effort, time, political connections and money of its members. That implies a certain bureaucratization: instead of members providing voluntary labour, paid staff do the work for the association and develop their own political connections for the association, rather than relying on those of the individual members. In this way an association may be able to develop positions in policy networks, independent of (large and important) member firms. The autonomy of an association is also served if this staff apparatus is not financed completely out of member contributions. Alternative sources of financial income may be amassed capital, proceeds of 'commercialization', that is the sale of goods or services, whether to members or also to non-members, and subsidies from other employers' associations or even the state. An association's position *vis-à-vis* its members will also be strengthened if it is able to acquire access to and recognition by opponents, interlocutors or the state, if it succeeds in obtaining seats on official advisory committees to governments or on bi- or tripartite sector boards, or if it may participate in the implementation of government policy. Such relations and positions can then be used to obtain certain resources, such as financing or information. Finally, a diversification of sources from which resources are obtained and external recognition by interlocutors often also require diversification of activities performed by the association. State financial or informational resources can usually only be obtained in exchange for certain activities from which the state can profit directly or indirectly, such as the collection and aggregation of sector statistics. The Swiss government, for example, has paid the trade association *Vorort* considerable sums of money in the past to hire people to collect statistical data from its members. The development of this service has enabled *Vorort* not only to build up a staff, but also to acquire an influential position with the federal government.

Often the demands which the function of control makes on the organization are contrary to those imposed by the function of representation. Members will tend to identify closer with a decentrally organized association, which considers member mobilization more important than negotiation and cooperation with interlocutors, which is less bureaucratized (except for the provision of services wanted by members) and which orientates itself in its activities more towards the members than the interlocutors.

That means that employers' associations and trade unions will need to find a compromise between these conflicting demands in their organizational structure. Box 4.2 summarizes some of the conflicting organizational demands which an interest association will have to satisfy.

Box 4.2 *Demands put upon the organizational structure of an interest association by the different functions of representation and control*

Representation requires/is aided by/ results in:	Control requires/is aided by/ results in:

Policy
- Close relationship between policy and particular individual member interests
  - • Reinterpretation of particular member interests to more general interests, taking into account interests and power of interlocutors
- Fluctuating short-term policy
  - • Stable long-term policy

Size
- Homogeneous interests, hence small size
  - • Large organizations and hence more interest heterogeneity

Differentiation and centralization
- Internal differentiation by subinterests
  - • No internal differentiation by subinterests (danger of centrifugal tendencies); possibly differentiation by tasks (division of labour)
- Decentralized decision-making
  - • Centralized decision-making

Integration in larger networks
- Only ad hoc coordination with other interests possible
  - • Durable institutionalized coordination and coalitions with other organized interests

Resources
- Low membership contributions
  - • High membership contributions
- Insecure resource acquisition because of dependence on continuous cost-benefit calculations of members
  - • Stable income

Activities
- Emphasis on production of selective goods (services only for members)
  - • Emphasis on production of public goods (lobbying) and self-regulation
  - • Diversification of activities

Formalization
- Formalization within limits
  - • Formalization

Professionalization
- Professionalization within limits
  - • Professional staff

Relative autonomy vis-à-vis members
- Limited autonomy
  - • High degree of autonomy

As an organization is able to satisfy the demands of the control function better, that is, has a higher capacity for self-discipline, it will tend to be a stronger organization, a more powerful instrument in the hands of the collectivity of members against its opponents. Such an interest association will show a relatively high degree of organizational development. However, as long as membership remains voluntary, it will have to retain elements of a representative organization, in order to offer members sufficient opportunities to identify with the association and to maintain its recruitment potential. The intensity of these conflicting demands on the association will depend on the environment, consisting of two main categories: the (prospective) members and the interlocutors. For employers' associations that is the trade unions and the state. As the external threats of strong unions and/or high strike frequency increase, the organizational structure will have to be remodelled to resemble a control organization. 'Closing the ranks' becomes more important. That implies centralization of decision-making, binding internal agreements and their effective implementation, including sanctioning of possible transgressors. However, when problems among members are more serious and urgent (for example, manifest interest heterogeneity and difference of opinion) than problems with opponents, an association will have to offer more space to representative functions in order to continue binding its members. The level of organizational development which an association has been able to acquire in the course of its history can hence be considered a function of the history of the member group (for example, the sector) as well as of the opponents, for example, the relevant trade unions.

What can now be said about the organizational development of employers' associations? How great is their authority, their relative autonomy *vis-à-vis* members? This question can only be answered here in relative terms, that is, by comparing employers' associations across countries and sectors. In which countries and sectors does one find the most highly developed employers' associations?

On the basis of the dimensions of organizational development just discussed – size, degree of centralization, member duties and sanction capacity, financial and personnel resources, resource dependency on members, diversification of sources from which resources are acquired, diversification of activities – the most important general employers' associations and the dominant sectoral associations have been ranked by degree of organizational development. The overall rank order scores are presented in Tables 4.6 and 4.7.

The aggregated rank order scores indicate that the most highly developed associations are to be found in the small corporatist countries: Sweden with the SAF and SHIO and the sector associations VF, BF and Ag-SAF in the lead; the Austrian BWK, which occupies the second leading position both among general and sectoral associations; the Dutch KNOV, NCW, VNO, FME, AWV and AVBB; and the Swiss construction association SBV. In the large countries, the Italian Confindustria and ANCE, the Canadian

Table 4.6   *Aggregated rank order scores on variables of organizational development: general peak employers' associations*

Country	Association	Rank order
High level of organizational development		
S	SAF	1
A	BWK	2
S	SHIO	3
NL	KNOV	4
NL	NCW	5
I	Confindustria	6
NL	VNO	7
CAN	CMA	8
E	CEOE	9
GB	CBI	10
D	BDA	11
S	SFO	12
D	ZDH	13
I	Confapi	14
GB	NFSESB	15
CAN	CCC	16
CAN	CFIB	17
CH	SGV	18
I	Intersind	19
CH	ZSAO	20
Low level of organizational development		

CMA and the British CBI and NFBTE score above average. Weakly developed by contrast are the Swiss peak associations ZSAO and SGV (perhaps because the regional associations in this extremely federalized country are more important and also because of its liberal tradition: even unorganized employers form an important force in this country) and sectoral associations ASM and VBCI, the German general as well as sectoral associations, the four Italian general and sectoral associations not yet mentioned, and all the Canadian associations except for the CMA. The British associations, both the general and sectoral ones, score around the average.

The most highly developed associations are also those that are most pronouncedly 'employers' associations'. The Swedish sector associations and the Dutch AWV and AVBB perform the greatest variety of activities typical for an employers' association, as distinct from a trade association. With the exception of the AVBB these are all pure employers' associations. They can concentrate on labour market interests. The latter are usually more homogeneous than the technical-commercial-economic interests of members. That not only facilitates the aggregation of larger groups of businesses into one association, but also aids consensus. The threat of

Table 4.7 *Aggregated rank order scores on variables of organizational development: sectoral employers' associations*

Country	Sector	Association	Rank order
High level of organizational development			
S	Constr.	BF	1
A	All	BWK	2
NL	Metal	FME	3
S	Metal	VF	4
GB	Constr.	NFBTE	5
CH	Constr.	SBV	6
S	Chemicals	Ag-SAF	7
NL	Constr.	AVBB	8
NI	Chemicals	AWV	9
I	Constr.	ANCE	10
GB	Metal	EEF	11
D	Constr.	ZDB	12
GB	Chemicals	CIA	13
CAN	Constr.	AECQ	14
CH	Metal	ASM	15
D	Constr.	HDB	16
D	Metal	Gesamtmetall	17
CH	Chemicals	VBCI	18
I	Chemicals	Asschimici	19
E	Chemicals	FEIQUE	20
I	Metal	Federmetal	21
Low level of organizational development			

trade union power and labour unrest has helped these associations develop into a well-organized counterforce. That threat also played an important role in the formation of employers' associations, both in the past (cf. for example the history of the Dutch AWV, van Waarden, 1987b) and more recently. It was not until 1972 that the Italian metalworking employers joined together to form the labour market organization Federmeccanica, first as a counter-weight against the trade unions in this sector, and secondly to facilitate the conclusion of collective wage agreements (Baglioni et al., 1972: 25). Specialization in interests thus seems to foster the organizational development of interest associations.

12   Possible explanations of national differences

Table 4.8 summarizes the various findings from the previous sections. Some countries score consistently across the different variables. Thus

Table 4.8   Summary of findings: high and low scores of the various countries on Tables 4.1 and 4.3–4.7

Variable (and table no.)	High scores	Low scores
Cohesion of system of general associations (4.1)	A, S, D, I	CAN, GB, NL, CH
Cohesion of system of sectoral associations (4.3)	A, D, CH	CAN, GB, NL, S, I
Representativeness of major general employers' association (4.4)	A, S, NL, CAN, I	CH, D (GB)
Representativeness of major sectoral employers' associations (4.5)	A, S, NL	CAN, CH, D, I (GB)
Organizational development general associations (4.6)	A, S, NL (I)	CAN, CH, D, I, (GB)
Organizational development sectoral associations (4.7)	A, S, NL	CAN, CH, D, I (GB)

Austria and Sweden have both cohesive associational systems and strongly developed individual associations (in Austria because of the unique position of the BWK). Canada, Britain and Italy score low on most variables, with some exceptions: the Italian Confindustria and the Canadian CMA are well-developed organizations, and although the UK systems score low on cohesion, the individual associations take up an intermediate position on the scale of organizational development.

A few other countries have quite different scores on associational systems and individual associations. Thus the Dutch associational systems are low in cohesion, because of the high degree of differentiation and competition. However, many individual associations are among the most highly developed associations of those investigated. In Germany the situation is the other way around. Here the various associational systems are rather cohesive, the dominant association BDA is quite comprehensive, but the individual associations score relatively low on organizational development. The Swiss situation is somewhat comparable to the German, that is, cohesive sectoral associational systems but weakly developed individual associations.

In short, in the smaller countries Austria, Sweden and the Netherlands (and, as far as cohesion of sectoral systems is concerned, also Switzerland) the employers are much more highly organized than in the larger countries Canada, Great Britain, Italy and Germany (the latter's individual associations). Why would this be the case? It seems obvious that there must be a relationship here to important factors in the past and present environment of employers' associations: the structure of the economy, the organization of the opponents, the trade unions, the tradition of state intervention in the economy. Space only allows a few suggestions here.

First, the small size of the country seems important. Smallness implies that there are fewer firms and that the business elite will be smaller, allowing for more personal contact. That might not only facilitate the aggregation of many particular interests towards more general group interests, but also offers the possibility of social control and more effective supervision of compliance with agreements made.

Secondly, the well-known argument of Katzenstein (1985) might be applicable here. Because the industry has a relatively small domestic market, it is more dependent on exports, forcing it to compete with firms which are able to produce under other, and sometimes cheaper, conditions. In the past, then, it was absolutely essential for the industry to secure moderate wage development and to avoid any labour unrest which might harm productivity. Originally, the employers thought to achieve this by forming strong organizations able to stand up to unions and break strikes: see, for example, the creation of the Swedish SAF. Later on attempts have been made to realize these goals through more positive measures, by negotiations, and a specific form thereof: preferably central negotiations with central unions. This is because, as has already been argued, the more comprehensive the associations and the more central the negotiations are, the more moderate policies and agreements tend to be. In the third place the economies of some of these small countries, notably Sweden and the Netherlands and, to a lesser extent, Switzerland, are dominated by large companies with important interests on export markets. They will have been able to impress upon their associations the importance of these interests. Because such companies are often active in more than one industry, they may also help overcome sectoral particularism, and in some instances they might even have an interest in developing a larger role for sector-unspecific employers' associations in wage negotiations (Sweden). Austria, Sweden and the Netherlands furthermore have a political and administrative culture of consensus, as opposed to a more adversarial one in, for example, the Anglo-Saxon countries. This culture also has an impact on the relationship between the state and interest associations. State agencies, which tend to include interest groups in the formulation and implementation of public policy, will have an interest in supporting those associations. In particular, they may want to strengthen the more comprehensive and central associations which tend to follow more moderate policies, perhaps closer to the interests of the state itself. Thus they may help such associations in organizational development. The involvement of interest groups in public policy is furthermore also supported by the corporatist ideology, which was such an important political force in various of these countries between the two world wars, a crucial period in the development of interest associations.

Such state support did not only come in the form of recognition and the provision of access to public policy-making, but also in the more active form of legal support: compulsory membership in Austria, a monopoly on the provision of important selective goods, or the willingness to declare collective labour contracts generally binding.

The state has also contributed to the strengthening of employers' associations in a negative way. The threat of state intervention, for example by the newly formed social-democratic governments in Sweden in the 1930s, brought employers closer together and induced them to prevent such intervention by self-regulation, either alone, or together with trade unions. That required well-organized interest associations.

13   Employers' associations and trade unions

What consequences does the organizational power of employers have on the system of industrial relations, particularly on the organizational pattern of their opponents, the trade unions? Is there any relationship between the patterns in which employers and employees have organized themselves? At first sight, there seems to be little similarity between the degrees of cohesion of the associational patterns of employers and workers. Table 4.9 shows the number of employers' associations and trade unions per country and branch of trade or industry. Generally speaking, there are many more employers' associations than trade unions, nearly twelve times as many. However, this figure is rather coloured by the high number of employers' associations in the German and Italian building industry. But even if these industries are left out, there are still almost 3.5 times as many employers' associations. Apparently, workers are more easily organized in inclusive associations than are employers. The latter clearly have more difficulty undertaking collective action. This confirms our earlier thesis that employers have more difficulty forming collective centres of power than other economic groups, among other reasons because they have significant individual sources of power at their disposal. Their individual economic power is at the same time their organizational and, hence, their political weakness – but the latter is again a point of strength in negotiations, as Streeck (1991) has pointed out. Because they are less well organized, they can make fewer concessions, so that the other party has to yield more (see also Traxler, 1991; van Waarden, 1989a: 36–44).

However, the theoretical organizational problems and possibilities of employers appear to be situation-bound, as differences between countries are considerable. The aggregated data on numbers of employers' associations and trade unions disguise substantial international differences. In the smaller European countries of Austria, Switzerland, Sweden and the Netherlands (the latter only in metalworking and chemicals), the number of employers' associations is smaller than or equals the number of trade unions. These are the countries which are characterized by cohesive systems of employers' associations and sometimes also by strongly developed individual associations. In large countries like Germany, Italy and Spain, the differences in number are, however, extremely large. Apparently, the factors which have supported employers' associations in the smaller countries – as discussed in the previous section – have influenced the associational patterns of both employers and workers. Moreover, in these

Table 4.9 *Numbers of trade unions and employers' associations by country and sector*

	No. of trade unions (TUs)	No. of employers' associations (EAs)	No. of EAs as % of TUs	% of workers subject to multifirm collective agreements (CAs)	No. of dominant CAs
A-Chemicals	2	1	50	100	0
A-Constr.	2	2	100	100	11
A-Metal	2	1	50	100	0
A-Total	6	4	66		
CAN-Chemicals	4	0	0	0	20
CAN-Constr.	16	46	288	95	414
CAN-Metal	6	0	0	0	29
CAN-Total	26	46	177		
CH-Chemicals	3	3	100	52	29
CH-Constr.	7	9	129	100	4
CH-Metal	7	1	14	?	2
CH-Total	17	13	76		
D-Chemicals	3	17	567	95	1
D-Constr.	4	791	19,775	100	9
D-Metal	2	45	2,250	95	15
D-Total	9	853	9,478		
E-Chemicals	4	14	350	25	36
E-Constr.	4	92	2,300	100	50
GB-Chemicals	11	2	18	19	14
GB-Constr.	16	9	56	76	6
GB-Metal	6	19	317	?	2
GB-Total	33	30	91		
I-Chemicals	3	33	1,100	100	3
I-Constr.	3	294	9,800	0	5
I-Metal	3	75	2,500	100	5
I-Total	9	402	4,467		
NL-Chemicals	4	2	50	4	93
NL-Constr.	4	31	775	100	3
NL-Metal	4	3	75	95	2
NL-Total	12	36	300		
S-Chemicals	2	3	150	100	2
S-Constr.	2	4	200	100	2
S-Metal	5	3	60	100	5
S-Total	9	10	111		
General total	129	1,500	11,628		
(excl. D+I constr.)	(122)	(415)	(340)		

'Total' per country means here the sum of the three sectors.

corporatist countries, the employers' associations and trade unions maintain much more intensive relations, particularly since the government has allowed them to participate in its policy-making process, so the mutual influencing of associational patterns is more pronounced here than in non-corporatist countries. The example of Sweden is again instructive (see Box 4.3).

Box 4.3   *The development of organizational structures of employers' associations and unions in Sweden*

The history of Swedish industrial relations is a fine example of that mutual influence. The Swedish central employers' association, SAF, has had a centralized organizational structure since the time of its inception in 1902. It had the power to impose lockouts, had funds available to support its members during strike action and could decide when a member was entitled to such support. Earlier, in 1898, the employees had established a central organization of their own called the LO (*Landsorganisation*). The LO had a strongly decentralized structure at first, so it could not call or support strikes. That power remained vested in the member unions. Similarly, it was the member unions which negotiated with the SAF. In the 1930s, talks began between the SAF and LO to limit the number of strikes through negotiations and so to prevent state intervention by the social democratic governments that had first come to power in 1932. The SAF demanded that the LO be granted the same powers as the SAF, including the right to conclude authoritative and irreversible agreements. This demand was supported by several individual unions, among them the textiles union. They saw centralization as the means to take a firm stand against the SAF. Under pressure of the war and imminent state intervention, the LO amended its articles at a conference in 1941. It was given a mandate to negotiate with the SAF and intervene in union activities that threatened to thwart central agreements. Unions which organized more than 3 per cent of the LO members could no longer call strikes without the LO's permission. Unions that refused to accept central collective bargaining agreements risked losing support from the LO's strike funds. This centralization has occasionally been challenged by individual unions in the years after the war, but under pressure from the SAF – which managed to close ranks against the individual unions – employees have again been forced to centralize (Bresky et al., 1981: 41–47).

In non-corporatist countries, the link between the associational structures of employers and workers is far less direct. In Italy and France, for example, the associational patterns of unions at the central level are highly differentiated into Christian, socialist and communist peak associations. The employers, on the other hand, are fairly centrally organized under the

Confindustria and the CNPF. In these countries, where internal contacts are less institutionalized, the logic of influence is less important to either party, and thus less decisive for their organizational structure. Employers' associations and trade unions tend rather to bow to the demands of the logic of membership, that is, the cleavages among the potential members – and these are of an ideological nature in the countries just mentioned.

14   Employers' associations and collective bargaining arenas

Is there also a relationship between the pattern of associations and the structure of bargaining arenas? Those countries with the fewest yet most highly developed employers' associations – Austria and Sweden – have the most central and inclusive negotiating systems. Table 4.9 shows that in these countries, 100 per cent of all employees are covered by a limited number of collective bargaining agreements. Similarly, in the Dutch and Swiss metalworking and building industries, comprehensive associational patterns of employers (Switzerland) or strongly developed individual associations (the Netherlands: FME and AVBB, Switzerland: SBV) go hand in hand with a limited number of collective bargaining agreements. Of all workers, 95–100 per cent are covered by two to four sectoral bargaining agreements.

Furthermore, the data indicate that systems made up of large numbers of less developed employers' associations (Italy, Germany) also go together, with only a few collective bargaining agreements covering nearly all employees. This could be explained by the fact that many employers' associations in these countries are not involved in wage bargaining. However, they nevertheless count as employers' associations because they perform other activities in the field of social interests, such as providing vocational training.

Furthermore, it also seems curious that exactly those sectors where employers have formed only one or very few associations, such as the Dutch, Swiss and British chemical industries, have such large numbers of bargaining agreements. The most likely explanation is that these are mainly company bargaining agreements. As employers conclude their own bargaining agreements, they have less need for collective contractual partners in their branch; hence the small number of associations.

The reverse is found in construction: few agreements but many employers' associations. One would expect that the limited number of agreements enhances the cohesion and centralization among employers, but that does not seem to be the case. This is probably because most associations in this sector promote both social and economic interests together. And the economic interests keep the various regions and building trades divided.

15   Consequences of the decentralization trend for employers' associations

What now might the consequences be of the fashionable trends of the day, that is more flexibility, deregulation, privatization and decentralization, for the position of employers' associations?

First of all it might be a good idea to point out that the impetus behind these trends is not all that new. In the history of industry and employers' associations, the dominant interest of business has fluctuated with some regularity. Businesses have always had an interest in flexibility, in individual freedom to make the most of their advantages in the competitive struggle. However, they also had an interest in regulation, in controlling competition so as to prevent it from becoming too cut-throat. These two needs, the need for freedom and for regulation, have alternated throughout history and have vied for dominance. The urgency of each one depended on the business cycle, that is, on the intensity of competition. When competition became too fierce, the need for regulation won out, and associations in countries such as Austria, Sweden and the Netherlands pressed for regulation, or regulated markets, including the labour market, on their own, sometimes assisted by the state. This trend has not only produced many forms of state intervention and state regulation, but has also supported the organizational development of employers' associations in those countries where the pressure for protective regulation was most intense or where it was well received by the state. The emergence of such well-developed interest associations in turn became a factor in its own right in the choice between freedom and regulation, often favouring regulation.

There is now evidence of a new phenomenon, with highly developed associations such as the SAF pushing for deregulation and decentralization (Myrdal, 1990; Pestoff, 1991), and, in a way, for their own redundancy as collective bargaining partners. It remains to be seen whether this trend is not again, as in the past, just a temporary and cyclical affair. Some authors maintain that it is more. They argue that the pressure to achieve greater flexibility is now arising from the internationalization of markets and the opening up of domestic economies. The resulting increased competition is forcing business to become more flexible, and the very process of internationalization is undercutting the national systems of regulation. The alternatives seem to be either completely open markets and competition, or interest organization and regulation at the international level, for example that of the EU.

However, those who present such arguments overlook the fact that the most highly developed and centralized systems of employers' associations and the most highly regulated economies were and are to be found precisely in those small countries like Austria, Sweden and the Netherlands which have been open to foreign markets or exposed to foreign competition through their sizeable export industries for a long time. Organization and regulation were precisely the strategies employed by these countries to increase the competitive position of industry. And not without success. Economic institutions, such as interest organizations, the degree of concertation between them, and regulations, produced gradual and moderate wage and price developments and provided the stability and predictability required for long-term investment. Associations and regulations thus enhanced economic performance and increased the competitive position of nations (see also Traxler and Unger, 1990). We may therefore question whether the internationalization of economies will really force the break-up of such institutions, among them business associations. One could also argue that it increases their importance – at least under certain conditions and in certain sectors.

Furthermore, even if the pressure to become more flexible in the 'post-Fordist' era continues, it does not necessarily make employers' associations redundant and less influential. If the desire for flexibility were to reduce the number of sector-wide collective wage agreements and increase the number of single-firm agreements, employers' associations would still play an important role, namely as a forum for the coordination of labour market policies behind the scenes, and as an advisor for firms or branch associations engaged in collective bargaining.

The example of the Dutch *Algemene Werkgevers Vereniging* (AWV) shows that this need not be an unimportant role. This association has never really been a contract partner itself. The sectors it organizes, the chemical and the food processing industries, do not have many sector-wide agreements. Company or branch agreements are more common. However, since its foundation in 1918 the AWV has been closely involved in such negotiations as an expert adviser, often even present at the bargaining tables, and has served as a forum for intersectoral concertation and consultation. In time, it has gathered a staff which possesses by far the greatest level of expertise on bargaining wages and employment conditions, and it has developed several widely used job classification systems. Even in this indirect capacity, the AWV has managed to become one of the most highly developed employers' organizations, both in the Netherlands and by international standards. Decentralization of negotiations does not necessarily have to reduce the importance and power of employers' associations.

Appendix

General (not sector-specific) employers' associations in various European countries, Canada and the USA

Principal general employers' associations

Canada	CMA	Canadian Manufacturers Association [mostly TA]
	CCC	Canadian Chamber of Commerce [mostly TA]
Germany	BDA	Bundesvereinigung der deutschen Arbeitgeberverbände [EA]
GB	CBI	Confederation of British Industry [mostly TA]
	IoD	Institute of Directors [mostly TA]
France	CNPF	Conseil National du Patronat Français [M]
Italy	Confindustria	Confederazione Generale dell'Industria Italiana [M]
Netherlands	VNO	Verbond van Nederlandse Ondernemingen [M]
	AWV	Algemene Werkgevers Vereniging [EA]
Austria	BWK	Bundeskammer der gewerblichen Wirtschaft [M]
Spain	CEOE	Confederación Española de Organizaciones Empresariales [M]
USA	NAM	National Association of Manufacturers [mostly TA]
	NCC	National Chamber of Commerce [mostly TA]
Sweden	SAF	Svenska Arbetsgivarförening [EA]
Switzerland	ZSAO	Zentralverband schweizerischer Arbeitgeber-Organisationen [EA]

Peak trade associations in those countries where separate specialized EAs exist

Germany	BDI	Bundesverband der deutschen Industrie [TA]
Sweden	SI	Federation of Swedish Industry [TA]
Switzerland	Vorort	Schweizerischer Handels- und Industrieverein (also called, after the place of foundation, Vorort) [TA]

General peak associations for small business and handicraft

| Canada | CFIB | Canadian Federation of Independent Business [TA] |
| | COSB | Canadian Organization of Small Business [TA] |

EA, employers' association, representing only labour market interests.
TA, trade association, representing technical and economic interests.
M, mixed business association, for both social and economic interests.

Germany	ZDH	Zentralverband des deutschen Handwerks [M]
	BDS/DGV	Bund der Selbständigen/Deutscher Gewerbeverband [M]
	ASU	Arbeitsgemeinschaft Selbständiger Unternehmer [M]
GB	NFSESB	National Federation of Self-Employed and Small Business [TA]
France	CGPME	Confédération Générale des Petites et Moyennes Entreprises [M]
	SNPMI	Syndicat National des Petites et Moyennes Industries [M]
	CGAF	Confédération Générale de l'Artisanat Français [M]
	UPA	Union Professionnelle d'Artisanat [M]
Italy	Confapi	Confederazione Italiana della Piccola e Media Industria [M]
	CASA	Confederazione Artigiana Sindicati Autonomi (independent handicraft) [M]
	Confartigianato	Confederazione Generale Italiana dell' Artigianato (Christian–democratic) [M]
	CNA	Confederazione Nazionale dell' Artigianato (communist–socialist) [M]
	CLAAI	Confederazione Libere Associazioni Artigiane Italiane (social–democratic/republican) [M]
Netherlands	KNOV	Koninklijk Nederlands Ondernemers Verbond [M]
	NCOV	Nederlands Christelijk Ondernemers Verbond [M]
Austria	ÖGV	Österreichischer Gewerbeverein [TA]
USA	NFIB	National Federation of Independent Business [mostly TA]
	NSB	National Small Businessmen Association [mostly TA]
Sweden	SHIO	SHIO–Familjeföretagen (Swedish Federation for Trade, Industry and Family Firms) [M]
Switzerland	SGV	Schweizerischer Gewerbeverband [M]

Associations only for large firms (sometimes semi-formal organizations)

Canada	BCNI	Business Council on National Issues [mostly TA]
France	AFEP	Association Française des Entreprises Privées [M]
	AGEF	Association des Grandes Entreprises Françaises [M]
Austria	VOEI	Vereinigung österreichischer Industrieller [TA]
USA	BRT	Business Round Table [mostly TA]
	CED	Committee of Economic Development [TA]

Important regional general associations (selection)

Canada	CMA-Q	Canadian Manufacturers Association – Quebec Division (practically independent regional peak) [M]
	CMA-O	Canadian Manufacturers Association – Ontario Division [mostly TA]
	CPQ	Conseil du Patronat du Québec [mostly TA]
	BCBC	Business Council of British Columbia [EA] regional Chambers of Commerce [mostly TA]
Germany		regional Handwerkskammern
Italy		large general provincial associations such as Assolombarda
USA		local and regional Chambers of Commerce [mostly TA]
Switzerland	ZAO	Züricher Arbeitgeberorganisationen [EA]
	ZGV	Züricher Gewerbeverband [M]
	BVWB	Basler Volkswirtschaftsbund [EA]
	FVE	Fédération Vaudoise des Entrepreneurs [EA]
	UAPG	Union des Associations Patronales Genevoises [EA]
	FSP	Fédération des Syndicats Patronaux (regional peak employers' association of the 'Gewerbe' sector, with emphasis in Geneva)

Employers' associations for firms with a specific ownership structure

Italy	AGCI	Associazione Generale delle Cooperative Italiane (social–democratic) [M]
	CCI	Confederazione Cooperative Italiana (Christian–democratic) [M]
	LNCM	Lega Nazionale delle Cooperative e Mutue (communist–socialist) [M]
	ASAP	Associazione Sindacale Aziende Petrolchimiche e Collegate (state-owned firms) [EA]
	Intersind	Associazione Sindacale Intersind (state-owned firms) [EA]
Netherlands	CECOIN	Centrale Vereniging voor de Coöperatieve Industrie [TA]
Austria	ADOEG	Arbeitsgemeinschaft der Österreichischen Gemeinwirtschaft (for state-owned companies and cooperatives) [TA]
	KONSUM	Konsumverband
	ÖRV	Österreichischer Raiffeisenverband
Sweden	KFO	Kooperationens Förhandlingsorganisation [EA] (cooperatives)
	SFO	Statens Förhandlingsorganisation [EA] (state companies)

Employers' associations by ideology, religion etc.

France	CFPC	Centre Chrétien des Patrons et Dirigeants d'Entreprise Française [M]
	CID–UNATI	Comité d'Information et de Défense – Union Nationale des Travailleurs Indépendants [M] (extreme right)
	EP	Entreprise et Progrès [M] ('leftist' employers)
Italy		See the party-affiliated associations of handicraft and cooperatives
Netherlands	NCW	Nederlands Christelijk Werkgeversverbond [M]
	NCOV	Nederlands Christelijk Ondernemersverbond [M]
	KNO	Vereniging van Kritische Nederlandse Ondernemers [M] (extreme right)
USA	NRWC	National-Right-to-Work-Committee (extreme right)

5 Government intervention in industrial relations

Frans van Waarden

1 The government as third actor in industrial relations

The role of the government as third actor in the system of industrial relations can hardly be overestimated. This prompts the question of precisely what interests, roles and duties the state has within the social and economic framework. In this section we shall discuss the potential roles of the government and the possibilities for government intervention. After that, we shall look at the way in which the different national governments interpret these roles.

Types of state intervention in industrial relations

The importance of state intervention only increased in the 1980s. This may seem a paradox, as at first glance this decade mainly saw governments withdrawing from economic and social processes. Many authors maintain that governments were forced to restrict their roles because of the economic recessions. As soaring unemployment put pressure on social security spending, the resulting budget deficits compelled governments to slash spending on social policy, trim the workforce in the public sector and reconsider existing rules and regulations characteristic of the welfare state. Deregulation, state withdrawal in favour of free market enterprise, and a cutting back on social expenditure in order to create a leaner welfare state were for many the key words of the 1980s.

Although the picture of a retreating government is in itself correct, it is also one-sided. It is probably better to say that governments recontemplated and redefined their roles. They have continued to intervene, but this time with a view to improving the competitiveness of their national trade and industry. Labour relations have been affected in the process. However, state intervention in Europe should not be brought under one common denominator. Some governments, like that of Germany, have been comparatively absent from the process of shaping terms and conditions of employment. Others have withdrawn somewhat from the social and economic negotiating table, as the Dutch government has done, or conversely, have taken regulation out of the hands of the social partners, like the Belgian government. In whatever way governments have intervened, they did so for quite different reasons. The British government took action to clear the way for free market forces, and did not shrink from attacking the position of the trade unions. In contrast, the French government introduced its Auroux reforms for the very reason that it wanted to strengthen the position of the trade unions in negotiations and in the workplace.

In this chapter we shall look particularly at the differences between countries in terms of the position and role of their governments in the system of industrial relations. The diverse systems of industrial relations in these countries can largely be put down to differences in the degree and nature of government intervention and the varying 'roles of the government' in the field of industrial relations. Besides the different types of intervention, there is a wide variety of issues with which governments will or will not be involved. Also, the extent to which regulations are detailed and require strict compliance differs from country to country. Clearly, it is beyond the scope of this chapter to compare and discuss all the roles and types of state regulation possible. Only a rough outline will be attempted here, focusing mainly on the 'rules of the game', that is, the formal rules making up the legal framework of industrial relations. We will concentrate on three general kinds of state action, and present the country most representative of the particular type of action. These types are:

1 *Liberal pluralism*: a passive state which upholds the principle of non-intervention. State regulation of industrial relations is confined to creating a (modest) legal framework within which private individuals and businesses can conclude agreements. The classic example in Europe is the United Kingdom.

2 *Corporatism*: active state interference, but usually in consultation with the social partners. This implies active support for their organizations

and their mutual relations. The archetype is Germany, closely followed by the Netherlands and Sweden.
3 *Statism*: active and direct state interference with terms of employment and working conditions. The country which best fits this description is France.

Interests and roles of the government in industrial relations

National systems of industrial relations have to a large extent been moulded by government action. The freedom and means of power of the contracting parties depend on the legal framework provided. Have the interest groups been officially recognized and do they have legal personality? Are contracts enforceable under civil law? Does the government have authority to declare collective bargaining agreements generally binding? How far-reaching is the right to strike and do employers have a right to lock out employees? Do the employers' and employees' organizations receive any other support from the government or have their activities been hindered by government measures? Labour relations are also substantially influenced by the degree of state intervention and state regulation of the labour market. Also, the degree of state intervention and regulation of the labour market has an influence on labour relations and on the position of trade unions and employers' associations. Public regulation of terms of employment, working conditions and social security may well further the cause of private interest groups, and may have even been taken after calls for action by these groups or, possibly, in consultation with them.

State intervention is, however, a double-edged sword. It may also put the brake on the development of private organizations, robbing them of the very tasks which justify their existence and keep their membership at acceptable levels. The threat of undesired government action may prompt employers' and/or employees' organizations to self-regulate their affairs. Thus, even by sitting back and uttering the occasional threat, governments can influence industrial relations.

The government has various interests in how the labour market and industrial relations develop. One such interest ensues first of all from the state's original, principal responsibility, which is to regulate general conflict. It must guarantee its citizens law and order. Strikes and other forms of labour unrest led to the first instances of government intervention in industrial relations. Initially, such intervention was of a repressive nature. Later, more positive measures were taken to secure law and order. The concern for what became known in the second half of the nineteenth century as the 'social question', the quest for some measure of social justice, was inspired particularly by the need to ward off labour unrest and possibly revolution. Later, with workers having obtained the right to vote, a more authentic concern for social justice emerged. Secondly, the government has an interest in a prospering economy. The more it intervened in the economy, the more it was held responsible for economic development. It acquired interests in economic growth, reduced unemployment and stimulated welfare for everyone. Derived interests were hence moderate pay rates, high labour productivity and, again, labour contentment, which enhanced growth and employment. Obviously, this economic interest goes back to the state's fundamental interest in law and order, its authentic concern for social justice, and not in the last instance its self-interest. In a mercantile sense, the economic riches of a state will increase its political power *vis-à-vis* other countries. But in an immediate financial sense as well, the government has an interest in economic growth. Its own (tax) income hinges on it.

Thirdly, as the state employs an ever-increasing number of civil servants and employees in the subsidized sectors, it has a direct interest in developments on the labour market. Pay rates in the private sector often serve as a guide for the terms of employment of its own workforce, and so quite directly affect its own budgetary options and limitations.

Interference with industrial relations is not only the result of the government's own initiatives. It has often been pressured to take action by private organizations in need of some support for their own organizations or activities, as without it they would be facing the considerable problems of collective action (see previous chapters). Outside parties, so-called free riders, may benefit from the actions of employers' and/or employees' organizations without paying any dues, this making it less attractive for those who do pay to keep up their dues. When a number of actors make use of collective services – which by definition are available to everyone – without contributing to the costs of those services, those who do contribute may well be discouraged from making further payments. Because free riding threatens the continuity of collective services, state support is usually the only way out. The state – which is in fact an all-embracing association with compulsory membership – has fewer free rider problems, thanks to its monopoly on the legitimate use of force, on taxation and on enacting generally binding rules and regulations. By allowing private organizations to share in its 'sovereignty' or otherwise supporting them, the state can reduce their Olsonian problems of collective action. The role of the state and the legal framework is hence in turn a reflection of the industrial relations system, of attempts by interest associations to exercise influence.

Government interventions which have a direct or indirect impact on industrial relations can be divided into five main categories.

1   The most sweeping interventions are concerned with the substantive binding rules which directly dictate terms of employment and working conditions: minimum wages, pay differences, absolute pay rates and pay rises, cost-of-living adjustments, working hours, holidays, shifts, social security, industrial health care, safety in the workplace, and so

on. In fact, a large number of the rules underpinning the welfare state belong to this category.

2   Less direct are the binding rules regarding the rules-of-the-game for industrial relations. They concern:

- the individual employment relationship: dismissal law, employment protection, workers' participation, and so on;
- the internal organization of the contracting partners: civil law, law of association, for example the rules governing internal trade union democracy, decision-making on strike action, and so on;
- the relations between employers' associations and trade unions: collective bargaining law, right to strike, right to lock out.

3   Even less far-reaching are those rules which, while supporting interest groups and/or their (inter-organizational) relations, are neither mandatory nor enforceable. Examples of these measures are the official recognition of and the grant of legal personality to interest groups if requested; the grant of privileged access to government bodies, like seats on social and economic advisory councils; recognition of the monopoly of organizations to represent a specified group of employers or employees; subsidies and tax relief; the right to implement statutory unemployment provisions. Apart from the organizations themselves, cooperation between them may be supported, for example, by the government assuming the role of mediator in collective bargaining negotiations, declaring collective bargaining agreements generally binding, or adjudicating disputes as an arbitrator.

4   Additionally, the state may provide collective goods which are not easily produced by the parties themselves because of free rider problems, but which are nevertheless important to them, such as vocational training and industrial health care.

5   Lastly, the state is a contracting party itself in its capacity as employer of public and semi-public servants.

Thus, the different sorts of state measures reflect the various roles of the state in the field of industrial relations: regulator, supporter, mediator, arbitrator, provider of collective services and employer.

2   Substantive regulation of terms of employment

Typical for French statism is that many secondary terms of employment, which are elsewhere the subject of collective bargaining agreements, are provided for by law: minimum wages, working week, length of holiday periods, social security provisions, child and family allowances, pensionable age and so on. Furthermore, employers are required to provide certain arrangements without the government specifying the precise content, for example, the duty to set up a profit-sharing scheme. Even the primary terms of employment, like pay rises, may be unilaterally dictated by the government, usually when the social partners fail to agree on the issue. If any such rules are to be imposed, it will be done only after consulting the social partners. Sometimes one has the impression that the social partners are not eager to reach agreement at all, letting the government do their dirty work and take what are considered necessary but unpopular measures. The fact that state intervention is relatively widely accepted as legitimate in France – even among those who in other countries would be appalled at such government interference, that is, the business community – is quite likely due to the possibility it offers interest organizations of ducking responsibilities.

Unlike the French government, the German authorities leave many more issues for regulation to the social partners. Although there is consensus in Germany that employees should be protected both by government rules and by collective bargaining agreements, the social partners are given much more leeway to regulate their affairs through collective bargaining. Working hours, holidays, dismissal protection and rationalization are usually laid down in collective bargaining agreements rather than in the law. In principle, pursuant to an Act passed in 1952, the German government has the right to impose minimum terms of employment upon any trade or branch of industry. Intervention is permitted if there is no collective bargaining agreement and/or there are no employers' or employees' associations operating in that sector. So far, the Act has never been used.

The German government has, however, actively been trying to influence the outcome of negotiations between the social partners, by making economic data available to confront them with the possible macro-economic effects of their actions. In the 1970s, the government even went as far as to develop this approach into a more or less formal coordination system of decision-making between regional governments and peak organizations. This system became known as the *konzertierte Aktion*.

If the German government has regulated other labour issues by law – like social security, health care or vocational training – its implementation has been partly entrusted to bodies in which both employers and employees are represented. Examples of these are the *Berufsgenossenschaften* (social security) and *Handwerkskammern* (vocational training). Private organizations thus play an important part in shaping and implementing rules governing the labour market in Germany. They were in a position to do so, firstly because German employers' associations and trade unions have a higher density rate, cohesion and internal disciplinary capacity than their French counterparts. Secondly, the delegation of regulatory tasks only went to strengthen their position. In other ways, too, the German government has lent support to employers' and employees' organizations. Their structure and operations have been placed within a legal framework. On this point, the German system differs from the British system.

In terms of regulating industrial relations, the British and French governments are poles apart. The British government adheres to the principle of non-intervention and voluntarism, which is particularly reflected in the freedom of the trade unions to negotiate and take industrial action. However, this principle is less easy to trace in the substantive regulation of terms of employment and working conditions.

Although Great Britain still has no statutory minimum wage, many secondary aspects of individual employment relationships have been laid down by law, ranging from health insurance and dismissal protection to health and safety at work. In the latter field, in particular, the British government has always been fairly active. Since the early nineteenth century, numerous statutory measures have been taken to regulate working conditions. In 1974, they were brought together under the Health and Safety at Work Act.

In addition, British governments, both Conservative and Labour, have in the 1970s made various attempts at controlling pay rates within the context of their macro-economic policies. As in Germany, this was to be realized by voluntary 'social contracts' between the government, TUC and CBI, or through so-called 'declarations of intent' which contained pay rate guidelines for the affiliated unions. A few times, wages and prices were mandatorily frozen for a limited period. The British government's voluntary income policy was not particularly successful because the peak organizations of employers and employees had insufficient authority over the affiliated associations that actually conducted the pay negotiations. State intervention in pay rates and prices, either direct or indirect, was extremely unpopular among employers and trade unions alike, even if the measures were taken by Labour governments who were associated with the unions. With this in mind, the Conservative Thatcher governments chose a different strategy to control wages: a stringent monetary policy, which has increased unemployment and weakened the position of employees on the labour market. This, too, is a form of state intervention in industrial relations.

State interference with primary terms of employment sometimes went beyond voluntarism. For some decades, some trades and branches of British industry were subject to statutorily binding pay rules. In sectors where there were no (strong) employers' and employees' organizations and/or no collective pay negotiations, the government established Wage Councils, which were to set minimum wages as well as other types of remuneration, like piece-rates, overtime bonuses and holiday pay. The Wage Inspectorate monitored compliance with these binding provisions. By the end of the 1970s, nearly 3 million workers in 500,000 companies were subject to the rules imposed by 40-odd Wages Councils. The Conservative government, however, abolished them in 1993.

As regards the implementation of government regulations, the social partners play a far less prominent role in Great Britain than in Germany. In Great Britain, there generally exists what the British perceive as a healthy distrust of particularistic interest groups implementing government policy. If in Germany health insurance is a matter for corporatist bodies to deal with, in Great Britain it is the task of the National Health Service, a government body. An important exception is the Safety Inspectors. The Health and Safety at Work Act 1974 is implemented with the aid of all parties involved. The Act imposes on trade unions the duty to appoint employees as Safety Representatives and as members of a Safety Commission on the workfloor, which is again an exception to the tradition of voluntarism. Moreover, the national peak Health and Safety Commission, which formulates the general policy on health and safety, comprises representatives from all three sides.

The fact that the British government has sometimes taken rather sweeping regulatory measures affecting the labour market is no doubt due to the close ties between the trade unions and the Labour party. In this way, the labour movement has two channels through which to attain its goals. The playing field of the unions (pay negotiations, right to strike and so on) is anxiously protected from state intervention. Where there are no (strong) unions or where no pay negotiations take place, state intervention is condoned. The marriage between the unions and Labour is sometimes an uneasy one, witness the conflicts which arose when different Labour governments made attempts at pursuing some kind of incomes policy. In Sweden, relations are more relaxed. Unions there more readily accept legislation by the Social Democratic government if employers will not budge during negotiations. Forty years of social democratic rule have strengthened the political position of the Swedish labour movement – until recently, that is.

3 Formal regulation: the rules-of-the-game governing industrial relations

Right to negotiate and conclude collective bargaining agreements

In France, the government not only directly exerts strong influence on the substance of terms of employment but terms of employment negotiated by the social partners are also influenced by the government, more so than in many other countries. French law specifies in great detail what provisions a collective bargaining agreement must and may contain. For example, it must confirm the freedom of association, be in line with the minimum wage rules, set out the procedures for employment and dismissal, specify the notice periods for dismissal, provide for paid holidays, and contain special arrangements for women and children, apprenticeship and the settlement of disputes. Additionally, the agreement may contain special terms of employment governing overtime and shifts, pay scales, seniority bonuses and performance, expense allowances, transfer allowances, compensation during slack periods and pension schemes.

National or regional collective bargaining agreements are standard, in any case in the private sector. Company-specific agreements are permitted by law only if they contain provisions which, from the employees' point of view, are an improvement on the collective bargaining agreement applying to the industry as a whole. Once concluded, the agreements must be officially registered with the *Registre de Conseil de Prud'hommes*. The nationalized industries are subject to different and more detailed rules and regulations, which among other things entitle workers to participate to some extent in formulating the companies' wage and labour policies.

Furthermore, the government often takes the initiative for negotiations, many of which take place in 'mixed committees' consisting of representatives of the employers and the 'most representative' unions. These committees are set up by the Minister of Employment, either at the request of one of the parties or at the Minister's own instigation. The committees are chaired by an *inspecteur du travail*. Only the collective bargaining agreements concluded by such a mixed committee instituted by the Minister can be declared generally binding by the government. In this way, private sector agreements become public law. French state interventionism is in stark contrast to the British tradition of non-intervention. The British government does not interfere with the substance of collective bargaining agreements or with the negotiating process. The parties have full freedom of negotiation. Nor can the British government declare a bargaining agreement generally binding. The agreement is not even statutorily binding on the contracting parties themselves. Compliance cannot be enforced in court. As recently as in 1969, the High Court held that collective bargaining agreements were 'binding in honour only' (Kennedy, 1980: 11). In this respect, British bargaining agreements differ from those in most other countries, where the state may be asked to help guarantee compliance with the arrangements made.

In the UK, collective bargaining agreements are not considered commercial contracts, which are legally enforceable in Great Britain, but rather a kind of 'industrial peace treaty and at the same time a source of rules for terms and conditions of employment, for the distribution of work and for the stability of jobs' (Kahn-Freund, 1977: 122). Voluntary compliance is a typical example of the more comprehensive British tradition of voluntarism, which is certainly supported by the trade unions. They strongly opposed the short-lived Industrial Relations Act 1971, which made collective bargaining agreements legally enforceable unless otherwise provided by the parties. In response to the Act, the TUC advised all its member unions to include provisions to that effect. In 1974, the government once again reversed the situation, so that collective bargaining agreements are not legally enforceable unless the parties agree in writing that they consider themselves bound by the agreement.

The German government takes up a middle position. Like the British government, it applies the principle of non-intervention. The German constitution provides that the social partners are autonomous and free to set rules through collective bargaining. It grants them a sphere of activity which is not regulated by the law. But unlike the British system and more like that in France, industrial relations in Germany are to some extent cast into a legal framework. For one, the contracting parties must meet specified legal requirements. In order to be able to conclude bargaining agreements, a union must be voluntary and operating independently from the employer (no 'company' unions). It must organize employees in different companies, have a democratic internal decision-making structure and one of its official objectives must be to conclude collective bargaining agreements. The *Tarifvertragsgesetz* of 1949 (as amended in 1969 and 1974) further provides that a collective bargaining agreement is a private-law contract and compliance is legally enforceable. It also prescribes the goals and substance of collective bargaining agreements, but not in as detailed a fashion as in France. Also, German collective bargaining agreements may be declared generally binding on a particular trade or industry and/or region at the request of the parties involved. This is actually common practice.

By declaring private-law agreements generally binding, the state turns them into public law, binding not only on the rank-and-file of the contracting partners but also on the unorganized employers and employees. It is a form of active support by the government aimed at resolving the problems of collective action and to some extent an alternative to the 'closed shop'. There is, therefore, a mechanism for preventing general pay regulations from being undercut by unorganized free riders, without the freedom of association being restricted. Apart from Germany, bargaining agreements can also be made generally binding in France, Belgium, the Netherlands, Austria, Spain and Switzerland. By means of the *procédure d'élargissement*, bargaining agreements in France may even be extended to a related industry or to a neighbouring region not covered by a collective bargaining agreement or where there are no employers' associations or unions. This option may be seen as a variation of the UK's Wage Councils.

Because of the more widespread tradition of voluntarism, collective agreements in Great Britain cannot be made generally binding. But the British unions used to have an alternative in the closed shop (see below). When a trade union makes a closed shop contract with an employer, all workers must join that union either before or immediately after joining the company, so any collective bargaining agreement concluded will in effect govern all workers. Of course, the closed shop is not a solution to the 'problem' of unorganized employers, but only to that of unorganized workers.

Neither can collective agreements be made generally binding in Italy. Alternatively, however, the Italian government may set statutory minimum standards for terms of employment (working hours, national holidays, individual dismissal procedures), all of which are based on existing collective bargaining agreements (negotiated legislation). In this way, provisions from collective agreements are occasionally extended to actors other than the members of the contracting parties.

These forms of state support – the ability to declare agreements generally binding, closed shop contracts and negotiated legislation – will not be found in the Scandinavian countries. Government support is not really necessary here because of the high density rates for both employers' associations and trade unions. Nearly all employers in any given trade or industry are bound by collective agreements. A high density rate reduces the problems of collective action to a minimum anyway, and with it the number of potential free riders.

Strikes, lockouts and the peace clause

The right to strike is probably nowhere as unlimited as it is in Great Britain. It has not always been like that. The trade unions have had to wage quite a battle in and outside Parliament to secure this freedom. During the 1980s, the Conservative governments have restricted the right to strike (outside one's own company).

Before 1824, the British courts interpreted the common law as viewing trade unions as criminal conspiracies. This changed after the Combinations Act was repealed in 1824, but the threat of the court holding trade unions criminally liable for certain activities remained immanent. Those activities included the calling and supporting of strikes. The Conspiracy and Protection of Property Act 1875 eliminated the threat of criminal prosecution. The courts, however, still held the unions civilly liable for damages caused by strike action. This gave the employers the possibility of recovering their losses from strike organizers.

With the Trade Disputes Act 1906, Parliament granted the unions immunity from civil claims for damages. 'Most Parliamentary statutes in the area of collective labour law have done little more than to restore to the trade unions and to their members some of the legal rights which had previously been taken away from them by judges' decisions. Indeed, trade unionists have often expressed the fear that the rights given to them by new statutes have been reduced or made invalid by the subsequent interpretations of the common law by the courts and by the judges' (Farnham and Pimlott, 1979: 186).

During the 1980s and 1990s, the right to strike became more limited. The consecutive Conservative governments attempted to restrict the freedom to strike. With the 1984 Trade Union Act, strikes became legitimate only if they had been voted on in advance by union members. The 1990 Employment Act gives employers greater freedom to dismiss people taking part in unlawful strike action; immunity is removed for union officials, including shop stewards, who organize support for people dismissed for taking part in unlawful strikes. All remaining forms of secondary action have been made unlawful. The 1993 Trade Union Reform and Employment Rights Act stipulates that the employer must be given a seven-day warning in advance before official industrial action; all pre-strike ballots must be postal and are subject to independent scrutiny, and users of public services have the right to seek injunction against unlawful strike action.

In Italy and France, there are no essential restrictions curbing the right to strike. In France, this right was embedded in the constitution of 1946. Workers on strike are normally protected by the law. Like those who are ill, they cannot be dismissed. In legal terms, a strike does not constitute a breach of contract, but rather a suspension of the individual employment contract. Although according to the constitution the right to strike is 'subject to the restrictions imposed by the law', only a few have been imposed. The most important restriction is that workers who misbehave (*faute lourde*) – for example, by aggressively picketing – are no longer protected under the law and can be dismissed. Also, political strikes directed against the government are prohibited. The trade unions involved may be held civilly liable by employers for any damage caused.

Unlike in other countries, there is no law in France prohibiting strikes which have not been announced in advance, or which have begun without first exhausting normal mediation procedures. This in spite of the fact that conciliation is mandatory under the Act on Collective Bargaining Agreements of 1950. Hence, the most important limitation on the right to strike is not a legal but a practical one. The French trade unions are too weak, in terms of density and financial resources, to be able to keep up a strike for a substantial period of time. Typically, although strikes in France are short-lived, their impact can be considerable.

Counter-action by employers in the form of lockouts is prohibited in France, unless they cannot continue operating due to circumstances beyond their control (*force majeure*). Employers have a considerable means of defence at their disposal, however, in that they can dismiss workers on strike providing they pay them the amount of wages payable during the notice period specified in the individual employment contracts. They can then hire strike breakers, who need not be replaced by the dismissed workers after the strike is over, because 'the employer now has obligations towards his new employees'. Germany and Sweden have more substantial limitations on the right to strike. In both countries, strike action is prohibited during the term of a collective bargaining agreement if the strike is aimed at changing (any provision of) the agreement. Thus, the trade unions are under a statutory peace obligation. The German law of 1949 requires every collective bargaining agreement to include such a peace clause. Similarly, employers are prohibited from organizing a lockout or boycott during the term of a collective bargaining agreement. Breach of contract entitles the other party to claim damages. As a further limitation, the German law provides that there must be a reasonable link between the means and the end. There must be *Verhältnismäßigkeit* and

Sozialadäquanz (Wolter, 1979: 232). The courts may test strikes against these criteria.

Unlike in France, lockouts by employers are generally permitted in Germany and Sweden. But again, the end must reasonably justify the means. Employers do sometimes resort to the lockout tactic. Lockouts were imposed in the German metallurgical industry in 1963, 1971 and 1978. In Sweden even the government used this instrument, when in 1971 it responded to strikes staged by highly qualified public servants who were demanding that differences in incomes should be restored. When government lockouts threatened to affect not only central government staff and railway employees, but also high-ranking army officers, the Swedish Parliament intervened by issuing a temporary strike prohibition.

One may say that limiting the right to strike fits in with the corporatist ideals of harmonious class relations, well-organized markets and politics based on consensus and cooperation. The restrictive regulation of conflicts is meant to encourage the parties involved to develop a working relationship. Allowing the imposition of lockouts as some kind of counterweight is also in line with these ideals, if only as a threat. In contrast, the unlimited freedom to strike in the UK reflects not only a liberal belief in the 'free exchange of societal forces' but also a tradition of adversarial political relations, as exemplified also in the British electoral system with its clear-cut alternatives and alternating governments.

Recognition, rights and facilities granted to trade unions

In most countries, official recognition requires trade unions and employers' associations to meet certain representational requirements. Once recognized, they are admitted to committees and other bodies and granted access to facilities. Recognition may also bestow certain privileges on them. All of this helps them fight off competitive unions and associations.

Even in Great Britain, where the government is very reluctant to interfere with trade unions and pay negotiations, legal procedures have been developed officially to recognize trade unions. Under the Trade Union Act 1871, unions could apply for registration with the Registrar of Friendly Societies. Registration was, however, voluntary and carried few advantages. Not surprisingly, few requirements were set. New legislation has been adopted since then, attaching some material benefits to recognition. Since the introduction of the Employment Protection Act 1975, only recognized unions have been entitled to receive business information for collective bargaining purposes. In order to be recognized, unions must apply for registration with the Certification Officer, the only condition being that they must be independent from the employer; 'company' unions will not receive recognition. What in fact happens is that the Officer merely confirms the applicant's independent status.

Because the social partners possess freedom of action and negotiation in the UK, recognition by the other party as a legitimate negotiating partner is often far more important, even from a legal point of view. The British government has supported the recognition process throughout. It set an example by recognizing the right of its own employees to join a trade union, and by subsequently entering into collective pay negotiations. The Employment Protection Act 1975 further specifies legal procedures by means of which certified unions can try to obtain official recognition from employers without having to take industrial action. But obviously, because of the tradition of voluntarism, employers cannot be forced to recognize unions or enter into negotiations with them. The Advisory Conciliation and Arbitration Service (ACAS), set up under the Act, can only act as a mediator and catalyst. If its mediation is unsuccessful, it may recommend recognition in a report. If the employer nevertheless ignores the report, the union in question may request that the Central Arbitration Committee (CAC) impose on the employer the terms of employment prevailing in that particular trade or industry. But this only rarely happens. Disputes over recognition are usually settled through ACAS.

Since the French government plays a larger part in collective pay negotiations than the British, official recognition there has far more consequences. Only those organizations recognized by the government may be invited to sit on 'mixed negotiating committees', have collective bargaining rights, propose candidates for representative advisory bodies in companies, or even be elected to consultative government committees. French trade unions may be recognized as 'most representative' unions. However, every trade, industry or company can have more than one such 'most representative' union. The requirements for recognition are stricter than in Great Britain. The unions must of course be independent from the employers, but there are additional criteria in terms of membership, regular payments of union contributions and the reputation, experience and age of union leaders. Even patriotism during the Second World War is a prerequisite, in that unions must not have collaborated with the Vichy government. Moreover, persons who have been convicted of specified crimes – such as joining illegal strikes – cannot be leaders of recognized unions (Seyfarth et al., 1972: 20). The representativeness of trade unions is determined on the basis of, among other things, the results of the elections for the *comités d'entreprise* and the *délégués du personnel*. Registration is applied for with the local mayor.

In Sweden, recognition has even more drastic implications and confers more extensive rights on the trade unions. Unlike British employers, their Swedish counterparts can be forced to acknowledge government-recognized unions and enter into negotiations with them. The trade unions in fact have a statutory right to negotiations, which obliges the employers to negotiate any issues which the unions have tabled. These issues may cover a wide range of labour aspects which elsewhere are determined unilaterally by employers: employment and dismissal, working methods, purchase of equipment, layout of workshops, working hours, industrial safety, transfer and so on. Moreover, employers are under a duty to supply the unions with information about the company's financial situation, staffing policy and proposed investments. Negotiations are regarded here in the broadest sense as a means to increase worker co-determination.

This active right to negotiate may be rather unique. However, in many countries the state supports recognized trade unions in more passive ways. For instance, the state may allow employers to check off, that is deduct, union dues from their employees' pay on behalf of the unions. The unions use this right to guarantee continuity of dues payment. Only in France is this procedure prohibited and is the prohibition defended by the unions themselves. The ensuing fact that many French trade unionists pay dues for only one or two months a year has landed the French unions in a weak financial position. Not surprisingly, they obtain nearly 60 per cent of their income directly or indirectly from the treasury or from friendly political parties.

The Italian government aids the collection of union contributions in still another way. The Italian Minister of Employment may give the national health and accident insurance companies permission to deduct union contributions from health benefits.

Also, trade unions may receive government support in that they are granted certain tasks in implementing social security policy, notably the payment of benefits. The Swedish and Belgian trade unions have these rights and duties, which explains the high union density rates in these countries.

Finally, trade unions in several countries, including France, Italy, Sweden and the Netherlands, have succeeded in securing facilities in the workplace: paid leave for union representatives for union activities, availability of conference rooms, right to put up notices, special protection of union representatives from dismissal and other sanctions by the employer. In this way, too, governments support trade unions.

Great Britain is the exception to the rule. Here, the shops stewards, who represent the unions in the workplace, have no statutory rights at all. But then again, they do not seem to need support from higher up in order to stand their ground. Shop stewardship has developed and become strong from the grass roots, instead of being imposed from above. Facilities are not obtained by referring to the law, but through direct negotiations with the employer. Added to this, shop floor trade unionism in Great Britain has a long tradition and employers have got used to its presence, so that facilities for shop floor activities have become accepted practice over time.

In continental Europe, shop floor presence of unions was not a matter of course at all. For quite some time, the unions were conspicuous by their absence from the workplace. Employers initially vehemently opposed attempts by the unions to attain facilities and protection for lay union officials on the shop floor. Because of such opposition, trade unions understandably sought the help of third parties at higher levels of aggregation, where their position was already strongly established – the state and sometimes also employers' associations – in order to acquire shop floor facilities.

Freedom of association and closed shop contracts

Recognition of trade unions implies the right of workers to join a trade union. In almost all countries, trade union membership is statutorily protected. There is freedom of association and freedom to choose a union. In Great Britain, however, the unions for a long time did not trust the law to protect union membership against hostile employers. They would rather rely on their organizational strength and militant action to secure this right. It was not until the adoption of the Employment Protection Act in 1975 that a statutory right to trade union membership came about. The Act not only enables unions to be recognized and acquire negotiating rights, but also entitles trade unionists to be exempted from work to conduct union activities and receive training.

The other side of the coin of freedom to join a union is the freedom to leave without suffering negative consequences. In most countries, these related aspects are embedded in the law. Strangely enough, for all its liberal tradition, for a long time this was not the case in Great Britain. Until recently, there was no freedom of association, one of many legal and political anomalies found there. In taking up employment, workers could be forced into trade union membership, and termination of their membership could result in dismissal by the employer. This was due to the closed shop contracts which trade unions could conclude with employers, and which either stipulated that jobs were available only to trade unionists (pre-entry closed shop) or that workers had to become members within a certain period after their employment (post-entry closed shop).

The closed shop system was the result of the high degree of job control exerted by the British trade unions, which have a strong presence in the workplace through their shop stewards. This situation is uncommon in the other European countries. Closed shops were common practice in the British coal industry, power industry, printing industry, in seafaring, ports and harbours, the railways and the haulage sector. In 1974, two-fifths of the British workforce had no choice. They had to become trade union members under some closed shop contract or other, although strictly speaking only 750,000 workers were subject to such a contract (Kennedy 1980: 4). Like collective bargaining agreements, closed shop contracts were not legally binding. They were usually no more than informal agreements between the trade unions and employers. However, the closed shop has become a thing of the past in Great Britain, outlawed by legislation introduced by the Thatcher government. Notwithstanding this legislation, some closed shop agreements continued to persist in practice for a time. By now, however, it is estimated that all closed arrangements have formally disappeared.

In most countries on the Continent, particularly France, Germany, Italy and Switzerland, closed shop contracts are either prohibited by law or not desired by the unions. Yet, they can be found in parts of the printing industry, which presumably has to do with another civil right, the freedom of the press.

In France, for example, the freedom of labour has been laid down in the constitution and was reinforced by the law of 1950, which provides that all collective bargaining agreements must contain a clause confirming the freedom of association. Workers may not in any way be pressured to join a (specific) trade union. This principle is also rooted in the consciousness of the social partners. A prominent member of the communist CGT once remarked that one would never come across a closed shop in France; the workers would not accept such an attack on their individual freedom (Seyfarth et al., 1972: 14).

Consequently, the trade unions in these countries have sought other ways to get unorganized workers to contribute towards union activities. When the Swiss supreme court declared closed shop contracts illegal in 1949, the unions managed to persuade employers to withhold about 50 per cent of the usual union dues from the wages of unorganized workers. This arrangement stood up in court and the legality of these 'solidarity contributions' was expressly laid down by law in 1956 (Kassalow, 1969: 144–145).

In Belgium, the trade unions achieved this aim when employers agreed to pay trade unionists an extra bonus. Employers thus subsidised a (substantial) portion of the union dues and the difference between membership and non-membership in money terms became quite small. In the Netherlands, employer-paid bonuses for trade unionists were prohibited. In the 1960s, however, the 'union tenner' was introduced; under the terms of the collective bargaining agreements, employers had to pay a specified sum for every employee (ten guilders, initially) into a fund, regardless of whether the employee was a trade unionist. This mechanism is still in place. Out of these funds, activities are paid for which generally benefit the particular trade or industry, like vocational training, industrial health care, research and so on. In some trades and industries, trade unions and employers' associations are allowed to draw substantial sums of money from these funds for their own purposes. The Dutch government actively supports these types of arrangement by also declaring these clauses in collective bargaining generally binding with the agreement as a whole, forcing unorganized employers to pay these levies as well.

4   The government as a mediator and arbitrator

In most countries, the government acts as a conciliator, mediator or arbitrator in conflicts between the social partners. What we see here, in fact, is the exercise of a very basic and original function of the state: the settlement of disputes within society. Mediation may be carried out at an informal level, where the government will try to get the top brass of the central organizations of employers and employees together to forge a social contract, or the government will intervene in strikes to encourage the parties to sit down and negotiate. At a formal level, however, special mediation services may be set up. Such services are available in most countries, but their powers vary greatly, which is reflected in the extent to which the parties concerned are free to choose to go to mediation.

Entirely in line with British tradition, mediation in the UK is based on voluntarism. The government merely offers an instrument, which the social partners may use if they please. They are not obliged to seek mediation. The reason why the British government nevertheless goes to such great lengths to provide mediation and arbitration is that it has no power to intervene directly in industrial disputes. The most important organizations are the Advisory Conciliation and Arbitration Service (ACAS), launched in 1974, and the Central Arbitration Committee (CAC), launched in 1976. Although ACAS has been set up by the government, it is to a very large extent not subject to direct government control. This was done in order to emphasize the neutrality of the service and inspire confidence among the social partners. After all, the British political system does, at times, raise doubts about the political impartiality of the British government. The chairman of ACAS is appointed by the Employment Secretary. Of the nine members, one-third are appointed by the TUC and one-third by the CBI; the others are 'independent' academics. Disputes may be referred to ACAS only if the settlement procedures voluntarily agreed between the parties prove unsuccessful. ACAS offers:

- conciliation, to help parties resolve their dispute in mutual consultation;
- mediation, to propose resolutions that may end the dispute;
- arbitration, to impose a final settlement of the dispute.

Conciliation will be attempted only at the request of at least one of the parties concerned, while arbitration requires the consent of all parties.

ACAS also arbitrates in matters like trade union recognition by employers. In addition, it gives advice on labour law, pay structures and dispute settlement procedures. It also publishes codes of practice concerning dismissal procedures or supply of information by employers related to wage negotiations. However, neither its awards nor its recommendations for trade union recognition are legally binding in any way. ACAS was considerably trimmed down by consecutive Conservative governments, whose confrontational policies apparently did not allow for organizations specialized in settling conflicts.

While in Great Britain mediation is possible, in France it is obligatory. The Act on Collective Bargaining Agreements of 1950 provides that all disputes concerning collective bargaining must be referred to mediation, which is provided by a tripartite committee set up by the government. Disputes may be referred by one of the parties concerned or by the Minister of Employment if the parties fail to act. The Act does not, however, impose mandatory arbitration on the parties involved in a dispute.

5   The government as a provider of collective services: vocational training

There are various services and provisions which are essential to employers and employees, but which are hard to come by via individual action or, indeed, the market. Examples are social security (insurance against such risks as illness, disablement and unemployment), industrial health care and vocational training.

Faced with the threat of free-riding competitors, few employers are willing to invest in provisions which may also benefit those who do not contribute towards the costs. These provisions are referred to as collective goods. Only a collective actor who can prevent free-riding practices will be able to provide these services. One such actor may be the government, but the employers' associations and unions may also take on this role. This is why collective services have become an issue requiring regulation within the industrial relations framework. The degree to which governments are involved in this varies widely, as will be illustrated by the issue of vocational training. We again come across a typically statist approach in France, where the government provides the majority of vocational training services. The social partners are merely the supporting actors. Basic vocational training is offered by state educational institutions (Crouch, 1991). There is a first level for 13- to 16-year-olds, which leads to the *Certificat d'Aptitude Professionnelle* (CAP), testifying that they are skilled workers. The second level for 15- to 18-year-olds leads to the technical 'baccalaureat', the CAP or the *Brévet d'Etudes Professionnelles* (BEP). The involvement of employers' representatives goes no further than the limited advisory role they have in designing the curriculum of such basic vocational training (Lane, 1989: 69).

Although further vocational education is partly provided in-house by companies, they do so under mild pressure from the government, which in 1971 introduced legislation – without prior consultations with the social partners by the way – obliging employers to spend no less than 1.1 per cent of their payroll costs on vocational training. They can either provide the education themselves or pay the sum into a state fund for vocational training. The Act also granted employees the right to educational leave. When it became clear that not much use was made of this right, the government passed additional legislation, forcing employers to pay 0.1 per cent of their payroll costs into a state fund which was then used to pay the wages of employees who took educational leave (Madigan, 1990: 32).

In this area, too, Germany displays all the typical features of the corporatist model. The German government and employers and employees carry joint responsibility for basic vocational training (15- to 18-year-olds), and have developed a dual educational system. Besides practical training on the shop floor, students receive theoretical education at school, for which employers must give them time off. Once they have passed the compulsory school age (15), the large majority of pupils enter into an apprenticeship contract with a company. All participating companies are obliged to have staff available who are capable of teaching students in the workshop.

The employers' associations and trade unions participate in this system in various ways. First, they operate in close contact with the *Bundesinstitut für Berufsbilding* in designing the curricula of some 380 recognized trades. Secondly, they have representatives in the *Handwerkskammern* or the *Industrie- und Handelskammern*, which register the apprenticeship contracts, monitor the various training facilities and are responsible for administering examinations. Thirdly, through these chambers employers and employees can put social pressure on companies refusing to participate in the system if need be. Companies that poach recently trained workers from other employers get pilloried in public. Fourthly, they establish the pay rates for apprentices during collective pay negotiations. They take care that the level remains low enough for employers to support the dual training system and take on apprentices. The collective bargaining agreements, moreover, link workers' wages and promotion prospects to their level of skills. This makes it difficult for other companies to lure skilled workers away by promising all sorts of financial bonuses.

The government's contribution consists mainly of financial support and some measure of statutory pressure. Companies are, for example, legally obliged to join an *Industriekammer* or *Handwerkskammer*. These chambers have public law status and their rights and duties are laid down by statute. Free riding is not an attractive option, since companies are prohibited from hiring workers under 18 without offering them an apprenticeship contract. The government, that is to say the *Länder*, also finance daytime education (Streeck, 1987). Government involvement in vocational training is lowest in Great Britain. However, the organizations of employers and employees do not concern themselves much with it either. Allocation and coordination are regulated through the 'market' rather than through the principles of 'state' or 'association' (see also Streeck and Schmitter, 1985).

Until the late 1960s, the British had a system which was still somewhat comparable to that in Germany. There were statutory Industry Training Boards on which employers and employees were represented. They operated various vocational training facilities, all of which were based on the apprenticeship system. The whole setup was financed out of compulsory contributions paid by the employers. The system collapsed as a result of consecutive recessions, when only few employers were prepared to take on apprentices. Their interest associations lacked enough authority to prevent this. Moreover, policy disputes arose between the interest organizations and the Conservative Thatcher government, which preferred more influence of market forces. There were various reorganizations, resulting in the establishment of local Training and Enterprise Councils (TECs), which are governed not by representatives of interest organizations, but by leading business people who sit on the Councils in a personal capacity. They have to raise voluntary funds from the business community. Interest groups are of little help in this respect. The actual organization of courses is mostly contracted out to commercial training institutions.

The role of the government does not stretch beyond establishing the TECs. It does not provide vocational training itself, nor does it exert statutory pressure on employers to do so or to contribute towards training facilities. If the government finances the TECs at all, it earmarks these resources mainly for re-training the unemployed. Thus, vocational training in Great Britain is largely left to the initiative of individual companies. These are, however, not much inclined to invest in general vocational training (as opposed to company-specific training) as employees in Great Britain are highly mobile and there is very little sanction on free-riding practice.

The Swedish and Italian systems of vocational training stand midway between the French and German models. At face value, the Swedish system resembles the French, in that basic vocational training is provided by state educational institutions. Unlike in France, however, Swedish employers' associations and unions are considerably involved in the Swedish government organization, including in state vocational education. For example, there is a tripartite body – the Labour Market Council – which gathers information about training needs in the business community and monitors training courses and facilities.

The Italian system of vocational training also parallels the French system. Vocational training here is organized by the government. However, at the local level, institutions based on cooperation between local governments, local political parties and local branches of trade unions and employers' associations have been set up with a view to promoting local industry. They have created new systems of apprenticeship under the joint responsibility of the business community and local government. Local government has even been the driving force behind the establishment of regional interest associations, in particular of small and medium-sized companies, for whom vocational training – more than for large companies – is a collective good which they cannot create for themselves individually.

6   The government as an employer

Having discussed the role of the government as a regulator and producer of collective services, we should not forget to mention a third, but certainly not its least important, role. The government also acts as a direct negotiating party in the field of industrial relations. In most countries, it is by far the largest employer, and has to deal with organizations representing its employees: civil servants, employees working in the subsidized sectors and those working in state companies. Over the years, it has introduced an ever-increasing number of rules determining the legal position and terms of employment of government employees.

We shall not provide an in-depth analysis of the special rules governing civil servants, labour relations in the public sector or the differences between countries in this area. However, we do want to highlight the signalling function which governments have in their capacity as employers. The terms of employment of public servants also have a bearing on those concluded in the private sector. Governments have tried through their own employment policies to set an example for private employers. The fact that the trade unions do not always appreciate the 'good' example may be clear from their response to government cuts in spending and staffing in the 1980s.

Even the British government has in the past endeavoured to set an example by recognizing the civil servants' trade unions and abiding by its self-imposed duty to negotiate. In Italy, state companies have been forced by Christian Democrat governments to pursue an exemplary social policy. To do that, they needed more freedom of action and had to leave the employers' confederation Confindustria to set up separate employers' associations for state companies (ASAP and Intersind). With this, the Italian government also tried to break down the omnipotence of Confindustria.

In the UK, in more recent decades, the Thatcher government used its influence in state-owned industries to attempt the opposite – to undermine the powerful position of the trade unions, by setting an example. In particular, British Leyland and the National Coal Board adopted a thoroughly uncompromising stance against the trade unions and their employees (Crouch, 1990b). An altogether different situation is found in France, where the government has attempted through its nationalized industries to encourage employers to enter into contracts of solidarity. Under these contracts, in exchange for government subsidies, companies must reduce working hours and allow longer holidays in order to boost employment.

7   Likely explanations for national differences

Governments intervene in industrial relations in many ways, and thus influence these relations to quite a large extent. Hence, differences between national systems of industrial relations can partly be related to the types of government intervention found in the various countries: paternalistic government intervention in France, non-intervention in Great Britain, active support and legal framework for corporatist structures in Germany –

statism, liberal pluralism and corporatism respectively – are the archetypes by which to describe government intervention in Europe.

Admittedly, none of these countries fully fits the mould which they are supposed to represent. However, on the essential points, the institutional patterns of conduct do apply. France is marked for its far-reaching nationwide regulation of terms of employment and the high degree of state interference with collective bargaining processes, vocational training, trade union recognition, and the imposition of a statutory duty on employers to seek mediation in disputes. In the UK, non-intervention, voluntarism and informality are the key words in such central areas of industrial relations as pay negotiations, industrial disputes and trade union rights. Compliance with collective bargaining agreements is unenforceable and the ability to make such contracts generally binding impossible. The trade unions and their shop stewards have no need for government support, mediation and arbitration are available but not compulsory, and vocational training is much less the concern of the government than in other countries. 'There is, perhaps, no major country in the world in which the law has played a less significant role in the shaping of industrial relations than in Great Britain,' wrote Kahn-Freund (1967: 44). In Germany, many issues are provided for in collective bargaining agreements. The social partners have a statutorily guaranteed autonomy and play an important part in regulating the labour market and managing services and facilities. In taking care of vocational training, they even implement public policy. However, their structures and operating methods are laid down in detail by the law. Restrictions have, for example, been imposed on the right to strike and formal requirements have been set for the recognition of employers' and employees' organizations and their contracts. This is the price to be paid for the benefits of corporatism.

This typification also applies to the broader social and economic policies in these three countries. In policy fields like industrial policy or product quality regulation, the policies of the French, British and German governments can be said to be statist, liberal pluralist and corporatist, respectively. These different ways in which a government looks upon society and confronts private interest groups are embedded in a country's political culture and in various divergent legal, political and administrative institutions, all of which can be traced to the early phases of state formation. It would go beyond the scope of this chapter to deal with these historical origins in detail, but some background information may be useful in order to argue that these various intervention styles are not ad hoc and incidental, but are deeply rooted in each of these societies.

Thus French statism is rooted in the far-reaching introduction of Roman codified law in this country. Roman law distinguishes rather sharply between public law and private law, between state and society, giving priority to the former over the latter (Badie and Birnbaum, 1983). Statism is also related to the general respect for *l'Etat* in French political culture, and is reflected in the power and authority of the President, all of this being the inheritance of an absolutist past. Statism is linked as well to the status and authority of top civil servants, an authority which is also respected in the business world, if only because there are close personal links and mobility between top civil servants and leading businessmen. Presumably, French statism is also the result of the success of government-led waves of industrialization and of the deep-rooted distrust of 'intermediary organiz-ations' which goes back to the time of the French Revolution, when the guilds, at that time the intermediary organizations, were seen as the epitome of particularist privileges. This general distrust is reinforced by the problem-atic relationship between church and state and the fear of ecclesiastical interference with state affairs. Certainly in the past, many interest organizations were catholic associations (Crouch, 1986).

Liberal pluralism in the UK has its roots in the common law tradition, which draws a rather thin line between state and society, and reflects the age-old tradition of unwritten rules originating in society and gradually evolving into rules of formal law (the similarity to collective bargaining agreements will probably not go unnoticed!). Also, the medieval British 'estates-state' (*Ständestaat*) (which represented a certain balance of power between the classes and between the classes and the monarch) never evolved into an absolutist state, thanks to the Magna Carta and the Glorious Revolution. Moreover, the fact that the early and successful industrialization was market-driven increased reliance on non-intervention and voluntarism, which has since been laid down in parliamentary statutes and court decisions. Furthermore, the first state interventions came in a period when *laisser-faire* was the dominant ideology. Current British social and economic policy still bears the marks of that philosophy. Another important factor was the late development and expansion of the British civil service, long after industrialization led to a dominant position of employers' organizations and trade unions.

The successful attempt by workers to build strong trade unions by themselves has boosted confidence in their own powers and increased their dislike of government support. Distrust of the state has also been kindled by the trade unions' negative experience with judges' conservative inter-pretations of the common law. 'Having gained these rights after long and difficult struggles against the common law, criminal and civil liability, bitterly hostile employers, and the decisions of judges, British trade unionists intuitively resist any form of legal limitation either on their freedom to bargain collectively or on their right to take part in industrial action' (Farnham and Pimlott, 1979: 187). This is why under Labour governments no changes were made to the liberal tradition of non-intervention in the affairs of interest organizations. The German prefer-ence for corporatist forms of intervention is largely the result of the early and strong establishment of private organizations with public functions, for example, the guilds. This development had everything to do with the importance of trading towns in this Middle European north–south corridor. As the French Revolution had less impact on Germany, this tradition was not essentially breached. Added to this was the fact that corporatist trade associations were the only political spokesmen allowed to represent the citizenry in the nineteenth-century absolutist German principalities. Also, post-war policy in the Federal Republic of Germany has been to establish a system of government which could not easily grow again into an all-powerful state. One instrument to achieve this goal was to resort to the old corporatist tradition of delegating state authority to private organizations. For this reason, the Allied forces at the time did not insist on breaking down the system of *Handwerkskammern*, even though they were formalized by the Nazi regime. Lastly, the German legal tradition of detailed rules and regulations has also left its mark on the legal framework of industrial relations.

PART 3

INSTITUTIONAL AND ORGANIZATIONAL CHANGE

6 Collective bargaining in transition
Rien Huiskamp

1 Introduction

The employment relationship can be arranged or given shape in a number of different ways: through individual contracts between employer and employee; through collective bargaining between trade unions and employers or employers' associations; or through legal provisions imposed by the state, acting either alone or in accordance with recommendations made by national consultation bodies. One type of arrangement does not preclude another; in most countries a kind of division of labour has developed. Pay levels are established in an individual agreement, pay rises are determined annually in collective agreements, and the state (sometimes after tripartite negotiations or consultations with union federations and employers' associations) establishes legal procedures for dismissal. In this chapter we will be concentrating on collective regulations pertaining to the employment relationship. We will study the significance of collective bargaining agreements and the way in which employers' associations and trade unions arrive at agreements in a number of European countries with respect to the employment relationship. One very important aspect is the degree of coordination between the industry level and the company level. The 1980s saw a number of remarkable changes in this regard: more flexible collective bargaining structures were created, so that the industry level was subject to less stringent regulations and management and trade unions or employee representatives had greater leeway to make (additional) agreements. Each European country has its own way of shaping such structures, however.

2   The structure and content of collective bargaining

Collective contracts – as a mechanism for regulating the employment relationship – are generally in the form of industry-wide agreements concluded by trade unions and employers' associations. This type of arrangement is typically European; its evolution was closely tied to that of the trade unions, employers' associations and social legislation, in short, to the social history of Europe. Employees unionized so that workers who practised the same profession or job in different companies enjoyed the same standards with respect to training, remuneration, sickness and dismissal. One important motive for employers to agree to industry-level negotiations was that such agreements minimized the chance that companies in the same industry would compete against one another in the area of employment conditions. In most European countries, the state upholds the industry-level agreement by a general decree making its terms binding on *all* firms in an industry, whether or not the company is a member of an employers' association or the employee a member of a recognized trade union. The industry-level agreement is not always the most obvious type of arrangement, however. Four other alternatives exist.

1   There may be little compliance with industry-level agreements, compliance being less strict than supposed, particularly in smaller companies; what appears on the surface to be a binding collective arrangement is actually replaced by numerous deviating arrangements.
2   The traditional industry-level agreement may be replaced by a different type of agreement, for example at the level of the corporation or company.
3   Internal regulatory devices replace the external ones; for example, agreements might be reached between management and works council, without the involvement of the trade union.
4   Collective bargaining may be dispensed with altogether in favour of individual employment contracts; in this case the trade unions or other employee representatives are no longer involved, but only the employer

and the employee (or groups of employees); the employment relationship is arranged entirely via individual employment contracts.

In addition, the relationship between the various regulatory forms may change. Not only can individual contracts replace collective bargaining, but the state can withdraw as regulatory partner in the employment relationship, or the importance of negotiations between the state, trade unions and employers can diminish. The decision to choose a particular type of arrangement is increasingly a strategic choice that must allow for changing circumstances. The question as to how this state of affairs came about is the main focus of this chapter.

Before discussing the strategic choices made in various countries, we will first take a look at bargaining structures in old and new industrial sectors and at changes in bargaining issues between employers and employees.

Bargaining structures in old and new industrial sectors

To begin, we will consider the evolution of industries, using the Netherlands as our example. Industry-level agreements in the Netherlands are still prevalent in traditional industries – printing and metal for example – which arose at the beginning of this century. In theory a collective bargaining agreement in one of these industries will be binding on all employees and companies in that particular industry. In practice, however, this is not always the case.

First of all, some companies are active in areas that straddle two different industries, or have shifted their activities to other products in the course of time; for example, a former metal processing firm once bound by collective agreements in the metal industry has gone over to plastics processing. Secondly, there are a number of companies that belong neither in one industry nor another. As a result, these companies are in fact free to pick and choose a collective agreement or to follow their own path, that is, internal regulation. Thirdly, there are companies that, although they fall under the terms of a collective agreement, nevertheless do not comply with them, using neither the pay scales nor the job evaluation schemes set in the industry-level agreement. There are quite a number of such companies, despite the binding nature of collective agreements. The reason lies in the company's size. Small firm management may resist complying with the job evaluation schemes established in collective agreements because many of the jobs described for large firms are not relevant for small ones. In addition, management in a small firm may be more dependent on wage levels in the local labour market. Branches of industry which came into existence at a later stage of the industrial revolution, such as the chemical industry, often have only company agreements. In this case a general binding decree is impossible, since no industry-wide agreement exists. If we distinguish between company agreements at large corporations and those at small firms, we see that the former increased sharply in number during the 1960s and 1970s, but that the latter decreased sharply. Because of this, the number of employees covered by a company agreement has increased, since a large corporation obviously has more employees than a small one. On the other hand, if we compare the number of chemical companies with a collective agreement to the total number of companies in the chemical industry, we see that many have no collective agreement at all. Given the increase in large corporations with a company agreement, most of these are probably small firms (Huiskamp, 1983a, b and c). What is the situation in newly developed industrial sectors, and how are employment conditions determined there? In the computer service and software industry, only a small minority of companies (approximately 27 per cent) has a collective agreement. The usual device, as in the chemicals industry, is the large corporation agreement which also covers the various subsidiaries. Most companies (50 per cent), however, make use of individual employment contracts; in 23 per cent of the cases wages are negotiated in works councils or in consultation with other employee representatives, instead of with the trade unions.

A strong correlation appears to exist between the way in which the employment relationship is regulated and the stages of industrial development. In the first stage (printing, textiles, tobacco, metal etc.) the industry-level agreement serves as a model. In the second stage (chemicals, oil etc.) the accent is on the large corporation agreement. In the third stage, which is now unfolding (for example the computer industry), emphasis has shifted to individual employment contracts, without the unions being involved in negotiations. Regulatory devices for the employment relationship appear to correspond with features such as the industry's age and the ratio of large to small companies.

Bargaining issues

The bargaining issues which determine the interplay between employers and employees are constantly in flux. To illustrate, we need only compare wage bargaining with bargaining on technological innovation.

First, the process of technological renewal is much more dynamic than the evolution of pay. Collective agreements eliminate wages as a factor in competition, because all companies bound by a particular industry-level agreement issue the same pay rises at the same point in time. Technological innovation is implemented precisely in order to capture an advantageous position before any one else. It is constantly being stimulated: company policy is directed toward accelerating it.

Secondly, collective agreements are often formulated at a great distance from the workplace, as most employees are subject to industry-wide or corporation-wide agreements. Negotiators pay the specific situation within a particular firm or plant little notice; indeed, they cannot do so. This is less of a problem in pay bargaining, because pay levels can be altered to a certain degree without also altering the way that work and production are organized and the power relations embedded there. This is not true in the case of new technology. Computerization often implies changing both the entire organization and the balance of power; as a result, this issue is not easily isolated and discussed at a distance. It is much more difficult to isolate from the workplace and the power relations prevalent there than the issue of pay. Consequently, the industry-wide agreement is not the best instrument for collective bargaining on technological innovation.

Finally, whereas pay fluctuations are quantifiable and related to the financial margin available in a company, negotiators seldom calculate the costs and benefits of implementing new technology in advance of implementation. Is it more expensive to implement employee-friendly techniques, or will this ultimately produce even greater benefits? Not until the answers to such questions are clear can negotiators recognize the issues at hand and their true place on their bargaining agenda.

The very nature of collective bargaining, then, means that the collective arrangements governing the introduction of new technology tend not to take account of company-specific circumstances and the particular characteristics of the relevant workplace. Above all, new technology is closely tied to the investment decisions that determine both the nature and the future of a company. Management sees this type of decision as part of its 'right to manage'. Collective bargaining is a bilateral process characterized by collective and shared responsibilities. From the management point of view, subjecting technological innovation to this process implies an undesirable expansion of the basic (albeit tacit) compromise restricting collective arrangements and shared responsibilities to specific aspects of the employment relationship, such as pay and working hours. In the computer and software industry, the establishment of new, generally small companies and the evolution of new bargaining issues have proceeded hand in hand. This new industry has scarcely developed any external and collective devices to regulate the employment relationship, the way other industries have. No institutional pattern of relations between unions and employers' associations has emerged to make collective arrangements possible.

Technological innovation can also affect older industries which emerged in the first stage of industrialization and whose industry-level agreement, set up within the context of an extensive institutional pattern, regulates various aspects of the employment relationship in great detail. The most outstanding example of this is the printing industry. In the UK, for example, the conflict between institutionalized, traditional types of arrangement and technological innovation became so intense that a large number of companies in the printing industry abandoned their industry-wide agreement, leaving management free to replace it by individual contracts after a drawn-out battle with the trade unions.

3 The significance of the collective bargaining agreement in Great Britain, Germany and France

Factors such as the 'age' of an industry and the nature of collective bargaining issues affect collective bargaining structures differently in each country. Nationally specific characteristics and the choices that actors make intensify these differences. We will examine the choices made with respect to the employment relationship more closely by looking at experiences in Great Britain, Germany and France.

Plant and company bargaining: the relations between shop stewards and management in Great Britain

The British engineering industry is often cited as the pioneer of the industry-level agreement (Berber, 1976). At the end of the nineteenth century it was one of the first branches of industry to embark upon an industry-wide agreement covering both substantive as well as procedural issues. The substantive agreements concerned pay levels, working hours, overtime etc., while the procedural agreements governed the relations between organized employees and employers' associations – in other words, the system of industrial relations. This written document included a switch in the 'right to manage' from skilled craftsmen to those who owned the means of production (management), in exchange for a bargaining monopoly on terms of employment for paid union officials.

However, even before the evolution of industry-wide negotiations, shop stewards had played an important role in bargaining within companies, first regionally, but later also at the company level. The industry-level agreement has never been able to edge out this type of bargaining completely, to the disappointment of trade union negotiators, who took on the role of official bargaining partner, sometimes in opposition to the shop stewards. Shop stewards were less likely to accept separating pay bargaining from bargaining over other issues such as the division of labour and work pace. They continued to follow in the footsteps of the skilled craftsmen, not only to exercise control over employment terms but also to resist changes in the production process. Mok (1990) has identified this distinction with the terms *arbeidsvoorwaardenbeheersing* (control of employment conditions) and *arbeidstaakbeheersing* (job control).

In the 1960s and 1970s bargaining at the company level grew more important, leading to double bargaining rounds, first at the industry level and then at the company level. Industry-level agreements set a 'floor' upon which local negotiators might construct additions. Larger companies within the employers' associations objected to this trend and, after extensive bargaining, the nature of the industry-level agreement changed. The essence of this change was the transformation of the industry-wide agreement into a 'safety net' (Brown and Terry, 1978), more flexible than a floor because it can move both up and down. Pay rises guaranteed by industry-level agreements apply only to those companies whose pay movements are at or under the level of the safety net, and not to companies with better employment terms, where wages lie above this level. The latter – generally the larger companies – conclude their own, company agreements. Pay rises negotiated in the industry-level agreement apply to companies, usually smaller ones, which are unwilling or unable to conduct their own negotiations. They are thus subject to the standard industry-level agreement.

The advantage of the safety net for employers is that their company agreements can deviate from the pay rises set in the industry-level agreement, not only upwards but downwards as well, until they reach the safety net level after a year or two. Then the industry-level agreement goes into effect again. The advantage for the unions is that the employment terms will not be allowed to drop below the safety net level set in the industry-wide agreement.

The pay clause in the collective agreement merely establishes a safety net rather than generally applicable provisions or a floor upon which additions can be constructed. Imagine, for example, that the pay level in such a company agreement drops a few years in a row, perhaps because of poor returns or because local negotiators are not sufficiently adept at bargaining. The conditions stipulated in the industry-level agreement will go into effect if the company approaches the safety net level, protecting employees against severe cuts but giving the company the necessary flexibility in less prosperous times.

The industry-wide agreement in the British engineering industry continues to provide for pensions and other secondary employment terms such as shift bonuses. For other issues, however, a layered collective agreement structure has evolved which not only offers downward flexibility with respect to wages, but upward flexibility as well. In other words, if trade unions fail to push through a 36–hour working week in the industry-level agreement, they can try again in a number of company agreements. If an increasing number of companies go over to a 36-hour working week, the expectation is that the industry-level agreement will follow this trend after a few years with provisions that are binding in small companies as well. In the meantime, the smaller companies have had time to adjust to this change. This strategy was used successfully by the British engineering unions in pushing through provisions on working time reduction, although their efforts were coupled with strikes in 1989–90.

This type of industry-level agreement has been given a positive response in Great Britain, so much so that it has captured almost the entire collective agreement 'market' in a short period of time. There are indications that the system of double bargaining rounds may have broken

---

Box 6.1   *Collective bargaining in the Dutch engineering industry*

In the Dutch engineering industry bargaining at the company level is subject to strict controls. Companies can set up their own job classification system based on the principles and provisions set forth in the industry-level agreement. Large companies in particular make use of this option. However, the question remains whether we can consider this a real case of independent bargaining alongside or above the industry level. In reality, a number of large companies apply the pay rises negotiated in the industry-level agreement to their own job classification pay scales, where levels are in fact already higher than those indicated in the collective agreement. In actual practice, then, the industry-level agreement acts as a standard agreement. Deviations are often marginal and continue to be determined by procedures and principles set up in the collective agreement.

---

down: a company is subject either to an industry-level agreement or to a company agreement, with the option of switching from one to the other. (See Box 6.1 for a comparison.)

According to data from the collective bargaining agreement database (Gregory et al., 1985, 1986) set up by the Confederation of British Industry (CBI) and the University of Oxford – the data are collected in an annual survey of managers involved in collective bargaining – almost half of all employees are covered by either an industry-level or a company agreement. Little more than 40 per cent of all employees, however, are now covered by a layered collective agreement structure. The combination of plant agreement and large company agreement is rare; the combination of large company agreement and industry-level agreement is clearly more common. But the most prevalent is a combination of industry-wide and plant agreement. Medium-sized businesses with 100–500 employees are particularly prone to layered structures; these also tend to be common in certain industries but noticeably absent in others. For several years in succession at the end of the 1980s, trade unions and employers' associations in the engineering industry were unable to reach agreement on each other's proposals. The continuous, annual or biennial bargaining process became an irregular, ad hoc one. The significance of the industry-wide agreement was undermined considerably as a result, particularly for the smaller companies. Some observers had been predicting this 'withering-away' of the industry-level agreement for years, and now their predictions were coming true. If the trend of replacing industry-wide negotiations by company bargaining is taken to the extreme, then the layered collective bargaining structure will be no more than a temporary phenomenon. After several years there will only be company agreements in the larger companies, while the whole process of collective bargaining in smaller firms will simply disappear, as it is clearly doing already. This trend is not limited to the engineering industry, as the 1990 'Workplace industrial relations survey' conducted by Millward, Stevens, Smart and Hawes (1992) indicates. Between 1980 and 1990, the number of workplaces with a recognized trade union dropped from two-thirds to slightly more than half. Most of this occurred in the smaller firms. There was a similar fall in the number of employees covered by a collective agreement, from 71 per cent in 1980 to 54 per cent in 1990. The decrease was closely related to the fact that among companies covered by a collective agreement, the share of those covered by an industry-wide agreement dropped from 40 per cent in 1984 to 25 per cent in 1990. Another background factor was the sharp decrease in the number of companies belonging to an employers' association. In 1980 a quarter of the workplaces were members; by 1990 this was a mere eighth.

Another relevant factor was the rise of single-union deals. Although not common enough in quantitative terms to be of real significance – there were scarcely a few dozen of such contracts – they were highly important in qualitative terms. In a single-union deal, the trade union is given the exclusive right to represent the employees in a company. In the traditional situation, management deals with four to six different trade unions.

Thirty-seven of these single-union deals were analysed on a number of features. The results showed that almost all of the agreements included provisions concerning complete job flexibility, and that in almost three-quarters of the agreements differences between blue-collar and white-collar positions were eliminated and consultation bodies were set up. In almost half of the companies a no-strike clause was included in the agreement.

Most of the companies in this survey were metal-industry related, for example car manufacturing, electronics and computers. The pioneers of the single-union concept were Japanese companies in greenfield sites. In the late 1980s, as many British or American companies introduced single-union deals, and those included existing firms (*European Industrial Relations Review*, 1993).

There was a great deal of discussion among researchers in the latter half of the 1980s concerning the position of the shop steward, the employee bargaining representative on the shop floor (Millward and Stevens, 1987). One school proposes that their bargaining position has weakened considerably. This argument is based on quantitative data concerning the number of shop stewards per employee, the number of issues that they bargain over, and the frequency of negotiations. There were some weak indications that the industry level began to recover its former significance in the engineering industry at the beginning of the 1980s. Wage provisions were more frequently applied without this leading to double bargaining rounds.

The other school believes that we cannot adequately describe bargaining positions with quantitative data such as mentioned above. The position of the shop steward may indeed have been weakened, if we consider the many closures affecting companies that played important trendsetting roles in regional and company negotiations. On the other hand, shop stewards retain their position of influence in many companies, and continue to link control of employment conditions with job control. The emphasis, however, is more on controlling and resisting any changes in the traditional working methods. Case studies from the early 1980s have shown that shop stewards will go no further than bargaining over the consequences of new technology. They do not wish to share responsibility for management's plans and investments.

Storey has reported a number of cases in the early 1990s in which company management has entered into a more or less serious love affair with HRM (human resource management) (Storey, 1992). In most of these companies management pursues what he calls a 'dual approach'. HRM initiatives are developed but no attempt is made to undermine collective bargaining. In fact, most of the companies do not pursue an explicit strategy on this point. The presence of a potential alternative, that is, HRM based on the individual employment relationship, does, however, have an impact. Remarkably, in many of the cases union members lose interest in applying for the position of shop steward. An important factor is that the shop steward, although still recognized in a formal sense by many managers, is frequently left out of discussions on new developments and is no longer asked for an opinion.

The result is that shop stewards are more concerned with their own survival than with negotiating. Data collected nationally has revealed that between 1984 and 1990 the number of workplaces with a shop steward fell by 10 per cent to 71 per cent. This drop was particularly sharp in the smaller firms (Millward et al., 1992).

Walsh believes that the fragmentation of collective bargaining, combined with the emphasis placed on the individual employment relationship, will bring the bargaining features of the latter to the fore. Such a development would undermine any effort on the part of management to present HRM as a harmonious approach. The fragmentation of collective bargaining arrangements will politicize the employment relationship (Walsh, 1993).

Supplementary negotiations: relations between trade union and Betriebsrat in Germany

The industry-level agreement is by far the most important type of contract between employers' associations and trade unions in Germany. Company agreements are only a marginal phenomenon. After the Second World War, British advisers called in to reestablish German industrial relations were able to achieve something that they had failed to achieve in their own country: a standard industry-level agreement binding in all companies, with a ban on local company bargaining. Does this mean that the institutional pattern is still intact, despite developments in industrial sectors and the rise of new bargaining issues? We can seek an answer to this question by investigating, first of all, whether companies adhere to the wages negotiated in the industry-level agreement, or whether they only use them as an indication of minimum levels. Increasingly the latter is the case.

One clear example is the collective agreement structure in the German engineering industry, which is split into a number of regional bargaining units. In some regions up to 40 per cent of earnings are determined at the company level, either by unilateral management decision or by an agreement, a *Betriebsvereinbarung*, between management and *Betriebsrat*. The industry-wide agreement indicates a minimum, and in actual practice only upward deviations occur. In short, a supplementary round of negotiations has evolved in Germany: in the first round, the industry union and employers' association reach an agreement at industry level, and in the second round, management consults with the *Betriebsrat* concerning a supplementary company agreement.

What is the attitude of the trade unions toward this phenomenon? In the 1960s German unions, in particular IG Metall, were already embroiled in a discussion over whether they should stimulate a 'second', supplementary bargaining round. Should they, in other words, go on to conduct supplementary bargaining in individual companies after completing their industry-level negotiations? The discussion never really reached a final conclusion. Proponents favoured recognizing the possibility of union activity at the company level in the trade union charter. Opponents were afraid that this would erode the authority of the industry-level agreement and diminish solidarity within the union. The issue remained undecided and trade union representatives in companies were left without official bargaining authority.

According to the German industrial sociologist Wolfgang Streeck (1984), the *Betriebsrat* has now taken over the bargaining task. First, although German law does not allow *Betriebsräte* to bargain about employment terms, there are a small number of articles which make it possible for them to get involved in arranging terms and conditions of employment, although on improper grounds. Secondly, many of the works councils in the metal industry are dominated by members of IG Metall. These union representatives conduct negotiations under the guise of their *Betriebsrat* membership. A symbiosis has in fact occurred between trade union activities at the company level and the activities carried out by the *Betriebsrat*. An important factor is that IG Metall no longer sees the development of union activities at the company level as an independent goal. The union has integrated its company-level activities into the work carried out by the *Betriebsrat*. In this way the union was able to avoid the tiresome internal discussion concerning official authorization of formal negotiating power at the company level in the union charter. What the trade union was unable and unwilling to resolve for itself, due to internal conflicts, has been delegated to an external body, the *Betriebsrat*, which is composed of union representatives. In this way German works councils are rapidly taking on the character of company unions. The symbiosis between the role of the trade union representative and the role of the works council member also gives union representatives in the company more autonomy from the trade union 'outside'. Because the *Betriebsrat* is obviously not regulated in the trade union charter but rather by law, the union is unable to impose its will upon it. (See Box 6.2 for a similar situation.)

Tension between *Betriebsrat* and trade union is most in evidence in bargaining structures such as they exist at IBM. Not long ago IG Metall took IBM's *Betriebsrat* to court because it had negotiated an agreement with management concerning Sunday work. The union claims that this agreement is contrary to provisions in the metal sector's collective agreement. The metal union is in fact attempting to secure its own bargaining position through legal channels. The supplementary pay rises agreed to in the *Betriebsvereinbarungen* are often counterbalanced by *Betriebsrat* concessions, for example on working hours, which are unacceptable to the union. In 1993 IBM introduced a new bargaining structure whereby only the manufacturing division was still covered by the industry-wide agreement, while other divisions, for example information systems and training, lay outside the bounds of the collective agreement. The debate now focuses on whether company agreements should be concluded with the unions or with the *Betriebsrat*.

How does the metal industry's employers' association feel about supplementary negotiations? What is their solution? First, they want to detach small firm bargaining from large company bargaining. Although supplementary bargaining rounds take place mainly in large companies, the trend eventually spreads to small companies as well. Secondly, they want both upward and downward flexibility in the industry-level agreement. Because the minimum agreement establishes a fixed floor, companies can only raise wages. The fascinating thing is that British metal employers faced with almost the same set of circumstances in the 1970s made similar proposals. According to Thelen (1991), the relationship between the trade union and the *Betriebsrat* in the metal industry has been very productive with respect to bargaining issues such as new technologies and the organization of work (multi-skill, task groups, skill-based pay). In cases where this type of issue was difficult to work out concretely in the industry-wide agreement, the *Betriebsrat* proved to be an excellent replacement forum (Thelen, 1991). In 1992 a company covered by the metal agreement (Teldec) concluded a supplementary company agreement with IG Metall concerning task groups, a simplified job and pay structure, training and industrial democracy in the form of employee participation meetings. The same agreement also provided for a greater role for the *Betriebsrat*. The remarkable thing is that this layered collective bargaining structure was not created in the form of a *Betriebsvereinbarung* with the *Betriebsrat*, but in a supplementary agreement with the trade union to the industry agreement.

Does a change in contract partner (from union to works council) mean a shift from collective bargaining to individual contract negotiations? In

---

Box 6.2   *The position of the* ondernemingsraad *in the Netherlands*

The position of the *ondernemingsraad* in the Netherlands with respect to employment terms and industrial unions is comparable to the situation in Germany (Huiskamp and Risseeuw, 1989), although a greater wealth of quantitative data is available there. Research, for example, has shown that the *ondernemingsraad* can be involved in establishing primary employment terms in a number of different ways. In some cases it plays an active role in drafting a list of demands, conducting negotiations and supervising the implementation of bargaining results in the company. In this case it acts as a true *negotiator* (8.8 per cent); management views the determination of employment terms as a bilateral process and agreements are arrived at in mutual consultations. In other cases the *ondernemingsraad* acts as a *sounding board* (10 per cent). Management takes unilateral decisions, but it does consider the wishes and comments of the *ondernemingsraad* and is interested in its opinion on implementing proposed changes in primary conditions. Finally, the *ondernemingsraad* may not be directly involved in setting up terms of employment as such, but it is involved indirectly due to the relationship between trade union and *ondernemingsraad*. Members of the latter, who also belong to a union, serve as *observers* in the bargaining delegation (14.5 per cent). Such members, sometimes united in a faction or company group, exchange ideas and information with trade unions concerning collective bargaining demands and the negotiations themselves. In short, the *ondernemingsraad* can play one of three different roles when involved in establishing employment terms: that of negotiator, that of sounding board, or that of observer. A large majority of *ondernemingsraden* (two-thirds), however, were not involved in any way in setting primary employment terms.

---

the Netherlands management may decide to conclude an internal but nevertheless collective agreement with the works council; this is not a real collective agreement in the legal sense of the word, of course, but it can function as such in practice. The collective nature of bargaining has not been undermined; only the contracting party has changed.

Another possibility is that management consults with the works council, but afterwards concludes only individual employment contracts. By using the works council as a sounding board, management can avoid having to bargain over employment terms with each individual employee. In this case, collective bargaining will gradually lose significance. Finally, the works council can play a role in supplementing the terms established in an industry-wide agreement. These supplements may be severely limited in character, but they may be so far-reaching that they in fact form an entirely new set of employment terms.

Besides the shift from trade union to works council as bargaining partner, a shift in the opposite direction, from works council to union, is also possible. In the Netherlands this trend has become evident in a number of companies in the past few years. For example, in companies that have experienced continuous growth since their foundation, agreement with the *ondernemingsraad* on employment conditions was relatively easy to reach. When economic reversals threaten the company's existence, and the bottom drops out of almost routine improvements in employment conditions, a different type of discussion is needed concerning the lagging wages and the cuts in personnel. The *ondernemingsraad* is not the appropriate interlocutor in this case; it, and/or management will often seek contact with the trade unions. Although it does not look as if the Dutch *ondernemingsraad* is attempting to take over the role of the unions on a large scale, research has indicated a link between their autonomous bargaining position concerning wages and their greater involvement in other issues such as personnel policy, bonuses and other secondary employment conditions. However, we must not discount the number of *ondernemingsraden*, particularly in industry, where the majority of seats are filled by union members. Their role works two ways: not only can the works council influence employment terms, but the unions can also influence collective bargaining issues through the channel of the works council.

State-sponsored company bargaining: legal intervention in France

In France a large number of employees (in 1981 an estimated 3 million workers in companies of more than 10 employees) were not covered by a collective agreement, particularly in small and medium-sized enterprises (SMEs). Bargaining at the company level lacked authority, despite a special 1971 amendment to the 1950 Collective Bargaining Act, a legacy of May 1968. Shortly after the Socialists entered office in 1982 under President Mitterand, four social reform laws went into effect. One of these four 'Auroux Laws' (named after the Minister of Labour) stipulated that in companies which had a *section syndicale* or official union representation, the representatives and management were obliged to negotiate a collective agreement, whether or not the industry was already covered by an industry-wide agreement. In the latter case the negotiations would focus on distributing the pay rises agreed to at industry level over the various personnel categories. Companies without a *section syndicale* or official union representation were considered exempt from the law. Almost half of companies with less than 50 employees do not employ a union member who acts as a *délégué syndical* or union delegate.

The Auroux law is aimed in particular at medium-sized companies and dictates that the *délégués syndicaux* must themselves do the bargaining, with paid union officials playing a supporting role. This was a remarkable provision for a government close to the labour movement. The goal was to strengthen the position of the *délégués syndicaux*, not only with respect to company management, but also with respect to union officials. *Délégués* may also conduct negotiations together with the *comité d'éntreprise* (works council) or in direct consultation with employees.

An important motive for encouraging bargaining at the company level was the goal of keeping pay developments more in line with each company's particular situation. To achieve this, pay rises negotiated in an industry-level agreement can be redistributed among the various job categories within the company. A second goal was to encourage bargaining over issues such as technological innovation, job content, qualifications and training. The number of company agreements rose immediately from 1,955 in 1983 to 5,165 in 1985. A high point was reached in 1991 with 6,754, with a slight decline the following year to 6,370. There was no similar decline in the number of employees covered by a company agreement but a rise between 1991 and 1992 by 10 per cent. Some 57 per cent of the agreements were in industry, and 30 per cent in the services sector.

It was large and, to a lesser extent, medium-sized companies which concluded collective bargaining agreements. Some 55 per cent of companies with less than 100 employees did not comply with the annual obligation to conduct negotiations, however. One of the most important reasons is the fall in the number of trade union members and trade union representatives in these smaller companies. The number of company agreements rose sharply, then, but the goal of stimulating negotiations in medium-sized companies was only achieved to a limited degree. Most of the agreements were concluded in large corporations and the falling union density rate in smaller firms widened rather than closed the gap between large and small companies with regard to collective bargaining.

Does this growth in company-level bargaining mean that collective arrangements at industry level will disappear? No, because a new division of labour has evolved between the various levels (Bamberger, 1989). At the national level a practice is developing in which parties arrive at a central accord or make recommendations on particular issues such as training or working-time reduction, to which the state sometimes responds with legislation.

Industry-level bargaining takes place less often and only intermittently. There are two reasons for this: first, the increase in the number of company agreements, and secondly, the decrease in the number of French employees and employers who are members of trade unions and employers' associations. There have also been changes in both the number and significance of wage agreements at the industry level. In 1992, wages constituted the subject of an agreement in only 61 per cent of the accords – the lowest percentage since 1982. Within this 61 per cent, each company was frequently able to redistribute the pay rise across the various categories of employees. Industry-level agreements still include various provisions concerning minimum wages, sick pay, working hours and employee representation. Finally, negotiators at the industry level can also thrash out the conditions under which deviation from statutory provisions is acceptable, for example shift work. In the past few years, employment and training have also become important issues.

We see, then, that the French government has expressly made use of legal interventions, first of all to stimulate company bargaining without sounding the death knell to the industry-level agreement and, secondly and simultaneously, to stimulate bargaining at the national level. What has not yet succeeded is the attempt to broaden the traditional field of collective bargaining to encompass new issues. Far and away the two most important issues covered in company agreements were wages and working hours. Agreements concerning working conditions, training and industrial democracy are very rare, although the importance of agreements concerning job classifications and employment has increased in the past few years. Agreements on new forms of work organization and task groups are exceptions to the rule (see Box 6.3).

Box 6.3   *Company agreement at Renault*

One instance where such an agreement has been made is at Renault. The substance and structure of the company's collective agreement, first implemented in 1956, has been completely overhauled. The new agreement describes the working unit as a task group with greater work autonomy and more responsibility for the quality of the product. Each unit can set its own working hours within certain limits. Non-standard working hours are compensated for with time off, remuneration, better working conditions and training. A new job classification system with more skilled worker categories has been implemented for assembly workers, while at the same time the number of supervisory levels has been cut from four to two. Wages are composed of a fixed and a variable portion based on the employee's performance. This portion can be as high as 15 per cent. In addition, there is a profit-sharing scheme based on the financial returns of the company and production per plant. Training is an important element of the new collective agreement. A requalification programme is being developed for 20,000 production workers who will be working in task groups.

Profit sharing is also being considered as a new approach to decentralizing wages. New legislation (1986/1987) once again played a crucial role in increasing the number of profit sharing schemes by offering fiscal advantages and by making disbursements exempt from social insurance contributions. Under the new law, the number of schemes increased from 1,300 involving 400,000 workers in 1985 to 4,600 involving a million workers in 1988. One remarkable aspect is the increase in the number of participating companies with less than 100 employees. In 1991 there were 8,840 schemes, after which the number dropped to 7,120, involving 1.8 million employees. Despite the remarkable growth, only a small minority of the total working population – approximately 13 per cent – participate in such schemes.

The law stipulates that a draft scheme must be developed within the company in consultation with the *comités d'entreprise*, trade unions or union delegates. The entire staff may also be involved in setting up the scheme; this varies from company to company, allowing each one to determine substance and procedure for itself. At present the state has put a ceiling on how large a contribution to the total pay level profit sharing schemes can make. Trade unions are afraid that profit sharing will increasingly edge out traditional pay rises negotiated in collective agreements.

The economic downturn is viewed as the reason for the drop in the number of schemes. Another factor is that in 1991 a quarter of the companies did not issue disbursements. After a fantastic start in the 1980s, profit sharing, not unexpectedly, has turned out to be an instrument sensitive to economic ups and downs.

4   Flexible collective bargaining structures

Developments in a number of European countries have shown that the industry-level agreement is no longer the most matter-of-course and all-pervasive regulatory device for the employment relationship. This is the result of the strategic choices made by actors with respect to:

- issues subject to the process of mutual regulation;
- the level at which such agreements should be made, the company, or above;
- the actors who should be involved and the role they play: the trade unions and employers' associations exclusively; or (also) management, works councils, company union representatives;
- the role of the state.

Important in this regard is whether or not new industries and new bargaining issues have a place within the context of existing arrangements and which actor has the initiative in the unfolding balance of power. If new industries and new issues lead to new types of arrangements, there may be repercussions for the power relations in existing sectors and for the historical compromises on traditional issues. Shifts in the balance of power occur in both inter-organizational and intra-organizational relations: witness the new confidence of employers and the subtle shifts between industrial union, works council and trade union members.

In recent years both the collective agreement and the position of the trade unions have been at issue in the United States (see Kochan et al., 1989). In many US companies it no longer goes without saying that management bargains with trade unions and that employment conditions are set forth in collective agreements. The number of companies in which the employees are not represented by trade unions is increasing and collective bargaining is giving way to individual contracts.

Such radical developments are by no means prevalent in Europe on a large scale. What is true is that the traditional regulatory device, the industry-level agreement, is undergoing a change in most West European countries. This trend has taken on many different forms, however. In the UK, through the efforts of management and shop stewards in particular, bargaining at the company level gained ground at the expense of industry-level agreements without forcing their disappearance altogether: they continued to play a supporting role with respect to internal regulation and remained valid in small firms that preferred not to embark on making their own internal arrangements. In the second half of the 1980s, however, a new trend emerged: the declining membership of both trade unions and employers' associations. The result is that fewer and fewer smaller firms are covered by industry-wide agreements. The industry-wide agreement loses ground on two fronts, then: on the one hand, larger companies are turning more and more to company agreements, and on the other, the smaller firms are withdrawing from collective agreements altogether. In this way the industry-wide agreement has got the worst of both worlds and is disappearing.

In Germany we saw the evolution of supplementary rounds of bargaining at the company level. Management continues to operate within the framework of an employers' association and union members, as works council members, provide a link with trade union policy. In reality there is a measure of symbiosis between traditional external arrangements at industry level and internal arrangements between the *Betriebsrat* and management. There are no signs in Germany that employers are trying to escape the regime of the employers' association by turning in their membership cards.

In France the government took the initiative toward expanding internal arrangements by encouraging bargaining between management and union officials at the company level, without seriously damaging the external arrangements. In France, as in the UK, the declining membership of both unions and employers' associations is beginning to undermine the application of industry-wide agreements in smaller companies.

Supplementary negotiations can quickly turn into independent negotiations, seriously damaging industry-level bargaining in the course of time. Is this a variation on the American trend, or is the increasing decentralization of collective bargaining in Western Europe taking place in the context of what we might call 'layered' collective bargaining structures? A layered collective bargaining structure means that alongside the industry-level agreement, each company has its own or supplementary collective agreement. Layered collective agreements can also come about in large companies or conglomerates: between the head office, for example, and the subsidiaries, business units or plants. Layered collective bargaining structures may help to prevent the disappearance of collective bargaining above the level of the company or prevent worker solidarity from being undermined by providing a common framework and general points of reference.

Compared with the more traditional arrangements, layered collective bargaining structures have undergone important changes in bargaining issues and negotiators. Company agreements make it possible to discuss new issues such as work content, qualifications and technology.

An important point for the trade unions is their identity as bargaining partner in the company: the union itself, the works council, or trade union lay officials. In Great Britain the position of bargaining partner has been taken over by shop stewards. In reality they constitute a company union that evolved as a result of union activities at the company level. In West Germany the *Betriebsrat* has adopted this role, although this body also shows signs of developing into a company union. In France one finds every conceivable variation; none the less the union delegate acting at the company level is the legally recognized partner.

Concerning the relations between national and local negotiators, the question arises as to who takes precedence at the negotiating table: local negotiators at the company level or national negotiators in sectors (or large companies). Sometimes negotiators from a sector or large company will thrash out all the important issues within the context of a nationally coordinated policy. This naturally leaves negotiators at the company level little room to bargain. This scenario can work in the opposite direction as well.

Who is the principal bargaining partner, at what moment in time does bargaining take place, and what are the bargaining issues? These are in fact the three crucial questions we must ask in evaluating bargaining structures. The answers can vary from company to company, from industry to industry and from country to country. Within sectors the balance between small, medium-sized and large companies is very important: who dominates in a sector, and is there a big difference in management styles between small and large companies, for example because of the presence of a personnel department? How many small companies do not have union representation? How many of these are trying to avoid having to take account of external arrangements? These are the questions that determine the strategic choices which trade unions and employers have to make.

The layered bargaining structure provides a means to make collective agreements more flexible. It is an attempt to maintain certain collective arrangements at the industry level while at the same time allowing companies more autonomy and more room to take the initiative themselves. We have seen in the countries considered above that country-specific historical development and institutions play a major role in this attempt. We must therefore guard against being too hasty in claiming that layered collective bargaining structures are a common European answer to management demands for greater flexibility. A sharp drop in union and employers' association membership may furthermore mean that the layered structure is an intermediate phase on the way to a situation in which the industry level disappears altogether or loses any real significance, with only company agreements in larger companies surviving.

7 Industrial democracy, employee participation and operational autonomy

Rien Huiskamp

1 Introduction

The previous chapter described how the employment relationship is regulated in collective negotiations between unions and employers' associations. In our view there is a very clear tension between the external rules derived from collective agreements or legislation and the ongoing process of interpreting, reinterpreting and applying such rules in the workplace. Which aspects of the employment relationship are regulated, by whom, when and in what fashion varies from country to country, from industry to industry and even from company to company. In this chapter our attention shifts to the level of the company. Here too we see that formal and institutionalized relationships have arisen between the employer and employee representatives or trade unions. The purpose of these relationships is to offer employees the opportunity to participate in company policy-making or certain aspects thereof, for example wage policy or the way in which the work is organized. When such participation takes place by means of legally established or otherwise formally prescribed bodies, we use the term 'industrial democracy'.

We will begin this chapter by comparing the formal arrangements made in various countries with respect to employee participation. We will then discuss a number of comparative studies which focus on formal employee participation and the degree of genuine influence that employees have on strategic decision-making in companies. Alongside formal industrial democracy schemes, countless companies also make use of other participation schemes implemented by the employer, often after consultations with employees: some examples are quality circles and semi-autonomous work groups. Such schemes are closely tied to the way the organization itself works. We will discuss the relationship between such participative schemes and industrial democracy.

2 Industrial democracy in Europe: a brief review

The first comparative studies on employee participation reviewed the formal, generally statutory arrangements made in various countries. A study conducted by the European Commission in 1979 is an example. Table 7.1 shows which bodies are responsible for which regulatory tasks in various countries. The columns indicate the most important actors: in addition to the trade unions, we see representative bodies (for example the Dutch *ondernemingsraad* or the German *Betriebsrat*) and officials (Great Britain's shop steward or Belgium's *syndicale afgevaardigden/délégués syndicaux*). A distinction can be made between employee representatives on the one hand and company union representatives on the other.

The works council falls into the category of employee representatives: the members are after all chosen from among the company's personnel and in most countries both union and non-union employees can stand for election. The shop stewards or *syndicale afgevaardigden* are typical examples of trade union representatives: they represent the unionized personnel on behalf of the trade union.

The columns in Table 7.1 show the issues or areas of jurisdiction of the various bodies. These include, first of all, joint establishment of rules

Table 7.1 *Formal industrial democracy schemes in a number of European countries*

Country	Determines employment conditions	Handles collec./ individ. grievance procedure	Advises on economic policy
Belgium	Trade union	*Syndicale delegatie*	*Ondernemingsraad*
France	Trade union (activity)	Personnel delegates	Works council
Germany	Trade union/*Betriebsrat*	*Betriebsrat*	*Betriebsrat*/ *Wirtschaftsausschluss*
GB	Shop stewards	Shop stewards	(Shop stewards)
Italy	Plant councils	Plant councils	(Plant councils)
Netherlands	Trade/*ondernemingsraad*	Trade union (activity)/ *ondernemingsraad*	*Ondernemingsraad*

Source: European Commission, 1979

related to conditions of employment in the broadest sense: wages, working hours, hiring and firing, training and job evaluation. The second issue concerns the role of employee representatives in grievance procedures. Such procedures permit the representatives to discuss employee grievances with various levels of management. Such grievances might include, for example, the amount of time available to carry out a particular task, inaccurately calculated wages or social security contributions, or the behaviour of a foreman. These discussions usually take place before the grievance becomes 'official' and is turned over to salaried union officials and upper management. The third area of jurisdiction is consultation: recommendations offered to management by the representative body which do not necessarily end in joint decisions. So we see that formal employee participation schemes cover a spectrum ranging from bargaining to consultation, with various gradations in between such as more legally prescribed forms of participation.

In most countries the union or its representatives – whether or not represented by a union body within the company – play a major role in the joint regulation of employment conditions (first area of jurisdiction). However, in the Netherlands and Germany, the employee representatives also play an important role. In most countries the salaried union official is not a significant party when it comes to handling individual or collective grievances (second area); such issues are dealt with either by union delegates (non-salaried) or by employee representatives. The third and final area mentioned above – consultation – does not apply in every country. The works council is the main player on this issue, and in countries where such a body does not exist, this particular aspect of industrial democracy is left blank.

The countries show a wide range of differences. For example, in Great Britain a single actor, the shop steward, is active in two of the three areas listed. In France each area has its own body or official. In the Netherlands or Germany, two actors may share competence in one area.

An important factor in explaining such differences in industrial democracy schemes is the historical background: how and in what way did such representation grow and develop? Did other representative structures spring up alongside or even above the existing ones?

In Great Britain the role of the shop steward in grievance procedures grew over the course of time to encompass the joint management of many different aspects of employment. Such an arrangement was formalized in procedural agreements between the trade unions and employers' associations, and was based on 'custom and practice'. Formal, statutory arrangements did not exist. The shop stewards were furthermore more concerned with shop floor activities and job control, and paid little attention to general company policy. Not until the 1970s did some British companies establish consultative bodies concerned with the general state of affairs within the enterprise.

The Federal Republic of Germany made a new start after the Second World War with the *Betriebsrat* as the company's consultative body. The *Betriebsrat* consists of representatives elected by the employees. Its authority has increased over the years, both in a formal sense and in actual practice. Trade union representatives in German companies, the *Vertrauensleute*, have never managed to capture a position of any significance. The *Betriebsräte* developed gradually in the direction of joint regulation of employment in a broad sense (see Chapter 6).

In Belgium the *syndicale afgevaardigde* (union delegate) was traditionally the most important employee representative in companies. Not until 1948 were statutory provisions made for an *ondernemingsraad* (works council) as well. Its role is much more limited than similar bodies in the Netherlands or Germany, however. Oddly enough, the *syndicale afgevaardigden* were not legally recognized until the 1970s, but that probably explains their strong and autonomous position.

These historical developments make it impossible to arrange the countries into a neat table with vertical divisions between employee and union representation and horizontal divisions between bargaining and consultation. We will therefore describe a new, fictitious country: the land of actual practice. In this country, employee representatives and union representatives have formally distinct tasks and jurisdictions, but in actual practice the two have merged within some companies. The employee representative body is a company institution, but because it is dominated by union members it is actually an extension of the union structure within the company. The difference between bargaining and consultation is blurred. Employee representatives are consulted according to statutory provisions, after which management, with or without their consent, can take a decision. A personal union arises: the members of the representative body are also trade union delegates. It is therefore easy for this body to effect a subtle shift from consultation as it is legally prescribed to bargaining over issues which are not really in its area of jurisdiction. Such shifts are often the result of the strategies of interest organizations choosing the most effective or desirable form of influence available. This in turn has an impact on the degree to which formal and statutory provisions are actually applied.

A striking example of the above can be found when comparing Great Britain and Germany. In Germany the *Betriebsrat* is active as the company consultative body; in Great Britain this role is assumed by the shop steward, an elected employee representative who also serves as the union representative and bargains at the company level. In Germany unions are organized according to industry; in Great Britain they form a patchwork of very different organizations. At first glance there seem to be huge differences between the institutional structures. These differences can be exaggerated, however; formal institutional diversity may obscure relative uniformity or equivalent practices. Such was the conclusion reached by the West German labour sociologist Streeck (1984) concerning the auto industry in Great Britain and Germany. In Germany, the *Betriebsrat* is not officially authorized to bargain over wages and conditions. In the metalworking sector that privilege rests exclusively with the trade union and the employers' association within the framework of collective bargaining. The situation in Great Britain appears to be otherwise. There the collective agreement in the metalworking sector is so loosely formulated that union representatives in automobile companies can conduct more or less autonomous negotiations with their employer. However, in Germany, the auto producers can offer their employees a higher wage than other types of company in the metalworking sector. As a result, lay union officials, disguised as members of the *Betriebsrat*, take part in additional bargaining rounds with management. This is not permitted according to the rules and the institutional framework, but it happens nevertheless. The position that the *Betriebsrat* has been able to assume in these wage negotiations strengthens its position in other areas as well – thereby creating British conditions in West German companies. Until well into the 1970s, the British auto industry set the trend for independent wage bargaining between shop stewards and management, by-passing unions and employers' associations altogether. The reason was that the auto industry was able (or thought it was able) to support higher wages relative to other types of company covered by collective agreements in the metalworking sector. Shop stewards used wage bargaining to introduce other issues into the sphere of bilateral decision-making.

The systems of industrial relations in the auto industry in Great Britain and Germany are more alike than their formal structures and institutions would have us believe. Perhaps the resemblance between such systems in the large car companies in these two countries is greater than it would be between a large car company and a small metalworking firm in the same country. The larger car manufacturers bargain autonomously with the *Betriebsrat* or shop steward, or conduct additional bargaining. The management of a small firm, on the other hand, tends to apply the rules set out by its employers' association rather strictly; the firm's representative body is not very effective and there is no sign of independent bargaining or a second wage round. We should keep in mind, then, that there can be huge differences between various industrial sectors and companies within one country. For example, there are companies in Great Britain where very little bargaining takes place; instead, representative consultative bodies have developed which resemble the German *Betriebsrat*.

We see that per country different formal arrangements can fulfil a similar function, or the same institution can operate quite differently from one company to the next within the same country. To illustrate this point, we have deliberately chosen the 1979 study by the European Commission as the starting point of our analysis, a study which explores only the formal participative structures and no more. Only later did other studies look at the impact of such formal arrangements at company level on the degree of influence that employees and their representatives actually have. This issue will be our main focus in the following sections.

3   The difference between participation and influence

The research project Industrial Democracy in Europe (IDE, 1981), the first large-scale comparative study on industrial democracy, went much further than investigating only the statutory and formal provisions for employee participation. The question posed in this project was whether participation in decision-making and the actual degree of influence on decision-making were determined by formal provisions and institutional structures of a country, or by other factors (as well).

The study focused on 12 countries. In each a number of companies were selected from the metalworking industry and from the banking and insurance industries, the latter serving to represent the service sector. In all 9000 interviews were conducted between 1976 and 1977 in 134 companies. Those interviewed included employees, foremen and middle and upper management.

The study plotted the decision-making process for two types of issues: first, short-term ones such as working conditions, holiday schedules, working hours, pay levels, and job classification, and secondly, long-term issues such as reorganization, large-scale investment and the introduction of new products. The first may be described as decisions which are directly related to dimensions of the employment relationship. The second tend to be economic decisions and involve the company as an organization.

For the various groups interviewed, the study explored to what extent they were involved in the two types of issues and how they assessed each other's impact. All those interviewed, in each country, stated that the involvement and influence of management was greater than that of the employees. Two remarks should be made regarding this statement.

First, a country's formal and statutory arrangements proved to be less important for the distribution of influence than the way authority is divided among the various hierarchical levels in the organization of a given firm. However, participative bodies have more influence in countries where statutory regulations or other formal provisions allow them more authority (for example Sweden or Germany) than those in countries where this is not the case.

Secondly, as decisions moved from short term to long term, the influence of employees and the representative bodies declined. In other words, they have a larger say in short-term decisions than they do in long-term ones. On the other hand, the more long-term the decision, the more influence management appeared to have. Here too there are differences between countries. In some, employee influence is extensive, both in long-term and short-term decision-making (for example in Denmark), whereas in others the degree of influence on both types of decision is minor (for example in Belgium). In addition, some countries demonstrate a mixed pattern of influence. In the Netherlands and France, for example, employees have a great deal of influence on short-term and very little influence on long-term decisions, whereas in countries such as Norway and Italy precisely the reverse is true.

The IDE study also asked those involved about their wishes for the future. Employees expressed a desire to increase their influence. Management, however, did not share this particular aspiration. Employees value participation as a goal in itself.

The study concludes that it is the distribution of authority within companies – made manifest in the hierarchy of positions and in the division of labour between management and employees – which determines the results of the degree of influence, regardless of the company's host country. Formal arrangements in a given country play only a secondary role: they stipulate who is involved, rather than determine the degree of actual influence. In addition, the researchers were able to identify patterns of influence on short-term and long-term decisions in the various countries.

The IDE study was repeated in 1987, providing a rare opportunity to explore how the formal and actual participation of employees and their representative bodies has developed under the influence of such factors as the economic recession which hit numerous European countries in the early 1980s or the introduction of new technologies (Koopman and Drenth, 1993). Most countries saw little change with respect to formal participation (legal framework) during this period. The hierarchical structure of the organization was once again a highly important factor in determining actual participation – indeed, more important than any other distinguishing factor between countries. The researchers therefore concluded that despite important contextual changes, actual participation is highly stable. In order to explain this phenomenon, they proposed two competing theoretical models. The 'system inertia model' predicted that those groups of employees who exercised a large measure of influence in 1977 would retain this degree of influence in 1987, even under unfavourable conditions, whereas groups which had little influence before would lose even more. The 'management strategic model' predicted that during periods of recession, management actively tries to reduce the influence of stronger groups, but pays little attention to weaker ones. Empirical findings support the second model. Under conditions of high unemployment, management is able to reduce the actual influence of powerful groups of employees and their representatives. However, the degree of actual influence exercised by strong groups scarcely alters when jobs are plentiful; neither does it change for those groups of employees who lacked any influence in the first place. Apparently the reduction is not across the board, but selective and limited in scale.

The participation paradox

In another comparative study, carried out under the auspices of the European Foundation for the Improvement of Living and Working Conditions, researchers focused on the degree of influence that employees have on one issue: the introduction of new technology. The study (Cressey and Williams, 1990) was conducted in 1982 in the 12 EC countries and involved 7,326 managers and employees working in companies where the introduction of new technologies had had a profound impact on the workplace. The degree of influence was charted by investigating the level of participation in product and market strategies and investment on the one hand, and the level of participation in decision-making on work organization, job classification and health and safety on the other.

Both managers and employees (for both groups 45 per cent) believed that employees were not involved in decision-making on product and market strategies and investment, while the greater majority (80 per cent for both groups) believed that they were involved in issues such as work organization, job evaluation and health and safety. The researchers explored this question in greater detail by introducing a distinction between all forms of participation and intense forms. By intense forms of participation they meant joint decision-making or true bargaining. The share of respondents who felt that product and market strategies and investment were subject to intense employee participation dropped to 6 per cent; for the other issues this percentage fell to 30 per cent.

Management motivated their views with the following, for example:

- management wished to retain the 'right to manage';
- centralization of internal decision-making within companies did not allow participation;
- many issues had as yet not been worked out in sufficient detail to allow participation;
- employees lacked the necessary expertise;
- there was no statutory obligation for participation.

The employees put forward motives such as:

- participation might lead to a confusion of roles (for example, with collective bargaining);
- employees might become 'hostages' of management;
- employees had no representatives at upper decision-making levels;
- employees had no legal rights to back up participation;
- the employees viewed the relevant changes positively, even without being allowed to participate.

A correlation between participation and the stage of the decision-making process also became evident. The researchers distinguished two stages: planning and implementation. All the respondents in each country believed that participation increased in the implementation stage. In the planning stage, however, three-quarters of the respondents indicated that participation was restricted to receiving information. The preference for participation in the implementation stage was motivated by referring to the 'visibility' of the change. For employees such 'visibility' was related to how familiar the issues were and whether they constituted a traditional employee concern. Management gave other, somewhat instrumental reasons: employee participation was a way of solving problems that arose during the implementation of new technologies and of fostering commitment and cooperation. Ultimately management saw it as a way of regulating change in the organization and in wages and conditions.

The researchers coined the term 'participation paradox' to describe their findings: participation is limited in the planning stage, when the possibility of having an impact is greatest, and increases in the implementation stage, when this possibility is much smaller. Participation increases precisely at the moment that the opportunity to exercise a fundamental influence decreases. According to the study, management and employees both view participation as a positive development. They disagree, however, when questioned about the degree of influence and intensity of employee involvement that they would like to see in future. Employees advocate greater participation, whereas management rejects any such development (particularly the intense forms of participation). The responses to this question also reveal an interesting difference between countries: employee aspirations for the future go furthest in those countries where they already enjoy an intense level of participation in the planning stage.

The researchers have established an important national difference related to the stage of involvement and intensity of participation. Denmark and Germany show a high level of participation in the planning and implementation stage, Italy and Spain show a low level in both stages, and Belgium and the UK fall somewhere in between. These differences become even more evident where intense forms of participation are concerned. By way of explanation, the researchers point out the presence of formal and statutory arrangements in such countries as Denmark and Germany.

Influence on strategic decision-making

A Swedish study (Levinson, 1991) explored the extent to which local trade union representatives participate in and influence strategic decision-making. The strategic changes are infrequent, but have a profound and lasting impact on the firm. Examples of such changes are: mergers and takeovers; setting up new companies; developing new product–market combinations; introducing new technologies; pushing through large-scale reorganizations; cutting back on or relocating production sites. Swedish law stipulates that industrial democracy is the province of trade union representatives who are elected by the company's employees (similar to the shop steward in Britain). The study distinguishes four stages in the decision-making process:

1   Initiating the decision.
2   Preparing the decision.
3   Taking the decision.
4   Implementing the decision.

The managers and employee representatives of 279 firms were questioned in the period 1982–83. All firms had undergone strategic changes as defined above. The most common changes were: cuts in production, changes in the work organization and introduction of new technologies. There were interesting differences in the length of the decision-making process. Initiation, preparation and decision-making with respect to relocating a company took two and a half years; mergers took 18 months and the acquisition of new technology took six months. This says nothing about actual implementation, however; if we take that into account, an entirely different picture emerges. The implementation stage for new technology lasted the longest: two years. For takeovers, implementation took only three months.

Management and local trade union representatives indicated that trade union representatives do indeed take part in decision-making on strategic changes. However, the degree varied from one stage to the next, increasing from the first to the third stage and then dropping again. Expressed in numbers, management and trade union representatives estimated the participation of the latter as 10 per cent and 24 per cent respectively in the initial stage, 20 per cent and 72 per cent in the preparation stage, 68 per cent and 94 per cent in the decision-making stage, and 42 per cent and 59 per cent in the implementation stage. In the first and second stages in particular the two groups gave widely different answers.

According to the researchers, the intense involvement in the third stage is due to the statutory and formal provisions of Sweden's Co-determination Act. In three-quarters of the cases, involvement in this stage was a direct result of this piece of legislation. Three-quarters of management described the influence of the trade union representatives as being of an 'advisory' nature; one-tenth viewed it as joint decision-making. The activities of local trade union representatives are described by the researchers as passive; they seldom take the initiative, do not propose alternatives and limit themselves to asking for additional information. Influence was found to be greatest when the decisions concerned cuts in production or issues affecting the shop floor directly. Concerning the future, management preferred leaving things as they were, whereas half of the representatives wanted a greater degree of influence for themselves.

The research team concluded that management still ran the show, and that the co-determination legislation had not led to dramatic changes. The legislation does safeguard the participation of local trade union representatives in the decision-making process, but it cannot guarantee that they will have a real impact on this process. Such an impact stems in part from the level of participation at an early stage of decision-making, which according to management estimates is not very high.

4   Interim evaluation

The conclusions reached in the Swedish study complement those of the two studies described previously.

- Statutory and formal arrangements do strengthen the influence exercised by employee representatives, but other factors, such as the distribution of authority between the parties and their hierarchical positions within the company, are more important.
- Employee influence in the formal stage of the decision-making process depends largely on involvement in an earlier stage.
- This influence increases when issues concern the shop floor more directly or, in other words, when they are more closely related to the employment relationship.
- Long-term or strategic decisions are more significant, but less likely to invite participation.
- Employee representatives would like to increase their degree of influence, whereas management would prefer that they do not.
- The differences between employee representation (works councils) and union representation (shop stewards or *syndicale afgevaardigden*) are not very significant when determining the degree of influence. We should take into account, however, the extent to which the roles of employee representatives and union representatives have become intertwined. Union representation within the company has the advantage that it stimulates greater coordination with (external) collective bargaining.

The studies have not uncovered any obvious patterns or models that can serve to categorize industrial democracy in different countries. There are also differences within countries between industrial sectors and firms. We cannot say, for instance, that non-statutory trade union representation within the firm, for example in a country such as Great Britain, exercises an influence only at the final stage of decision-making and only then on the consequences of proposed changes for wage levels. This may well be the case in one plant, but not in the other; moreover, the influence of the statutory *ondernemingsraad* in a Dutch firm may be equally small and equally restricted to a later stage of decision-making and to the immediate concerns of the employees. Our concern is that the influence of statutory and formal arrangements is often only of a limited significance. Extensive regulations do in fact encourage participation and consequently offer more opportunities for employees to exert an influence, but the regulation of the employment relationship can take on different forms and be expressed in various ways within the same national context.

5   Industrial democracy and operational autonomy

As we have seen, the tension between an employment relationship which is unilaterally dictated by management on the one hand, and the aim of employees to subject this employment relationship to a bilaterally determined set of rules on the other, gives rise to various regulatory options. Alongside prescribed institutional forms of employee representation, actors may develop other structures, closely tied to the specific work organization in a company, for example shop floor consultations, quality circles and semi-autonomous task groups.

The question is to what extent such types of work-related participation are dominated and restricted by management. In other words, are the rules for non-institutional participative channels set unilaterally by management? Are they merely a means to improve the product or production? Or do they also, almost as a matter of course, involve aspects of the employment relationship, for example working hours or work pace? What is the connection between these forms of participation and the institutional forms? Do institutional organs have any influence on the implementation of new types of consultation? Do the two structures complement one another or compete? We will explore these questions by considering the experience of semi-autonomous task groups.

The operational autonomy of task groups

One important aspect of work organization within (semi-)autonomous task groups is that groups of employees take joint decisions with respect to important aspects of the production process, such as product quality, work preparation, maintenance etc. Employees must be familiar with a large number of the tasks allocated to the group and be able to perform them. They are also responsible for coordinating their work with other departments and with management. This might even involve making the group accountable for expenses and profits. It becomes a budgetary unit, a 'company within a company', bearing responsibility for certain costs, for example hiring temporary workers. There is internal flexibility and operational autonomy within the task group coupled with a minimal specification of rules imposed 'from outside'.

Does this ideal, self-governing unit exist in the real world? If we consider task groups in companies in the Netherlands, France, Germany and Sweden, then the answer is no (see for example Joosse et al., 1990; Van Ruysseveldt and Janssens, 1989). For example, task groups in a large number of these companies have had problems related to the rotation of tasks: production may fluctuate too sharply for adequate rotation or group members may consistently refuse to carry out low-status tasks. Shop floor consultations might also take place only irregularly, for example because of high production demands. Task groups do more than allocate and arrange work. They can in theory also be responsible for training and for scheduling individual working hours and holidays; remuneration may be on a group basis rather than on an individual one; and the group may also be involved in hiring temporary workers or lending task group members to other groups. These aspects are directly related to the employment relationship; they refer to pay, qualifications and working hours. In actual practice, again, there have been problems. Production is not allowed to suffer because of training; the remuneration system as stipulated in a collective agreement is based on individual job categories and does not fit in well with group work; and when a group has spare time, it is not allowed to take a break due to management interference. The ideal concept of the autonomous task group is seldom achieved in practice.

Limitations have to do not only with the hierarchy of management and employees, but also with the relationship between staff departments and the shop floor. Greater operational autonomy on the shop floor implies that tasks are removed from staff departments. Such decentralization of autonomy often meets with great resistance on the part of staff workers. An arrangement which allows for operational autonomy on work, hours etc. and with minimal outside interference would affect not only the position and tasks of the personnel department as a staff department, but also of the works council, trade union officials, and so on.

Employee participation and task group implementation

Some evidence of the involvement of employees in introducing task groups can be derived from three separate research projects in the Netherlands exploring technological and organizational innovation in companies. Each of the projects made use of case studies. The first investigated the consequences of implementing computer numerical controlled (CNC) machines for work and organization (six cases); the second investigated practical experiences with autonomous task groups (AT) (14 cases), and the third investigated computerized production control systems (PC) and changes in work organization (six cases). The three projects explored 26 cases in all, in the metal industry, the electronics industry, the processing industry and the services sector. Part of the analysis focused on the involvement of the employees in making technological and organizational changes. We can characterize the changes in work organization within the case firms in the following manner (see Table 7.2).

1   A shift from a Taylorist form of organization to an increased division of labour.
2   A shift from Taylorist organization to job enrichment.
3   A shift from Taylorist organization to task groups.

**Table 7.2   *Changes in work organization seen in 26 case
studies***

	Autonomous task (AT) groups (n = 14)	CNC machines (n = 6)	Production control (PC) systems (n = 6)
Taylor to increased division of labour	n.a.	3	5
Taylor to job enrichment	5	3	1
Taylor to task group	9	–	–

Table 7.3   *Stage of employee involvement*

	AT (n = 14)		CNC (n = 6)		PC (n = 6)	
	Works council	Users	Works council	Users	Works council	Users
None	–	1	2	3	–	5
Late	1	7	4	2	5	–
Early	7	6	–	1	1	1

In the CNC study, three of the six companies had taken steps to extend the tasks of machine operators, while the other three sharpened the division of labour by introducing new jobs for programming and adjusting machines. In all cases but one, a change to computerized production control systems led to a more rigidly Taylorist work organization. In the study concerned with autonomous task groups in five companies the change in work organization goes no further than introducing elements of job enrichment.

The involvement of the employees has been operationalized in the study by considering.

• the stage of involvement: early (during the initiating or planning stage) or late (during the implementation stage) (see Table 7.3);
• the nature of the involvement: advisory versus merely informed of the pending changes (see Table 7.4).

Involvement has been plotted for both works councils and actual users (employees). The case material does not permit further distinctions.

Involvement by works councils and users early on in the process of introducing technological change was only incidental. Involvement in the implementation of autonomous task groups, however, came at an early stage in half the cases. We see the same pattern when it comes to the nature of the involvement: only task group implementation showed any involvement in the form of advice, and then only in a minority of cases. It is

Table 7.4   *Nature of employee involvement*

	AT (*n* = 14)		CNC (*n* = 6)		PC (*n* = 6)	
	Works council	Users	Works council	Users	Works council	Users
None	–	1	2	3	–	5
Advisory	8	9	3	2	6	1
Early	6	4	1	1	–	–

Table 7.5   *Involvement scores*

Score	AT (*n* = 14)	CNC (*n* = 6)	PC (*n* = 6)
0–3	1	3	5
4–6	9	3	1
7–8	4	–	–

important to determine whether there was a connection between the involvement of the works councils and that of the users within a firm. In four firms the works council and the users were equal in a positive sense: that is, both had an advisory role at an early stage. In three companies they were equal in a negative sense: that is, involvement was at a late stage and they only received information. In none of the cases were the users intensely involved in implementation while the works council was not.

Another way to represent involvement is by means of scores. A company scored:

- 1 point for late involvement
- 2 points for early involvement
- 1 point when employees received information
- 2 points when employees were asked for their advice.

Depending on whether the works council and the users were involved singly (1 point) or together (2 points), the maximum score is eight points ([2 + 2] × 2 = 8). A score of zero indicates no involvement whatsoever (see Table 7.5). A score of 4 shows a minimum degree of involvement: for both works council and the users, involvement is late and limited to being informed. Less than 4 points indicates that involvement was below even this minimum level. A score of 4–6 represents a minimum to somewhat higher degree of involvement, while only a score of 7 or 8 points shows that both works council and users were involved early on in the game in an advisory capacity.

With respect to the implementation of CNC technology and PC systems, many firms did not even meet the minimum standards of involvement. CNC technology is frequently limited to 'island computerization', and in the eyes of both management and employees has few consequences for the organization as a whole. The computerization of PC systems often involved computerizing a portion of the administrative procedures in stock-keeping or materials supply. These were viewed as isolated administrative changes. That implementing CNC machines implied a greater degree of involvement than computerized PC systems is understandable when we consider that CNC computerization affects the shop floor more directly. Nevertheless, even among those firms that started up autonomous task groups, a change with far-reaching consequences, there were only a few where the employees got involved at an early stage and were asked to give advice in the planning stage.

6 Conclusion: supplementing or eroding industrial democracy?

At this point we will repeat the questions summed up above: do the non-institutional employee participation channels which have been initiated by management threaten the institutional employee representative bodies or the trade unions? Or do they simply offer employees more opportunities to influence the terms of their employment relationship?

There is almost no empirical material on which to base an evaluation. There are, however, theoretical reflections on this topic. As for the role of representative bodies, such as the works council, in innovations in production technology and the quality of work, de Sitter (1981) writes that the works council is not a suitable place to discuss work and organizational restructuring. Such discussions should take place in 'functional' groups: groups of people who work as a team to perform a particular function within production. One might mention crews, product groups or staff departments. The works council, in de Sitter's view, is composed of categories of interest groups. Once employees in the new organizational structure possess sufficient operational autonomy, he sees little need for formal structures such as the works council.

A good example of the profound impact that task groups can have on the structure of employee representation can be found in the case studies given in Box 7.1. In Great Britain, groups of employees who have the same task in the production process choose their own trade union representative, the shop steward. The decentralized structure ensures that the shop stewards are independent of management. Strike action can quickly and effectively cripple the most vulnerable parts of the production process.

Evidence from two (unpublished) Dutch case studies has shown that employees are involved to a limited extent in planning and implementing task groups. There is no hard evidence that a new model of participation is developing in which cooperation is intense from the earliest stages of change. From all appearances, the operational autonomy of the task group does not provide such a strong foundation for self-regulation of the

Box 7.1   *Industrial democracy and new forms of work organization: three case studies*

As early as the 1970s, the management of the **Herberts Machine Tools** factory in Coventry began to convert the traditional line organization to one structured around autonomous task groups. This also brought changes to bear on trade union representation: the composition of the group to be represented had changed, and each new task group (formed by management) in the new setup chose a new shop steward. Innovations in work organization had direct consequences for shop floor representation. Old demarcation lines between unions disappeared and the boundaries between shop steward constituencies were altered. The employees had trouble accepting this, because the production process was now organized into a series of parallel production lines. It no longer hinged on one or two 'bottlenecks' controlled by the employees. On the other hand, the link between interest representation and operational autonomy presumably became quite strong, because the shop steward was now also task group coordinator in the management structure, appointed by his own group.

British car manufacturer **Rover** began to introduce 'Total Quality Improvement' programmes in the late 1980s, combining this move with working in teams. At the start of the 1990s negotiators agreed in a collective agreement on more radical innovations in work organization, including a far-reaching restructuring programme for industrial relations. The proposals were highly controversial among the union rank-and-file. When the votes were in, 11,961 employees had voted for the agreement and 11,793 against – a majority of less than 200! Part of the agreement involved the maximum devolution of authority and accountability to cells, each cell consisting of 40–50 employees and reporting to a team leader. The teams were not only held responsible for work-related issues such as quality of work, routine maintenance, process improvements, cost control and control of consumable tools and materials, but also issues which directly impinged on the employment relationship – work allocation, job rotation and training. Employees were also to become involved in discussion groups, quality action teams and suggestion schemes aimed at improving company performance. Continuous improvement was required for everyone. Consultations with representatives of recognized trade unions were to be enhanced to include company performance, products and long-term corporate plans.

The German company **Teldec** has also stipulated the participation of individual employees, teams and the *Betriebsrat* in a supplementary agreement to its industry-level collective agreement. Each employee on an individual basis and the works council on a collective basis were given the right to raise issues regarding working conditions, job grading, the allocation of work within a team, workload and staffing levels. Work teams and joint committees (consisting of three employer and three employee representatives, appointed by the works council) would deal with such matters as overall job design and technology design; occupational health, hygiene and worker protection; working procedures and the organization of work. If differences of opinion arose within a joint committee, the matter would be taken up in negotiations between the employer and the works council. The agreement is quite recent, but so far employee involvement at the individual and joint committee level has proved to be a very difficult point.

employment relationship that the institutional forms of participation will disappear. The examples cited above show that, even when the participation of workers is stipulated in formal rules, employees are still extremely hesitant when it comes to extending their own level of influence by means of task groups. Task groups are, after all, embedded in a particular social structure within a company, based on the hierarchical position of management, and the formal position of employee representatives or trade union bodies.

The most important development that could grow out of these new forms of work organization is a shift (albeit a minor one) from centralized bargaining to decentralized consultation. The introduction of operational autonomy on the shop floor might blur the traditional divisions between production and representation.

PART 4

WAGES, WORKING TIME AND QUALIFICATIONS

8 Wages from a European perspective

David Marsden

1 Introduction

Labour differs from other commodities exchanged within the economic system because it cannot be separated from the workers supplying it, and they take their social values and norms with them into the workplace. In our societies, wages fulfil a large number of different functions which may often not all be compatible one with another. For firms, wages are, in the first instance, a cost of production, and the more competitive their product markets become, the greater the need to minimize wage costs. But they are also a source of motivation, a means by which managers can persuade workers to carry out the tasks they want, and increasingly, to the level of quality they require. For workers, wages are primarily a source of income, but they can also be a source of social prestige, and may be judged according to their fairness. For economists, they are seen additionally as the chief mechanism in a decentralized market economy whereby labour is allocated to the jobs in which it will be most productive. There are doubtless many other social functions that are fulfilled by wages. These are just a few principal ones, and it is clear that they may often conflict, making wages an easy target of conflict and social struggle.

This chapter starts by looking at wage differences between various categories of workers. By analysing these differences, we hope to gain insight into the various mechanisms that influence wage determination. We will discuss wage differences between countries in the European Union, between sectors of trade and industry, between occupational categories and between male and female employees. Throughout our discussion, we will be investigating possible backgrounds and reasons for the differences we come across. In the third section, we will explore whether wage differences change over the course of time, focusing specifically on wage movements in the 1970s and 1980s. In section 4, we will once again look for explanations for these movements. Time and again, we will discover that a complex range of factors influences wage determination. On the one hand, market fluctuations play a role, although the game of labour market supply and demand – played out against the backdrop of economic growth or decline – is not the dominating factor. On the other hand, we should be aware of the strategic behaviour of the various actors involved: collective bargaining between organized employers and employees, governmental incomes policy, and employer personnel policies all exercise an influence on the process of wage determination and on the relative wage positions of various categories of employees (pay differences). Such strategic behaviour must be seen in a wider context which includes social institutions such as the system of education, country-specific traditions associated with industrial relations and politics, and economic, technological and organizational trends.

2 Wages compared

Wage differences among countries within the European Union

The creation of the Single European Market is reducing the level of barriers to trade among Union countries, and exposing many firms and whole sectors to a higher level of competition. One of the fears of many firms and their workers is that in the new environment they will no longer be able to compete or that the price of competition will be too high. Indeed, one of the reasons why many unions are in strong support of the European Union's Social Chapter is that they would like to see limits set on the intensity of cost competition among European firms. They fear that economic competition will ultimately undermine a number of hard-won social gains.

Table 8.1 *Labour costs and unit labour costs in 1991 (whole economy) as a percentage of EC average*

	Labour costs/employee	Unit labour costs
Netherlands	110.6	101.4
Germany	110.9	105.7
France	110.6	101.0
Luxembourg	113.0	124.4
Belgium	116.5	104.1
Denmark	103.7	103.3
Italy	109.1	87.2
Ireland	86.5	98.9
UK	86.7	111.3
Spain	84.5	89.0
Greece	46.4	74.3
Portugal	37.3	87.6

Labour costs (compensation) include gross wages and salaries, employers' actual social contributions, and imputed social contributions; unit labour costs are calculated as labour costs per 1000 Ecu GDP.
The figures for Germany date from before reunification.

Source: Eurostat, 1993: National Accounts ESA Aggregates 1970–91

The fear has arisen that European competition will encourage social dumping: companies might be inclined to set up production in those countries where labour is cheap. Wage costs and the level of social protection would therefore become an important element in competition.

The scale of differences in hourly labour costs among member countries is indeed great: such differences include gross wages and salaries, employers' actual social contributions and other premiums (see Table 8.1). Recent estimates based on national accounts data for the whole economy show that the range of difference extended from Portugal, whose hourly labour costs were only 37 per cent of the Union average, to Belgium, whose labour costs were about 17 per cent above it and more than three times the level in Portugal. These of course are the extremes, and the majority of the Union countries lie within a smaller range, but it is still large enough for workers in some of the higher cost countries to fear significant loss of jobs. However, these large labour cost differences are to some extent offset by differences in productivity. Labour costs must be seen in the context of worker productivity: a more expensive employee may ultimately cost a company less because he or she performs better, for example by producing more products per unit of time than a less expensive employee (see Table 8.1, unit labour costs).

If we adjust the difference between Belgium and Portugal to take account of the difference in productivity between the two countries, then the gap drops from nearly 80 points to under 20. Belgian firms could then remain competitive because they may have advantages in transportation costs to the markets they supply, and in the type of products sold. It might nevertheless be said that when multinational firms invest in low labour cost countries they do so in the expectation that they will achieve much higher productivity levels than those of local firms. They will probably bring better management, and different technology, and they will have better access to design and marketing skills. So the low cost/low productivity countries will continue to look attractive, although one should also remember that part of the productivity gap is due to the quality of the local infrastructure (for example the road network), and local skills (labour market supply) and training systems, and there is little that multinationals can do about that in the short run.

Thus, one can expect differences in labour cost levels between countries to remain a factor in the location of new investment. There is, of course, a conflict of interest between labour in the low and in the high labour cost countries. Low labour costs are one of the means by which unions and political parties in these countries hope that they can attract new investment, and so gradually reduce the gap in production, and living standards, between themselves and the established industrial countries of the European Union.

What matters to firms when they are competing is the total cost of employing labour, and not just the wage levels. In many EU countries, wages represent only between 50 per cent and 60 per cent of the total cost of employing labour, although in others the figure is much higher (Table 8.2). In the Netherlands, for example, wages paid for work actually undertaken represented a little over half of total monthly labour costs, and even including annual bonuses, and paid absences such as annual vacations, remuneration accounted for just over 70 per cent of labour costs. The remaining 30 per cent was made up of employers' social security contributions, supplementary pension contributions, and so on. The exceptions to this pattern were the UK, Ireland and Denmark, the reason being that social security and pensions are funded to a greater extent out of direct taxation on employees. However, in all countries, there has been a gradual upward movement of so-called 'non-wage' labour costs. One important question this raises concerns the distribution of employment, as high employer social security contributions are effectively a tax on employment, and one fear is that the increased competition of the Single European Market will encourage governments with high employer contributions to reduce social security coverage in order to reduce the burden on employers. They could also switch the burden to direct taxation, following the model of the UK, Ireland and Denmark, but this may be electorally unappealing to governments. One of the provisions of the Social Chapter is to maintain the level of social security provision so that governments refrain from taking this path in order to maintain the competitiveness of their countries' industries.

Apart from establishing more unified product markets across the EU, part of the process of Economic and Monetary Union (EMU) is concerned

Table 8.2 The structure of monthly labour costs in industry in 1988, as a percentage of total monthly labour costs[1]

	Belgium	Denmark	Germany	Greece	Spain	France	Ireland	Italy	Lux.	NL	Portugal	UK
Direct earnings	49.1	83.1	56.0	61.0	55.3	51.4	70.4	50.3	67.7	54.6	56.0	73.0
Bonuses and premiums[2]	11.0	0.8	8.8	11.0	7.0	6.2	1.4	7.9	4.1	7.2	11.8	1.3
Pay for days not worked	9.2	12.3	11.4	7.0	12.4	9.4	10.3	11.4	11.2	11.0	6.0	11.0
Pay in kind	0.1	0.0	0.2	1.0	0.2	1.0	0.2	0.4	0.2	0.1	0.4	0.2
Total direct costs	69.4	96.2	76.4	80.0	74.9	68.0	82.3	70.0	83.2	72.9	74.2	85.5
Social security payments												
Statutory	25.6	1.9	16.9	18.0	22.9	19.1	8.1	30.6	13.3	16.2	18.9	7.3
Voluntary/agreed	3.3	1.1	4.6	1.0	1.7	9.4	7.0	1.4	2.6	7.5	2.8	4.6
Other	1.6	0.8	2.2	0.0	0.6	3.4	2.7	-2.0	0.9	3.4	4.2	2.6
Total	99.9	100.0	100.1	99.0	100.0	99.9	100.1	100.0	100.0	100.0	100.1	100.0

[1]Establishments with 10 or more employees. Coverage: NACE 1–5, industry and construction.
[2]Eurostat defines these as 'bonuses and gratuities not paid regularly at each pay period'. They include employee share ownership schemes.

Source: Eurostat, 1988, Table 201.A

Table 8.3   *Hourly earnings of manual workers in industry,*
October 1992, as a percentage of EC unweighted average

	At current exchange rates (Ecu)	Adjusted for differences in living costs
Denmark	169.1	129.3
Germany	147.3	129.5
Luxembourg	n.a.	n.a.
Netherlands	118.8	113.6
Belgium	118.4	117.0
UK	97.1	115.8
Ireland	98.7	108.4
France	92.7	88.8
Italy	n.a.	n.a.
Spain	81.5	91.7
Greece	46.0	63.5
Portugal	30.4	42.4

Coverage: NACE 1–5 excl. NACE 16 and 17.

Source: Eurostat, 1993: Earnings: Industry and Services

with the guarantee of opportunities for labour mobility among member countries. The Treaty of Rome establishes the principle of free circulation of workers within the EU, and the CEDEFOP has worked hard to make this a reality by promoting agreement among countries to recognize each other's educational and training qualifications. In addition, the increased pace of mergers and acquisitions among Union-based firms means that many of them will be faced with the task of building integrated teams of managers and of technical specialists from across Europe. Already, a high proportion of inter-regional labour mobility within countries takes place within firms (more than by people quitting jobs in one region to look for a job in another). As European companies integrate their workforces, one can expect that they too will become vehicles for the movement of labour between regions within the EU. Thus, differences in the levels of pay workers can get among EU countries could be one factor encouraging inter-country labour mobility.

As a rough guide to the differences in workers' pay levels, we might take the average earnings of manual workers in industry for which there are roughly comparable data across the European Union (see Table 8.3), comparing wages at current exchange rates, and in terms of their purchasing power in each country, that is, after allowing for differences in the cost of living among countries. At current exchange rates, Denmark and Germany offer the highest wages in Europe. The lowest average wages are to be found in Greece and Portugal.

Manual workers' wages in Denmark are about 70 per cent above the EU average. Some of this will be to the benefit of Danish workers, particularly as concerns goods and services purchased from abroad. However, a good proportion of their pay will be spent upon services which

are provided locally, such as housing, schooling and health, and these will
have to be paid for at local levels of wages. Thus, when account is taken of
the purchasing power of each country's wages, the gap between them is
considerably reduced. Danish workers are then only 30 per cent better off
than the EU average, and Portuguese workers improve from being at 30
per cent to more than 40 per cent of the EU average, not a fortune, but not
as bad as it seemed at first. It would be possible to take the comparison
further and estimate disposable income after tax, but then a number of
difficult conceptual problems emerge. For example, it is not clear that
workers who pay taxes for their medical care are worse off than those who
pay their medical expenses by means of private insurance schemes. Thus,
assuming Portuguese workers have the requisite skills, can speak Danish,
and suitable arrangements can be made for social security, then there is a
considerable potential for labour mobility, especially among younger
workers who do not yet have family responsibilities. These are all big
assumptions, so it is unlikely that there should be a great wave of migrant
workers, but the incentives nevertheless exist. In fact, the main large scale
migratory pressures are expected from North Africa and Eastern Europe.
Up until now, we have looked only at national and European averages,
assuming that all workers were paid the same, but there are also
considerable variations within countries, for example, among industries,
occupations and between females and males. It is to these that we now
turn.

The industrial wage structure

One of the remarkable features of average pay levels in different industries
is the similarity of the rank order industry pay levels over time, and among
countries. On the whole, the same industries that are highly paid in one
country tend to be so in others, and the same is true, by and large, of the
low paid industries (see Table 8.4). The picture shown here has been
confined to the European Union countries, but a survey of the evidence for
a range of countries in other parts of the world confirms a similar picture of
which are the high and low paid industries (Dickens and Lang, 1987;
OECD, 1965).

Notable among the high paid industries are oil refining, computers,
electricity and gas, chemicals, aerospace and ships. Among the factors
which might explain this are the levels of skill required of the workforce in
the industries, the danger or difficulty of the work, and the firm's position
on its product market. The strength of union organization might be
another. We shall look at a number of these factors in more detail later,
but at least at first sight, some of these industries would appear to have
high skill requirements, especially computers, aerospace and gas and
electricity. Danger could also be a factor in the energy sectors and in
chemicals as the products handled are often highly toxic and explosive.
Difficulty of working conditions is a further factor as many of them are

Table 8.4   Hourly labour costs in Ecu in five high- and five low-paid industries in 1988

	NACE	Belgium	Denmark	Germany	Greece	Spain	France	Ireland	Italy	Lux.	NL	Portugal	UK
Oil refining	14	27.9	15.0	30.4	7.5	n.a.	23.3	n.a.	17.5	n.a.	24.3	8.8	20.1
Computers	33	17.3	17.6	26.3	n.a.	12.3	27.2	11.3	16.7	10.0	18.5	n.a.	16.0
Electricity and gas	16	n.a.	17.6	24.2	7.2	15.9	25.0	15.0	19.3	n.a.	18.3	7.5	13.5
Chemicals	25	19.9	17.6	22.7	6.5	11.4	20.2	13.4	16.3	13.7	20.8	5.0	13.4
Aerospace and shipbuilding	36	16.7	15.7	21.5	7.2	11.2	19.9	10.8	14.5	n.a.	15.9	4.6	12.6
Textiles	43	11.8	13.4	13.4	4.7	7.3	12.0	8.0	11.5	n.a.	14.1	2.3	7.3
Leather	44	11.8	13.5	11.7	4.6	7.5	11.5	6.6	11.1	n.a.	11.7	2.3	7.8
Wood and furniture	46	12.5	13.2	14.6	4.4	5.9	11.4	7.7	10.9	9.5	12.8	2.1	9.3
Clothing and footwear	45	10.1	11.7	11.5	3.7	6.4	10.4	5.5	10.0	13.7	10.4	2.0	6.3
Miscellaneous	49	9.8	14.6	14.1	4.0	7.7	13.1	8.8	11.3	n.a.	13.0	2.4	9.6
All industries	1–5	17.0	15.5	18.3	5.4	9.1	15.3	10.6	14.2	13.6	16.4	3.0	11.0

Manual and non-manual workers included.

Source: Eurostat, 1988: Table 17

process industries, and so require round-the-clock supervision and maintenance. On the whole, these industries also have stable (and largely male) workforces, and so tend to be more highly unionized. In Great Britain, for example, for an average union membership density of 58 per cent in manufacturing, the sectors including these industries had either average or above average rates of unionization (Millward and Stevens, 1986).

Finally, the position of firms in the highly paid sectors *vis-à-vis* their product markets tends to be exceptional. In a number of countries, large parts of these industries are in the public sector, for example electricity and gas, and in oil refining. In some cases, the public visibility, and being part of the public sector, places an obligation on the employer to provide a model for other employers. This has certainly been the case in France where many of the employment conditions of the core of the public sector were extended to employees in these branches so that they became known as *secteurs à statut* (CERC, 1989).

Even non-public sector firms in these branches occupy an oligopolistic position. There is generally a small number of large firms, each aware that their actions will directly influence the behaviour of the others. For example, in pricing decisions, the oil companies tend to move together, and even if they do not collude directly, which in any case might be difficult given the vigilant eye of public regulatory bodies, no one will want to 'spoil the market'. This means that in such sectors, there is plenty of opportunity for earning so-called monopoly rents, as competition does not force the producers to pass on the full gains of increased efficiency to consumers. These rents may then be shared with the workers as a result either of the companies' personnel policies, which may favour a high wage/high quality workforce, or of collective bargaining. Either way, the end result is that the high wages of some of these sectors may be the result of market power in the firms' product markets. Turning to the low wage industries, these tend also to be the same from one country to another, and generally include such branches as textiles, leather goods, wood and furniture, and clothing. A first glance at the skill structure of these industries suggests that low skill levels explain a large part of the low wage levels. The large proportion of young workers under 21 years of age would seem to bear this out because at such ages they would normally be undergoing training. It is sometimes argued that the high proportion of female workers is also a sign of low skill levels. However, although most of the women in these branches are indeed classified as unskilled, there is some debate as to whether these areas of work are so classified because little training and dexterity is involved, or because they are done by women. Recent work has shown that in some plants, women – although classified as unskilled – were undertaking work that was technically as demanding as that done by their male colleagues. Such comparisons can only be done by means of detailed case studies, so it is hard to assess their generality. Nevertheless, the evidence is sufficient to warn against too literal an interpretation of the skill categories of large scale wage surveys.

Working conditions in these industries might be thought to be less dangerous than those of some of the high paid industries. Nevertheless, there are considerable occupational hazards, for example damage to the respiratory system from breathing the dust of textiles or wood sawings.

Finally, the competitive structure of these industries is generally very different from that of the high wage ones. Small firms are much more dominant, although there are some large textile firms, and the markets tend to be more competitive. Indeed, it is hard to picture a more competitive market than that for fashion clothing and footwear.

The fact that there are noticeable differences between the (average) wages paid in various industries, and that these differences carry through to all of the various countries surveyed, indicates that sector-specific economic and technological factors do have an impact on wage determination. Specifically, the market position (public sector/oligopoly) seems to be a significant factor in determining the profit margin and the wage level. Other factors include the nature of the work itself, for example the required qualifications and the working conditions. These are highly important in the exchange of wages for performance. The nature of the work is also closely related to sector-specific characteristics, such as the level of technology, the organization of the production process and the product features. It seems that market position and profit margins dominate, since objectionable working conditions can be found in a number of low wage industries as well. Such working conditions are not compensated for in wages.

Differences in earnings among occupations

Until this point we have been comparing average wages paid in member states of the EU and in various sectors of industry. Such comparisons are analytically useful; they tell us something about the country- or sector-specific factors that influence wages. At a lower level, however, we can also compare wages according to occupation. First, however, a remark concerning methodology is appropriate.

Whereas industries share certain similarities in terms of the kind of technology used and the type of product marketed, so that it is relatively straightforward to apply a common industrial classification across many countries, the problem is quite different for occupations. Even though workers in many countries may be using similar production technologies, in practice the way in which work tasks are divided between the job categories used in the enterprise varies greatly. For example, a major study (Maurice et al., 1982/1986) comparing the division of labour in a sample of French and German manufacturing plants found that the range of technical tasks undertaken by skilled workers was markedly narrower in France than in Germany. They also found that the French skilled workers had a much smaller margin for making decisions in their work, and they had often to refer upwards to management, whereas German management devolved many more job-related decisions to skilled workers. As a result, the German skilled workers both undertook a wider range of technical tasks in their normal work, and exercised considerably greater discretion in deciding how to solve problems. Thus, jobs may vary between countries both in terms of the horizontal division of technical tasks, and in the vertical distribution of authority or decision-making power.

Faced with such variation among countries, any attempt to compare occupational pay structures between countries is fraught with difficulties. One cannot, after all, compare apples and oranges: skilled workers in France and those in Germany are comparable in name only. Their range of responsibilities and authority are otherwise highly dissimilar.

The only roughly comparable data for comparisons between EU countries are from Eurostat's *Structure of Earnings Surveys* which used a hierarchical classification based on a mixture of criteria relating to skill level and the amount of responsibility exercised (figures are from the *Structure of Earnings Survey*, 1978; unfortunately an updated version of this report will not be available before 1996). It is unavoidable with such a classification system that some differences in pay structure may arise simply because the statisticians in one country draw the line between say 'managers' and 'executives' at a slightly different level (see Tables 8.5 and 8.6). Even if we assume that the division of labour is identical between two countries, it is possible that classifying more of the low paid managers among executives in one country than in another will produce apparently higher average pay for managers in the country in which the junior managers are counted as 'executives' by the survey.

A glance at the figures on employment by occupation in Tables 8.5 and 8.6 gives some confidence in the consistency of the occupational classification, although there are significant variations among countries. Some of these may indeed reflect underlying differences in the division of labour, such as the larger percentage of foremen and supervisors in France as compared with Germany. This observation is compatible with the results of the enterprise level comparisons by Maurice et al. (1978) that the French firms had a much higher ratio of supervisory to skilled workers than did their German counterparts. Likewise, the high percentage of skilled manual workers in Germany is a reflection of the large numbers of qualified apprentice-trained workers in that country. However, in the absence of such corroborating evidence for the other countries, considerable caution is needed to interpret the results sensibly. The figures nevertheless give some broad indication of degree of pay levels by occupation, and receive some corroboration from comparisons with other national sources (Marsden and Redlbacher, 1984). Of the five countries, if we look at the gap between managerial pay and that of other categories, it appears that France and Italy are the most inegalitarian, whereas Germany, the Netherlands and the UK are the least inegalitarian. Two countries in particular experienced major changes during the 1970s and

Table 8.5 *Occupational differentials in industry and construction in 1978*

	% of average gross monthly earnings (full time)				
	France	Germany	Italy	NL	UK
Men					
1a Higher management	314.3	215.6	280.6	209.8	204.8
2 Executives	216.3	159.4	158.3	172.7	152.1
3 Assistants	134.1	122.9	122.3	130.2	114.0
4 Clerical	103.0	93.9	101.7	98.7	90.1
5 Foremen	130.5	134.1	116.9	119.9	118.4
All non-manual men	154.5	138.8	139.5	129.5	124.5
1 Skilled	93.4	102.8	101.7	97.5	111.7
2 Semi-skilled	77.5	92.4	91.1	89.2	101.6
3 Unskilled	68.7	84.4	87.1	81.3	89.5
All manual men	87.5	97.9	95.4	91.4	103.4
All men	108.1	108.3	105.5	103.0	109.8
Women					
1a Higher management	221.1	180.1	236.0	145.3	n.a.
2 Executives	169.5	133.1	140.2	123.7	100.1
3 Assistants	117.5	99.7	110.3	100.1	78.7
4 Clerical	85.6	73.5	90.4	69.2	63.8
5 Foremen	101.7	97.8	95.5	93.8	69.2
All non-manual women	95.8	89.4	102.4	75.3	67.7
1 Skilled	72.6	74.4	81.6	73.6	66.4
2 Semi-skilled	64.8	66.4	76.9	60.7	64.6
3 Unskilled	61.2	64.8	77.3	61.6	60.0
All manual women	65.7	66.1	77.6	63.0	62.8
All women	76.6	74.2	83.7	68.8	64.8
Total M+F	100.0	100.0	100.0	100.0	100.0
(National currency)	3,927.6	2,459.1	524,237.4	2,767.5	388.6

Source: Eurostat, 1978

1980s. In Italy, the impact of the strongly egalitarian wage indexation system (*scala mobile*), which gave the same flat-rate monetary increase to all workers irrespective of the level of their pay, greatly reduced wage differentials among employees, as did the egalitarian wage bargaining policies of the early 1970s. In Great Britain also, the figures for 1978 represent something of a trough as they came at the end of a long period of compression of white-collar and managerial differentials as a result of the incomes policies of the 1970s. This movement was completely reversed during Mrs Thatcher's period of office. Just as France had the highest managerial differentials, so it also had the largest difference between skilled and unskilled workers. This was a distinction it shared with Italy in the early 1970s, but which was eliminated in Italy by the effects of bargaining policies and indexation (Saunders and Marsden, 1981).

Table 8.6 *Employment by occupation (% share of total)*

	% of average gross monthly earnings				
	France	Germany	Italy	NL	UK
Men					
1a Higher management	0.1	0.2	n.a.	0.1	n.a.
1b Management	1.3	1.1	1.0	1.6	1.1
2 Executives	4.5	5.9	5.1	5.1	4.6
3 Assistants	6.4	7.7	6.1	5.6	8.4
4 Clerical	4.5	1.6	2.6	8.2	2.4
5 Foremen	5.9	2.7	2.1	6.9	8.0
All non-manual men	22.6	19.2	16.8	27.4	25.6
1 Skilled	34.1	34.1	24.9	25.9	22.0
2 Semi-skilled	12.3	15.1	26.4	26.9	20.4
3 Unskilled	5.4	6.7	6.6	11.1	11.5
All manual men	51.8	56.0	57.9	64.0	54.0
All men	74.4	75.2	74.8	91.3	78.2
% part-time	0.3	0.4	0.9	0.9	1.0
Women					
1a Higher management	n.a.	n.a.	n.a.	n.a.	n.a.
1b Management	0.1	n.a.	n.a.	n.a.	0.1
2 Executives	0.5	0.5	0.4	0.1	0.2
3 Assistants	1.1	3.7	2.1	0.3	1.3
4 Clerical	7.2	4.4	3.0	3.4	6.3
5 Foremen	0.4	n.a.	0.2	0.2	1.3
All non-manual women	9.3	8.8	5.8	4.1	9.4
1 Skilled	3.4	1.0	2.3	0.6	1.1
2 Semi-skilled	8.5	6.6	14.1	1.9	6.6
3 Unskilled	4.5	8.4	3.1	2.1	4.9
All manual women	16.3	16.0	19.4	4.6	12.6
All women	25.6	24.1	25.2	8.7	21.8
% part-time	0.9	4.9	0.8	20.9	17.5
Total M+F	100.0	100.0	100.0	100.0	100.0
Total ('000)	5,966.6	8,404.3	3,516.8	1,260.3	8,025.7

NL and UK data: full-time only, other countries full- and part-time.
Establishments with 10 or more employees.
n.a. = not available, mostly because sample numbers too small.

Source: Eurostat, 1978

One can only speculate on the causes of the larger spread of differentials. The first possible cause might be differences among countries in the availability of labour for work in the different occupations. If there is little work available in a particular occupational category as compared with the number of qualified workers, then the price of labour (wages) falls. If, on the other hand, there is a large demand for a small number of qualified workers, then wages rise. Thus, as compared with their German counterparts, French firms might pay their foremen and managers a bigger differential over manual workers because they are relatively more scarce than in Germany. However, if we look at the employment shares of foremen in each of the two countries, it is clear that the French firms employ relatively more of the more expensive factor of production. So it seems that the standard supply and demand analysis does not provide the answer, in this case at least.

One notable feature of the occupational pay structures is that, in some countries, skilled workers are more highly paid than clerical staff, while in others they are not. This is particularly true of Germany and Great Britain where there is a great deal of overlap between the blue- and white-collar pay hierarchies. In contrast, in Italy and the Netherlands, there is no such overlap, and in France, there is a considerable gap between the two hierarchies. This was also true in 1972. This might be taken as an indication that the organizational structures underlying pay differ in some systematic way among these countries. Indeed, again we might take a cue from the detailed plant level comparisons of Maurice and Sellier (1979, 1980: the latter also included Great Britain).

One notable difference between the organization of French and German firms is the much greater reliance in the former upon enterprise internal labour markets than in the latter. In France, young people are more likely to take up jobs below their level of qualification, and there is more extensive use of upgrading between job classifications. Although there has been a big increase in the number of young people entering the labour market with vocational qualifications for skilled work in France, especially since the early 1970s, these young people still have to start work in semi-skilled or unskilled jobs and wait for an opportunity to be upgraded. In the meantime, they gain on-the-job experience. Positions higher up the ladder are filled by promoting company employees. In addition to work experience, then, loyalty to the company plays an important role. There is also more frequent upgrading from blue- to white-collar jobs in France than in Germany. In contrast, in Germany, most skilled workers reached their current status by serving an apprenticeship at the start of their working lives which gave them access to a widely recognized occupation, and gave them a skill that was recognized by a large number of employers, and so could be transferred between enterprises. In contrast then to the vertically structured internal labour markets in French enterprises, German firms make greater use of horizontally structured occupational labour markets. There is a good deal of evidence that Italian firms use similar kinds of organization to those of French firms, and that British firms approximate to the German model (Marsden, 1990a). The Dutch case seems to fall somewhere in between, possibly because the Dutch vocational training system is something of a hybrid between the German and the French models (Marsden and Ryan, 1991).

What then is the link between enterprise organization and occupational pay differentials? Again, only a tentative answer can be given, but it would seem to rest on the marketability of skill qualifications in systems with occupational labour markets. In such cases, skilled workers are not dependent upon their current employers and so are in a better position to defend their relative pay levels *vis-à-vis* white-collar workers. They are much more mobile. If their position in the company comes under threat, they can easily take a job at another company. This gives them a strong bargaining position when it comes to negotiating wages. In countries dominated by occupational labour markets for skilled workers (Germany and the UK, for example), they are in a much better wage position than in countries dominated by internal labour markets (Italy and France, for example). In contrast, in enterprise internal labour markets, skills are more narrowly dependent on the worker's current firm, and are more under the control of management. The qualifications acquired are usually company-specific and do not necessarily have to be recognized by other companies, which may have different job categories or organizational structure. Employees in internal labour markets such as these can only cash in on their training or retraining within that specific company. The lower market value of qualifications acquired internally puts the employee in a much weaker bargaining position. Maurice et al. showed that control over the allocation of training remained strongly with management in France, with management spotting talent it would subsequently train, whereas in Germany it was the subject of an individual decision.

Comparing pay differentials by occupational categories, we see that wages are influenced by country-specific characteristics, including social institutions such as the system of vocational training, the organization of the production process and personnel. The best example is perhaps the market value of skilled labour. The wages of skilled workers are not only determined by labour market supply and demand. Also important is how such workers acquire their qualifications – in a generally recognized vocational programme or within the company itself – and how employers select their employees, organize their companies and set out career paths.

There are noticeable differences between countries in this respect. In those countries where skilled workers end up in occupational labour markets and assume a wider variety of tasks with more responsibilities, their bargaining position is much stronger and manifests itself in their favourable wage level. In countries where skilled workers enter internal labour markets, are less likely to take on technical tasks and have fewer responsibilities assigned to them, their bargaining position is weaker and their wage position disadvantageous.

Differences between women's and men's earnings

We can see that social factors influence the wages of specific categories of employees if we compare men's and women's wages. The subordinate position of women in both the family and society carries through in their position in the working world. On the other hand, there is a movement in society to emancipate women; at various policy levels, steps have been taken to encourage the equal treatment of men and women. Two directives have been adopted by the European Union which are to eliminate differences between men and women in the labour process. The first focuses on equal pay for men and women (Directive 75/117 of 10 February 1975), while the second encourages the equal treatment of men and women in the labour process, in occupational training, in promotion and with respect to terms of employment (Directive 76/207 of 9 February 1976).

Despite the acceptance throughout the European Union of the principle of equal pay for women and men, on average, women's pay remains substantially less than that of men in all EU countries. Currently, if women do identical jobs to those of men, it is unlikely that they will be paid at a lower wage, indeed, it would be illegal. However, to a great extent, women are segregated into different jobs, and tend to be less often promoted than their male colleagues. Employment segregation results from two main factors: the application of employment rules which make it difficult for women to conform to the norms of the jobs in question; and a tendency for society to undervalue jobs done mainly by women.

These two problems may be related because of the general social (and male) expectation that women who undertake market work should maintain their role in the household as mother, carer and family organizer. Combining these roles often limits women's ability to apply for jobs which require a high degree of geographical mobility, or long journeys to work, and it can reduce their availability to meet the demands of jobs with a heavy responsibility. Thus many women face a more restricted choice of jobs, and are disadvantaged in the stiff competition for managerial and certain professional jobs. This then crowds women into seeking certain types of work, and the large supply of labour then depresses the wage levels that they can command. As males have a wider choice of jobs, it is relatively easier for them to refuse such low wage 'women's jobs', and so a degree of wage differentiation and job segregation arises. Such segregation in employment can of course reinforce gender stereotypes of women's and men's abilities.

Of the five countries discussed in the last section, in industry, the UK, the Netherlands and Germany pay their women least well, whereas the two 'Latin countries' pay them rather better (Tables 8.7 and 8.8). Because Eurostat's structure of earnings survey is the latest source available for detailed comparative data, we are confined to 1978 as our 'benchmark'. However, the rank order of inequality between women and men among these countries was the same in the early 1970s (Saunders and Marsden, 1981), and updating the figures from national sources suggests that it has not changed much since 1978. Women's relative pay remains better in Italy and France than it does in the other three countries, and the UK remains in worst position.

Averages for the whole of industry conceal a great deal of difference among occupations, and in the access of women to higher paid occu-

Table 8.7 *Women's employment and monthly earnings as a percentage of men's in industry*

	France	Germany	Italy	NL	UK
Employment					
1a Higher management	6.2	3.0	2.2	1.8	4.3
2 Executives	9.2	8.0	7.8	2.7	4.5
3 Assistants	14.1	32.6	25.7	5.5	13.8
4 Clerical	61.8	73.0	54.0	29.1	72.6
5 Foremen	6.8	1.5	10.5	3.4	14.4
All non-manual	29.1	31.5	25.7	13.1	27.9
1 Skilled	9.1	2.9	8.4	2.3	4.6
2 Semi-skilled	40.8	30.4	34.8	6.7	24.4
3 Unskilled	45.4	55.5	31.7	15.8	29.8
All manual	24.0	22.3	25.1	6.8	19.0
All workers	25.6	24.2	25.2	8.7	21.8
Monthly earnings					
1a Higher management	70.3	83.5	84.1	69.2	n.a.
2 Executives	78.3	83.5	88.5	71.6	65.8
3 Assistants	87.6	81.1	90.2	76.8	69.1
4 Clerical	83.1	78.3	88.7	70.1	70.9
5 Foremen	77.9	73.0	81.7	78.2	58.5
All non-manual	62.0	64.4	73.4	58.1	54.3
1 Skilled	77.8	72.4	80.3	75.5	59.4
2 Semi-skilled	83.7	71.9	84.3	68.0	63.5
3 Unskilled	89.1	76.8	88.7	75.8	67.0
All manual	75.0	67.5	81.4	68.9	60.7

Source: Eurostat, 1978

Table 8.8 *Effect of occupational distribution of women's and men's earnings differential (women's pay as percentage of men's)*

	France	Germany	Italy	NL	UK
Current structure	71.1	68.5	79.2	66.8	59.0
Same structure for both women and men	80.87	75.7	84.7	72.8	62.4

Source: Eurostat, 1978

pations. The difference between women's and men's pay is markedly smaller within the broad occupational groups (Tables 8.5 and 8.6) than the overall average. For example, among non-manual workers in the Netherlands, women's average pay is only 58 per cent of that of men, whereas within each of the individual non-manual occupations, it ranges from 11 points higher than this for higher management to about 20 points higher for assistants and foremen (Table 8.7). The same picture can be seen in each of the other countries.

These differences between women's and men's pay are mainly indicative. The occupational categories used are very broad, and include a large number of different occupations within each. Hence, one cannot deduce that the big differences within the occupations shown represent equivalent differences in rates of pay for the same jobs. A finer occupational classification would reveal smaller differences between men's and women's pay (Saunders and Marsden, 1981), although it would not remove them completely because of differences in length of service and in levels of responsibility, and premium payments, for example.

The overall inequality in pay is the product of both differences of pay within the same occupations, and differences in men's and women's share of employment in different occupations. Looking across the five countries, among white-collar jobs women are concentrated in clerical work; in all five, between one-half and three-quarters of white-collar women are in such jobs. Among blue-collar workers, they are heavily concentrated in unskilled and semi-skilled manual jobs. Skilled, supervisory and managerial jobs remain the preserve of men. The country in which women appear to have got closest to breaking through the 'glass ceiling' is France, where they have the highest employment share of the five countries in the top two non-manual occupations. One factor helping women progress further in France is the high level of provision of childcare facilities and junior schools for very young children which enable women to compete more equally with men for the better jobs.

Also of interest is the higher proportion of women in skilled manual jobs in France and Italy, as compared with the three other countries. One potential reason, particularly as compared with Germany and the UK, is that in France and Italy employers make greater use of enterprise internal labour markets as means of organizing their workforces, and for skill formation. In contrast, in Great Britain and Germany, greater use is made of occupational labour markets based on apprenticeship training, which combines theoretical instruction with practical work experience in a real production process (Marsden, 1990a). Apprenticeship training has remained fairly closed to young women, especially in industrial occupations, in both countries. This is partly due to the masculine ethos of the jobs to which it leads, but also to the organization of training, and notably its concentration in the first years of a person's working life. After this period, it is difficult to enter apprenticeship because of the low level of earnings during the training period. In contrast, training in internal labour markets relies more heavily upon the gradual accumulation of skill and experience on the job, leading to promotion to skilled jobs. This may be started at later periods in a person's working life. In view of the break in labour market activity of most women around their middle twenties, it would seem that the more gradual and diffuse training process of internal markets is less of a barrier for women seeking access to skilled manual employment than the apprentice-ship system used in Germany and Great Britain.

The overall effect of unequal access to skilled and managerial jobs in industry varies among the countries. In most of the countries, women's overall average pay, compared with men's, would be considerably higher if workers of both sexes were equally represented in all occupations. In France, women's average pay would rise from 71 to 81 per cent of men's. Again the contrast between France and Germany is of interest, as women's overall position, compared with men, benefits from the larger pay gap between blue- and white-collar pay.

Apart from occupational differences between women's and men's employment, in most EU countries women tend to be concentrated in the lower paid industries, such as clothing and footwear, textiles, leather goods and electrical engineering, and relatively absent from the high paid sectors such as the energy sector, oil refining, and ship and aircraft construction. Women's pay relative to men's is not especially worse in the low paid than in the higher paid industries. The important fact is that the low paid industries are also low paid for men. Adjusting the female/male pay differential for this industrial concentration of women's employment would remove between four and six percentage points from the overall differen-tial for manual workers, but hardly anything for non-manual workers.

It is possible to extend the comparison of women's and men's pay to certain services, notably distribution and the financial sector. In the former women tend to be less well paid than in industry, and in the latter better paid. A broadly similar pattern of occupational segregation can also be found in these sectors. Even though women have a much larger employ-ment share in these two sectors compared with industry, they are still greatly under-represented in managerial and other higher paid white-collar jobs.

Dispersions of earnings

Differences in pay between occupations, industries and between women and men capture only part of the total amount of variation in earnings among individual workers. Within each of these categories there remains a considerable amount of variation among individuals. The dispersion coefficients in Table 8.9 indicate the scale of wage inequality for manual and non-manual workers for the five countries. For non-manual workers

Table 8.9 *Dispersions of monthly earnings in industry in 1978*

	France	Germany	Italy	NL	UK
Manual	27.1	26.5	21.4	26.1	38.9
Non-manual	53.9	34.6	39.5	39.9	46.8

Source: Eurostat, 1978

the dispersions provide some indication of the amount of inequality within occupations, and in particular within that of higher management. They thus give a view of the extent to which managerial pay extends above the averages for that particular grade. It is notable therefore that the greatest amount of variation among white-collar workers was to be found in France, reflecting the high levels of pay relative to other workers received by higher management. In the UK, the coefficient of variation is also fairly high, but a large part of this is due to the big difference in pay between women and men. The data are for 1978, one of the last years in which higher paid workers in the UK saw their position eroded, and before the big increase in inequalities under Mrs Thatcher. As indicated above, however, more recent data will not be available until 1996.

Among blue-collar workers, dispersions of earnings were smaller than among their white-collar colleagues, generally reflecting the more limited opportunities open to them. One potential reason for the larger dispersion in the UK is that, of the five countries, it has the least comprehensive form of minimum wage coverage. Both France and the Netherlands have national minimum wages for adult workers, which means all those over 18 in France, while there is special provision for 'young' workers aged under 23 in the Netherlands. In Germany and Italy, a fairly effective minimum wage is provided by the possibility of extending the minimum rates of pay negotiated in industry agreements to all workers in the appropriate industry. Moreover, the system of indexation in Italy has been particularly favourable to the lower paid, as it provides fixed monetary increases for each percentage increase in the price index. In contrast, in Britain, sectoral minimum wages were established for those industries in which it was deemed that workers are too weakly organized to engage in collective bargaining. This took place in wages councils, which came under pressure from the Thatcher government and were abolished in 1993. Even with this system there were weakly organized workers in all sectors who slipped through the net of low wage protection. This shows that the wage structure is determined to some extent by industrial relations. In those countries where labour and management agree on collective agreement provisions on minimum wages which apply throughout the entire sector, or where the government introduces compulsory schemes, the dispersion between manual workers is smaller than in other countries. We will consider the significance of collective bargaining for the wage structure in greater detail when we discuss changes in wage structures in the 1970s and 1980s.

3   Changes in wage structures during the 1970s and 1980s

In this section we will explore whether the wage differences discussed earlier vary over the course of time. Has wage inequality increased or decreased? Which factors have an impact on this process?

Across much of the Western industrial world, the 1970s were a period of reduction of wage inequalities, and the 1980s a period of increase or 'restoration' of inequality. The scale of changes varied from country to country, with workers in Italy and the UK experiencing among the greatest reductions in wage inequalities in the 1970s, and those in the UK and the United States seeing the strongest reassertion of wage inequalities during the 1980s.

The contrast between the two decades is of considerable interest from both a theoretical and a practical point of view because wage structures are, on the whole, fairly stable apart from a few rather exceptional periods of history. That means that the relative wage position of various categories of employees changes very little over time. From a theoretical perspective, the important question is how to explain this stability. The discussion of the various theories presented in Box 8.1 leads us to deduce that wage structures are influenced by a mixture of economic and social factors.

The stability between the various wage categories is in sharp contrast with what we established earlier: in the 1970s, dispersions of earnings fell dramatically, only to reassert themselves or even increase in the 1980s. This observation leads us to search for factors that might offer an explanation. Although the experience of the 1970s and 1980s has not as yet produced any study that enables us to choose one way or the other, it does offer a very interesting mixture of different economic and social pressures on pay structures. The 1970s witnessed incomes policies and union wage bargaining policies designed to protect the lower paid from the worst ravages of inflation, union policies to promote greater equality more generally, and government policies to reduce the inequality between women's and men's pay, to mention only the main ones. The 1980s witnessed a steep rise in unemployment in most industrial countries, and in some, a collapse in industrial employment, plus a reassertion of the view that wage incentives were necessary to encourage workers and their managers to achieve higher productivity and to take greater economic risks. The period also witnessed a crisis in established methods of large scale mass production, a faltering in the growth of mass consumption, the rise of Japanese competition, and discontent in the workplace causing the 'regulationist' writers to speak of a crisis of 'Fordism'. Thus, within a relatively short space of time, pay structures have been subject to intense pressures from shifts in labour supply and demand as well as from changes in the social acceptability of differing degrees of inequality. The groups of workers between which differentials can be measured are many. Those chosen in this section relate to dispersions, which measure overall amount of inequality among individual workers; occupations, which in most published statistics relate to the levels of skill and responsibility exercised; industries, which relate to the types of economic activity in which people are engaged; and between women and men. A detailed analysis of most of the statistics on which this section is based can be found in an ILO study of differentials (Marsden, 1990b), but for the present, and because of the

Box 8.1   *The stability of wage structures: explanations*

Compared with the prices of other goods, wage structures have proved to be remarkably stable over long periods of time, and are fairly insensitive to short-run changes in labour demand and supply. For example, Phelps Brown and Hopkins (1955) showed that the wage differential between skilled and unskilled construction workers had remained very stable over seven centuries in England, until the dramatic reduction in the differential in the period during and immediately after the First World War (Knowles and Robertson, 1951). Across a wider range of occupations, Routh (1980) showed that occupational differentials in Britain were remarkably stable through much of the twentieth century, until the 1970s, despite the major economic upheavals, except during and immediately after the two world wars. There are three competing types of explanation of this broad stability of wage differentials.

1   The neoclassical economic theory: implicit contracts
The first explanation is based on the neoclassical economic theory. The idea is that the wage levels prevailing for different categories of workers correspond more or less to the long-run equilibrium positions as predicted by competitive labour market theory. Some recent developments of economic theory stress the importance of 'implicit' contracts which offer stable wages in the short-run also.

Employment relations are characterized by a kind of implicit contract whereby employers offer workers stable wages in exchange for a risk of lay-off. The contract is 'implicit' because it is nowhere written down, and cannot be enforced legally, so it has to rely on the mutual interest of those concerned. Firms behave as if they are offering workers a dual contract, a fixed wage contract and an insurance contract. The former is like the traditional employment contract; however, although workers' remuneration may be fixed, the value of their marginal product varies over the economic cycle. In boom periods it is above their fixed wage, and the employer benefits, and in recession it is below the fixed wage, and the workers gain. It is as if workers contribute to an insurance fund, managed by the employer, against the impact of economic fluctuations on their income during the boom, and receive pay-outs from the fund in recession (Azariadis and Stiglitz, 1983). It is argued that workers prefer this kind of arrangement because they have only their human capital as a source of income and so need to protect themselves against fluctuations in its value, whereas firms hold a wide range of financial assets and so can more easily spread their risks.

2   The regulation and segmentation theory: mass production, the monopolistic method and internal labour markets
The second explanation derives from the 'regulation' and the 'labour market segmentation' schools. About the turn of the century in many industrial countries, the organization of production underwent a fundamental change with the shift from small-scale market coordinated

production to large-scale mass production of the kind illustrated by Henry Ford's innovations in the automobile industry (for example, Aglietta, 1976; Boyer and Mistral, 1983). Small-scale market-coordinated production fostered competition on all markets. Under the competitive mode, labour markets functioned like ordinary competitive goods markets: wages were flexible in response to employment fluctuations because firms competed to recruit workers, and workers competed for jobs. The employment relation was not very stable because most firms were small and exposed to often quite violent economic fluctuations. The rise of mass production and economies of scale favoured the development of giant firms which sought to plan production and sales to a far greater extent. These firms competed for a dominant share of the stable section of product markets, enabling them to plan their capital investment and the building of their labour forces. As many of the skills required were specific to production processes used, internal labour markets became the preferred pattern of workforce organization; in this way, expertise based on work experience, as acquired in company-specific production processes, ultimately became more important than any skills acquired in occupational training. This more modern kind of production required predictable relations between managers and workers. Stability of production relations required also a certain stability of pay relations as pay became more the result of administrative decision than the interplay of labour supply and demand. In general, then, the employment relation became more stable, and employers gained a greater measure of clarity and predictability with respect to future career paths and wages.

3   The social wage structure theory: 'fair pay'
The third explanation is that the broad stability of wage structures over time derives from the way in which the pay of different categories is embedded in the social norms of 'fair pay' and in the power structure of any society (see Akerlof, 1982; Hicks, 1955, 1974; Kahneman et al., 1986; Wood, 1978; and Wootton, 1955). It is these factors which serve to insulate pay from labour market pressures to a very great extent. Fair pay also implies that other points of departure apply in addition to the relationship between supply and demand: there are social and normative judgements as well.

The wars of 1914–18 and 1939–45 were also periods of major change in social and economic structure, which could explain the coincidence of these periods with change in wage structures.

Contrasting the three families of theories, the great strength of the competitive theory lies in its ability to provide quantitative answers as to the levels of pay to be expected for different categories of labour, notably human capital theory, although it remains weak in explaining stability. The 'regulationist' theories score better on explaining stability than levels of pay differentials, as do the social and institutional theories of wage structure. Each seems to explain an important but different aspect of the phenomenon.

Table 8.10 *Summary of the main changes in wage structure, 1970–88*

Country	Dispersions 1970s	Dispersions 1980s	Occupations 1970s	Occupations 1980s	Industries 1970s	Industries 1980s	Male/female 1970s	Male/female 1980s
France	−	+('84)	−	+('86)	−	+('84)	−	−
Germany	−	n.a.	=	−('84)	+	+	−	−
Italy	−	n.a.	−	+('84)	−	+	−	?
Netherlands	?	++	?	n.a.	?	?	−	−
Sweden	−	+(83)	−	−	+	+	?	+
UK	−	++	−	++	−	+	−	+
USA	−	++	−/+	+	+	+	=	−

+ increase; − decrease; = not much change; +/− changes in different directions depending on categories; double sign, major changes; n.a. not available.
Where the turning points in trends are known to deviate markedly from the turn of the decade, the dates are indicated.

strong similarity of changes among countries, the main focus will be on the overall picture (see Table 8.10).

In all of the countries shown in Table 8.10, dispersions of earnings decreased during the 1970s, the strongest fall occurring in Italy. That was also the country in which earnings differentials between skill levels were most severely reduced. The other dimension of pay structure that displayed a fairly uniform reduction during the 1970s was the adverse differential against women's pay where notable improvements were achieved in the UK and the Netherlands. The picture for industry differentials was less uniform, with industry differentials declining except in Germany, Sweden and the USA, where they increased. Nevertheless, the rank order of industry pay levels remained virtually unchanged (see previous section). In the UK, the two most notable changes were the rise of coal mining wages, driven by a mixture of the first oil shock and two successful miners' strikes, and the demise of car workers' pay, arguably the victim of the successive oil shocks.

During the 1980s, the picture was less uniform than in the 1970s, but it was nevertheless predominantly one of increasing differentials on all of the dimensions shown except between females and males where the advance of the 1970s was checked, but on the whole, not widely reversed. In the UK, women lost some ground against men overall, in part because of the surge of pay in higher paid managerial occupations in which men are heavily over-represented. Also notable in Table 8.10 is the spread of dates from which pay differentials began to increase again. In the UK and the United States the watershed years are very much those of the turn of the decade, 1979–80. In most of the other countries, the switch occurred somewhat later, between 1983 and 1986.

4   The main causes of the change

The main factors for explaining the changes in pay structures during the 1970s and 1980s would seem to be the following:

- the oil shocks with their impact through rising unemployment;
- technical change which is partly autonomous, and partly driven by the increased competition;
- government policies to restrain inflation;
- union bargaining policies;
- employer remuneration policies;
- policies to promote greater equality of pay between women and men.

All of these pressures have been strong at various times during the two decades, although the simultaneity of their action makes it exceedingly difficult to disentangle patterns of causation. In reality, it was a complex interplay between economic and technological changes and the strategic behaviour of the various actors – the government, employers and interest organizations.

Unemployment

The rise of unemployment over the two decades was steady in France and Italy, but strongly fluctuating in the UK, Germany and the United States (see Figures 8.1 and 8.2). Changes in unemployment are only likely to affect pay differentials if they represent differential movements in excess supply of different categories of labour. If they affect all categories equally, then inflation-adjusted wages might fall in aggregate, but wages of one

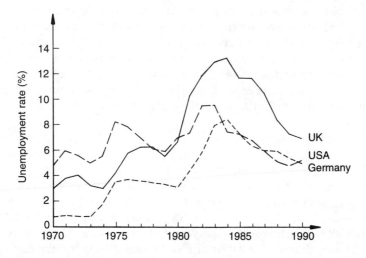

Figure 8.1   *Unemployment rates 1970–90 in (West) Germany, the UK and the United States*

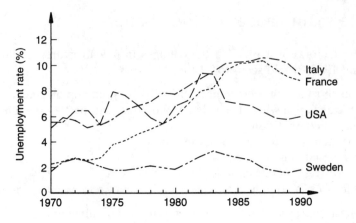

Figure 8.2 *Unemployment rates 1970–90 in France, Italy, Sweden and the United States*

category relative to another should remain unchanged. However, the impact could vary, for example, between skilled and unskilled workers because firms are more reluctant to lay off their skilled than their unskilled workers in a recession (Oi, 1962). This is because many firms invest in the training of their skilled workers, and because even qualified workers usually have to undergo a period of adaptation after hiring so that there is a delay before they are fully effective in their new jobs. Unskilled labour is usually more readily available and requires less preparation so employers can more easily afford to lay them off at the onset of recession and rehire later. An additional reason for such hiring policies is that providing a degree of employment security to skilled workers turns labour from a variable into an overhead cost, and this may induce employers to seek greater variability elsewhere, notably in unskilled employment. If firms tend to retain skilled and lay off unskilled labour at the approach of a recession, then the competition for unskilled jobs increases more than for skilled jobs, and so leads to a bidding down of unskilled pay more than for skilled pay. Hence, according to Oi, a rise in unemployment should produce an increase in the pay differentials between skilled and unskilled workers.

An alternative view, put forward by Reder (1955), argues that pay differentials should increase during a recession because the supply of skilled workers is more flexible than that of unskilled workers. Reder's model relies on the idea that access to skilled positions is mostly by upgrading, so that in a boom workers are upgraded to meet the increase in the demand for skilled labour, and in a recession, they are downgraded, the least skilled entering unemployment. This practice used to be common in the United States where it was called 'bumping'. On leaving a recession, new skilled positions are filled, and workers upgraded. As the boom continues, the pool of unemployed unskilled workers is progressively drained so that the supply of unskilled labour dries up faster than that of labour for upgrading to skilled jobs. In European countries, this model would seem to be more applicable in those firms which rely heavily upon upgrading to skilled positions, although generally, even in those countries in which such practices are more widespread, downgrading in a recession is much less common. Hence, Reder's model of differing movements in supply of skilled and unskilled labour may be less applicable in a European context.

Overall, one would expect, on both Oi's and Reder's theories, that pay differentials should have risen overall during the two decades, and in particular, have risen especially sharply at the time of the two oil shocks when unemployment rose most steeply (see Figures 8.1 and 8.2). However, short-run (year to year) changes in pay differentials prove to have been fairly insensitive to all but the steepest rises in aggregate unemployment. Only in the United States and the UK was there much evidence of cyclicality in blue-collar pay differentials, and even in these two countries the inverse correlation between pay differentials and unemployment change was really only visible in the 1980s. In the other countries, although there was an increase in occupational differentials and in dispersions during the 1980s, the timing of the changes does not coincide well with that of those in unemployment. This suggests a number of possible conclusions. First, that Reder's and Oi's hypothesis about the link between movements in aggregate unemployment and relative unemployment rates of skilled and unskilled workers is mistaken. According to Oi and Reder, unskilled workers are relatively harder hit by recession. It is possible that the rise of unemployment in some countries, notably the UK, was so severe in the early 1980s that whole plants closed down, cutting jobs for workers of all occupations. This may have been true of the US also, but it was not so severe in many of the other European countries. More detailed analysis of unemployment *changes* by occupation have proved very difficult on account of differences between the statistical concepts and occupational classifications used in employment and unemployment statistics (OECD, 1987). Nevertheless, there is some evidence that employers have developed systems that enable them to provide greater job security to their more valuable employees (for example, Atkinson and Meager, 1986), and it is common for employers to use natural wastage as a means of reducing their work forces, taking advantage of the higher turnover rates of less skilled and more junior employees.

Technical change

A second explanation for changes in the wage structure points to technological progress. There has been a shift in the demand for labour towards more skilled categories during the 1980s, and this has caused skilled pay to rise relative to that of the less skilled. The regulation school mentioned earlier also explains higher wage dispersions between occupational categories by pointing to the move from Fordist to post-Fordist production concepts (see Box 8.2).

Box 8.2 *The regulation school and post-Fordism*

The regulation school has its own insights to cast on the developments of the 1970s and 1980s. So-called 'Fordist' production methods depended upon continued acceptance by the workforce of a highly subdivided system of work organization and the oppressive nature of the work environment. This proved to be less and less acceptable to European and US workers during the 1960s, witness the growing proportion of immigrant workers in automobile production in France and Germany during the 1960s, and the problems of absenteeism in Sweden which triggered the famous Volvo experiments in work organization. To some extent, the crisis of industrial relations of the late 1960s and early 1970s was also a crisis for this pattern of work organization (Butera, 1974). The erosion of skilled workers' wage differentials was due in part to the erosion of the legitimacy of their status. As traditional ideas of skill gave way to skill based on on-the-job experience, semi-skilled workers saw less reason why they should be paid less. The challenge was strongest in Italy because there the changes had been most rapid and intense, and the immigrant workers in the factories, albeit from the south, were still Italian (Paci, 1973). The restoration of skill and managerial differentials in the 1980s, following these theories, then reflects a shift in management orientation away from large scale mass production to smaller and more flexible systems in which skill and quality play a larger role (Piore and Sabel, 1984). Post-Fordist production methods emphasize differentiated quality production for customer-specific demand. Management under 'Fordism' could rely on crude methods because the tasks to be undertaken were often relatively simple and standardized. When quality comes to the fore, and capital equipment is more sensitive, then management has to rely more upon winning the support and motivation of the workforce, hence its interest in more individualized remuneration systems (Reynaud, 1989).

The main shortcoming of these theories with respect to the changes in wage differentials in the 1970s and 1980s is that they rely heavily upon developments that occurred in a small number of important economic sectors, especially the automobile industry.

Although there are many reports of firms introducing new microprocessor controlled technology during the 1980s, and there is little reason to doubt that this is widespread, the impact upon the demand for skilled labour is less evident. It is clear that the technical knowledge demanded of some jobs has greatly increased, and that some former skilled jobs have been almost completely eliminated (for example, traditional draughtsmen eliminated by computer aided design). However, the balance of these two tendencies is uncertainty. One indicator of a shift in the demand for qualified relative to unqualified labour (for Great Britain, cited by Bean et al., 1987) is that both the relative pay and the employment share of university graduates has increased over recent years. This could then lie behind the increase in occupational pay differentials during the 1980s, as the pay differential of skilled over unskilled blue-collar labour rose, notably in the metal industry (CERC, 1988, 1989; Marsden, 1990c), as did that of higher paid white-collar workers over other groups.

Again, although the argument seems appealing in principle, it seems unlikely to provide the whole story as technical change is present in all of the countries; indeed, Britain's reputation is that of a laggard in this process, but the increase in occupational pay differentials began in Great Britain before it began anywhere else. In fact, the timing and the degree of increase of differentials differs greatly among countries.

Government incomes policies

By pursuing incomes policies, governments can affect wages and wage differentials. Indeed, this is precisely what governments did during the 1970s and 1980s. The two decades differed in terms of the basic policy premises, however. In the 1970s, the emphasis was on pursuing greater equality and protecting the wages of low paid workers; in the 1980s, the accent shifted to improving the labour market position of skilled workers.

One of the presumptions of the years of campaigning against inflation was that lower paid workers were hit hardest by price rises. Thus, it was felt that the low paid should be protected by allowing them larger proportionate increases than those allowed to the higher paid under government incomes policies. Such provisions were included in the incomes policies of the 1970s in the UK, and France at various points, but most strongly in the former. There the policies of the Conservative government of Edward Heath, and the following Labour government under first Harold Wilson and then James Callaghan involved at various points both provisions for maximum cash increases (for example, £6 per week under the Social Contract between 1975 and 1976), and the specification of levels of annual income above which no increase at all should be received. These policies squeezed pay differentials (Brown and Terry, 1978), and by virtue of the general limitations on percentage increases at other stages of the policy, prevented the higher paid from 'restoring' their differentials. In France, Prime Minister Barre's austerity package of 1976 included restrictions on increases for higher paid workers, but it applied only to a small proportion of earners. Government policies on low paid workers have also been influential. In France, the minimum wage (the SMIC) has been the government's main instrument for protecting the wages of low paid workers. Apart from major reevaluations in 1968 (+35 per cent), in 1973 (+12 per cent), and on the socialist government's election in 1981 (+10 per cent), there have been a series of minor nudges (*coups de pouce*) which have helped it maintain its role as an effective floor for earnings. Particularly during the 1980s, when the increments in the

SMIC were excepted from the general austerity imposed by the socialist government after 1983, the SMIC has compressed blue-collar pay differentials (Benveniste, 1987; Glaude and Hernu, 1986).

Both of these sets of policies held sway during the 1970s, and in Britain, at least, appear to have contributed to the reduction in pay inequalities. However, during the 1980s, government policies have tended to work in the opposite direction, encouraging employers to reduce the pay of the least qualified sections of the workforce. This time improving access to jobs was given priority over equality and decency of living standards.

In the United States, the Reagan administration's policy on the minimum wage was to allow it to decline slowly as a proportion of average earnings in order to prevent it from pricing low skilled workers out of jobs. It dropped from 43 to 45 per cent of average non-farm earnings in 1981 to 34 per cent by 1987.

In both the UK and France, public policies to boost youth employment may have helped to make lower pay more acceptable to young workers. In both countries, there are special employment and training schemes for unemployed young workers (in the UK the Youth Training Scheme, YTS, and now the Employment Training scheme, ET; and in France the Travaux d'Utilité Collective, TUC), both of which encourage employers to provide places for young workers who are paid a small allowance instead of a wage. Such schemes reduce alternative earnings available to young job seekers, as do restrictions on social security entitlements, so that their pay expectations are diminished.

Trade union bargaining policies

Even more than the government, the various interest organizations (employers and employees) are highly significant in regulating wages. Collective bargaining agreements determine a major share of the wages. Countries differ, however, as to the significance of collective bargaining. Specifically, trade union policies have been an important feature in West Germany, Italy, and Sweden, although one should also recognize the strong role of the unions in Great Britain and France in promoting some of the government policies just discussed. Indeed, in Great Britain, the Social Contract (1975–9) was the brainchild of the then leader of the largest trade union, the Transport and General Workers' Union.

In Germany, Italy and Sweden, collective agreements have a special role in setting minimum rates of pay. In Germany, firms which are not party to the collective agreement commonly still follow it, and in any case, the public authorities have the power to extend agreements if necessary. In Italy, industry agreements set minimum rates which are compulsory for all firms in the industry thus providing a form of bargained minimum wage. In Sweden too, collective agreements are strongly influential across most firms. This gives unions a great deal of direct influence on low paid workers' incomes, and has been used by the German unions, for example, to eliminate gradually the lowest pay levels from industry agreements during the 1970s. In Italy also in the late 1960s and early 1970s, industry agreements were progressively simplified by eliminating regional variation and reducing the number of separate industries and skill grades. Sweden, however, provides the most dramatic example of union policies to reduce wage inequalities in the LO's Solidarity Wage Policy. The union's argument was that workers should not subsidize inefficient firms by accepting low pay. Instead, the union should deliberately price labour out of low productivity jobs, and use labour market placement and retraining services to enable displaced labour to move to more productive employment. The policy was successful through the 1960s and into the 1970s when the whole philosophy of the Swedish model of linking wage bargaining to macro-economic coordination began to falter.

Seeking to reduce wage inequalities in industry level agreements always runs the risk that skilled workers will succeed in restoring their pay differentials at the plant and company level. Local skill shortages will often leave employers sympathetic to the demands of skilled workers for more pay, and locally conceded bonuses and other types of payment may compensate for reduced pay differentials in basic pay rates negotiated nationally. This indeed seems to have occurred to some extent in both West Germany and in Sweden. In West Germany the reduced skill differentials in industry-regional agreements during the 1970s contrasts with their stability in terms of earnings (Marsden, 1981). In Sweden, wage drift, arising from local bargaining over pay at the plant level, also threatened the achievement of goals set by national level bargaining (Gourevitch et al., 1984). However, unlike in Germany, the LO's policy on pay differentials, and those between white- and blue-collar workers caused a considerable compression during the 1960s and middle 1970s (Hibbs, 1990). Italy witnessed action at all levels during the 1970s. From the shop floor, after the emergence of a strong shop steward (*delegati*) movement from the Hot Autumn of 1969–70, there came strong demands for a reduction of the skill hierarchies in the work place from which newly arrived workers were excluded. The radicalized members of the rank-and-file argued that such hierarchies only served to divide and rule the workers. Under strong pressure from the newly militant semi-skilled workers, the skilled who had formerly dominated the unions gave ground; the skilled workers accepted *egualitarismo* in order to keep the semi-skilled within their own organizations (Santi, 1981). Apart from action on skill differentials, the unions also pressed for the amalgamation of the pay scales for blue- and white-collar workers, extending the compression up the hierarchy to include also foremen and junior white-collar workers.

As the pressure from the egalitarian wave was easing, the reform of the system of wage indexation, the *scala mobile*, introduced the idea of compensating workers for increases in the cost of living by means of fixed monetary increases, the same for all irrespective of their level of basic pay. This was introduced as part of the social contract of the mid-1970s when the Communist Party entered into tacit alliance with the Christian Democrats. The flat rate provisions of the new agreement between the employers and unions took effect fully from 1977, and with the unanticipated inflation that followed, there came a strong compression of all collectively bargained differentials. By the early 1980s, the amounts received from the *scala mobile* accounted for nearly half of the average worker's gross pay. The symbolic break came in October 1980 when the foremen and skilled workers at Fiat rebelled against the unions' line, and marched in protest against the erosion of their position in pay and in their unions.

Pressures on union bargainers for a 'restoration' of pay differentials for their skilled members built up in both Great Britain and Italy towards the end of the 1970s. The revolt at Fiat was symbolic of a wider discontent by more qualified workers, and stirred a more determined effort by the unions to regain the confidence of their skilled membership. However, modest attempts to adjust basic rates of pay in industry agreements in their favour in the early 1980s were insufficient to offset the strongly equalizing pressures of the indexation system, which for the unions, and especially the CGIL, remained one of the few tangible gains from the social contract of the mid-1970s. In 1983 and 1984, under the auspices of the then Minister of Labour, Signor Scotti, the unions and employers met to consider a reduction in the coverage of the indexation system. This seemed to end the compression of skill differentials and to set it into a modest reverse. In Great Britain, the revolt of the skilled took the form of increasing pressures within unions for a 'restoration of differentials' and subsequently, of a large scale electoral defection in the 1979 election from the Labour Party to vote Conservative for the first time.

Employer remuneration policies

Employers had more of the initiative during the 1980s to determine pay strategy than they had in the 1970s, when the overriding concerns were the fight against inflation, and adjusting to a radicalization of the shop floor.

During the 1980s, this greater initiative has taken the form of moves to restore financial incentives for skill and responsibility, and to allow management greater scope to link pay to the performance of both individual workers, task groups, production divisions and to the enterprise as a whole. In many countries they have sought to decentralize pay bargaining away from industry negotiations towards the company level. There has also been a move to centralize pay bargaining within the firm, reducing the autonomy of local managers to make concessions to shop floor representatives, particularly in Great Britain and Italy.

Two of the most discussed employer initiatives in remuneration systems have been those of linking pay increases to the performance of individual employees ('merit pay'), and those of linking pay to performance of the enterprise or a part of it, notably by profit sharing and employee share ownership schemes. Both of these policies represent a departure from the idea that pay should be largely determined by the demands of the job (the 'rate for the job') rather than by the particular efforts or qualities of the individual worker occupying it.

Merit pay has been most widely canvassed in Great Britain, France and Italy. In the two former countries, its spread is likely to have contributed to the increased dispersions of earnings, notably within occupations, and possibly also to the increase in occupational differentials as managements have often insisted that merit pay should be attributable in response both to individual performance and to market needs (CERC, 1989). It is now quite widely used according to surveys of employers: in the middle to late 1980s, in France some form of merit pay extended to nearly half of all employees and in Great Britain it was used in about a quarter of manufacturing establishments and about half of those in private sector services. In Italy, it is estimated that employers have managed to reduce the share of workers' gross pay that is fixed by collective bargaining at various levels from about 90 per cent to below 80 per cent as a result of the reduced coverage of indexation and greater use of merit pay (Dell'Aringa and Lucifora, 1990). Nevertheless, it is hard to assess how much merit pay has altered pay structures because it has generally involved only a small proportion of the pay of beneficiaries, except possibly among senior managers.

There are several reasons why the progress of merit pay should have been limited. First, unless it is based on an effective system of employee performance appraisal, it is likely that many employees will consider it arbitrary and unfair. Under such conditions, it is unlikely to increase motivation. Secondly, it can easily arouse union opposition as it is perceived as a means for management to undermine union loyalties: after all, a portion of the wages depends on one's own performance and not on the bargaining power of the trade unions. Without union support, again employee distrust is likely to be higher. Finally, good appraisal systems place heavy demands on management time and training, thus considerably raising the cost of introducing merit pay schemes.

Profit sharing and employee share ownership schemes have also increased in popularity among managers as a means of promoting an atmosphere of greater cooperation among employees, and of fostering greater employee commitment to the enterprise. They are regarded by some as superior to individualized merit pay which may cause rivalries among staff, and so reduce cooperation and flexibility as staff wish to take individual credit for success and fear work assignments in which they may perform less well. Evidence on the impact of profit sharing schemes on employee performance provides at best mixed support for it. There is some evidence that it may enhance productivity (FitzRoy, 1991), and there is some recent British evidence that employee share ownership schemes may help performance (Richardson and Nejad, 1986). Both kinds of scheme are likely to increase the amount of variation of earnings, and so could have contributed to the increase in dispersions, and in so far as more highly paid employees, especially managers, benefit more often from such schemes then they could increase occupational pay differentials.

Equal pay

The implementation of EU equal pay legislation had a significant impact in reducing the gap between women's and men's pay in Great Britain during the 1970s (Tzannatos and Zabalza, 1984). The 1970 Equal Pay Act, which came into force in 1975, provided only for equal pay for equal work, and so it still left British women with a smaller percentage of men's earnings than in other European countries, where the principle of equal pay for work of equal value was in force. The British law was challenged on the ground that it fell short of the European Union Directive on Equal Pay, and in 1983 it was amended to take account of equal value. Unlike the initial impact of the Act, the equal value amendment is yet to have any major impact on women's relative pay. One of the main reasons seems to be that equal value applies only within the same establishment, so that women employed in low wage establishments cannot claim equal value with men in high wage establishments.

5   Conclusion

This brief review of the causes of the changes in pay structures during the 1970s and 1980s highlights the variety of factors at work, ranging from the labour market pressures of supply and demand, through technical change, to government and union and employer policies. The diverse nature of the pressures, and the difficulty of disentangling their respective influences, mean that it is not possible to apportion a particular amount of the change in pay structures to any given factor.

Government incomes and union bargaining policies have not always had a simple and direct impact on differentials. Although the restriction of pay increases to a maximum of £6 a week in the first year of the British Social Contract (1975–6) appears to have caused a reduction in differentials, the average rate of increase was above that level. In Sweden, wage drift arising from local negotiations was always a threat to the integrity of the central bargainers. Thus, one cannot presume that deliberate policies of the main actors to alter differentials always achieve the desired results. Indeed, government, union and employer association policies usually require a degree of consensus over objectives if they are to be successful. Providing some general direction to pay negotiations usually requires a degree of central coordination, and the organizations providing this, be they unions, employers or governments, have to manage coalitions of groups with different interests. On the union side, pressing for reduced skill differentials requires the support or at least acquiescence of skilled workers, which in both Great Britain and Italy was eventually withdrawn. On the employer side, restraint usually means that firms that wish to pay above average increases in order to pay for greater productivity have to delay their programmes, which they are not prepared to do indefinitely. That is why, despite the principles set forth in the central policy, extra pay bargaining rounds are sometimes organized at company level.

So it seems that even if the most important actors undertake to pursue a well-considered policy to change the wage structure, we cannot assume that they will always reach their intended goal. Wages continue to feel the impact of market fluctuations, whether or not set in motion by techno-logical change. And at the end of the day, employers want to have a big enough margin within their own companies to pursue a company-specific wage policy. After all, their own wage initiatives during the 1980s were at times quite far-reaching.

9 Working time and time resource management

Willem de Lange

1 Introduction

If there is one subject that has aroused emotions in the field of industrial relations in the past few decades, it is the shorter working week. In some countries, former West Germany in particular, an impressive number of working days have been lost to strikes in favour of a shorter working week. That is not a new phenomenon in and of itself. Since 1870, the working week has slowly become shorter. At the start of the century trade unions took up the gauntlet of an eight-hour working day (Karsten, 1990), a goal achieved in most countries after the 1917 Russian Revolution. Employers and governments were afraid that revolutionary ideas would get the upper hand if social conditions led to unrest among the working classes. That is why they gave in to one of the most important trade union demands, the shorter working week (Lamers et al., 1989).

Since then the length of the working week has been a constant topic of debate and, at times, of conflict. In the 1950s and 1960s the working week as established in collective agreements was slowly cut back, first from six days to five when Saturday became a day off, and then to 40 hours a week. The number of paid vacation days also increased steadily. All these interventions led to fewer hours spent at work each year, on average. We will use the general term 'working time reduction' to refer to the reduction in the amount of time during which labour, whether paid or not, is performed during a specific period, measured either per day, per week or per year (for a further explanation, see de Lange, 1989).

This chapter will present a summary of the developments in the configuration of work in the 1970s, 1980s and, whenever possible, at the beginning of the 1990s. 'Configuration of work' is taken to mean arrangements concerning working time, operating or opening hours and working time patterns. It is not our intention to draw a complete picture of all of the relevant developments in this field in Europe. That would be impossible within the scope of this chapter. Our goal is rather to present a general picture of the most relevant events against the background of industrial relations. That is why section 2 will present some quantitative data, and section 3 will describe what has happened in this particular field in six different countries: Belgium, former West Germany, France, Sweden, Italy and Great Britain.

Section 4 will offer an explanation for the shift from collective working time reduction to more flexible working hours and longer company operating hours. This shift became evident in most West European countries in the mid-1980s. Recently the term 'time resource management' has become popular. Time has been 'discovered' as a manipulable factor of production by management. Time resource management increases the efficiency and effectiveness of organizations. The demands of the customers can be better satisfied by making working time more flexible. The past 20 years have seen the large-scale introduction of a great number of new working time patterns: contracts based on annual number of hours worked, the compressed working week, teleworking and so on. The configuration of work that emerges is a multifaceted one; the uniformity which characterized the *mise en scène* until approximately 1970 is behind us, once and for all.

2   Comments on the use of statistical material

For an initial and well-organized look at the configuration of work in Western Europe, we will make use of statistical material. This raises some (methodological) problems, however. The data are collected by numerous countries and institutes which by no means use the same definitions and methods of measurement. The data cannot therefore be compared just as they are.

This applies, for example, to part-time work and sickness leave. Certain countries set an upper limit of 35 hours for part-time work (Japan, Sweden, the United States), in other countries this is 30 hours (France, the United Kingdom), and still others classify any person who works shorter hours than normal as a 'part-timer' (Italy). The question pertaining to sickness leave is: when are sick employees included in the statistics? Does the first day of leave count or are employees only classified as sick after several days' absence? To what extent are those on long-term sick leave or those with an industrial disability covered by the statistics? In some countries maternity and parental leave are calculated as part of sick leave, but in others they are not. We must therefore interpret the data with caution. Whenever possible we will specify where definitions and other factors differ. The data are intended to serve, first of all, as an indication of the various trends over time and to point out striking differences between countries.

Another problem is that there simply are no data available in many countries. Shift work and operating hours are two 'infamous' examples. In the Netherlands and Germany, for example, there is a flood of statistical data available, whereas Italy and the United Kingdom offer only a trickle. Even the geographical areas to which the data refer should be viewed with the necessary degree of caution: the data discussed in this section were taken from the UK (that is to say, England, Scotland, Wales and Northern Ireland), but in section 4, because of the limited availability of statistical data, we will be describing the situation in Great Britain (England, Scotland and Wales).

To arrive at a satisfactory comparison of (actual) working hours, we must take a number of elements into consideration:

- the maximum number of working hours as prescribed by law and as set forth in collective bargaining agreements;
- overtime work;
- bank holidays;
- days off, paid vacation;
- absenteeism in all its possible forms;
- part-time work.

Unfortunately it is beyond the scope of this chapter to discuss all of these various facets in any detail. We will therefore restrict ourselves to certain significant themes: the legal, contractual and actual number of working hours, part-time employment, and operating hours. The remainder of this chapter will show that both unemployment and employment (especially as pertaining to women) have a major impact on the configuration of work.

We will, incidentally, not restrict ourselves in this section to the six countries discussed in section 4. A comparison that includes a few other countries (Japan and the USA) or which focuses on a larger unit (EU, OECD) produces points of reference.

3   Comparing working hours: statistical data

Working time

One of the most important gauges for working time is the number of hours worked per week. We must distinguish between what is legally permissible and laid down in collective bargaining agreements on the one hand and the actual number of hours worked on the other, including overtime. Table 9.1 shows the working week as prescribed by law and as set forth in collective agreements. In many countries there is a large difference between the legal maximum number of hours and the contractual number of hours. The legal specifications have been adjusted to conform with actual practice. In other countries, legislation has paved the way for changes in practice. France introduced legislation on working time reduction in 1981. The same occurred in Austria, Belgium, Luxembourg, Norway, Spain, Sweden and Switzerland in the 1970s.

Collective bargaining is generally more important than legislation in determining the (average) working week. Table 9.1 also shows that in countries where working time reduction has been introduced by law, the contractual working week in many sectors is shorter. The maximum number of hours permitted by law says nothing about the contractual working week. In countries with a high legal maximum, the contractual working week is no longer than in countries with a low legal maximum. Indeed, the big gaps between countries in the first column do not carry through to the second column. The European countries indicated are more or less consistent, but other countries in Europe, such as Switzerland and Portugal, have a much longer contractual working week.

Table 9.1   Legally prescribed and contractual working week

	Legally prescribed maximum[1] (1991/92)	Contractual bandwidth[2]
Belgium	40	36–39
France	39	35–39
Germany	48	38–40
Italy	48	36–40
Netherlands	48	36–40
Sweden	40	35–40
UK	–	35–40
Japan	46	40–48
USA	40	–

Sources: [1]ILO, 1989; [2]Eurostat, 1993

Table 9.2   *Developments in the contractual number of working hours and the number of hours actually worked, 1970–87*

	Contractual working time 1987	Percentile change in contractual working time 1970–80	Percentile change in contractual working time 1980–87	Actual working time per employee 1987	Percentile change in actual working time 1970–80	Percentile change in actual working time 1980–87
Belgium	1,759	−9.2	−5.0	1,550	−12.2	−3.0
France	1,767	0.0	−4.6	1,696	−9.5	−3.3
Germany	1,712	−5.9	−4.7	1,672	−5.6	−3.7
Netherlands	1,744	−9.1	−7.0	1,645	−8.2	−4.5
Sweden	1,796	−8.2	0.0	1,482	−11.7	+3.1
UK	1,782	−2.1	−4.6	1,730	−6.7	+2.4
Japan	2,121	−5.9	0.0	2,085	+3.1	−1.3
USA	1,916	−0.0	0.0	1,770	−1.0	+2.0

Sources: Bosch, 1989; ILO, 1989 (percentile change in actual number of working hours 1970–80 and UK in final column 1980–87)

Most collective agreements establish not only the number of hours worked per week, but also per year, including paid leave and bank holidays. There are major differences between countries on this point. Table 9.2 outlines the annual number of working hours established in collective agreements and changes in these figures.

Although the commotion raised by the introduction of a shorter working week in the 1980s was extraordinary, the actual reduction in the number of working hours was even more significant in the preceding decade. If we look more closely at the situation in the 1970s, we see that there was a sharp reduction in the first half of the 1970s in particular – a reduction that was not accompanied by labour unrest! Working time reduction was introduced more or less without a hitch. It almost seems as if the furore surrounding this subject had an adverse effect, but in reality the two oil crises and subsequent economic recessions blocked further progress in working time reduction for some years thereafter.

Belgium and the Netherlands saw the largest reduction in the contractual number of working hours between 1970 and 1987. This trend did not result in a much smaller number of hours in these countries than in others, however, because they started out with a relatively long working week; the reductions merely served to bring them into line with the others. Countries which saw smaller reductions (France, the UK) traditionally had fewer hours to begin with and are no longer exceptional in this respect.

More remarkable yet is that Sweden, by not introducing working time reduction in the 1980s, has the longest contractual working time among the European countries investigated here. In terms of the actual number of hours worked, Sweden's position is again exceptional, this time along with that of the UK. Unlike the other European countries, these two have seen an increase in actual working time; in the UK this has happened despite a reduction in the number of contractual working hours! This increase is largely due to overtime.

On average, the actual number of hours worked was reduced by only 4 per cent in the UK between 1970 and 1987. The high level of absenteeism means that in Sweden the actual number of hours worked is far below the overall average (see section 4). The gap between contractual and actual number of working hours in that country is huge: more than 300 hours. This may explain why Sweden did not introduce working time reduction in the 1980s. In general we can observe that the EU countries described here have presented a relatively consistent image from 1980 onwards. With the exception of the actual number of hours worked in the UK, these countries are more or less in line in terms of both the contractual and the actual number of working hours.

Operating hours

The attention given to operating hours and extended operating hours is a recent phenomenon. Hence, there are very few statistical data available, making longitudinal research impossible. In 1989, the European Union investigated opening hours and operating hours in the retail trade and in industry. Table 9.3 refers to the retail sector and shows huge differences in opening hours (see column 1). Shops in the UK are open longer than in the other countries, while German shops are open the least number of hours. There is only a two-hour margin in working hours, however. The Netherlands stands out as the only country on the list where the retail sector has not passed the 40-hour limit. In Spain and Portugal, retail trade working hours are much longer (43 and 44 hours respectively). All of the countries – in particular France and the UK – show a huge gap between opening hours and number of working hours.

Table 9.3   *Opening hours and working hours in the retail trade, 1989*

	Average opening hr per week	Average contractual working hr	Difference opening/ working hr	Reduced opening hr	Extended opening hr
Belgium	51	38	13	9	2
France	56	38	18	5	48
Germany	48	39	9	18	8
Italy	49	38	11	4	75
Netherlands	52	40	12	8	13
UK	58	39	19	5	59
Europe	53	39	14	9	38

Source: *European Economy*, March, 1991

Table 9.4 *Operating hours and working hours in industry, 1989*

	Average operating hr per week	Average contractual working hr	Difference operating/ working hr	Shift work	Reduced operating hr	Extended operating hr
Belgium	77	37	40	80	45	21
France	69	39	30	74	23	43
Germany	53	38	15	65	43	15
Italy	73	39	34	83	13	16
Netherlands	74	39	35	63	17	30
UK	76	47	39	73	24	43
Europe	66	39	27	70	29	26

Source: European Economy, March, 1991

Columns 4 and 5 indicate whether opening hours have altered in recent years. The figures refer to the percentage of businesses which have introduced either reduced or extended opening hours. The EU table includes businesses which did not respond (an average of 2 per cent), but these are not incorporated here. The results speak for themselves.

Asked to predict what will happen in the near future (1–2 years down the road), 27 per cent of the retailers questioned responded that they expected to see further extended opening hours. Almost no one expected a reduction. Bosch (1994) disagrees with the figure for Germany. He claims that researchers in Germany use a different method of measurement than in the others, and that West Germany is actually somewhat above the EU average. This debate once again underlines what was stated in section 2: we should proceed with caution when dealing with international comparative research. The same study in industry led to the results shown in Table 9.4.

As in the retail trade, there are major differences between countries, with Germany once again trailing behind and the UK forging ahead of the rest. Belgium has surpassed the British, however, with the Netherlands and Italy close at their heels.

The average contractual number of working hours shows only minor variations in industry, as it did in retail. The Netherlands has fallen into line with the rest and matches the European average, which is kept high by member states with a relatively low standard of living: Greece, Spain, Ireland, and above all Portugal. The position of Germany is particularly striking. Given the extraordinary degree of technological progress in industry in the Federal Republic, we would expect to see a relatively large amount of shift work and a large number of companies with extended rather than reduced operating hours. In fact, the opposite has occurred.

We would expect that a large difference between average operating hours and average contractual working time would be accompanied by exccssive shift work. Although this appears to be the case to some extent, it is by no means a hard and fast rule. In Belgium and the UK shift work is indeed quite common, but in West Germany it is relatively rare in industry. Italy relies on shift work to a major extent, but the Netherlands does not.

Another striking aspect is the number of companies that have reduced their operating hours in the past five years. On average this figure even exceeds the number of companies in Europe which have introduced extended hours. The discrepancy is very obvious in Belgium and West Germany in particular, whereas in France, the UK and to a lesser extent the Netherlands more companies have introduced extended hours.

We can probably attribute the reduction in operating hours to working time reduction to a large extent. Whether operating hours were reduced or not depended on the type of reduction introduced (see, for example, Great Britain in section 4). As far as we know, there has not yet been an international comparative study on this subject.

Working time patterns

The phenomenon of shift work has led us to the subject of working time patterns. Slowly but surely, statistical material has become available, some of it useful for international comparisons. Table 9.5 shows the number of temporary contracts for full-time and part-time employees. It shows that there are large differences

- between full-time and part-time employees: except in Germany (1991), part-timers are much more likely to be employed on temporary contracts;
- between countries: in Belgium, the UK and Italy temporary employment is relatively rare, whereas in France and Germany it is more common;

Table 9.5 *Proportion of wage and salary earners in temporary employment, categorized by full-time and part-time status*

	Years	Full-time	Part-time	Total
Belgium	1983	4.1	19.5	5.4
	1991	3.7	13.9	6.1
France	1983	3.2	4.3	3.3
	1991	8.7	21.1	10.2
Germany	1984	9.7	12.3	10.0
	1991	9.5	9.4	9.5
Italy	1983	4.9	54.1	6.6
	1991	2.9	50.0	5.3
Netherlands	1983	3.8	13.4	5.8
	1991	5.2	12.9	7.7
UK	1983	3.1	15.2	5.5
	1991	2.4	15.0	5.3

Source: OECD, 1993

- (for a number of countries) between the 1983 figures and the 1991 figures. France in particular has seen a sharp rise.

Nevertheless, overall growth between 1983 and 1991 was slower than one would have expected. A sharp rise in the number of temporary contracts seemed to be a natural consequence of the emphasis placed on flexible working practices in European countries, but except for France no such increase was seen. In several countries the number of temporary contracts even declined! One possible explanation for this might be the economic recession. After all, in periods of recession, the employees on contracts for a specified period of time lose their jobs first, and those that survive the cuts generally have contracts for an indefinite period of time. An expansion in personnel is generally approached with great caution; in other words, by contracting a large number of temporary employees.

One type of contract that we should consider within the context of this chapter is the part-time contract. The importance of part-time work for the emancipation of women and for the re-division of labour was acknowledged early on. Table 9.6 clearly shows how this trend has developed.

The figures for the various countries cannot be compared just as they are because, as we indicated in section 2, not every country uses the same definitions. Nevertheless, we can draw a few conclusions from the enormous differences between countries. There is, for example, a striking contrast between the extremely high percentage of part-time employment in the Netherlands and the very low level of part-time employment in Italy. Other southern European countries – that is, Spain and Greece – follow Italy's example. The parallel between part-time work and working hours is also striking. Countries whose average number of contractual working hours is high have a small percentage of part-time jobs. The reverse is not always true, however. Italy and Luxembourg have relatively few part-time jobs, but their working hours are average for the EU.

The Netherlands take a leading position in more than one respect. For both men and women the number of part-timers is exceptionally large.

Table 9.6 *Part-time workers as a share of the total workforce*

| | Women | | Men | | Total | |
	1983	1992	1983	1992	1983	1992
Belgium	19.7	27.4*	2.0	2.1*	8.1	11.8*
France	20.0	24.5	2.6	3.6	9.7	12.7
Germany	30.0	34.3*	1.7	2.7*	12.6	15.5*
Italy	9.4	10.5	2.4	2.7	4.6	5.4
Netherlands	50.1	62.2*	7.2	16.7*	21.4	34.3*
Sweden	45.9	41.3	6.3	8.4	24.8	24.3
UK	42.4	44.6	3.3	6.1	19.4	23.3
Japan	29.8	34.8	7.3	10.6	16.2	20.5
USA	28.1	25.4	10.8	10.8	18.4	17.5

Sources: OECD, 1993; *OECD, 1991

This position was attained within a very short period of time. In 1977 the Netherlands still occupied a modest position on the list. The growth in part-time employment can be attributed to the decline in overall employment, particularly full-time employment, at the beginning of the 1980s. From 1981 to 1985, the number of full-time jobs held by men declined by 4 per cent and by women by 6 per cent. The number of part-time jobs, on the other hand, grew by 33 per cent and 32 per cent respectively.

Various countries show evidence of relatively rapid growth, especially when we consider the short period of time during which such growth took place. In addition to the Netherlands, that has been the case in Belgium, Germany and France. Sweden has a long tradition of part-time employment. Remarkably, however, in the 1980s the number of part-timers declined. The same trend occurred in a few other OECD countries, for example Denmark, Finland and the USA.

Table 9.6 also reveals that the growth in part-time employment was not restricted to women alone. In almost every country, men also took up part-time work more frequently. In some countries, for example Denmark, the Netherlands and the UK, the increase in male part-time employment led to a decline in the share of overall part-time employment held by women (OECD, 1994).

4   Six countries: a survey

Introduction

This section will describe the situation in six countries, including Sweden. In many respects Sweden is an exception when it comes to the configuration of work and labour market policy in Europe. The main focus will be on developments in legal and contractual prescriptions concerning working time and working time patterns between 1975 and 1990. The descriptions and the statistical data presented in the previous section serve as a basis for the analysis in section 5.

(West) Germany

In the 1970s and 1980s, former West Germany served as a pathfinder on almost every front with respect to the configuration of work (Bosch, 1988/1989; Bosch et al., 1988/1989; de Bruin, 1979; Lallement, 1988/1989). It did not always assume this role without a struggle, however. The issue of working time reduction in particular gave rise to pitched battles, some of them quite fierce. After the economic recession set in around 1975, employers refused to cooperate further in reducing the number of working hours. From 1950, the annual number of hours worked had gradually fallen from 2,316 (1950) to 1,737 (1975). A further reduction would mean dropping below the 40-hour working week, a move which companies labelled irresponsible. We can see how heated the controversy surrounding this issue became by the number of working days lost to strikes: more than 11 million between 1975 and 1985. Almost all of the conflicts were related to working time reduction and flexible work. In the preceding 40 years, 7 million days were lost to strikes and neither of these issues had been the focus of strike action.

In Germany, as in the Netherlands, the metal industry set the trend in collective bargaining. In 1978–9 this sector endured a 6-week-long strike related to the 35-hour working week. Partly because employers succeeded in closing ranks, the unions were unsuccessful in their bid. Their only victory was the introduction of early retirement and an increase in the number of days of paid leave.

The unions were divided on what the following step should be. After a while, however, it became clear that the measures that had been agreed were not enough to stem the tide of unemployment. That resulted in a new offensive in 1983 in favour of the 35-hour working week. Employers, on the other hand, wanted more flexible working hours and extended operating hours. In the spring of 1984 the disagreement erupted into a surprisingly bitter struggle, especially in the printing sector and the metal industry. Unions in the first called a national three-month-long strike, while the metal sector struck for six weeks. It was the most serious industrial conflict since the Second World War. Finally employers gave in and working time reduction was introduced. From 1 April 1985 the working week was shortened to 38.5 hours. An interesting difference between Germany and the Netherlands is that in Germany the 38.5 hours were taken as an average per company whereas in the Netherlands the working week was set at 38 hours per employee. Individual employees could work between 37 and 40 hours. In this way, employers still managed to gain a measure of flexibility. The length of the working day could vary, as long as the average number of hours over the course of two months did not exceed 38.5. Further arrangements were left to the company's works council.

In the years thereafter, working time reduction, flexible work and extended operating hours continued to be important collective bargaining issues. The atmosphere was much less strained, however. The various interest organizations began to realize that their demands would be met if they were prepared to make concessions themselves. In 1987, for example, the printing industry and metal sector, once more setting a trend, negotiated new agreements in relative harmony. The core of these agreements was the introduction of a flexible 37-hour working week as of 1 April 1989. The metal industry went the furthest in exploiting the possibility of flexible work. The working week of individual employees varied from 36 to 39 hours, and the length of the working day could vary as well. The average over a period of six months was not to exceed 37 hours. These margins allowed management more room to manipulate working and operating hours. They also explain the intense interest in the new phenomenon of time resource management.

Another remarkable fact related to this collective agreement was its period of validity: three years. This brought peace to the labour front and that alone made all of the various parties happy . . . until 1989, when prices jumped 3 per cent, exceeding the wage rises agreed.

In 1990, the same sectors again concluded agreements for a longer period. Wages were not included, however – there were to be separate wage bargaining rounds every year. The agreement provides for a 36-hour working week in 1993 and a 35-hour working week in 1995, in this way achieving the ideal level proposed by the unions in 1978. The unions were, however, made to promise that they would not raise the issue again until 1998. Once again, concessions were made on the issue of flexible work and wages. Thirteen per cent of the employees may volunteer to work a 40-hour working week (without receiving overtime compensation). The collective agreement also provides for sabbatical leave, variable working hours and parental leave. We will not discuss these in detail here.

We can see how trendsetting these industries are when we compare them to the rest of Germany. In 1994 the average contractual working week in Germany came to 38.14. With an average of 1,667 working hours a year, Germany nevertheless presently has the shortest contractual working time in the world.

Before 1990, the year of Germany's reunification, East and West Germany differed sharply with respect to contractual working hours: East Germany exceeded West Germany by some 300 hours annually. The high level of sickness-related absenteeism in the DDR, however, meant that the difference in actual working time was considerably smaller. Rejecting the idea of a 'low-wage country' within Germany's borders, the unions brought pressure to bear and the differences were rapidly evened out. In many sectors the standard working week has been reduced to 40 hours. Nevertheless, Bosch expects that Germany will remain a divided nation with respect to employment conditions until the year 2000 at the very least. The former DDR simply lagged too far behind West Germany to be brought in line any sooner. In 1991, for example, a metalworker in East Germany earned only 40 per cent of what his counterpart in the West took home.

We have seen here that working time reduction, extended operating hours and flexible work are closely intertwined. The period of time within which a company must reach a certain average is becoming longer and longer, sometimes being extended to a year, such as in the metal industry. More and more opportunities are being created to work evenings or on Saturday. A form of working time reduction that is growing increasingly popular is the shorter working day. The company operating hours are extended to 70 hours per week by introducing two shifts of 2 × 7 hours, five days per week. The unions find this an attractive alternative because it allows them to reduce working hours to 35 per week. Employers also find it attractive. West German industry is technologically highly advanced. Capital-intensive companies must be in operation for longer hours if they

---

Box 9.1   *Volkswagen's 1993 collective bargaining agreement*

The economic crisis at the beginning of the 1990s had a very definite impact on Germany and influenced the configuration of work in a number of different sectors. Volkswagen is a good example.

At Volkswagen, the dramatic decline in automobile purchases in 1993 threatened to lead to mass redundancies. Some 30,000 Volkswagen employees were to be made redundant. At the end of 1993, the company reached an accord with the unions which attracted a great deal of attention. As of 1 March 1994, 100,000 employees began to work a four-day working week of 28.8 hours; in return, the company promised that it would not force any employee to become redundant for a period of two years. The reduction in working hours meant a 10 per cent drop in wages, which meant losing the '13th month' bonus, holiday pay and other secondary employment terms. The base monthly salary remained at the same level. The agreement will remain in effect for a period of two years (Ministry of Social Affairs and Employment, 1994).

---

are to be profitable. Longer operating hours can improve a company's competitive position. (See Box 9.1.)

The description above makes no mention of the German government. That is typical of German post-war industrial relations. Terms and conditions of employment are negotiated collectively at sectoral level and, to a lesser extent, at company level. Facing each other across the bargaining table are the employers' associations and the trade unions, both of which are generally close-knit and well-organized. Neither party is afraid to use whatever means it has available, including strikes and lockouts. In March 1991, the Bundestag adopted a new Law on Working Hours (*Arbeitszeitrecht*). The old law dates from 1938, and a number of its provisions from 1981. The most important amendments concern creating more scope for flexible work practices, the individualization of work, Sunday work and the equal treatment of men and women. The international competitive position plays an important role in the new law.

Great Britain

One of the most notable features of the British situation[1] is the extremely modest degree to which working time is subject to any type of regulation whatsoever (see Garnsey and Roberts, 1988/1989; Rubery et al., 1990). Indeed, there are no generally applicable restrictions placed on working hours for adult males. Women and children have been legally protected since the nineteenth century, but it is precisely in this area that deregu-

---

[1] My thanks to Mr P. Blyton and Mr C. Gratton for their contribution to this section of the chapter. It is reiterated that this section applies to the situation in England, Scotland and Wales only, owing to a lack of statistical data for Northern Ireland.

lation has recently been introduced. Right now only children aged 16 years and under and subject to compulsory education are still subject to legal protection.

There are some indirect protective measures, for example the rules pertaining to lorry drivers and to opening hours for shops, banks and other organizations. Nevertheless, Great Britain, which also lacks legislation governing paid leave, is without a doubt the champion of voluntarism. This has been more than confirmed within the context of the European Union. The rejection of the EC's draft Directive on working hours (part of a broader Charter of Fundamental Social Rights of Workers, the Social Chapter) by the UK government in 1991 has put the country into an exceptional category. Working time arrangements – organized by day, week, year or over the course of a lifetime – are laid down in collective bargaining agreements or by custom and practice. Employers are not obligated to adhere to the collective agreements that apply to their sector, but they usually do. The agreement governing the metal industry has once again been the trendsetter. In 1947 the industry introduced the 44-hour working week, in 1960 the 42-hour working week, five years later the 40-hour working week and finally, in 1979, the 39-hour working week. Most of the other sectors followed its lead. Collective agreements include provisions pertaining to the number of days of paid leave and the number of hours to be worked per week. Sometimes they also provide for shift work, overtime, and work on Saturdays and Sundays, but such provisions generally focus on the financial side of these issues: the extra pay. In general there are no restrictions on the actual number of hours, an important point in the context of the evolution in working time, as we will see below. Another point is that there has been an obvious shift in collective bargaining away from the sector to the company level. This shift has made it possible for companies to make working time arrangements that best suit their specific situation. Employers' associations have taken on a different role. Instead of a contracting party, they are becoming advisory bodies.

Another important development is that a decreasing number of employees are actually covered by collective agreements. This trend is related to a shift in employment from the secondary to the tertiary sector, which is regulated more by tradition and custom than by collective agreements.

Great Britain suffered serious setbacks during the economic crisis at the beginning of the 1980s, reaching an unemployment figure of 12 per cent. After 1983 the economic tide turned, but there was no improvement in the labour market situation. Unemployment remained high for a number of years. Encouraged by the economic recovery, large groups of newcomers entered the market, particularly women. In previous years they had been discouraged and remained on the sidelines. In addition, there were increasing signs of an old and truly British phenomenon: overtime work increased dramatically. Partly as a result of this trend, productivity per employee rose sharply, so that growth in production did not lead to more jobs during the early years of the economic recovery. Core personnel were expected to carry an increasingly heavy burden.

Having now sketched the context, we can focus our attention more specifically on the configuration of work. As a consequence of the excessive number of overtime hours, the number of actual hours worked in Great Britain is relatively large. Even in 1981, when the recession was at its worst, male production workers worked an average of 4 hours a week of overtime. In 1988 this had risen to 6 hours per week, bringing the actual number of hours worked to its highest level in the 1980s. There was no improvement in the 1990s. In 1992 the contractual number of hours worked averaged 39 hours per week, but the actual number (in the month of April) came to an average of 44.5 (Blyton, 1994). More than 15 per cent of the workforce generally work more than 48 hours per week. (See Box 9.2.)

The annual number of days of paid leave is no smaller than in other West European countries. Most collective agreements provide for 4–5 weeks of holiday, with a growing tendency to exceed the 5-week limit. Neither does Great Britain differ excessively from the others when it comes to the contractual number of hours worked per year. It is overtime in particular, then, which gives Great Britain its exceptional position with respect to the annual number of hours actually worked.

If we consider the length of the working life, we see that the British employee works a relatively long time. The most important reasons are:

- the relatively small number of people who go on to continuing and higher education – the majority of employees enter the labour market early on in life;
- the advanced age of retirement, which delays staff departures;
- the rather high participation rate of both women and men in the labour market.

The foregoing should not lead us to assume that the British trade unions are very powerful. In fact, the opposite is increasingly the case. The crumbling power of the trade union movement means that work is becoming more flexible. In the private services sector, extended operating hours play an important role. The Shops Act allows stores to remain open later in the evening, on Sundays and on bank holidays. An increasing number of companies are making grateful use of this opportunity. Banks have extended their opening hours to Saturdays, and have introduced a wide variety of flexible work, including overtime, weekend shifts, rotating working days, staggered working hours, contracts for specified periods of time, on-call contracts etc. Staff who work irregular hours do not always receive compensation pay, and it is female staff in particular who work on the basis of flexible contracts.

The public and semi-public sector has been dominated by traditional working time patterns, but even here flexible work is making inroads. More and more hospital staff work part-time and schools are increasingly

Box 9.2   *Developments in working time in Great Britain, 1979–90*

The debate on working time reduction was much less tumultuous in Great Britain than in most of the other EU member states. In 1979 the TUC (Trades Union Congress) argued for a 35-hour working week, 6 weeks of paid leave, early retirement and restrictions on overtime. But the TUC does not take part in contract negotiations, and its arguments were little more than a declaration of intent. A further point is that certain sectors (specifically the tertiary sector) and professional groups (civil servants) had already introduced a working week of less than 40 hours, robbing the TUC's plea for working time reduction of wider support. Most of the unions have adopted a pragmatic attitude, supporting working time reduction only if it fits into the overall package of employment terms. Wages are still the unions' greatest priority, with working time as the most important non-pay issue (Millward et al., 1992).

The metal industry is a front runner on the issue of working time reduction. In 1979, after strike action had been initiated by the AEU (Amalgamated Engineering Union), the 39-hour working week was pushed through. Once the metal industry had dropped below the 40-hour limit, almost all other sectors followed. The 39-hour working week became the new standard. Few sectors introduced further reductions. An exception was the printing industry, which introduced a 37.5-hour working week after a strike in 1981. Some companies went further than the provisions set forth in the sector agreement, trading working time reduction for flexibility, extended operating hours or other things. Some employers viewed it as a painless, one-off way of reducing personnel. Sectors supported by a high level of technological development were particularly keen to introduce working time reduction in more extreme forms in several firms, although they were not prepared to do so collectively for the entire sector.

The biggest reductions in working time took place between 1981 and 1984. After this period the pace slowed considerably as a consequence of the economic recovery. Companies that restricted reductions in working time to one hour a week generally used this hour on Friday afternoon, decreasing both working time and operating hours. Companies that introduced further cuts in working time sometimes implemented other major changes in the configuration of work, including contracts based on the annual number of hours worked (annual hours contracts) and other forms of flexible work, shift work and weekend work.

In 1990, 13 per cent of full-time manual workers had a basic working week of below 39 hours. The most notable development in working hours in recent years has been seen in the engineering industry (Blyton, 1994). In 1989, the Confederation of Shipbuilding and Engineering Unions (CSEN) started a campaign of industrial action for a further reduction of working time. In November 1990, the union had reached agreements with over 1,200 firms (for instance British Aerospace and Rolls-Royce) concerning working time reduction, mostly to 37 hours. This is seen as an interim step to achieving a 35-hour working week.

making use of contracts for a specified period of time. More unusual is the situation of state-owned companies which have been or will be privatized. To make these companies more attractive to investors, the government has attempted to cut costs, in part by introducing flexible work (see Box 9.3). These efforts have met with resistance, however. The unions have mobilized railway employees (against flexible schedules), miners (against the 6-day working week) and postal workers (against Sunday shifts).

Still, compared with other countries, Great Britain does not have an abnormally large amount of atypical work. The number of employees on contracts for a specified period of time is relatively small. On the other hand, many employees work irregular hours, not so much at night, but in the evenings and weekends, including Sundays. This, and overtime, have made it possible to extend operating hours to a considerable degree.

Box 9.3   *Use of Japanese management techniques and intensification of working time*

Management is presently emphasizing the intensification of working time by making use of Japanese management techniques (such as *kanban* and just-in-time). Blyton (1994) reports that a relatively large number of collective bargaining agreements have supplementary provisions attached to them concerning the transfer of duties between shifts, for example changing and washing outside of working hours. This is known as 'bell-to-bell working'. Other arrangements concern staggered breaks and refreshment breaks at the work station.

In general, Blyton concludes that intensification of working time and the increased utilization of the working period received more attention than temporal flexibility. We can also mention the compressed working week consisting of 12-hour shifts, a system which is not permitted in most other European countries but is very common in Great Britain, largely because there is a singular lack of regulations there with respect to maximum number of working hours and minimum periods of rest. For example, a company like Frigoscandia may order its workforce on an 84-hour working week for several weeks a year! In the mining industry 12-hour shifts reduce the time lost in transporting miners below ground and back. Only two shifts descend per 24-hour period instead of three. Blyton is correct in questioning these practices. It is highly doubtful whether it is responsible to work such long days, certainly considering the heavy work involved.

Looking at the overall picture, we may conclude that the changes in the configuration of work in Great Britain were not excessively drastic. In general, a major turnabout failed to materialize, while existing trends endured. The contractual number of working hours was reduced, the trend toward flexible work grew, and deregulation in this area gained momentum.

The British configuration of work can be described as liberal, pluriform, pragmatic and conservative.

- Liberal because there are very few regulations and because fewer and fewer employees are covered by collective agreements.
- Pluriform because of the new working time patterns introduced in the past few years and because of the tremendous variety between and even within individual sectors.
- Pragmatic because agreements governing working time, flexibility and operating hours are generally linked to one another and to other employment terms and presented as an overall package. The point of departure is usually the specific situation within a single company or industry at that particular moment, leading to customized agreements.
- Conservative because compared with most other West European countries, Great Britain is by no means a trendsetter in the configuration of work.

Belgium

The economic crisis set important changes in motion in Belgian industrial relations at the beginning of the 1980s. The most visible among them were changes in the configuration of work (Leroy et al., 1988/1989).

A series of interprofessional agreements gradually shortened the working week to 40 hours in 1975. The first oil crisis prompted a serious debate on the shorter working week which focused on the redistribution of labour as a means of creating employment. In 1976, both the catholic and socialist union confederations announced that they wanted to reduce the working week to 36 hours. Their attempt to do so in 1977 under the terms of an interprofessional agreement failed. The failure to arrive at a central agreement signified a break with a long-established tradition (a tradition which had also played an important role in maintaining social stability).

After 1977, unemployment continued to rise hand over fist. This led after 1981 to a more active role on the part of the government, although unions and employers' associations were still involved to some extent. The most striking measure was the '5-3-3' operation. Unions and employers were to arrive at collective agreements providing for a 5 per cent reduction in working time, a 3 per cent cut in wages and a 3 per cent increase in the number of jobs. The results of this measure were also disappointing.

It is at this point that the 'Hansenne experiments' enter the picture (named after the Minister of Labour and Employment). By combining working time reduction and restaffing, companies were allowed to deviate from labour laws and collective agreements. Many of the companies involved introduced some form of compressed working week. Weekend shifts were particularly popular. For example, companies switched from semi-continuous to continuous shift work by having two crews work two weekend shifts of 2×12 hours. At times the weekend crews were forced to work on Fridays as well, increasing their average working week to 30 hours.

In 1987 the Hansenne experiments were replaced by legislation governing the introduction of new working schemes in companies. The Hansenne experiments were the jumping-off point for this legislation, which provided a more solid legal basis for the introduction of new working time patterns. The new law made it possible, for example, for General Motors in Antwerp to introduce a 6-day working week based on two daily shifts of ten hours each. Employees worked 11 days straight in a three-week cycle. The average number of hours was cut back to 36.4 a week.

It is important to note that, both in the case of the Hansenne experiments and in the case of the 1987 Act, unions and employers' associations continued to play an important role. Specifically, they were needed to approve any deviation in standard working time arrangements. It is true that between 1983 and 1987 the emphasis shifted from working time reduction to extended operating hours. There was no change in the actual goal, however, which was to use measures such as those discussed above to reduce unemployment – a goal which seemed impossible to achieve.

Government measures to stimulate employment were largely ineffectual. This does not imply that the configuration of work did not undergo changes, however. As early as 1981, an interprofessional agreement was reached providing for the introduction of a 38-hour working week, further promoting a trend which began in the 1950s. Economic growth had gradually led to a shorter working week. From 1965 to 1975, the pace increased thanks to the economic boom. The extent to which working time reduction was linked to the economy became very obvious in the years thereafter. The process stagnated in 1980 but political pressure jump-started it again, as described above. (See Box 9.4)

This policy was continued in the 1990s. In November 1993, the Belgian government presented its 'General plan for employment, competitive power and social security'. The essence of the plan is to drive down unemployment by means of a redistribution of labour (once again). Companies are being called upon to draft business plans aimed at stimulating employment, for example by means of compressed working weeks, annual hours contracts, shift work, part-time pension plans, restrictions on overtime, part-time employment, collective working time reduction and sabbatical leave.

Once a business plan has been approved by the Ministry of Labour and Employment, the company has a sum of 100,000 Belgian francs (approximately £2,000) deducted from the contribution it pays into social security for each additional job created (Ministry of Social Affairs and Employment, 1994).

The outline presented here has made it clear that Belgium offers companies a relatively large number of opportunities to extend operating and opening hours. The law covering this area is much more liberal than in many other EU countries. Another important observation is that unions and employers' associations both play an important role in regulating

---

Box 9.4 *Operating hours in the Belgian retail sector*

Belgian regulations governing opening hours are much more liberal than those of its neighbouring country, the Netherlands. There is in fact no law prescribing shop closing times. Shopping hours are generally determined locally. In general terms this means that shops may remain open until 8.00 p.m. from Monday to Thursday and on Saturdays, and until 9.00 p.m. on Fridays. One notable feature is that shops are classified according to size so that small retailers have a better chance of surviving competition from larger stores. Large grocery stores may not open on Sundays, whereas smaller shops are allowed to open their doors for a few hours. Shops of whatever size may open a few Sundays in the year, but they are obligated to remain closed at least one working day every week.

---

working time, although the government has been much more active in the field in recent decades.

France

France experienced a sharp increase in flexible configuration of work in the 1970s (see Boulin, 1988/1989; Lallement, 1988/1989; Michon, 1987; Taddei, 1988/1989). The trend expressed itself in particular in a variety of non-permanent contracts, but employers put pressure on employees to make 'regular' work more flexible as well. The economic recession hit France in 1975 and unemployment grew by leaps and bounds. At the end of the decade the rising level of unemployment led to demands for a redistribution of labour by means of working time reduction. This debate was not linked to flexibility, however, and the two issues remained separate.

When macro-economic interventions proved ineffective, France turned in 1980 to a policy of regulating and reducing working hours. The agenda for interprofessional bargaining included working time as an issue for the first time in 1981. The most important breakthrough came in 1982, however, when legislation was passed establishing the 39-hour working week. Companies were to introduce this shorter working week in subsequent years, and labour and management were to thrash out the details. The government hoped to encourage the negotiating partners to agree on even further reductions. At the same time, the number of days of paid leave was increased to 25 and limits were placed on overtime work. Even the use of non-permanent contracts and temporary employees was restricted. Flexible working hours were preferred to flexible employment contracts.

In the years thereafter, the bargaining parties did indeed engage in frequent negotiations on the subject of working time reduction. In addition, the bargaining level shifted markedly from the sector to the company. In 1985 the 39-hour working week became a fact in industry, but its impact on employment was extremely disappointing. The entire operation was ultimately viewed as a failure in this respect, and the bargaining partners lost further interest in working time reduction. The only measure that continued to make good progress was early retirement, but it proved to be a financial drain on the government. The disappointing results meant that forms of flexible work rose in popularity at the expense of the shorter working week.

Such was the climate when the Delabarre Act came into force in 1986. By then a change of government had taken place, made obvious in this piece of legislation: the rules governing the length of the working week were made more flexible. The working week could be extended to 41 or 42 hours without any form of compensation being paid, as long as the average number of hours per week remained at 38 or 37.5 respectively. The law established a direct link between flexibility and working time reduction.

The Delabarre Act did not last long, however; in 1987 it was replaced by the Seguin Act. No longer was there a link between flexibility and working time; instead, the law paved the way for further flexibility. The most important points covered in this Act are as follows.

- The working week could be extended to 44 hours, provided that the average week calculated over the course of a year did not exceed 39 hours; the 44-hour limit could be exceeded in collective agreements.
- Employers and employees could establish modular systems by collective agreement, granting employees a certain minimum number of working hours per year, and allowing an increase in this number as required by the employer or employee.
- Collective agreements could provide for Sunday work for economic reasons (Sunday work for economic reasons was forbidden before then).
- Women were henceforth permitted to work nights.
- Legal specifications governing breaks were abolished (except for minors under 18).
- Industry was given the opportunity to introduce weekend shifts similar to the system used in Belgium (12-hour shifts on 1 or 2 days).
- The bargaining partners were given the right to make further agreements on flexible work.

It will be clear that the Seguin Act went a long way in the direction of deregulation and flexibilization. In the years following the introduction of this law, companies made grateful use of the opportunities it presented. In 1987, 42 per cent of the almost 7,000 collective agreements arrived at included provisions governing working time. Most of these provisions concerned greater flexibility and extended operating hours. The average length of the working week scarcely changed.

Very little has changed in the interim. In their 1989 central agreement, employers and employees continued to adhere to the policy set forth in the 1987 Seguin Act; the only exception was that the shorter working week was dusted off and put on display again. Employees proposed reduced working hours as a possible concession on the part of management in exchange for flexible work or longer operating hours. The government had the same idea; its employment plan of September 1989 awarded fiscal benefits to companies that shortened their working week without shortening operating hours.

The economic crisis of the early 1990s has led to a 'Five-year Act Governing Employment' which came into force in December 1993. The purpose of the law is to create employment, for example by lowering the cost of labour, by introducing flexible working practices and collective working time reduction, and by stimulating part-time employment. All of this is entirely in keeping with the 1987 Act. One striking feature is the experimental working time reduction scheme in relation to flexible working practices. Companies wishing to take part in this experiment must reduce working hours by at least 15 per cent with an accompanying salary reduction (not specified). A minimum of 10 per cent additional staff must be hired. In return, the government will make a sizeable contribution to the company's social security expenses. In addition, the company can allow weekly working hours to fluctuate along with peaks and lulls in production, provided that agreement has been reached on this matter in the relevant collective bargaining agreement (Ministry of Social Affairs and Employment, 1994).

Looking at the above, we may conclude that the configuration of work has been a very important issue in France since 1982, playing a leading role both in legislation and as a bargaining issue. The government was responsible for two important breakthroughs. The first came in 1982 when it made the 39-hour working week obligatory, overcoming the 40-hour psychological barrier. The second was in 1987, when it introduced far-reaching measures encouraging flexible work and extended operating hours. These two milestones also marked a shift in political thinking. The emphasis at the beginning was on employment through the redistribution of labour. When this approach failed, the accent shifted to ensuring efficiency and effectiveness in trade and industry, in the hope that this would have an indirect effect on unemployment.

Despite the important role of government in encouraging and steering such changes, the actual configuration of work will henceforth be determined at the industry and company level. In fact, the law supports this move. Bargaining outcomes (and, incidentally, legislation) show that in the 1980s, employers were more successful at protecting their interests than employees. Low union density and union fragmentation are particularly to blame.

More than in other EU countries, developments in France have been determined by politics. As a consequence, these developments have been more turbulent. The past few years have seen a trend toward liberalization, resulting in more variety in working time patterns.

Italy

We can distinguish three phases in post-war Italy on the issue of the configuration of work (Garonna and Reboani, 1989; Gasparini, 1988/ 1989). In the first phase (1945–75), working hours were standardized and rigid. The emphasis was on protecting and improving the position of the employee. That is why in collective bargaining, trade unions deliberately tried to restrict the freedom of employers to vary working hours or introduce differences between groups of employees. In the 1960s, Italy's robust economy led to a tight labour market. The trade unions occupied a position of power and were able to make demands. As a consequence, overtime and 'alternative' contracts, for example part-time contracts and contracts for a specified period of time, were subject to restrictions. There was also progress made on the issue of the shorter working week, which the unions included in their struggle to improve employment terms and protect employees.

Italy was hard hit by the first oil crisis and experienced large-scale unemployment, particularly among women and young men. Companies found their competitive position worsening by the day and their profits decreasing. In macro-economic terms, inflation was just as big a problem as unemployment. In short, the various interest organizations and the government all had an interest in working together, avoiding conflict and introducing changes.

This brings us to the second phase. To give the weakest groups a chance in the labour market, the unions softened their position on rigid and standard working hours, clearing the path for an increase in part-time and other working time patterns. The shorter working week also became an important issue. Employers did not view working time reduction as negative because it allowed them to lower the cost of labour. Redundancies could be avoided, slowing the rate of increase in unemployment. The government not only contributed by participating in tripartite negotiations, but also introduced a number of statutory measures. The most important of these was the Cassa Integrazione Guadagni (CIG), implemented in 1975 specifically to serve as a weapon in the war against the economic crisis. The CIG governed working time reduction, allowing sectors or regions that had a temporary overcapacity to suspend all or part of a company's production for a while. During the period of suspension, employees received curtailed wages which were supplemented by a government benefit. By getting involved in the requests for CIG applications and in the CIG's implementation, the trade unions were able to influence the industrial restructuring process. This made it possible for them to force concessions on issues like the shorter working week, training, employment and so on.

It was generally accepted that the CIG played an important role in surmounting the economic crisis, but the measure was called into question during the third phase. The system protected those who already had work against unemployment, but provided fewer opportunities to newcomers to the labour market, meaning women and young people. In addition, bureaucratization became a problem. Anyone who wanted to make use of the CIG had to follow all kinds of rules and procedures. The trade unions began to lose their grip and the government viewed the intensive use of the CIG as an increasingly ominous problem. The financial burden created by the measure became a millstone around their neck and added to the budget deficit. There were calls to alter the CIG from all sides. Only employers resisted any change, as the current system allowed them a wide measure of flexibility.

In 1983 Italy began to recover gradually from the effects of the economic crisis. Inflation was reined in, profits rose and investments grew. Production did not increase enough to raise employment to an acceptable level, however. The unemployment rate rose to 11 per cent in 1988.

In 1983 the government, labour and management arrived at a central agreement which provided for a shorter working week and longer operating hours. The agreement was that the annual working time would be reduced by 40 hours over the course of 1984/5. This agreement followed the example set by the metal industry in 1979 and the textile industry in 1981: reductions in the number of hours worked would be agreed on a year-by-year basis. In subsequent collective bargaining rounds, the parties did in fact generally agree to a working time reduction of five days, and employers were given the opportunity to extend operating hours. The general consensus was that reducing the number of working hours barely made any contribution to economic recovery, though it made the labour market more flexible. It was popular neither among employees nor among employers, at least not any more. It disappeared from the agenda, making way for flexible work, not only as a response to the economic crisis, but as a permanent bargaining issue. The increase in the number of atypical working time patterns, which began in the second phase, continued unabated and was given the legal seal of approval in 1984. This trend also encouraged early retirement or semi-retirement.

The reduction in working hours took on the following proportions during the three phases described. In the first phase, reductions were quite far-reaching. In industry alone, the contractual number of working hours dropped from 2,000 to approximately 1,800 per year between 1970 and 1975. In the second phase the process stabilized, to be continued from 1982 on, but at a more measured pace. In fact, the actual number of hours worked increased during the final phase! Another feature is that the differences between sectors grew less significant, especially in the 1970s. That was equally true of the differences between white-collar and blue-collar workers. The greater degree of uniformity with respect to the reductions themselves was countered by the increased variety in working time patterns.

If we attempt to describe the situation in Italy in just a few key words, then 'regulatory' and 'conservative' are the first to spring to mind. Even though the country has witnessed slow but steady progress in the field of flexibility and differentiation, it is by no means a trendsetter, especially when compared with most other West European countries. As in France, the government played a dominant role.

Sweden

The Swedish situation is unique in several respects, even by West European standards (see Petterson, 1988/1989).[2] Unemployment levels have been very low for quite some time, partly thanks to the government's extremely active labour market policy. The participation rate of women is extremely high. Almost half (48 per cent) of the working population in Sweden is female. The powerful position of the trade unions is also highly significant. More than 80 per cent of employees are organized. The largest trade union, the LO, is closely allied with the Social Democratic Party, which has been in power, almost without a break, for the past 50 years. Against this background it is certainly no mystery why the trend in working time, especially the shorter working week, has followed a different course in Sweden than in the other countries discussed in this chapter. Working time reduction in Sweden has never been linked to the redistribution of labour. It gained ground first as a means of protecting workers; then, from the 1950s onward, it was linked to improvements in welfare. This link was never broken, and in this way too, Sweden differs from the rest of Europe after 1975.

The 40-hour working week became standard in 1973 and was established by law in 1982. Since then, most sectors have reduced the contractual number of working hours. Shift workers work an average of 35–38 hours a week. For day-time employees, only the banking and insurance industry is an exception in having introduced a shorter working week.

In 1978, the majority of collective bargaining agreements provided for 25 days of paid leave, a number set by law in 1982. There has been a great deal of progress on this issue since then. At the present time 40 per cent of employees have more than 25 paid days off. There is little possibility of collective working time reduction at present, except perhaps for shift work.

Sweden is also exceptional when it comes to the actual number of hours worked. After 1981, the number of hours actually worked per employee increased. Opinions differ as to why this happened. Some say that the most important reason was the reduction in the upper marginal tax rates. Others point out that real wages declined between 1975 and 1983, causing employees to 'catch up' by working longer hours. Another possibility is the increased demand on the labour market. Finally, we should mention that the tax system makes work outside the home an attractive alternative for women. All of these factors probably contributed. The actual number of

[2] I would like to thank Mrs B. Vighurd for her comments on a previous version of this section of the chapter.

hours worked is, in fact, no higher than in other West European countries, thanks to various forms of leave (see Box 9.5), the large number of days off and part-time work. Taking account of these factors, the average number of hours actually worked drops below 1,500 annually, the lowest among Western industrialized countries (see Table 9.2).

Box 9.5   *Measures targeting work and family in Sweden: parental leave and childcare*

With respect to leave, we should first of all mention leave related to childcare, which accounts for 3 per cent of all cases of absence. Swedish legislation on childcare, which came into effect in 1974, surpasses all others. Parents are currently allowed to take 15 months of leave at 80 per cent of their salary and three months at 50 per cent of their salary. The government is responsible for implementing the law and making the payments. The right to parental leave is not restricted to women alone. Men are permitted to take leave as well, or it can be shared between the two partners. One of the parents must take at least one month that is otherwise not granted to the other. There is another sense in which this law has shown itself to be very flexible and highly advantageous to parents: leave can be stretched out over a longer period of time (until the child reaches the age of eight) or taken up in combination with part-time work. If parents have 'used up' their leave, they can still absent themselves from work for 25 per cent of the time, counted as unpaid leave. Until a child turns 12, the parents are also allowed to take time off if the child becomes ill (to a maximum of 90 days per year), and their wages on those days will only be reduced by 10 per cent. The extent to which Swedish society encourages the participation of women in the workforce becomes obvious when we look at their child-care arrangements. The government guarantees childcare for all children between the age of 1 and school-age. More than 80 per cent of all children up to the age of 7 currently make use of this arrangement in one way or another.

The excellent provisions and high rate of participation of women have not (yet) led to complete equality between the sexes. We can see this by looking in greater detail at the ratio of men to women according to job level, and by considering the distribution of full- and part-time jobs. Compared with other countries, the number of men working in part-time positions is relatively high (8.4 per cent in 1992: see Table 9.6). The number of women who hold down part-time jobs is much higher, however (41.3 per cent). Nevertheless, part-time work is thought to have an emancipatory effect and is encouraged. That is why part-timers with a job of 17 hours a week or more have the same rights as full-time employees.

A special form of part-time work is flexible retirement. Employees who have reached the age of 61 may cut the number of hours they work each week, and receive 65 per cent of their regular salary for the hours not worked. This arrangement was extended in 1980 to include the self-employed.

The schemes described above are without exception highly advantageous to employees, but they offer little or no compensation to companies with respect to flexible work or longer operating hours. Sweden still upholds a general ban on night work from midnight to 5 a.m. (with certain exceptions), and overtime is restricted to 200 hours annually. On the other hand, there is no prohibition placed on Sunday work. Employees must have 36 uninterrupted hours of rest each week; the days themselves are unimportant.

Bargaining partners are allowed to deviate from these rules and agree to implement more flexible forms of work, and indeed, employers and employees often do. Civil servants, for example, work longer hours in winter than in summer, and in the metal industry there is a more flexible agreement concerning overtime.

Even night work can be arranged by collective agreement. This opportunity was partly responsible for the increase in night work, weekend work and irregular shifts in the 1980s. One-third of employees work on Saturdays and/or Sundays (either occasionally or frequently) and more than a quarter have irregular working hours. It is striking that women are more likely to have irregular working hours than men. Such work is usually associated with the tertiary sector – many shops are open until 8 p.m. (or later) and on Sunday. There are no legal restrictions governing opening hours.

Our observation must once again be that most of these arrangements, both statutory measures and collective agreement provisions, are greatly to the advantage of the employees. As indicated previously, the government frequently contributes financially to maintaining such schemes, and this has led to a relatively high tax burden. Overall taxes account for approximately 55 per cent of Sweden's GNP! Attractive social systems have their dark sides as well. The situation in Sweden can therefore be typified as employee-oriented. The Swedish model can also be described as progressive and regulatory. Nevertheless, the tide does seem to be turning in Sweden. Unemployment is no longer almost unheard of. 'Regular' unemployment has risen to 7 per cent, and a comparable part of the labour force is enrolled in employment projects. A major part of this group is locked into a vicious circle: from unemployment to retraining, from retraining to temporary work, and then back to unemployment again. Measures to stimulate employment are no match for what is in Sweden an extremely high unemployment rate.

Other developments also indicate that a change is under way. For example, the number of days of paid leave established by law had been increased to 27 some years ago, but has now been brought back down to 25. Another suggestion has been to raise the legal retirement age from 65 to 66 or 67. Early retirement used to be possible at 60 years of age; this has now been raised to 61. Finally, we should mention that the maximum number of overtime hours has been raised from 150 to 200 hours a year.

5 Analysis

Working time reduction

If, in a few decades, we look back on the evolution of the working week, then the years 1975–93 are more likely to be identified as a period of stagnation than as a period during which great strides were made with respect to working time reduction. In a sense that is remarkable, if we consider how industrial relations in various European countries were dominated by battles over the shorter working week. If we look more closely at the past few decades, however, then we see that they can be divided into four different phases. The first began in the 1950s and featured the 'spontaneously' shorter working week (Boulin, 1988/1989). Prosperity was on the rise, leading not only to greater profits, investment and wages, but also to a reduction in the annual number of hours worked because of an increase in the number of days of paid leave, the introduction of the five-day working week and the shorter working day. Bit by bit, the 40-hour working week became a fact and was hailed as the new standard. It seemed that a 'natural floor' had been reached; at the very least, 40 hours constituted a psychological barrier.

About 1975 the process began to stagnate, not only for psychological but also for economic reasons. The economic recession, brought on in part by the first oil crisis, made further improvements in employment terms impossible. Most countries in Europe found themselves struggling with rising unemployment, plummeting profits, inflation, a growing state budget deficit and an unfavourable balance of trade. Many saw the shorter working week as an important instrument in the fight against recession. The trade unions were unanimous on this score, but governments (depending on the party in power) and employers resisted. In general, it was the employees who took up the banner of the shorter working week, with West German employees leading the way.

Large-scale strikes in 1979 ushered in the third phase. The issue of the shorter working week became dominated by the redistribution of labour. With or without the help of government and/or statutory regulations, the process of cutting back the number of working hours was started up again and the 40-hour limit was broken. The hoped-for impact on employment never materialized, however. In 1981–2, the economic crisis was at its height and the unemployment rate recalled memories of the 1930s. Even after the tide had turned, employment still failed to climb back up to acceptable levels, undermining the credibility of the shorter working week as a policy instrument (Baglioni and Crouch, 1990). Employees saw higher profits but at the same time an increase in work pressure, and no positive results in terms of employment. Consequently, only a few countries could be mobilized to fight for a further reduction in working time. The third phase ended about 1985. From that year on, the issue of working time came to resemble the first phase again; in other words, it became just one more issue among many to be negotiated periodically between employers and employees.

The most striking thing about this summary is how heavily the issue of working time is dominated by macro-economic developments. This is not surprising. Working time does after all fall under terms and conditions of employment, and these terms and conditions are determined by economic developments. In particular, we might mention the major role played by the 1973 and 1979 oil crises. The first led to the start of the economic recession, put an end to the luxury of full employment in many countries and caused progress in working time reduction to stagnate temporarily, albeit indirectly. The second crisis marked the beginning of mass unemployment and, precisely for this reason, led to new advances in working time reduction.

Flexibility and extended operating hours

In general we can divide the history of flexible work into the same phases as those used for working time reduction. Until 1975, there was little movement on this subject. Working time patterns were highly rigid and uniform. There were of course deviating patterns, for example part-time work and temporary jobs, but for the majority of employees permanent, full-time jobs were the rule. In addition, there was very little variety within organizations, with the exception of shift work. Working time and working time patterns were not even considered a policy issue by employers. This state of affairs changed in 1975. The number of new working time patterns increased and rapidly found general application. In addition, employers increasingly began to insist on more flexible approaches to staffing. During the third phase (1980–85), when working time reduction became a major bargaining issue, employers in many countries (including Belgium, West Germany, Italy, the Netherlands and to a lesser extent France) saw it as a chance to introduce flexible work and extended operating hours.

After 1985, the shorter working week became less of a bargaining priority, but employers nevertheless continued to promote greater flexibility and extended operating hours. They had begun to realize just how important the configuration of work is for management. 'Time resource management' was the new battle cry. Flexible work and extended operating hours showed up on the list of bargaining issues each year like clockwork. We should be cautious in drawing conclusions, given the scarcity of reliable statistical material on this point, but it seems that there has been a shift in the nature of flexibility. If in the third phase the emphasis was on a variety of different temporary arrangements (external numerical flexibility), after 1985 the accent shifted to the flexible use of permanent employees, both in the form of functional flexibility (employees competent in carrying out a range of different tasks) and internal numerical flexibility (varied working hours). The role of national governments has been to create the conditions to do so, specifically by relaxing legislation. For example, women are now able to work nights and there are greater opportunities to work at the weekend. The weekend shifts introduced in Belgium and France are typical examples.

One of the most important points of debate with respect to operating hours has been work on Sunday. In most countries Sunday work is still prohibited by law (*Der Arbeitgeber*, 1988). The United Kingdom and the Scandinavian countries of Denmark, Finland and Sweden are the most important exceptions. Where prohibitions do exist, however, Sunday labour is permitted out of technical or social necessity. The debate between employers' associations and trade unions focuses on whether Sunday work should be permitted for economic reasons. The law or licensing policy in various countries (Belgium, France and the Netherlands) has become less stringent, so that Sunday work is now allowed in these countries for economic reasons.

The opportunities for flexible work and extended operating hours are increasing everywhere; a wide range of different working time patterns has arisen; and the decentralization of collective bargaining and break with working time reduction gives organizations the opportunity to seek best-fit solutions for their own specific situation. The overriding idea comes down to business economics: strengthening the company's competitive position by making better use of capital goods and by responding more rapidly (for which, read flexibly) to the market.

There are countries that deviate to some extent from the picture sketched above, of course. This is particularly true for Sweden and Italy, where flexible working time patterns have not increased as dramatically as in other countries, at least not yet. In Sweden we can attribute this hesitancy to the tight labour market, which does not give employers the room to introduce less attractive patterns. In Italy the trade unions have stemmed the tide of all-too-deviant working time patterns, although they have been less insistent on standardization since 1975.

The extent to which the ideas surrounding flexible work have also undergone a change becomes apparent if we look at a number of OECD publications (Michon, 1987). In 1973, flexible work was still dominated by the idea that individual employees should have a free choice (flexible working hours). In 1982, flexibility was seen as the flexible use of capital and labour to achieve greater efficiency within companies.

Technology, the economy and the labour market

Technical advances have fuelled efforts to extend operating hours and, whether in conjunction or not, have prompted a shift in working time patterns. Automation has increased the capital intensity of the production process. In addition, rapid technological advancements have shortened the economic life cycle of capital goods. Companies are being forced to make more intensive use of their capital goods (in other words: for more hours during a fixed period of time). Weekend work in Belgium and France is an obvious example. Nevertheless, practice is more recalcitrant than theory. In so far as we can determine from the limited data available, our impression is that shift work, for example, has not increased dramatically in the past few years. The compressed (4-day) working week, another working time pattern that makes extended operating hours possible, has had a very slow and drawn-out introduction.

Teleworking is perhaps the clearest example of a working time pattern associated with technology – but it also confirms the statement that practice lags behind theory. Toffler (1980) forecast a spectacular explosion in teleworking in the 1980s, but these predictions did not materialize then. Even now, teleworking is still used on only a very limited scale.

More dramatic has been the influence of macro- and micro-economic developments on the configuration of work. In macro-economic terms, the dramatic shifts in employment played a highly important role. Unemployment was the motor driving the shorter working week in the first half of the 1980s. When working time reduction failed to bring about the hoped-for increase in employment, it was quickly dropped as a policy measure. We should mention, however, that the shorter working week undoubtedly made an indirect contribution to economic recovery, if not a direct one. In most countries, the shorter working week was coupled with a reduction in real wages or with more moderate wage demands, in any event. In addition, smaller staff numbers (reduced by working time reduction schemes) made it possible to increase worker productivity. Companies recovered their revenues and consequently their room for investment, bringing a halt to the economic decline and clearing the way for economic recovery. It is impossible to quantify the effect on employment, but we may safely assume that working time reduction contributed to this recovery.

At the company level, it was a decrease in the return on investments that first prompted efficiency measures. In fact, many sectors welcomed the shorter working week, seeing it as a chance to cut back on their workforce without suffering too much (and without tarnishing their image). Also important was that competition became fiercer in a number of markets, partly because trade barriers were being lifted. In addition to efficiency, there were greater demands made on quality and flexibility. There were also the following related developments.

- The life cycle of many products (for example, audio-visual equipment) is becoming increasingly shorter; companies must be able to switch as soon as product innovations are introduced.
- Customers are making more demands on products, and their demands are becoming more specific; this implies a large measure of product differentiation and customized production.

- Delivery times are becoming shorter and shorter, making more rapid routing and turnabout times necessary.

In addition to the extension of operating hours discussed previously, these developments have forced organizations to expand or cut back on capacity, depending on fluctuations in production and sales (numerical flexibility), and to ensure that their personnel can take on a variety of tasks (functional flexibility). Numerical flexibility is possible by making use of a variety of arrangements for temporary work (employment contracts for a specified period of time, help from temporary employment agencies etc.), but also by being more 'flexible' when it comes to hiring and firing personnel. The 'hire-and-fire' approach is an accepted phenomenon in the United States. The average period of time that an American employee remains with the same employer is considerably shorter than in Japan or Germany, for example, and external mobility (changing employers) is much higher (Bosch et al., 1988/1989). The large gaps in the social 'safety net' mean that employees who have been made redundant must find other employment as quickly as possible, if necessary even accepting a cut in pay. This also explains the relatively low number of long-term unemployed and the extensive degree to which men and women both participate in employment, making for a highly flexible labour market.

Experts have pointed out the consequences of these changes in working time patterns and the contractual conditions of employment for the segmentation of the labour market. Most countries have seen an increase in the number of 'precarious jobs', as they are called, particularly in small production firms (sweatshops) and in the services sector (Baglioni and Crouch, 1990). The labour force has been divided in two. On the one hand, we have a group of employees with permanent employment contracts, legal protection, a secure income and skilled work. These employees are the core of the company, and are referred to as 'core workers'. On the other hand, we have a group with the opposite characteristics, known as 'peripheral workers'. This group has a low union density, meaning that the trade unions are faced with a dilemma: should they champion the interests of their members (who already have a stronger legal position) or show their solidarity with the weak? Their decision becomes obvious when we consider their stance on the shorter working week in the 1980s. They were clearly less insistent about working time reduction in the latter half of the decade, mostly, as we indicated, because the effect on employment was ultimately disappointing. However, pressure from their rank-and-file, who were not prepared to make still further concessions in exchange for a shorter working week, played a role as well. In the majority of countries (Germany was an exception), the trade unions decided in favour of the material interests of their members.

Bosch et al. (1988/1989) distinguish the following three further lines of demarcation.

1   *Between civil servants and workers*   In a number of countries where white-collar civil servants have their own unions or where the 'unions of workers' are weaker, white-collar employees work shorter hours than their blue-collar colleagues. This is true in the United Kingdom and Portugal, for example.

2   *Between large companies and small firms*   In some countries (the United States, Japan), collective agreements do not cover smaller firms, so that employees there work longer hours, sometimes much longer, than the employees of large companies, where collective agreements do apply.

3   *Between job categories*   The division between core and periphery workers mentioned previously is more subtle when it comes to the number of working hours. Skilled employees, especially at staff and management level, usually work long days, do not take up all of their paid leave and work weekends. This group consequently does a great deal of overtime work, both paid and unpaid.

Industrial relations and the role of the government

Baglioni and Crouch (1990) have observed that throughout Western Europe, industrial relations and politics are becoming increasingly intertwined. Governments intervene more often and more actively than before. That is why we will be discussing these two spheres of influence in conjunction in this section.

Baglioni's proposition seems to go a step too far, however. In Sweden, for example, trade unions and government have always been closely involved with each another, while in the United Kingdom the government has not altered its highly passive stance, at least with respect to the configuration of work. Nevertheless, we must accept his proposition for the majority of West European countries, certainly if we consider the period 1980–87. Statutory regulations on working time in the various countries of the European Union are being harmonized. Table 9.1 shows that there are still major differences in the maximum number of hours that an employee is legally permitted to work each week. The current widespread trend toward deregulation and destandardization has, somewhat paradoxically, led to legal harmonization in a number of countries. Recent changes in legislation in Belgium and France and the new regulations being prepared in Germany and the Netherlands are highly similar, at least in character. The emphasis is on expanding the opportunities for flexibility and extended operating hours by increasing the maximum number of working hours per day and per week, and by relaxing licensing requirements for Sunday work and for night work for women (Bosch et al., 1988/1989).

Legal harmonization does not mean harmonization in actual practice, however. The extent to which countries still differ in actual practice became apparent in the country studies covered in section 4. The discrepancies become obvious when we look at differences in the contractual and actual number of working hours, and in working time patterns, for example flexible work in Belgium and France, overtime in the UK, and informal work in Italy. Each country has its own specific patterns and will no doubt retain them for the time being. In summary, then, we can say that there have been more or less general trends (working time reduction, flexibilization, expanded operating hours and governmental deregulation) on the one hand, and a large measure of variety in the concrete shaping of these trends on the other. With regard to deregulation, the prevailing opinion seems to be that the protective role of government and legislation governing working time can be diminished. Regulations continue to be necessary to combat certain excesses, specifically in the informal economy. But for the majority of employees, the end of the 'second wave' (Toffler, 1980) has carried them to a situation in which the protective hand of government can rest somewhat more lightly on the shoulders of society.

6   Epilogue

For researchers investigating the configuration of work, the 1980s were an exceptionally exciting decade thanks to major advances in this field. International comparative research is extremely important: participants in national debates, whether political or scholarly, often defend their standpoints by referring to foreign countries. Unfortunately, the arguments presented are rather careless at times; they fail to take into consideration the context in which certain developments have arisen, and they tend to focus on a single development and ignore the rest, even though such trends clearly have a reciprocal impact etc. In short, the comparisons and arguments rest on incomplete information. It is of course beyond the scope of this chapter to provide a complete picture; the material is much too complex and all-encompassing. An attempt has been made here to sketch the most important developments and to provide a reliable picture of the various contexts in which these developments have come about, in the hope of increasing the reader's understanding of the material in this way.

   For the time being, the emphasis in the configuration of work will be or remain on flexibility and extended operating hours as opposed to the shorter working week. It may be that the recent events in Germany and France will encourage further reductions in working time in Europe, but on the other hand, Japan and the United States, which lag behind in this respect, will probably inhibit further progress. European countries with longer working times, such as Portugal and Switzerland, can be expected to reduce the working week to 40 or 38 hours, at least as regards the contractual number of working hours. Within the context of European unification, statutory regulations on working time will be harmonized further. It is not unlikely that the majority of EU countries will pass more or less the same legislation on this matter during the 1990s.

   The actual number of hours worked will probably continue to differ dramatically from one country to the next. Such 'traditions' as overtime in

Great Britain are deeply rooted. They are furthermore bound up with the wage structure and are more difficult to regulate (if regulation were indeed desired). We can also expect to see greater variety in the area of working time patterns. Employers learned the value of time resource management in the 1980s. Taking advantage of the benefits presented by this concept means greater pressure to decentralize collective bargaining. And we can realistically predict that their efforts in this direction may at times be accompanied by the introduction of a shorter working week.

10 Labour relations, organization and qualifications

Arndt Sorge

1 The societal effect approach

The societal effect (SE) (*effet sociétal*) approach is based on one central proposition: whatever happens in one sector of society is always connected to events or to structures in other sectors. This means that social institutions such as industrial relations are related to other institutions such as vocational training, education, work organization, organizational structures, the legal system, politics, social stratification, and so on. The approach which we will be applying here emphasizes the role of social actors, but these actors always operate within specific social structures, and the choices they make can be explained by looking at these relatively stable social structures. The purpose of this chapter is to explore to what extent one can substantiate the central proposition of the SE approach empirically. We will discuss a number of comparative research projects at the company or meso-level. Research into organizations has revealed that differences in the way that companies (or governmental institutions) are organized can largely be attributed to differences in size, in the technology used to transform incoming goods, people or information ('inputs') into products or services ('outputs'), in the degree to which the company depends on its environment, and in the nature of this dependence. In addition to this technological and economic effect (contingencies), there is also a country or societal effect. For example, if we compare companies from different societies (countries) which resemble one another on the variables 'size', 'technology' and 'dependence', then we will still find differences in how they are organized. These differences are specific to that particular society. They do not arise by coincidence, but are systematically interrelated. Indeed, these interrelations should also form an object of investigation. The nature of the mutual connection should be specified: are the variables dependent or independent, which variables apply, or is there interaction, reciprocal influence? The SE approach defends the proposition that social institutions exercise a reciprocal influence on one another. The interaction between them – the societal effect – has an impact on how companies are organized and differs from one society to the next. Research into the societal effect starts with a somewhat static analysis focusing on the existence or non-existence of momentary but nevertheless temporarily stable social structures and connections. On the other hand, it is undeniably true that societies undergo social, economic and technological change. The question then is to what extent these changes are also subject to the societal effect. We will deal with this question in the following chapter. The present chapter is based on a comparative study of companies and social institutions in Great Britain, Germany and France. Most of the available research material was drawn from these countries. Readers are encouraged, however, to think about the interaction between companies and social context – in other words: the societal effect – in their own countries (and differences between their own country and the countries being discussed).

2   Methodological and conceptual aspects of cross-national comparisons

Key terms

Employment is given shape within the context of an industrial relations system. This system, in turn, is shaped by the relationship between the government, employers and employees. The institutional structure – the system that emerges as a result of such activities and which makes these activities and the relationships between the various parties durable – is to some extent specific to the particular sectors of industry, companies and corporations. The resulting variety is related to differences in the size of the company, in the socioeconomic circumstances surrounding it and in the strategies pursued by the relevant actors. Institutions are also rooted in the wider society, however, which is relatively independent of such factors. In general the sources of this variety in industrial relations systems are usually differentiated in the following way.

- Universal factors, such as the economic, technological and organizational objectives and strategies of the various actors; in theory these factors apply to each country in the same way.
- Societal factors, such as laws, norms and customs, the balance of power, values and priorities of individuals and groups; these factors are specific to a particular society.

To understand the impact of societal factors, it is necessary to explore differences between companies with the same universal factors. This means comparing companies of the same size which produce the same type of product, using the same type of production technique, subject to the same type of market structure and dependent to the same degree on the administrative environment (owners, corporate management etc.). We cannot compare apples and oranges; the goal is to choose research units which resemble one another quite closely, and then to compare them on specific variables and characteristics expressing socially specific factors.

Theoretically, every structural element of the society and indeed the companies can qualify. We will focus here on the following four groups of variables and characteristics.

1 The organizational structure of the companies: relative size of personnel categories and departments, number of subordinates relative to the number of supervisors (the 'span of control'), number of levels in the hierarchical structure.
2 Differentiation and integration mechanisms: in the first, organizations divide and distribute tasks according to jobs, individuals, professions, departments, work groups or other production divisions. In the second, organizations coordinate and integrate these differentiated positions. Integration mechanisms may take the form of careers, transfers to another job, group or department, mutual coordination, leadership and hierarchical structures.
3 Education and training: these variables refer to everything related to the socialization of employers and employees, including schooling and university training, general and vocational training, in-company training and more latent, unconscious or informal forms of training and education.
4 Industrial relations, specifically company-level collective labour relations, such as forms of compensation and compensation structures, employee representation (works councils, trade unions), consultation and bargain-

ing structures between employers and employees or their respective representatives.

The first two groups of factors are organizational, the third refers to the process of acquiring qualifications, and the final group to industrial relations – hence the title of this chapter.

Methodology

Comparative research on differences between countries with respect to the societal effect has concentrated largely on France, Germany and Great Britain. The initiative for these comparisons was taken by the Laboratoire d'Economie et de Sociologie du Travail (LEST) in Aix-en-Provence, culminating in a book by Maurice, Sellier and Silvestre (1982). A second study conducted by Sorge and Warner (1986) focused on a German–British comparison. The empirical data presented in this chapter are drawn from this publication and from a joint French–British–German comparison by Maurice et al. (1980). The companies involved in the comparison were selected according to the method described above. They display similar characteristics with respect to products, size, production techniques and dependence. The features of the German and British companies are given in Table 10.1. The variable 'technique' has been operationalized according to Woodward's well-known classification system (1965), in which a distinction is made between small-scale production, mass production and continuous production (for example, the chemicals industry). The French study also involved similar types of companies, and focused in particular on the four groups of variables and characteristics mentioned, supplemented by other relevant research material and statistical references. Various methods were used to collect the data:

- analysis of company data, including organization charts, statistics (personnel, compensation, qualifications, careers), collective agreements, trade union structures, and so on;

Table 10.1 *Company characteristics in a comparative study*

Technique	Country	Products	Size (no. of employees)
Single units Small series	Germany	Pressure vessels, heat exchangers, heavy, large vessels	1,700
	GB	Pressure vessels, boiler drums, pipework, nuclear waste containers	700
Mass production	Germany	Steel tubes (straight, welded)	800
	GB		600
Continuous process	Germany	Ethylene, polyethylene, acrylonitrile	2,600
	GB	and other chemical, semi-manufactures	2,200

- interviews with managers and employee/employer representatives focusing on general conditions in the company;
- interviews with staff members in specific posts about their work, the relationship to other jobs, groups and departments, their careers and their views on working conditions in the company.

The following observations are based largely on the studies mentioned previously. Readers are advised to consult Lane (1989) for a good summary of the various comparative studies.

3   Organizational forms

The structure of companies

A company can be organized according to various different principles. The following classification systems should be distinguished.

- *Classification into personnel categories*   for example, blue-collar and white-collar workers, which in turn encompass managers and 'regular' employees, technical and commercial/administrative staff. Such classifications are often stipulated by collective or company-level agreements or by law.
- *Classification according to the various operations carried out in a company* An industrial concern might perform the following operations, for example: production (including direct production, preparation and planning), supervision, maintenance, research and development, sales and marketing, accounting, personnel. Other sectors of the economy or government would have different categories.
- *Classification according to levels of authority*   for example hierarchical positions, operatives, staff positions and support staff.

The classification systems mentioned above not only differ between companies but also from one society to the next. For example, in Germany workers involved in production planning (and sometimes even those who work in development) are classified as manual workers, even though their jobs consist almost exclusively of office or white-collar work. This would be unimaginable in other countries. Another example is France, where hierarchical authority is the exclusive domain of white-collar employees, the first step above the common worker being the *chef d'équipe* (the chargehand). In Germany, by contrast, the *Vorarbeiter* is still classified as a manual worker.

Alongside similar qualitative national differences, we also find that there are quantitative differences between countries. For example, we can measure the number of subordinates to superiors, known as the span of control. Another method is to calculate various indices – for example, relative staff size in a specific department, job or job category. It is also customary to count the number of clearly differentiated hierarchical levels, from the common worker up to and including the head of the company.

These types of measurements make it possible to describe the structure of the organization in numerical terms.

Differences between countries

What follows is a description of quantitative differences in organizational structure between France, Great Britain and Germany (for a more detailed description, see Maurice et al., 1980: 66–69). If we measure the proportion of manual workers in relation to the staff size of the companies investigated, then we see the following:

- In the small-scale production companies, manual workers constitute 47.6 per cent in France, 52.9 per cent in Great Britain and 61.2 per cent in Germany of the total staff;
- In the mass production companies, these figures are 76 per cent for France, 72.4 per cent for Great Britain and 88 per cent for Germany.
- In the processing industry, the relative proportion of manual workers comes to 51.8 per cent in France, 63.9 per cent in Great Britain and 66.4 per cent in Germany; other indices reveal even larger differences.

How can we account for these enormous differences between companies of a similar size, using similar technology, providing a similar range of products, and with a similar level of dependence? First, there are major differences in the way that employees in comparable positions or jobs are classified. In Germany, draughtsmen, employees involved in production planning, foremen, lower technical personnel and laboratory staff are often categorized as workers. They are trained to be manual craftsmen and they remain so. German job categories for blue-collar workers are much broader than in other countries; on top of that, white-collar workers do not necessarily enjoy any advantages in terms of overtime compensation or social status. Moreover, German companies very much appreciate the advantages of bridging social differences between the shop floor and the office, and see the benefits of making staff (both shop floor and office) multifunctional.

Classification is only part of the explanation, however. Another important key is the division of labour. The countries investigated differ sharply with respect to the tendency to bar manual workers on the shop floor from preparatory, planning and supervisory jobs or tasks and delegate them instead to special technical positions, groups or departments. Quite apart from the technical level of development, a German company clearly has more workers, fewer technicians and fewer engineers than a British and, to an even greater extent, than a French company. Indeed, in France any non-manual tasks are siphoned off to individual, specialized offices, laboratories and service divisions consisting of technicians and engineers.

Research results on organizational structure are presented in Table 10.2. This table can be explained in the following manner. In Germany there has been a smaller increase in the number of separate job and personnel

Table 10.2   *Organizational structure in France, Germany and Great Britain*

	Low	Medium	High
White-collar employees as % of total personnel	G	GB	F
Production and maintenance superiors as % of total number of manual workers	G	GB	F
All hierarchical superiors as % of number of manual workers	GB	G	F
Technicians and engineers as % of number of manual workers	G	GB	F

Source: Maurice et al., 1980: 69

categories above and beyond those found on the shop floor or factory and in production work than in either Great Britain or, especially, France. This is particularly true of technical departments. On the other hand, the ratio of hierarchical line positions to staff positions in Germany is relatively high, and the ratio of technical managers to workers relatively low.

Great Britain shows average growth in the number of white-collar jobs, but there are very few hierarchical line positions (managers and supervisors) compared with the number of workers and compared with the size of the departments. The growth within the factory and on the shop floor has been the sharpest in France. This has led to a proportional increase in both supervisory, line managerial and staff positions. Because growth has affected all sectors, the ratio between hierarchical line positions and specialists in staff departments is balanced; all of these categories of personnel can claim a large share. The British organization is weighted in particular towards technical staff departments. The German organization leans towards manual workers and technical management.

4   Differentiation and integration mechanisms

Companies impose a certain degree of differentiation on their organization. The division into jobs, positions, professions, task groups and departments is to some extent determined by the organization itself or by specific circumstances (industrial sectors, products, markets, technology, size). On the other hand, such a division also reflects social features. The result of differentiation, however, is that in the interest of directing all efforts towards achieving the predetermined company goals, integration mechanisms must be instituted in the organization. Because differentiation mechanisms differ from country to country, we may correctly expect that integration mechanisms are also determined by social influences. We can use management, personnel policy and career models to determine which differentiation and integration mechanisms are typical of a particular country. The results of similar studies are described in the following sections, each one focusing on an individual country.

Germany

The most prevalent image of Germany and German organizations is that of an inflexible, bureaucratic management, a restricted measure of personal autonomy and highly formal hierarchies. According to this stereotype, German industry has achieved its success by applying authoritarian methods. The results of comparative research present an entirely different picture, however: German companies turned out to be no more bureau-cratic than companies in other countries. Indeed they were often less so. In the first place, the organizational division into separate units, professions, jobs and hierarchical levels was much less extensive than in France and Great Britain. The delineation between separate elements and levels was furthermore less strict and rigid than in the other countries. The researchers themselves were surprised to discover that it was much harder to obtain organization charts from German companies than from French or British ones. A classic rule of organizational theory is that staff and line positions or departments must be clearly delineated. It should be entirely clear whether someone has the right to give orders (line) or whether they may only advise on the basis of experience and expertise (staff). German companies are more guilty than others of breaking this rule; the distinction between line and staff positions is weakest there. The tasks performed by employees in line positions are more explicitly technical-craft than in the other countries; specialists have a quasi-hierarchical role and the distinction between these two categories of personnel is highly ambiguous.

In theory the restricted degree of differentiation in German organiz-ations should simplify hierarchical control, and so it does. But informal agreements and consultations between co-workers function as a co-ordination mechanism in Germany, much more so than in France. In addition, specific professional qualifications play a bigger role in German companies; specialist know-how, skills and responsibilities are generally applicable and not specific to any one company. But professionals are by no means strictly segregated; one of the responsibilities of a professional is to acquire knowledge of subjects beyond his or her own field. On the other hand, professionalism does not conflict with a company-specific orien-tation. The contrast between the importance of the profession and that of the organization, so prominent in British companies, is much less acute in German ones, although it continues to be present as a structural conflict.

The peculiar thing about German professional culture, which encom-passes different levels and positions, from the lowest production worker to the managing director, is that the job- and occupation-specific obligations are relatively comprehensive, so that their formal descriptions are not entirely clear or strict. In this way, formal and informal obligations, specialist and generalist, as well as different jobs, occupations and parts of the organization are nevertheless linked. And this phenomenon once again appears highly typical of Germany in the eyes of foreigners.

Great Britain

A popular impression of British company culture is that it is generally messy, pragmatic and fixated on status. This impression was confirmed, at least in part, by research, but not without a few nuances and further details being required. In the first place, British companies typically have a strict division between management and non-management jobs and careers. Nowhere else is the difference between managers (line) and specialists (staff), between hierarchical authority and expertise sharper than here. British managers are generalists, and their approach to management is more likely to be generally administrative and financial than technical. This puts a greater distance between managers and other categories, especially technical ones. A management focused on administrative and financial goals is the most important coordination mechanism.

In addition, informal agreements and consultation within the technical staff and service departments are highly important. This is particularly true of maintenance, preparatory, production technique and development divisions. Departments, task groups, jobs and professions are more sharply delineated. Each can claim a large measure of autonomy based on specialist knowledge and skills. Coordination between the various positions can be problematic. Management has little understanding of the individual professional fields and does not possess the necessary competence required in each area. Neither do the individual areas, professions and jobs have much in common. Modern British managers have tried to correct this problem by introducing matrix organizations and by decentralizing administrative/financial responsibilities.

British organizations, then, are much closer to resembling loose con- federations of individual, highly differentiated units than are German organizations. This does not necessarily imply that the vertical differences in status and the power gaps are bigger. In the first place, differentiation is more often horizontal. Secondly, the degree of professional autonomy and the status of the various different organizational units and professions are much greater than in Germany. In particular there is a huge difference between shop floor workers who are directly involved in production, and maintenance, preparatory and other technical staff. Employees in the maintenance division, specialist staff positions and in upper management have much more professional autonomy and a higher status than employees directly involved in production and than foremen and super- visors. We could mention numerous examples of such divisions and differences in status: for example, trainee production workers in a chemical company were not allowed to do preventive maintenance work. Except for unit and small-batch production work, coordination by spontaneous reciprocal adjustment is very rare. In some instances management even finds such consultation illegal.

To outsiders, Great Britain seems like a 'class society'. This cliché is somewhat misleading, however. Those in Great Britain who consider themselves members of the 'working class' include technicians and administrative employees. One's subjective identification with a particular class is determined as much by background as by occupation and type of work. Both in their backgrounds, careers and subjective identification, production managers, preparatory positions and other technicians categorize themselves as manual workers. Class differences *within* the area of production are certainly no greater in Great Britain than elsewhere, but all those involved in production – and this includes technicians and engineers to a certain extent as well as workers – have an inferior status, lower wages, less power and fewer career prospects. It is the people in financial, commercial and accountancy positions who have the career advantages, power and influence. In addition, the 'working class', while offering its members something positive to identify with as an overall concept, is sharply differentiated internally. This becomes evident if we take a look inside the British factory. The relationship between an employee and his company is determined by the 'cash nexus', whereas in departments, working groups and personal relationships the focus is on external autonomy and internal cohesion and solidarity. The entire panorama is coordinated by a generalist and financially orientated management.

France

To North Europeans, France seems a strange mixture of colourful, 'devil-may-care' individualism combined with authoritarianism and bureaucracy. Initially the French companies investigated did indeed seem organized along formal, hierarchical and bureaucratic lines supported by formal rules. They had the most explicit and differentiated pay scales, organization charts, planning systems and policy procedures, and the most autocratic approach to management.

Alongside these features, however, there were also coordination mechanisms in the form of informal and reciprocal agreements. They served mainly to mitigate or overcome the negative consequences of bureaucratic and hierarchical coordination (for example, fossilization). However, the bureaucratic and hierarchical principles carried more weight than company or professional rules or regulations. The terms denoting occupation (both *métier* and *profession* are used) emphasize both the specific know-how of a sector or company and the special knowledge of the employee. There are very few semi-autonomous *professionals à l'anglaise*; neither are there many German-style professionals who, with a transcendent sense of duty, allow the interests of their company and those of their profession to overlap.

It is not the case, however, that lower-level employees – in particular the manual workers – spend their lives beaten down by oppression and small-mindedness. French companies consistently offer their employees more opportunities for promotion than German companies do, because French organizations are broad at the top and can accommodate talented or experienced people there. There are clearly more administrative, supervisory and technical positions in French companies than there are in the other two countries. The same applies, for that matter, to French society as a whole: people are encouraged, either at school or at work, to escape the inferior status of worker as quickly as they can. Bureaucratic differentiation, while restricting individual autonomy, also offers a wider ladder which can accommodate more people who wish to increase their position of power, autonomy and earnings.

In France then, the concerns of a rational and authoritarian organization match the interests of the individual much more closely than most North Europeans would believe. Quite apart from the opportunities for promotion, the bureaucratic order uses its rules to ensure the individual of an almost inviolable autonomy. This gives paid employment in France an entirely different structure than in Germany or Great Britain. In this sense, the colourful individualists have more to gain from an impersonal bureaucracy than outsiders might initially suspect.

5   Education and vocational training

It is the task of companies not only to differentiate and coordinate activities, but also to ensure that there are enough qualified people to carry out these activities. The way in which companies do this differs from one country to the next, and these differences are closely related to variations in organizational structure. In theory a company can:

- itself make sure that it has qualified employees, for example through in-house training (or training provided by third parties), or by structuring the organization in such a fashion that employees are able to learn 'on the job';
- let others (for example the government or school boards) provide the necessary training and select its employees from the resulting supply; that means that the company's jobs, positions and career paths have to be adapted to the employees' knowledge and skills.

Companies employ a mix of different strategies, and the mix itself varies, not only from country to country but from sector to sector and even from company to company. The decision to pursue a specific strategy ultimately depends on the institutional order: the system of education and training. We will begin by surveying the distribution of personnel into various levels of qualification in the German, French and British companies investigated.

Table 10.3   *Qualifications of managerial personnel in chemical companies*

France	%	Germany	%	UK	%
No formal professional qualifications	19	No formal professional qualifications	3	No formal professional qualifications	42
Technique courte	11				
Technique professionnelle	8	*Facharbeiter*	42	Craft worker	21
Technique longue	12			City & Guilds Ordinary National (OND)	4
BTS, PST, CNAM	14	*Meister, Techniker*	30		
		Fachhochschulingenieur	17	Higher National (HND)	8
				State engineering	4
Supérieur, grandes écoles	36	*Universitätsdiplom*	8	University/CNAA degree	21

Source: Maurice et al., 1980: 79

The concrete significance of the qualifications described will not be considered here, but will be examined more closely for each individual country later. Table 10.3 reports the percentage of individuals who obtain the 'highest' qualifications in each category. The data are taken from the chemical industry and cover all employees in the hierarchical line – managers, supervisors, foremen etc. This means that the comparison is consistent with respect to immediate context (products, company size etc.), and that the impact of any variations in organizational structure is neutralized. The focus is exclusively on company hierarchy. The most interesting aspect is that these companies are part of the same corporation. They had even undertaken to bring their personnel policy and organization into line with one another. Any differences found between the companies can therefore be attributed to the societal effect.

Table 10.3 shows the lowest educational level (no formal training) at the top, and the highest (university education) at the bottom. Educational differences in 'level' are represented by each row. This makes it easier to read the table, since many of the terms will be unfamiliar and an explanation of each would be cumbersome. Note, however, that the table covers not only external or internal training – it shows all of the various important forms of vocational training.

There are remarkable differences in how employees are distributed over the various qualification levels. In France, the higher the qualification, the more common it is; France has the largest share of university-level graduates. Another striking aspect is the vertical distribution of the qualifications. In Germany, the lower the qualification, the more common it is; the employees at one particular qualification level are selected from an ample pool of employees at a lower qualification level. The various levels are built up from the *Facharbeiter* diploma, the most common qualification. In Great Britain, the frequency of the craft worker diploma lies somewhere between the French and the German qualifications at this levcl. The same is true of university degrees. On the other hand, the proportion of staff without any sort of formal qualification is excessively high. We will now explore in detail the characteristic systems of education and training in these three countries.

Germany

The qualification structure in German companies is typified by the presence of a broad stratum of personnel who have completed their apprenticeship training. In this system, students spend two to three and a half years acquiring work experience while attending a vocational training class one or two days a week. This system is quite distinct from similar structures abroad in a number of different ways: it not only covers the industrial crafts, but also all the various sectors of the economy, including government. In addition, it is not only young people with little schooling who enter apprenticeship programmes, but also those who have successfully completed secondary school or pre-university programmes.

The apprenticeship system does not exist in a vacuum; it constitutes an important step up on the way to various forms of higher or vocational education. In some branches of industry, and in trade, banking and insurance, companies view job candidates who have both a university degree and an apprenticeship qualification in a highly positive light. Indeed, German higher vocational education requires practical and academic training to be closely linked. This group is shown in Table 10.3 under the term *Fachhochschulingenieur*. In the past students entering a technical *Fachhochschule* were required to have an apprenticeship qualification and several years' work experience.

Achieving the level of *Techniker* once again comes down to first acquiring an apprenticeship qualification and work experience. In addition, there are schools and training programmes preparing skilled or technical employees, or those directly involved in production (for example painters, electricians, construction workers and metalworkers), to work independently or assume supervisory responsibilities. Employees take such courses in their spare time, spreading them out over two to three years, and round them off with a *Meister* examination and diploma. *Meister* constitute a special group in German society and enjoy much more prestige than similar groups in other countries. The German system of vocational training is therefore distinct not only because of the broad stratum of qualified workers, but because it allows for the possibility of moving vertically between different educational programmes and levels. The continuity this provides is particularly effective with respect to the combination of apprenticeship training and some other, higher, qualification, whether vocational or general. Even in institutions of higher education there are close links between academic and practical training. There is, for example, no distinction made between business economics and business administration, such as occurs in the Netherlands.

It is, of course, true that Germany, like other countries, continues to apply vertical segmentation in its system of education and training. Programmes of higher education are becoming more popular and their share of the education pie is becoming quantitatively more important. They no longer rely on lower levels of training as much as they once did. *Fach*, *Meister* and *Techniker* training programmes are also expanding, however, and the growth in higher education has often been accompanied by closer ties with vocational training. Despite the recent trend to separate education and training, in international terms Germany's educational programmes are still the most highly coordinated and are widely supported.

Great Britain

The British system of education is perhaps the most difficult for outsiders to understand. British pupils do not 'fail' classes; they do not necessarily sit exams at the end of their school careers; and they are not obligated to study a prescribed 'core' of subjects to the same extent as in other countries. This means that the system tends to produce a contingent of school-leavers who, lacking the basic knowledge, have few opportunities to continue their formal education. On the other hand, graduates of the better schools must satisfy exacting requirements and have often studied a specific, individualized selection of subjects based on their own talents or interests. Differences in performance and knowledge are already enormous by the time pupils reach secondary school, in terms of both level and area of specialization.

Students who complete grammar school are not automatically accepted at university. Each university has its own unique, individualized admissions policy. In addition to older universities, there are the former polytechnics which are now also counted as universities, where some of the courses are similar to those given at higher vocational schools in other countries while others resemble university-level courses. Most polytechnics have evolved from technical colleges, somewhat general technical educational institutions offering a variety of different courses ranging from day-release education for apprenticeships and vocational training at junior level to specific pre-university training based on contracts with companies.

In addition to the university examinations in the narrow sense (leading to a BA or BSc), there are similar qualifications known as National Academic Awards, which apply mainly to students at polytechnics. A step below these we find Higher National and Ordinary National programmes and qualifications, obtained by full-time and part-time students at technical colleges. As in Germany, technical training used to be an extension of the craft apprenticeship system, but this changed in the 1960s, when craft apprenticeships and technician apprenticeships were differentiated at a much earlier stage.

Apprenticeships may or may not be concluded with an examination. Once again, there are huge gaps between the various programmes with respect to actual know-how and course content; the specific arrangements vary from one company to the next and from one apprentice to the next, and the system tolerates individual interpretations and results. Pupils can take craft and technical examinations at the City & Guilds of London Institute, or aim for the slightly more advanced technical programmes and examinations (Ordinary and Higher National Diploma). The City & Guilds programmes are more academic in nature. They do not involve practical work, as in Germany. All in all, there is very little standardization in the way training and practical experience are linked. The prevailing social norm dictates that individual arrangements must be accepted because prior knowledge and acquired skills already differ at the start.

Educational programmes take relatively less time than in Germany; in England and Wales three years and in Scotland a year longer. Many students have completed their studies by the age of 21. The relatively short duration means that programmes are sometimes more specialized and sometimes more general than in other countries. There is generally no obligation to undergo practical training. The stronger the link between academic knowledge and practical experience, the less prestigious the educational programme; for example, this link is stronger at polytechnics than at universities, and stronger at 'regular' universities than at Oxbridge. This link is also stronger for administrative or technical programmes (especially those focusing on production) than academic ones. Technical programmes are consistently rated as inferior in Great Britain. They attract fewer qualified students, are organized by less prestigious institutions, and lead to occupations that pay less well than comparable positions in financial or commercial management. As contradictory as it may seem, the birthplace of the Industrial Revolution has never given engineers their proper due as a group, precisely because their careers are so closely linked to industrial practice. An additional factor is that the link between higher education and professional practice has become weaker in the course of time. Indeed, students enrolled on specialized programmes at prestigious institutions only acquire practical experience after graduation.

Great Britain, then, has a relatively differentiated, individualized and elite system of education and training. This can be attributed, among other things, to the lack of concern for student performance in general basic education, to the autonomy of the various schools and institutions of higher education, and to the prevailing social stratification. In general the reputation and status of the various technical-industrial training programmes are much lower than those of commercial, financial, scientific and general managerial programmes. In this respect, Great Britain and Germany are worlds apart. There are also differences related to the apprenticeship system and the opportunity to move on from an apprenticeship programme to pre-university education. Specifically, the number of young people who complete apprenticeship training is much smaller in Great Britain, and has even dropped in recent years; the number of employees who have had no formal training whatsoever is quite high, as we saw in Table 10.3. The system has little appreciation for technical and production-oriented training; neither does it value a combination of practical and academic education.

France

The French system of education and training differs from the British and German systems in quite a number of respects. The contrast with Great Britain is the greatest with respect to the selection, training and status of engineers, both socially and in companies. In France, more than in any other European country, engineers enjoy a privileged position, are subject to the strictest and most differentiated selection process, attend the best schools and exercise the most influence in companies. Engineers, upper administrative and managerial personnel and senior commercial and financial managers do not train at universities but in special *grandes écoles*, which are not under the jurisdiction of the Ministry of Education but rather of other ministries (defence, post office, industry etc.) and other important bodies, specifically the chambers of commerce. Students require more than the usual final examination to be admitted to these schools; an additional examination is necessary after having taken *classes préparatoires* at special grammar schools. For engineers the accent is on mastering subjects such as mathematics, physics and logic. The landscape of the *grandes écoles* is a richly varied one, however. The selection is more stringent for programmes in mathematics or physics than for more technical programmes. Unlike Great Britain, France does see its engineers as part of a social elite, but a highly differentiated one. Technical and practical skills are acquired in less prestigious specialist schools. Academic performance makes it easier to gain admission to somewhat more prestigious general schools. To be accepted to a programme or even a career in government or in one of several large companies, students must participate in a public *concours* (a selection procedure and examination). State schools are a very important part of the vocational training system. There is almost no apprenticeship system to speak of, with the exception of training programmes for small businesses. France differs most sharply from Germany in this respect. While companies affiliated with the German chambers of commerce concentrate on the broad apprenticeship base and further training for apprentices (*Meister* for the technical-managerial and *Fachwirte* for the commercial-administrative fields), the French chambers of commerce focus on managing state institutions of higher education, with the Parisian chamber of commerce taking responsibility for the most prestigious of these institutions.

In general, vocational training in France is the province of the *collèges techniques* and the *lycées techniques*, which also include the *lycées d'état techniques*, leading to the more advanced title of *technicien supérieur* (BTS), and the *instituts universitaires de technologie* (IUT), leading to the *diplôme universitaire de technologie* (DUT).

French technical programmes are differentiated, both vertically and horizontally. The *lycée technique* may be rounded off with a technical final examination (*baccalauréat technique*) which allows admission to higher technical training, although young people with this degree generally go on to specialist technical schools rather than to one of the prominent general scientific institutions. In addition, the *lycée technique* programme also leads to the *brevet de technicien* or technical certificate, which is more career preparatory. In recent years an increasing number of young people have gone straight from the *lycée technique* into jobs on the shop floor; in the past this was much less the case. Vocational qualifications beneath this level are equally differentiated. Employers, pupils and parents are showing less and less interest in the CAP (*certificat d'aptitude professionnelle*), which used to be immensely important.

In France, education and training always precede the start of a career. Adult education based on practical experience is relatively rare and has little prestige; the majority of adult education programmes are organized by the *Conservatoire National des Arts et Métiers* and are not accorded the status of equivalent programmes at the *grandes écoles*. It is almost as if the sweeping, differentiated system of education which precedes working life is intended to prevent people with work experience from having to undertake additional training. This is diametrically opposed to the principles of the German system, but also, in part, to those of the British, in which management training takes place largely by means of 'post-experience' courses. In France, on the other hand, as in Great Britain, the level and social status of an educational programme is related directly to its academic, general and general-technical nature. Unlike in Great Britain, however, French general-technical programmes do lead to prestigious and advanced positions in companies.

Summary

Without reducing the various systems to caricature, we can, however, state the following: in each of the three countries, a university-trained engineer at the upper echelons of a large company would be proud of different aspects of his educational background.

- In Germany he would take satisfaction from the fact that he had completed his apprenticeship training and had learned his trade 'from the bottom up'.
- In Great Britain he would emphasize the fact that he had completed supplementary management training and in this respect had kept pace with other top managers; in other words, he would be pleased that he was not 'just an engineer'.
- In France he would stress the fact that he had studied at a prestigious technical *grande école* and that he had completed his exams there successfully.

On the other side of the training ladder, that is, the lower occupational categories, we see similar differences. A young German would in any event try to finish secondary school, and might even try to sit the final exams successfully. After finishing school, he would be strongly inclined to enter into an apprenticeship, even if he planned to attend a technical school or higher technical training programme later. His biggest motive would be that practical training can offer him the best basis for a successful career.

In Great Britain, on the other hand, young people are motivated by the desire to be financially independent as quickly as possible and to find a well-paying job. No matter which educational programme a young British student chooses, even a university degree, in many cases that student's full-time educational career will be finished by the age of 21. There are also large numbers of young people who, lacking any training whatsoever, must resort to short-term employment (with government assistance), and/or temporary jobs or odd jobs that, with a little luck and effort on their part, might lead to a permanent position.

In France young people attempt to achieve the highest educational level available to them. If they cannot gain admission to general education (at higher prestige educational institutions), vocational education offers them an opportunity to achieve this.

6 Labour relations

Industrial relations have already been discussed in previous chapters in some detail. In this chapter we will focus on collective labour relations at the company level – specifically, we will be looking at how the structures of specific systems of industrial relations are reflected in the organization and personnel structure of similar companies in the countries being considered. We will be exploring company-level labour relations using a general grid which can be applied to all three of the countries in relatively the same way. The horizontal dimension of this grid shows the functional distribution of the organization into divisions, groups, services, and so on. This dimension differs, however, according to hierarchical level, company size and technology, and it is therefore difficult to standardize across the various companies. The other, vertical dimension of the grid shows the hierarchical pattern of the personnel structure. With the exception of a few particularities within the companies, we can describe this pattern as follows:

- production manager
- product division manager (for larger elements of the product line)
- works manager, service manager (preparatory departments)
- departmental manager (for example metalworking, installation, and so on)
- supervisor, foreman

- chargehand
- worker.

Germany

In the ideal German company, all employees, up to the works manager or even the product division manager, are represented by the *Betriebsrat*. Upper management (product division manager and production manager, and staff at comparable levels in other positions) are not represented by the *Betriebsrat* and their employment terms are not covered by collective agreement. There are cases where managers have employment contracts which are not covered by collective agreement but they are nevertheless represented by the *Betriebsrat*. Collective bargaining agreements and company agreements (between management and the *Betriebsrat*) are differentiated according to the various categories of employees: workers, supervisors, technical staff and commercial-administrative staff.

The pay scales for workers generally also include the position of foreman. The single exception in the study was the chemical company, where shift foremen were classified under the lowest pay scale for supervisors (the M-scale for *Meister*). It is unusual for management-level union members who, through promotion, are no longer covered by collective agreement to turn in their union cards.

Great Britain

Labour relations in British companies are completely the opposite of those in German companies in almost every respect. The most characteristic feature is the minimal degree of formalization with respect to agreements. Agreements are relatively short and make use of vague terms and settlements. For example, they may refer to a frame of reference provided by 'custom and practice'; declarations of intent are included stating that the parties will solve problems in 'a spirit of mutual cooperation'. Agreements are more precise when it comes to job demarcation. The chemical company agreement, for example, stated which tools a production worker was allowed to use without trespassing on the territory of the maintenance worker. A further typical characteristic is that serious problems arise not so much because of conflicts between management and workers but rather because of procedural uncertainties and ambiguities in the negotiations conducted between management and the various trade unions.

British companies usually have four or more trade unions representing the personnel or segments of it. The unions concentrate on specific groups within the company, with the following delineations being important:

- divisions between crafts, specifically between mechanical engineers and metalworkers on the one hand and electricians on the other;
- direct production work versus maintenance work;
- operational work versus supervision, management and planning;
- the shop floor versus the technical divisions or laboratories.

In addition to divisions between the unions, there are also important divisions within unions. The Amalgamated Engineering Union (AEU), for example, had a separate section for technical personnel (TASS) which conducted autonomous negotiations. The organization of trade unions in British companies is furthermore generally quite different from that found in German or French companies: representatives are chosen initially by working groups or departments and maintain remarkably close ties with them. In the companies investigated, industry-level agreements were insignificant; they covered only the most elementary aspects, for example the basic right to holiday leave. All of the important aspects of the employment relationship were settled via company-level negotiations and agreements, and further agreements pertaining to each specific category of personnel. A distinction is made between bargaining (between management and shop steward) and consultations (in consultation committees). In the largest company (chemical production), labour relations are split into the following categories:

- process workers and general labourers;
- maintenance workers (craft force);
- laboratory staff;
- supervisory and service personnel;
- professional (engineers) and managerial staff;
- senior management.

The fragmentary nature of trade union activity at company level is not necessarily a sign of weakness. Both unit/small-batch and mass production companies have closed shops, meaning that company management makes sure that every employee in a job category covered by the collective bargaining agreement belongs to the union. The same is more or less true of the chemical company, although here the closed shop is informal. Management acknowledges that the closed shop principle can work to its advantage: after all, it guarantees the presence of employee representatives whose authority is clearly defined.

British managers spend an important part of their time dealing with labour relations issues – indeed, lower and middle managers spend up to a third of their working hours on labour relations problems, which are generally related to the following areas: pay levels, transfers and establishing time standards and bonuses for abnormal working conditions. Shop stewards and managers generally solve these problems together, but they get passed on to the upper echelons of the hierarchy when employees (or their representatives) appeal the lower-level decision.

France

It is unusual or indeed impossible to find trade unions in Great Britain or Germany based on ideological or religious principles. The attitude of both unions and employers is relatively pragmatic, despite the conflict-prone tenor of their relationship. In France, on the other hand (Gallie, 1978), the trade unions are much more concerned with ideological convictions. In addition, industry-level bargaining and agreements are more important for labour relations within the company than is the case in Great Britain, although they are not as significant as in Germany. There is also a greater degree of formalization and a stricter legal framework. Labour relations in French companies are by no means highly integrated, however. Unlike in Great Britain, the dividing lines do not parallel divisions between departments or occupations. There are distinct bodies with sharply delineated jurisdictions: the *comités d'entreprise* or *comités d'établissement* are consultative bodies, the *délégués du personnel* and the *sections syndicales* belonging to the representative union federations have bargaining functions.

Labour relations are also differentiated or specified along hierarchical lines, with the white-collar electorate beginning at the foreman level. Upper managers or *cadres* have their own trade union (CGC), a large-scale, broad grouping of managers and highly skilled specialists. The CGT, which claimed a large proportion of the union members in the companies investigated, also has a subsidiary organization for *cadres* whose members have principally come up from the ranks of workers. *Cadres* begin at the level of departmental management, approximately the same as British managers but lower down the ladder than Germany's *leitende Angestellten*. Promotion or appointment to a *cadre* position in France is similar to being dubbed a knight or to being promoted to the rank of officer. The CGC recruits members from among the supervisors, which demonstrates how attractive this status is. In France company management determines company policy (including personnel policy) more unilaterally than in Germany. French supervisors have little say in decisions on conflict-inducing issues, such as pay scales, transfers and adherence to employment terms. As in Great Britain, conflicts are more likely to require the intervention of the upper levels of the hierarchy. Management thus spends a great deal of its time sorting out such problems.

7   Interpretation and conclusions

The societal effect

The issues discussed above show obvious parallels within each individual country: in each, there is a specific relationship between such social institutions as the organizational structure, the differentiation and integration mechanisms, the qualification structure and labour relations. We previously called this relationship the societal effect. We will now describe this societal effect for each country in general terms.

Germany

Of the three countries, Germany is least inclined to separate operational, planning, preparatory and management tasks. Practical training and career mobility, both horizontally and vertically, are the important prerequisites. There are no strict dividing lines between differentiated organizational components, careers and educational processes. The same phenomenon can be found in Germany's labour relations. There is very little differentiation here; instead, labour relations are integrated at company level by linking career paths, qualifications and tasks. Company-level labour relations are further linked to those at industry level and higher: the situation within a company is never entirely divorced from the social standards which determine the structure of occupations, careers, industrial relations and organizational practice. Occupations still maintain general rather than company-specific standards, such as rules and regulations concerning exams and diplomas. Examples demonstrating the extensive degree of formalization and social standardization are: the legislation governing vocational training; legal specifications regarding entrepreneurship and the framework for collective agreements; the immense importance of the industry-level agreement and its connection with company agreements (through the opening clause); and the tightly organized trade unions and employers' associations. In addition, informal cooperation between the various divisions within companies and between the authorities, employers' associations and trade unions is also common.

Great Britain

In Great Britain, on the other hand, we see looser ties between the differentiated segments within a company. The internal labour market keeps the various career paths separate and independent of one another. British society allows more room for the individual approach, that is, specific to one particular company, division or position as opposed to another, or the autonomy of one profession with respect to another. As in Germany, then, occupation is important, but occupational training does not take place within the same socially regulated framework and the various occupations are not as closely linked.

Whereas production companies in Germany are closely knit units that fit comfortably into the social framework, in Great Britain they are looser and subject to financial controls. Characteristic of Great Britain is the limited number of regulations and the minor degree of formalization, except when job demarcation is at issue. Job demarcation provides a balance between the various divisions within the organization, between the various training and career patterns, and within the system of labour relations.

France

Of the three countries, France displays the most far-reaching differentiation. Nevertheless, labour relations in French companies are less differentiated than in British companies. How can we explain this? Occupation has always played a much bigger role in Great Britain as an organizing principle for companies and trade unions. That is not the case in

France. The significance of a rationally ordered hierarchy as a mechanism for coordinating jobs and for apportioning career prospects, and the growing prominence of academic training over apprenticeship training have undermined the importance of the occupation in educational and organizational structures more than they have in Great Britain. Professions are kept alive by professional organizations or existing interest organizations, which may demand that certain jobs, training programmes and career paths should be set up according to a specific plan that has no connection to the specific company. This principle of cooperation is quite weak in French society, however. An explanation can be found in the events of history: after the Revolution of 1789, the Jacobites and the infamous *loi le Chapelier* forbade every cooperative or corporate association as a crime against democracy. The central government and the individual company came to play an increasingly important role in the dynamics of society. At the same time, the system of industrial relations and the trade unions grew along strongly hierarchical lines, so that centralization and the internal hierarchical structure came to dominate the CGT.

This description makes clear that we must seek other explanations for some country-specific characteristics. The ideological divisions between French trade unions and between European trade unions and employers' associations should not immediately be explained by pointing to organizational and educational factors. In this case, the political history of the country is a necessary part of the explanation (see for example Poole, 1986).

Causality and interaction

The question now is: to what extent is there a causal connection between organizational structures, coordination and integration mechanisms, education and training, and labour relations? Can we propose that one factor explains another? If so, then which factors explain which? If not, then what exactly is the relationship between the groups of factors mentioned?

For the majority of observers, the British example is the most obvious. Trade unions in Great Britain impose their own policy on companies in order to demarcate the various occupations. It would not be unusual to find employees spontaneously walking out on the job because a mechanical engineer tried to repair electrical machinery. In this case, our inclination would be to choose a model in which labour relations explain how occupations, careers, organizational structures and qualification processes are set up.

But it is precisely the British example that demonstrates the limits of this type of explanation. In the past, British employers made an important contribution to instituting labour relations through their own organizational and strategic policy. The loose organizational ties which typify Great Britain are rooted in the way in which employers structured their companies. They preferred to hire in groups of temporary workers who functioned more like subcontractors than real employees. Control over the implementation and organization of the work, and occupational qualifications and standards were deliberately left to institutions that operated independently of the company. There is ample evidence that this type of 'preindustrial' tradition was stronger and enjoyed a longer existence in Great Britain than elsewhere (Loveridge and Mok, 1979). But it is also conceivable that this type of organizational strategy (focusing on avoiding internal problems by contracting out work and on evading production policy) was influenced by the characteristics of labour relations as they already existed in the 'community culture', as Loveridge and Mok call it. And so the arguments go back and forth. At the most refined level, a discussion such as the present one leads us back in history, making the boundaries between industrial relations, organizational policy and qualifications ever more blurred. What does become clear, however, is that the characteristics of such social institutions show very specific parallels within a country. It is furthermore obvious that there is an interaction between groups of factors. They seem to influence one another, with the interaction consisting of a series of causal influences going first in one direction and then in the other. This interaction exists in each society, but it always has a socially specific character. According to the societal effect approach, it is that specificity which never changes.

Stability and change

The conclusion drawn may come across as conservative. It presents a picture of a social coherence in which existing structures are constantly being reproduced and in which subsidiary (functional) events are constantly getting in one another's way. On the other hand, there is no denying that societies do in fact undergo technical, economic and social change. The passage of time brings changes to the structures described, and after a while they are not precisely the same as before. In the next chapter we will explore how stability and change are related and how the undeniable fact of social change can be brought into line with the societal effect approach.

PART 5

NEW TECHNOLOGIES, ORGANIZATIONAL CHANGE AND EMPLOYMENT RELATIONS

---

11 New production technologies and changing work systems

Arndt Sorge

---

1 Labour relations and change

The fact that labour relations change under the influence of technological innovation, organizational change and changing qualification structures is considered self-evident. Indeed, this type of influence arouses the most interest in the literature. Although mention is sometimes made of the impact of labour relations on innovations in technology, organization and qualifications, the overriding inclination is to view labour relations as an obstacle to or brake on progress. The classic example is that of the brakesman, who, in accordance with collective bargaining agreements, had to form part of the crew on British and American trains, even though his presence on electrical or diesel trains was totally superfluous from a technical point of view.

In this chapter, we attempt to demonstrate that the influence of labour relations on innovation is not so simple and one-sided as the prevailing notions and models would have it. The situation is more complex and – as the ideas presented by the societal effect approach suggest – differs somewhat according to country.

Another widespread misconception is that technological change leads to converging economic and social processes in the different countries. In this school of thought, permanent and persistent differences between societies are seen as signs of backwardness or underdevelopment. In this chapter, we will show that (even highly comparable) innovations or changes may generate new differences between countries, and that these differences can be explained on the basis of earlier diversity.

Labour relations: cause or effect?

Observers agree that technology, organizational methods and professional qualifications are subject to constant changes. It is also clear that such changes are linked to labour relations in one way or another. But this simple statement is not the end of the matter. The question then arises as to precisely what role labour relations play in such issues as technological innovation, organizational change and the process of qualification acquisition. There are different lines of reasoning.

First, it may be argued that labour relations have an impact on technological progress and changes in organization and qualifications. In this analysis, labour relations constitute the independent and explanatory variable. Their structure sets all these changes in motion, or conversely, prevents such changes. A well-known example of this occurred in Great Britain, where the unions of printers and compositors jointly regulated the employment relationship in the printing divisions of Fleet Street newspaper publishers. This practice for a long time prevented the introduction of new composing techniques (electronic instead of ordinary typesetting machines). Another example is the ease with which certain types of labour relations permit the introduction of new techniques. The Japanese unions are often purely company unions. Since their organizational structure to some extent reflects the existing corporate hierarchy, disputes over new technologies hardly arise.

It should be noted, however, that relations are much more complex than suggested here. The opposition of the Fleet Street compositors and their unions not only frustrated the introduction of new techniques, but also triggered a counter-attack from some employers. Composing and printing offices moved to other areas where there was little or no union presence (rural areas or the London Docklands). Existing offices were gradually closed down or forced to adapt. Thus, the 'negative' impact of labour relations on technological progress may in time very well result in accelerated innovation. But even then, the buildup of arguments still starts with existing labour relations. They are the independent variable.

The argument can also be reversed, however, in the sense that changes in technology or organizational methodology are considered the independent variables. They generate changes in labour relations. In this second scenario, labour relations emerge as the dependent variable requiring analysis.

We again come across an example from the printing industry. The gradual switch from mechanical to electronic typesetters is, one may argue, a consequence of the micro-electronic revolution. Digital information processing has become easier and less expensive than analogical processing. It has also, however, downgraded the work of qualified compositors. Operating electronic typesetters rather resembles working on a typewriter, so the work may as well be done by secretarial staff who need not be paid as 'craftsmen'. Compositors regard themselves as qualified craftsmen and are organized in trade unions which boast an old and rich tradition; a sort of elite among the working classes. They are now being replaced mostly by female workers, who are paid lower wages and are less likely to seek solidarity within the framework of a union. The fraternity of compositors, which used to have a monopoly on filling vacancies and determining pay and conditions, is no more. This would not have happened without the development and application of micro-electronics.

Thus, the argument is reversed: labour relations are determined by outside developments. Who is right, then? Examples supporting both theories abound. And since the same example – changing labour relations and application of micro-electronics in the printing industry – permits two different interpretations, it might be a good idea not to let either one prevail. The longer the period of time covered by the analysis and the greater the number of examples analysed, the more pressing is the need to link both lines of reasoning.

The third, and integrated, hypothesis is based on mutual effects. It suggests that there is an interaction between labour relations and changes in technology, organization and qualifications. This does not mean that in individual cases the one factor may not be the result of the other, but a broader analysis is likely to show some kind of interaction. What precisely do we mean by interaction? In its true form, interaction means that there is a mutual dependence between at least two different elements of a system, and between the system and its environment. Each change in an element of the system or the environment triggers changes in all other elements. This eliminates the distinction made earlier between dependent and independent variables.

The role of labour relations

The three perspectives described above may seem at odds with each other. But irrespective of the precise relationship between organization, technological innovation, qualifications and labour relations, the following factors should in any case be analysed in order to gain sufficient insight into their interaction (Sorge and Streeck, 1988: 38–42):

- the introduction of new techniques (technological innovation);
- changes in the organizational structure;
- changes in qualification requirements;
- trends in labour relations;
- changes on product markets;
- changes in product market strategies.

The next section deals with the first three factors, and discusses their connection with developments in labour relations. We shall also show in what way work systems (that is, technology, organization, qualifications and labour relations combined) may differ and develop in different directions. The other factors (changed product markets and product market strategies) and their interrelation with changes in work systems will be analysed in the last section of this chapter. These issues will be linked to those discussed in the previous chapter. We shall also examine which of the three hypotheses described above can best be used to interpret the relations found.

2   Changes in technology, organization and qualifications

Technological innovation

Technological progress is an ongoing process. There is no reason to believe that technology advances at a quicker pace nowadays than in the past. However, accelerations do tend to occur when new techniques are introduced. Microelectronics was one of the technical innovations to gain momentum in the 1970s. Since then, micro-electronic circuits have become increasingly integrated, information processing time has been reduced, and the price of switching functions, millions of which were recently integrated on one component, has fallen proportionally. Improved computer performance has led to the incorporation of computers in equipment, installations and machinery in order to expand, improve and accelerate processing capacity. The use of new and upgraded micro-electronic applications has become particularly widespread since the late 1970s. Controlling and information processing capacity has improved greatly for the following applications.

- Data processing equipment and computers, which are now easily integrated into large networks.
- On-line data processing by means of stand-alone or network-integrated computers, designed for various clerical and commercial purposes and supported by a growing series of application-specific software.
- CNC-controlled processing machines (metal, plastic, wood, etc.) incorporating programs in which the parameters of the targeted process are stored, and which are run by an electronic controlling system (CNC = computer numerical control).

- CAD (computer aided design): equipment for designing and drawing technical component parts.
- Flexible manufacturing systems and flexible manufacturing cells: processing equipment (possibly connected in a series) which automatically controls the loading, transporting and sorting of component parts.
- Industrial robots to perform such activities as welding, handling, painting, fitting and so on.
- Automatic control devices for engines, lifts and so on.
- Other applications in the never-ending CA-series, intended to at least partly link and integrate separate functions with the aid of computers.

The introduction of new technologies often coincides with cutbacks in staffing. This effect must, however, also be seen in the light of possible increases or decreases in the demand for products produced by the company, division or working group concerned. Any judgement about the effects of technological innovation in terms of staffing levels is only warranted when taking into account changes in labour productivity and changes in output. If the increase in demand compensates for the labour-saving effect, the introduction of new techniques is often considered less problematic than if demand remains below the level of the cutbacks.

To assess the qualitative effects of technological innovation, we must first explore to what extent jobs and qualifications have changed. Are new forms of expertise and skills required and have the old forms of work organization, task structuring and qualification disappeared? Cases have been reported where the simplification and schematization of duties as a result of technological innovation have led to lower job requirements and an increased number of downgraded and/or stress-inducing work situations. Still, technological progress may also increase the level of qualifications required in technical and preparatory departments. And there have, of course, been cases where innovation has changed the substance rather than the level of qualifications and task structures.

Also, the privacy of employees is likely to be affected. Their activities become increasingly transparent as a result of the information and data available, which can be efficiently and systematically processed and analysed. This creates the spectre of the 'glass' employee, whose performance, mistakes, disciplinary offences, habits and movements within the company are meticulously monitored.

However, the results of studies into technological innovation indicate that the changes listed above are not only caused purely by changes in technology. They are to a very large extent determined by the individual situation and policy of a company in terms of the following:

- the organizational concepts used (integration and expansion of duties as opposed to task segmentation and differentiation);
- the distribution of qualifications among employees (egalitarian or unequal);
- the structure and quality of training facilities;

- the purchase of suitable and tailor-made equipment to support choices made concerning organization and qualifications;
- retraining possibilities, and the relocation of staff from the scaled-down segments of the organization;
- protection of privacy by technical means (code words and cards, blocked access to data files) and organizational means (regulations);
- the company's strategy, designed to expand its range of products and production, or aimed solely at productivity increases and payroll cutbacks;
- the market, cost and competitive position of the company and the particular branch of industry *vis-à-vis* competitors in the country and abroad.

Clearly, labour relations have a bearing on most of these intervening factors. Rules contained in statutes, collective bargaining agreements and company-specific agreements may influence decisions on what techniques to use in practice and in what way. They may be explicitly aimed at a specific technology. The fitting of computer screens, for example, is subject to technical requirements and governed by rules on working conditions. Then there are rules which do not directly target technological innovation, but nevertheless have an effect. For example, it may be provided that employees working in divisions which are subject to cutbacks cannot be dismissed, and must be retrained and relocated to other divisions, while retaining all their vested rights as regards terms of employment.

Also, pay structures and job assessment systems may offer negative as well as positive incentives. They enhance the introduction of new applications of existing techniques and influence their practical effects. For example, Sweden has the largest number of industrial robots per employee. This is the result of the comparatively high wages for unskilled labour, which in turn is the result of the solidaristic incomes policy promoted by unions. In Sweden, the purchase of robots produces larger cost-savings and the purchase price can be written off more rapidly. In countries with large numbers of skilled workers (like Germany), investment in training prompts employers to utilize all of the various skills available. The development and application of new techniques there is less geared to separating the planning and preparatory tasks from the purely implementing ones.

Moreover, arrangements regarding the introduction of new technology are laid down in collective bargaining agreements in many countries. The contracting partners may also negotiate rules governing the effects of technological innovation. Bamber summarizes the results of a survey conducted in different countries as follows:

> It can be argued . . . that in countries with adversarial traditions of industrial relations (most English-speaking countries), unions are less likely to cooperate

with technological change than their counterparts in countries with recent traditions of social partnership in industrial relations (West Germany and the Scandinavian countries). To a considerable extent, current differences in union behaviour reflect contrasting legacies of employers' attitudes . . . . For example, American and British unions have traditionally placed more emphasis on bargaining after decisions have been made, rather than on participation in making decisions, in contrast with many of their German and Scandinavian counterparts, which face more paternalistic employers. (Bamber, 1988: 212)

It should be added that German and Scandinavian employers are certainly not the most paternalistic. Paternalistic styles of management are also found in the French and southern European cultures, but decision-making there is rarely a matter of close cooperation and worker participation. Also, fewer agreements are concluded between employers and employee representatives on the introduction and impact of new technologies. Table 11.1 presents the situation found in the different countries.

The situation depicted in this table more or less reflects labour relations in the different countries. Strikingly, industry-wide agreements do not exist in Great Britain, except in parts of the public sector. Regulations and negotiations are at their most decentralized here, down to the level of companies and businesses. The most centralized collective bargaining and regulations are found in Sweden, where local bodies merely fill in the space left by national legislation and collective bargaining agreements. Germany again shows a tapestry of statutory rules, industry-wide bargaining agreements and company bargaining agreements. The statutory rules provide general standards for job security, health and working conditions; the industry-wide agreements (*Rationalisierungsschutzabkommen*) protect against lower wages and dismissal in the case of technological innovation. The company agreements regulate additional and company-specific aspects. Moreover, government programmes to promote new technologies are influenced by trade union demands. The German government, for example, supports the development of control systems for processing machines which preserve craftsmanship in manufacturing to the maximum.

In France, increasing weight is attached to industry-wide agreements to govern working conditions and the impact of technological change. The same can be said of the formal involvement of the *comités d'entreprise* and the *comités d'hygiène et de santé*. The fact remains, however, that the bargaining provisions are general in nature and the committees only have a right to be informed and consulted. Although there is a tendency to encourage consultations and negotiations, worker participation is still non-existent (Tallard, 1988: 290–93).

This summary shows that there is an overall tendency to make (the impact of) technological innovation an item on the negotiating agenda. Yet the way in which the different countries go about it varies strongly, as do the intensity and efficiency of the rules they introduce. The existing differences between the countries remain in place.

Table 11.1 Approaches to the joint regulation of technological change

Country	Average density rate	Legislation	Collective bargaining agreements		
			Nationwide	Industry	Company
West Germany	40	Works Constitution Act 1972; Works Safety Act 1973, and rules on working with computer screens, 1981	None	Job security in the metallurgical, textile, shoe, leather, paper-processing and printing industries	Over 100 agreements
Norway	45	Working Environment Act and rules on working with computer screens, 1982	Computer-controlled systems, 1975	Banking industry	Trade, industry and services largely come under local bargaining agreements
Sweden	73	Working Environment Act 1977 and rules on working with computer screens, 1981; Co-Determination Act 1977	Working conditions, 1976	Technology in the printing industry; workers' participation in national and local public sector, and private sector	Exercise of statutory rights
Italy	43	Statute of Workers' Rights 1970, Health and Safety Act 1978	None	Agreements in the metallurgical industry contain provisions	Various agreements contain clauses (Fiat, Olivetti, Alfa Romeo)
USA	<20	Occupational Safety and Health Act 1970	None	Bargaining agreements contain provisions on technological changes	
Canada	30	Recommendations on statutory rights	None	Existing agreements contain limited provisions	
UK	50	Health and Safety at Work Act 1974	None	Parts of the public sector	Over 100 agreements
Australia	55	None	Decisions of the Federal Conciliation & Arbitration Commission (e.g. job security)	Telecommunications	Parts of the printing industry and public sector

Source: Bamber, 1988: 210–211

Organizational change

In each country, technological change is associated with organizational change. The following are among the most innovative organizational concepts advocated in the literature.

- Semi-autonomous working groups, which themselves decide on the division of tasks among their members; they are often entrusted with responsibilities and tasks previously reserved for production foremen and supporting and planning departments.
- Quality circles, which are established within or across working groups and departments to improve product quality and the efficiency of the work organization as a whole; they rely heavily on the expertise and working experience of employees.
- Job enrichment at the individual level, that is, tasks which were previously hived off from more comprehensive jobs (preventive maintenance, work planning, quality control) are partially re-integrated.
- Just-in-time management of product flows, that is, component parts are supplied by the other company departments or by suppliers 'just in time', when they are needed and at the responsibility of the department or working group concerned, so as to reduce the costs of storage and stock control.
- Simplification of the organizational structure, that is the existing hierarchy is flattened out or specialized divisions or working groups are dissolved.
- Contracting out the production of component parts or services.

Trade unions have for some time been recommending some of the organizational changes described above, notably job enrichment and the creation of semi-autonomous working groups. This innovation-orientated approach is reflected particularly in the demands of the Swedish and German unions. In these countries, the government, employers and employees have worked together to develop national schemes. In other countries, such schemes either do not exist or have little practical significance. The British unions had been at pains to protect the division of labour, which has developed from custom and practice, and to preserve the autonomy of the various crafts in the workplace. There has as yet been no movement aimed at changing the existing organization of labour issuing from the unions themselves.

It is difficult to determine the scope and significance of the trends found in the different countries. The situation is not quite clear because of a propaganda wave launched by employers. The innovation drive has been initiated by company managers, despite (earlier) attempts at innovation by trade unions eager to accept changes. As a result, the changes introduced thus far mainly concern cost reductions and are supposed to improve the competitive position of companies.

Organizational change often causes tension between employers and employee representatives, as it considerably affects job descriptions and pay classifications. An added problem is that local trade union representatives consider the representatives of working groups elected to quality circles as unfair competition. This has also to do with the absence of company agreements detailing the relationship between these parallel representational structures. With control authority decentralized and planning and implementation merged, there remains only a thin line between employee representation and employee supervision. For example, the spokesman for a semi-autonomous working group may not only promote the interests of the group members but also be in charge of the group.

In Anglo-Saxon countries, the United States in particular, this trend creates much more tension than in northern European countries, as it stands in stark contrast to the cherished principle of a strict separation between management and worker representation. American companies involved in organizational changes often wish to steer clear of disputes with trade unions and therefore practically prohibit trade unionism in the workplace. At the same time, they avoid having to conclude collective bargaining agreements. Not surprisingly, in American usage, 'human resources management' (HRM) and 'industrial relations' are ideological opposites. If you use the one term, you are viewed with suspicion by those who use the other, and vice versa. In France, the 1982 Auroux legislation was an attempt at institutionalizing (by means of semi-autonomous working groups and quality circles) consultation between employers and employee representatives about organizational innovation. However, since the Act does not render consultation compulsory, very few companies provide for consultations as envisaged by the Act (d'Iribarne and Fossati, 1986).

There certainly is tension in this area in Great Britain. Employers have staged several attempts at undermining or indeed eliminating trade unionism by introducing technological and organizational changes. An extreme example of this is the establishment by newspaper companies of new publishing and printing offices in the London Docklands. Since these offices are not governed by the Fleet Street agreements, the unions have had to start all over again. Also, there is a trend among companies which establish facilities in 'greenfield sites' (new and poorly industrialized areas), particularly Japanese companies, to enter into contracts whereby flexible working practices and no-strike deals are accepted by one union at a time in exchange for a workplace representation monopoly. The Electrical, Electronic, Telecommunication and Plumbing Union (EETPU) has considerably enhanced this development. Unions are now fighting each other to obtain monopolies in the workplace (Bamber, 1988: 212). As a result, multi-unionism is disappearing, as is the profession-based differentiation between unions.

Still, this development does not necessarily constitute a move towards the Continental principle of industry-based trade unionism. What we see emerge in Great Britain is the situation where the name of a trade union no longer denotes either the category of affiliated workers, or the branch of trade or industry. Extreme examples are also found in the United States, where the United Auto Workers (UAW), originally an industry-wide union operating in the car industry, nowadays recruits its members from any organization that invites them. On a smaller scale, this is also happening in Britain. There is a general shift taking place from industrial and craft unions towards competitive general unions.

Changes in qualifications

In some cases, technological and organizational innovation goes hand in hand with the disappearance of craftsmanship, and sometimes an increase in unskilled jobs. Consider the manufacture of watches, electronic tills, typewriters, telephone exchanges and similar products. In these sectors, the replacement of complex (electro)mechanical tools with highly integrated, easy-to-use electronic equipment has reduced the number of jobs for skilled craftsmen.

In most cases, however, the number of skilled workers increases. Most organizations have seen a structural shift towards jobs for white-collar workers, technicians, skilled commercial/clerical staff, engineers and executive staff. This applies to nearly every country. The move towards higher qualifications already began before the introduction of micro-electronic applications. At the macro-level, the shift is taking place very gradually, without any abrupt rift or sudden acceleration. Yet, this development is not so much due to higher technical and economic job requirements as to the endeavours of young people (and their parents) to become as highly qualified as possible. Many financial and cultural obstacles previously restricting access to (higher) education have been removed.

Although this development has been seen across the board, we should not lose sight of the differences that still remain, and which have everything to do with domestic industrial relations. We will explore these differences by comparing the status of the skilled craftsman in the different countries. In the 1960s and 1970s, wages of unskilled and craft-skilled workers were gradually assimilated in Britain. A similar trend was set in motion in Sweden by the solidary incomes policy pursued by the government with the support of the LO union. This development was less strong in Germany and virtually non-existent in France.

Throughout British history, the (craft) unions have shown little interest in boosting the number of skilled workers in the different trades and industries. They argued that limited access to the profession only increased the market value of those who already had a job. For a long time, the unions used the apprenticeship system as a means to curb such access. No wonder the Conservative Thatcher government saw the corporatist bodies which had managed the apprenticeship system since the 1960s (Industrial Training Boards, Manpower Services Commission) as meddlesome anti-market relics from a chapter which needed closing. The link between trade unions and apprenticeship schemes has led to a fall in the number of craftsmen, and apprenticeships have fallen since the late 1970s, along with employment in the manufacturing industry. The increase in student enrolment at institutions of higher education had also halted, but this has changed recently.

An altogether different situation is found in Germany. Here, craft-skilled workers count as the backbone of the industrial unions. The more craftsmen find employment in a particular industry, the stronger a trade union becomes. The German unions have always urged employers and the government to increase the number of apprentices. As a result, the apprenticeship system has a corporatist structure, but it is not subject to any of the restrictions imposed by the craft unions in Great Britain. The system is shouldered by the influential employers' federations and is regarded as a cornerstone of economic success. Also, apprenticeship training and higher education do not compete with each other. In Germany, the number of apprentices more or less keeps pace with the number of students in higher education. The situation is again different in France, where craft-skilled workers also constitute the backbone of the industrial unions, but the unions are ideologically divided. Moreover, the size and power of the corporate hierarchy and technical staff departments, the availability of vocational training outside companies, and the hierarchical segregation of personnel and trade union structures adversely affect the status of the craftsman. The French unions endeavour to improve vertical mobility by demanding greater access to better schools. The decline of the French unions in general and the CGT in particular, and of the French craft-skilled worker, coincides with the growing attraction of higher education. All of this adversely affects the apprenticeship system.

The small wage bands specified in collective industrial agreements for craftsmen prove an added obstacle (scales P1–P3). The highest P3 scale represents the same level of experience and expertise as the lowest craft scales in German bargaining agreements. This is considered a serious problem, as the need is growing for a greater appreciation for manual and production work. In the 1980s, more wage scales were introduced for craftsmen and new wage categories were added, similar to those for lower technical staff. The new categories are referred to as *techniciens d'atelier*. Apparently, shop floor employees with slightly higher technical qualifications and more responsibilities had to be called 'technicians' and recruited from levels lying above ordinary vocational education. These developments also show how difficult it is in France to secure a stable pool of craft-skilled workers. This problem has a considerable bearing on the introduction of new technology in the workplace.

Thus, the problems triggered by changes in qualifications differ strongly according to country. In Germany, a large-scale offensive has been mounted to encourage young people in times of high (youth) unemployment to enrol as apprentices. Also, the quality of vocational training has been upgraded (introduction of courses for new occupations, instructions during basic and advanced training on how to deal with new techniques). However, structural changes have hardly been made.

In Great Britain, access to craft apprenticeships has been restricted as it is associated with trade union interference, job demarcation and high payroll costs. Market forces are given free rein to set up training courses. The institutionalized apprenticeship system is being scaled down. Public institutions increasingly act as commercial providers of training courses and related services to apprentices and students, often sponsored by the business community. The institutional changes have affected both the educational system and trade union structures. Qualifications are increasingly associated with corporate individualism and the principles of a free market.

In France too, the status of the craftsman is dependent on the mechanics of trade unionism and apprenticeship schemes. Here, however, state schools provide courses free of charge, so training is less commercially motivated. The winners of the educational power game are the government and employers; the biggest losers are the trade unions who represent the craft-skilled workers. Admittedly, qualifications are upgraded due to the shift towards jobs in the technical and commercial services sector. Attracting properly qualified employees in the workplace is a different matter. This will require structural changes in collective bargaining agreements, for example, a rethink of wage scales.

The Swedish situation is conspicuous for its steady increase in white-collar workers who, instead of being organized in the LO union, which had dominated the scene thus far, have massively joined the TCO. This, and the growing discontent among highly paid skilled workers over the solidaristic incomes policy, have rendered the joint management of the Swedish economy by the powerful LO and the Social Democrats increasingly difficult. Clearly, the problem is not so much the availability of qualifications as the impact of structural shifts in employment on the management of the economy.

3   Changes in work systems and labour relations

In the previous section, we have explained what role labour relations play in the different countries with respect to problems caused by technological change and the introduction of new organizational and qualification structures. We shall now look at whether it is possible to find a universal

definition of these problems. Is there evidence of a general trend? In order
to answer this question, we must find out:

- whether the changes described have a universal dimension;
- how work systems (that is, the combination of organizational structures, differentiation and coordination mechanisms and qualifications)
  change and how these changes relate to general trends;
- how labour relations change and how these changes relate to changes in
  work systems and general changes.

Work systems and their environment

In general, the choice of organizational and qualification structures and of
differentiation and coordination mechanisms largely depends on the
company's objectives and the setup of the branch of trade or industry
where it operates. These structures and mechanisms are also rooted in a
country's political and institutional traditions and balance of power (see
the previous chapter). This is certainly true for labour relations. It also
means that we must first define a framework in which to place these
structures and changes. In this section, we shall refer to this framework as
the environment of work systems. The characteristics of a work system
(and partly those of labour relations) are to a considerable extent
determined by two elements from the production environment: the size of
a company or business, and its range of products. Organizational sociologists
and management consultants regard the different size of businesses (as
measured by their workforce) as the most important reason for differences
in organizational structure. If production techniques are similar, business
size is further related to output, that is to say, the quantity of goods and/or
services produced.

The second factor should be looked at more closely. We can distinguish
between two types of product, market and strategy. A company may
decide to concentrate on market segments where customer preferences are
highly divergent. Its objective will, then, be to accommodate individual
wishes and needs. The products it designs, develops and manufactures will
be tailor-made. The company's competitive position will hinge on product
quality and product diversification. Proceeds will increase as wider profit
margins are included in the selling price. Alternatively, a company may
target segments of the market where customers have comparable needs, so
a standard range of products can be offered. A competitive edge may be
gained by reducing product costs. Moreover, standardized products and
services enable companies to make maximum use of automation and
benefit from economies of scale. Thus, there are two types of corporate
strategy, market segment and product.

- The first is distinguished by individualized customer demand, tailor-
  made supply, and competition on the basis of product quality and
  diversification.

Market segment/production strategy

		Standardized, competitive prices	Customized, competitive quality
	Low	1 Specialized component parts	2 Craft production
Production output			
	High	3 Mass production ('Fordism')	4 Diversified quality production

Figure 11.1 *Categorization of work systems (Sorge and Streeck, 1988: 30)*

- The second is characterized by a highly standardized supply and demand, and competition on the basis of scale economies.

We find both types of strategy in nearly all markets. To take the car industry as an example, the up-market Rolls–Royce and Mercedes–Benz models – which customers may order to be tailored to their specific needs – represent the first type perfectly. The second strategy stands for classic mass production of such cars as the Ford Model-T, Volkswagen Beetle, Citroen 2CV and Renault R4.

Some products almost necessarily belong to the first type of market segment. Consider large and heavy investment goods like chemical installations and steel-rolling mills. Consumer goods fit the second type. But generally speaking, variations of all products can be found in both market segments and be classified under both production strategies. In Figure 11.1 this differentiation of segments and strategies is further delineated by production output. So we see two dimensions emerge: business size (large versus small) and market segment/production strategy (standardization versus customization). The combination of the two creates a typology of work systems. In this way, a link is established between labour relations, the context in which organizations operate (product, market, strategy, business size) and the work systems described.

Section 1 in Figure 11.1 mainly comprises small and specialized suppliers. Section 2 covers the classic crafts, like a smithy, where every possible iron product can be ordered. It should be noted, however, that small software companies in fact also fall into this category, as they usually cater for very individual needs. The absence of manual labour does not detract from the principle of craft-skilled production.

Section 3 represents the large-scale manufacturing industry, geared to mass production. Section 4 combines high output with customized development and production of goods and services. This combination is sometimes

Table 11.2 *Union policy*

Company policy	Efficiency-orientated	Market-orientated
Emphasis	Quantity	Quality
Business	Cost factor	Market factor
Workforce	Cost factor	Innovation factor
Short-term	Increased proceeds	Increasing costs
Long-term	Increased expenditure	Increasing return on investment
Technological change	End	Means
Labour	Task differentiation	Task integration
Training	Ad hoc, partial	Integral

Source: Pot, 1988: 66

overlooked in the literature and by researchers. However, we often find this type of work system in producers of investment goods, like the steel-rolling mill mentioned earlier, or any other machinery and equipment offered in many variations and models and with highly customized features. Think of machine tools and textile and printing machines.

In this way, changes in production and work systems can be related to environmental changes. A mass manufacturer (section 3) who focuses increasingly on market segments where there is a strongly customized demand will gradually move into section 4. He will presumably develop production systems incorporating features of diversified quality production. A craft business (section 2) which no longer wishes to accommodate customer-specific needs is likely to lose its craft production characteristics and shift to section 1, to produce specialized component parts.

The effect which changes in work systems have on the policies of employers and unions has been put in a nutshell by Pot (1988). He distinguishes between efficiency-orientated and market-orientated production systems (see Table 11.2), which nicely corresponds with the dividing line between the sections on the left-hand and right-hand side of Figure 11.1. Efficiency-orientated systems are designed for efficient bulk production, market-orientated systems for craft or differentiated quality production. Table 11.2 shows the business–economic logic of each system as well as its impact on technology, organization of labour, training systems and labour relations.

There is a third important element to be extracted from the business environment. Companies may choose to carry out certain operations (production of component parts, services like cleaning, sales or development) themselves or contract them out (make or buy). For example, they may concentrate on their core activities and contract out all other operations. Conversely, they may decide to produce in-house component parts and services previously provided by outside suppliers. Oil companies internalize an exceptionally large number of operations, from oil drilling down to selling petrol. Large garment companies, by contrast, tend to contract out many of their operations.

A fourth element concerns the power position of employers' and employees' associations. Union power increases in times of labour shortage, as does the power of employers in times of unemployment. Still, highly formalized and institutionalized systems of labour relations can break the link between the power resources of any particular interest organization and labour market fluctuations. The interest organizations themselves may influence labour market forces (as in the case of the Swedish labour market policy). Also, the colour of the ruling political party(ies) is important. The closer its ties with the unions, the greater the power of the unions. The same goes, of course, for conservative governments and their relationship with employers' associations.

Organizational structure

One of the least controversial results from investigations into the effects of technological change is that, in terms of organizational structure, a gradual shift is taking place towards indirect production. This shift was not only pointed out in recent studies of (the introduction of) micro-electronics, but had already come to light in research on conventional automation. The number of workers in direct production jobs, on the shop floor and in offices is on the decline. Either their work is automated right out of existence or labour productivity is increased by the introduction of new technologies. The increase in labour productivity is consistently highest in direct jobs. On the other hand, the number of workers in indirect production positions is gradually increasing: maintenance, sales, customer service, preparatory work, research and development, personnel management and training, as well as on the managerial front, from the foreman up to the managing director. Not surprisingly, this has led to frantic attempts by companies to automate manual work in indirect jobs. Indirect production and overhead costs are increasingly viewed as obstacles, although they were paid little attention in the past when they had a less prominent share in overall expenditure. Number one on the famous McKinsey consultancy charts is a methodology to stunt the growth of overhead costs and reduce staffing levels. Notwithstanding these efforts, we may conclude that although companies are putting the brakes on growth with regard to the percentage of indirect workers, the tide has yet to turn. Some companies contract out many operations which they believe do not belong to their core activities. Not only is the manufacture of components contracted out, but also such services as cleaning, maintenance, billing, financial management, accounting, technical advice and research and development. Depending on what production operations are contracted out, the number of direct or indirect production jobs decreases. As a result, cooperation between businesses, within and between industries, has taken on considerable importance.

Furthermore, in managerial publications, authors increasingly express the wish or need for flattening out and slimming corporate structures (less vertical and horizontal differentiation). This response has been prompted by the excessive complexity of companies. Complex, broad and hierarchically deep organizations are not considered flexible enough. Such structures prevent a quick response to fluctuations in demand, changes in products and market trends. Although they allow companies to operate efficiently in a stable working environment, complex structures are not at all suited for craft or differentiated production systems (see Figure 11.1). Studies do highlight a trend, though, towards strong fluctuations in demand, differentiated quality production, expanded product ranges and customized products and services. Different terms are used to describe this trend: flexible specialization, new production concepts and differentiated quality production. The question remains, however, as to whether corporate structures have in fact become simpler and hierarchies flattened out and slimmed. The empirical evidence available is insufficient to support this theory. There is still a world of difference between management theory and corporate practice.

It is likely that organizational complexity is increasing at a slower pace than before, and that in some cases it may even be reduced. Companies can simplify their organizational structure either by integrating operations which were previously differentiated, or by contracting out production operations. An alternative option is to combine the two strategies. However, reverse developments towards increased complexity also exist. Electronics are now being applied in trades and industries where computers were hardly used before. Sales companies are focusing more closely on different groups of customers and services are diversified. These developments may well render corporate structures more complicated, but eventually, attempts will be made to curb organizational growth, because of its downward pressure on flexibility. The comparative growth of indirect jobs entails an increase in highly educated workers. Conversely, the number of manual workers and less educated workers falls. The effect on labour relations is considerable and will be discussed in greater detail elsewhere in this chapter.

Given the substantial differences between countries in terms of organizational structure, it is only logical that the general trends highlighted here should have diverse effects. German companies tend to have a smaller setup, a simpler hierarchy and a comparatively weighty basis (direct production jobs). They are therefore better prepared and equipped to absorb recent trends towards smaller structures and transparent hierarchies. British and, especially, French companies are more complex, hierarchically differentiated and broader. Their centre of gravity lies above the basis, so they will have greater difficulty reforming and trimming intermediate and top management levels.

Now, is it the case that organizational structures are converging as a result of these recent developments? Although some movements point in this direction, it is clear from the literature cited by Sorge and Streeck (1988) that differences between countries remain in place. A tentative conclusion may be that societies are developing in the same direction, but the distance between them remains the same. Metaphorically, the idea is that if several ships set sail along the same course and at the same speed but from different starting points, the distances between them will remain unchanged.

Differentiation and coordination mechanisms

The organizational consequences of the trend towards craft and differentiated quality production are reasonably clear. As organizational theory has it, responding to a changing environment requires adaptation: decentralization of power, de-specialization or job enrichment, team work, and fine-tuning operations and divisions as a coordination mechanism (Mintzberg, 1983; de Sitter, 1981). This list is a good summary of postmodern slogans which have been coined by management experts since the late 1970s. These slogans are quite different from those of the 1950s and 1960s. The key words then were: product specialization, large-scale production, rational organization, formalization and rigid automation of manual operations. Strikingly, the German and, to a lesser extent, British differentiation and coordination mechanisms already enable a better response to recent developments. In both countries, the importance of close cooperation and consultation was recognized at a far earlier stage.

Germany, moreover, has a professional bureaucracy which, due to the intensity and quality of vocational education, is found mainly in the operative heart of the company, that is, in the production jobs and the hierarchical line from foreman to general director. This situation has given German industry a dominant role, particularly in market sectors which are characterized by customer service and varied product and service patterns; in other words, markets where investment goods and capital-intensive durable consumer goods are sold. The other side of the picture is that many German mass-producers of consumer electronics have been purchased by foreign companies: Grundig by Philips, Nordmende and others by French concerns; even the Japanese have bought one or two.

The patterns of differentiation and coordination mechanisms, coupled with the vocational training system, enable German industry to respond fairly easily to changing markets, without undermining its organizational discipline and coherence. The British situation in this regard is less rosy due to the breakup of companies into semi-autonomous divisions and the gradual disappearance of craft-skilled workers from direct production units (Sorge, 1991).

When comparing German and British companies which have introduced CNC (computer numerical control) controlled machines, it is striking that in both countries there is a trend towards flexible production. Still, the existing work systems have not consistently been adjusted to the changing situation. Differentiation and coordination mechanisms have been preserved and further developed according to initial company policy. The dividing line between production management and production techniques, and between work preparation and work implementation, is still firmly in place in the British companies. Although they recognize that the CNC-controlled machines can also be used to involve workers on the shop floor in programming operations, it is not their immediate objective.

Shutt and Whittington (1991) observe that British companies do endeavour to make production operations more flexible. However, instead of rendering their in-house work systems more flexible, they contract out production elements and services. These moves are inspired by the belief that smaller or newly established businesses, to whom operations are contracted out, are less bothered by trade unionism and traditional forms of worker representation, and are thus better able to deploy and utilize their workforce flexibly.

Flexibilization in Great Britain is realized according to the country-specific pattern which we earlier found to be typical of British society (see Chapter 10). The financial and accounting management determines the relationship between the stand-alone production units; employers rather regard trade unionism as an obstacle to flexibilization; and putting out operations is often a very attractive option given the comparative unimportance of industry-wide collective bargaining agreements, especially if expensive company agreements have been negotiated for one's own company.

In Germany, the possibility of having programming operations performed by shopfloor workers is an essential reason for purchasing these machines. In fact, CNC-controlled and peripheral equipment is used as a (technical) means to integrate production-technical operations straight across divisions and personnel categories. In Germany, more than in any other country, traditional technical and hierarchical coordination concepts have come under attack from alternative concepts, aimed at an even greater integration of tasks on the shop floor (Sorge et al., 1983). The introduction of a flexible organization does not usually take place outside the framework of existing labour relations. Operations are contracted out and companies do sometimes concentrate on core activities, but German companies are rather reluctant to hive off technical and production operations. In their view, the costs associated with worker participation, union involvement and internal coordination are more than compensated for by improved customization and product quality.

A comparison between German and French companies shows that the application of CNC techniques in France does not essentially reduce the importance attached to hierarchical differentiation and coordination. What catches the eye is that technical expertise has increased at all levels and hierarchical coordination must meet stricter requirements. This is how the French try to respond to changes in the task environment.

The preliminary conclusion may be drawn that changes in the task environment have confronted companies in different countries with similar problems and challenges. However, due to different strategies, traditional institutions and other aspects of the general task environment (government policy, balance of power), they have applied different solutions.

Qualifications and personnel management

All countries are witnessing an increased use of qualifications, a shift towards higher qualifications and an upsurge in personnel management. These developments reflect the following underlying changes.

1   With the introduction of new technologies, existing expertise and skills become obsolete, in any case partially. This creates problems in the field of retraining and adjustment to new equipment and procedures. It is possible, however, that after the initial retraining, practice and habituation period, the need for training and qualifications eases off.
2   New technologies require a more competent handling of abstract data and pre-structured information. Skills must be developed to understand and implement programmed processes. Workers must be increasingly alert, concentrated and possess a general ability to learn. Purely physical exertion is no longer needed. The demand for upgraded skills and expertise calls for school training instead of learning by experience. Such training is provided by vocational educational institutions, the apprenticeship system and tailor-made courses provided in-house or by outside institutions.
3   Work systems which produce craft and differentiated quality products demand higher qualifications for manual work. In particular, there is a need for combined cognitive/abstract and technical/practical skills. The flexible production of goods and services does not permit a strict division between planning and implementing operations. Also, fewer staff have to be hired as routine jobs are increasingly automated.

The process of change mentioned under (1) usually occurs in times when new technologies are rapidly introduced. However, the ensuing need for advanced qualifications and training eventually becomes less urgent, as operations and types of work again turn into routine. To illustrate this point, for a long time working with computers and automated information systems was the privilege of experts. Nowadays, with procedures and systems becoming simpler, small-scale and user-friendly, almost everyone can control such systems, provided they have had a proper introduction.

The factors mentioned under (2) have a long-term impact. They have led to vocational education assigning more time and space to courses which, in geographical and substantive terms, are far removed from the workplace, where the expertise and skills acquired will actually be applied later. There is also a tendency, however, to link school education and actual working processes more effectively (consider the importance of apprenticeship in some countries).

The changes described under (3) are linked to developments on the product markets. Although they have a long-term impact, the practical effects differ with the specific circumstances of the trade, industry or company concerned. In fact, in some industries and product markets we see developments going the way of standardized production and economies of scale. Also, the growth of differentiated production may be delayed or indeed reversed. In the post-war period, for example, different countries experienced a comprehensive and protracted movement towards mass production.

Moreover, differences may occur in the nature and intensity of these developments. The degree of intensity depends very much on the features of and traditions underlying the structure of work systems, which, in turn, are influenced by social institutions. The German work systems and institutions are pre-eminently suited to apply models of differentiated quality production. The French work systems and institutions tend to favour large-scale production and forms of production based on government-dependent demand or on a large proportion of highly qualified staff (arms, aircraft, energy, nuclear power, electronics). British society has been subject to a prolonged process of change. Once the workshop of the world, Great Britain has developed a hybrid structure of suppliers, producers of standardized goods, financial and commercial services, and exports of arms, aircraft and R&D-intensive products.

Clearly, the effects of technological change should not be explained as ensuing from the new techniques themselves. Rather, they are created by the environment where technology has developed and is applied. Only on this basis can we properly analyse the differences found between countries. As for Germany, it is likely to intensify its vocational training system, both quantitatively and qualitatively. Despite the growing numbers of highly educated workers, elementary vocational education will probably remain important. This prophecy has already partially come true. At any given moment, over half the population has attended an apprenticeship course. Apprenticeship is increasingly combined with further technical studies, a *Meister* diploma, a university degree or higher vocational diploma as an engineer, business administrator and so on. Compared to their counterparts in other countries, German craftsmen are on average better able smoothly and independently to handle CNC-controlled machines or other innovative devices. The shift from junior secondary vocational education and apprenticeship training towards senior vocational education, as seen in the Netherlands and notably in France and Great Britain, has not taken place in Germany, or in any case not as thoroughly.

As stated, France has seen a change towards vocational training at a higher (senior) level. Once CNC technology arrives on the scene, companies recruit young workers who are educated (far) above the 'ordinary' level of craft training, even though they initially have limited duties and powers. If the number of workers with lower vocational training increased in the past, many companies nowadays consider that level insufficient to deal with new technologies (Maurice et al., 1986). In France, technological progress has triggered an exodus to more vocational education. At the same time, it has upgraded the status of technicians and led to tighter supervision of selective operations by technicians and planners.

Different yet again is the situation in Great Britain. Here, too, the need is felt for higher vocational qualifications. The companies surveyed in the German–British comparison, however, had not tackled the problem by intensifying apprenticeship training. British companies increasingly differentiate between craft-skilled workers, semi-skilled workers (with little or no training) and company-skilled workers (in between craft- and semi-skilled), and satisfy their need for qualified workers in two ways. On the one hand, they provide apprenticeship training for technicians supplemented by a technical college course, and on the other, they set up company-specific training courses designed to acquire company skills (Sorge et al., 1983). Thus, the manner in which qualification processes adjust to technological changes and market developments differs from country to country.

Labour relations

Of the environmental factors specified earlier, considerable importance must be attached to the relative position of power of employees, employers and their organizations. The sustained shortage of jobs has substantially reinforced the position of employers, and put pressure on employees and trade unions. Strikingly, changes in this balance of power again differ greatly according to country. In France, the number of trade unionists as a proportion of the working population has plunged to 10 per cent. In numerical terms, the trade union movement has become virtually unimportant. In the Scandinavian countries, in contrast, density rates have gone up, despite the already high numbers of trade unionists.

As trade unions are embedded in different ways in different societies, the extent to which the position of employees has weakened differs considerably, as do the institutional responses.

In Great Britain, union membership has not undergone any drastic change, but the actual power of union representatives and the opportunities for them to support their demands by industrial action and organize their members have been checked by the Conservative government. Competition between unions has been intensified by the government's attempts to introduce single-union deals. The very character of the unions may change due to the ongoing shift from craft and industrial unions towards general unions. In France, density rates have plummeted dramatically in heavy industry. The CGT has been the most affected. Union power has been strongly undermined, despite the fact that the country for a long time had a Socialist government. All of this is in keeping with a classic French pattern: central government legislation becomes increasingly important, while collective bargaining agreements are no longer the obvious tool to promote employee interests. In Germany, IG Metall continues to exercise its dominant position. The fact that trade unionism is alive and well in Germany was demonstrated by the nationwide dispute over shorter working hours. Membership has not dropped substantially.

Having explained these differences, it would appear as if new technologies and changes in the economic framework do not play a role at all. Or do they? After all, the societal effect approach suggests that there is such an interrelation. The shift towards craft-skilled and differentiated quality production and market-orientated policies (see Figure 11.1 and Table 11.2) certainly affects the workforce, as training and qualifications become increasingly important. More flexible and market-orientated production systems also require more efficient staffing policies and harmonious labour relations. And indeed, both policy areas have taken up a firm position in overall company policy. We need only mention the term human resource management.

Not everywhere has this shift resulted in the reinforcement or preservation of the position of trade unions and works councils. This already became clear when we discussed the impact of labour relations on technological and organizational changes. We shall now analyse the situation in the different countries.

In France, the trade unions and *comités d'entreprise* have only a marginal share in the innovation movement. The 'market' for innovative personnel management, based on mutual trust and sensible negotiations, has remained small. Innovation is often pushed through by the one-sided policy of company management. If such a policy establishes an informal relationship between those involved, it does so outside formalized labour relations, without involving the bodies formally set up to shape these relations. The fact that the Auroux legislation, aimed at increasing worker participation, is hardly applied in practice only underlines this trend. Indeed, the intensification of personnel management has played into the hands of company management, which, because of the autonomy so acquired – or conquered – is better able to push through its decisions.

In the UK, attempts to pursue an innovative staffing policy are often made within the framework of collective labour relations. But there are exceptions to this rule, as the printing and publishing industry has shown. The traditional practice of large companies to enter into *de facto* closed shop contracts has remained unchanged. The struggle to integrate negotiations between the management and all the trade union representatives working in the company (single union bargaining), and to limit job demarcation/control and other restrictive practices, sometimes has strange results. Trade unions increasingly find themselves having to fight for company-specific monopolies instead of craft or division-specific monopolies. Still, the position of the unions has stayed more or less the same. In fact, unions which adopt a cooperative attitude may even succeed in strengthening their position in the workplace, and claim the benefits of the company's refurbished staffing policy. In addition, the traditional segmentation of

British labour relations on the shop floor is being reduced. Fierce competition between unions on the market for local representation monopolies is the price they have to pay.

Few changes have been reported for Germany. Gradually, despite opposition from employers, aspects of technological and organizational innovation have been included in collective bargaining agreements or company agreements. Another important element has been the efforts of trade unions to increase the number of apprentices. Union policy has also been aimed at the quality of basic training, even though the numbers and qualifications achieved clearly exceed industry's immediate needs. Partly under pressure from the government, employers have adopted the unions' policy, especially as regards apprentice enrolment. Besides the general argument that employers should assume more social responsibility, a sufficient supply of craftsmen must be secured in the long run, as the 1990s will see a decline in the number of young people.

The unions are also endeavouring to maintain the independence of craftsmen. IG Metall wants to preserve the wage system, which is largely based on professional qualifications. They expect that the high pay rates for craft-skilled workers will force employers to make maximum use of the qualifications available, and thus keep intact the independence of craftsmen on the shop floor. The unions have also been lobbying the government, sometimes backed by employers, to ensure that technical equipment (notably CNC-controlled machines) is developed in such a way that it stabilizes workers' independence and competence. Here too, we see that developments unroll along typically German lines: the craftsmen trained under the apprenticeship system constitute the foundation of corporate structures and, indeed, of career development.

Recent events in Germany, following the hangover after the reunification party, have altered this picture somewhat. As the country pulls out of its recession and is faced with the increased 'emigration' of large-scale production to Eastern Europe, we can expect that the institutions linked with diversified quality production will reassert themselves.

4   An overall perspective

Our analysis appears to justify the following conclusions.

1   Developments in the area of technology, organization and qualifications partly have a common denominator, and thus occur in all the countries under review. Companies must improve their ability to respond flexibly and readily to constantly changing product markets, and to successfully introduce new technology.

2   These developments and resulting changes in production and work systems are often indirectly and to a limited extent influenced by labour relations. This is especially true for the involvement of trade unions and the various consultative and negotiating bodies. Indirectly, however,

the general production environment (including labour relations) does play an important role. Labour relations (and other elements of the general environment in which companies operate, like government policy), the task environment, organization of labour and qualification processes are interrelated.

Consciously or subconsciously, employers act within existing country-specific relations and institutions. Even if all participants in the different countries endeavour to realize the same goals and pursue the same strategies, the result will still be characteristic of the society where they operate. Moreover, there is a link between the institutional relations in a society and the task environment. For example, the patterns found in Germany in terms of organization, qualifications and labour relations are better suited for differentiated quality production.

We believe that this analysis, and our findings, demonstrate that the societal effect not only comes to light when we take a random picture or provide a static description of society (see Chapter 10). Placed in a dynamic perspective, against the backdrop of processes of change and innovation, the societal effect is still visible; it influences the nature, direction and degree of change. Thus, despite developments in markets, products, technology, training systems and organization forms, the existing social diversity does not disappear. It merely continues in a slightly different form.

12 The crisis of Fordism: restructuring in the automobile industry

Ben Dankbaar

1 Introduction

This chapter will provide a detailed consideration of developments in one specific sector: the automobile industry. In addition to its economic significance, this sector merits close study for a wide variety of other reasons. In recent decades, most car manufacturers have seen the need to engage in often extensive restructuring. New production standards have placed very different demands on both the organization and design of the work process. As a result, employment relationships in the automobile industry have undergone drastic changes. The inquiry undertaken here addresses the role industrial relations play in this process: do they act as constraints on changes in the employment relationship or do they change along with it?

The automobile industry is also noteworthy for other reasons. Automobile manufacturers operate and compete with each other on a global scale and are necessarily confronted with institutional diversity between continents and countries. This chapter will also consider how companies respond to these inconsistencies: do the specific industrial relations systems within various countries exert a fundamental influence on employment policies of multinational production enterprises? Or does the international orientation of the parent company's management circumvent the differences between countries? To pose the question in another manner: does the automobile industry engender a characteristic form of employment relationship unique to that industry as a whole, or does the organization of work within the industry exhibit varying attributes distinctly associated with the social institutions of the country in which the manufacturers operate?

2 The automobile industry and industrial relations: issues

The period following the 1970s has been a tumultuous one for the automobile industry world-wide. Two oil crises in 1973 and 1979, continuing controversy over safety and environmental pollution, accelerated technological development, as well as the rapid ascendancy of new manufacturers in Japan and Korea, have sorely tested the responsiveness of the traditional producers of passenger vehicles in the United States and Western Europe. The demands and needs of consumers have shifted, the product has evolved, and the manufacturers – as well as the environment in which they operate – have been transformed. And there is as yet no end in sight to this process of change. It is self-evident that such unsettled conditions also strain existing industrial relations systems. In some cases, management of the involved enterprises regard existing understandings with labour organizations and works councils as serious impediments to attempts to adapt to new circumstances. In other instances, proposed changes in the configuration of the work process are at odds with existing organizational structures. As a result, labour relations which are based on historic organizational arrangements may be unintentionally undermined. In yet other scenarios, labour relations are severely tested by wholesale shutdowns of individual factories as well as entire companies. The construction of new factories in regions previously unfamiliar with the automobile industry, and the importation of so-called Japanese management concepts, pose entirely new challenges for unions. New job requirements, in concert with new technologies, displace existing demarcations between occupational groups and task descriptions. Finally, increasing internationalization creates tremendous problems for the nationally orientated labour movement.

Against the backdrop of these complex adaptive and restructuring processes in the automobile industry, this chapter will specifically address the following three questions.

1 How and to what extent do the national industrial relations of a country influence the manner in which enterprises react to changes in their environment?
2 How and to what extent do the strategies for change adopted by enterprises influence the development of industrial relations in a country?
3 Does the now global scope of the involved enterprises, in concert with world-wide technological development and Japanese competition, indicate a trend toward structural convergence of national and regional industrial relations systems?

The organization of the rest of this chapter is as follows: sections 3 and 4 contain a closer analysis of the automobile industry and its historic significance, particularly with respect to the area of industrial relations and the challenges which automobile manufacturers have faced in recent decades. Section 5 reviews various adaptive strategies undertaken by enterprises, with specific attention focused on new notions of work organization and the 'Japanese model'. Section 6 follows up with the interplay between changes in work organization and industrial relations in a number of countries (relating to questions 1 and 2 above). Section 7 takes up the question of whether a trend toward convergence of industrial relations approaches may be identified in recent developments.

3   The automobile industry as a symbol of mass production

The automobile industry has played a key role in the economic and social history of the twentieth century. In 1886, Carl Benz obtained a patent for a three-box vehicle with an internal combustion engine. The succeeding decades saw a boom in technical development, which, among other changes, transformed the vehicle from a coach without horses to the three-box model, typically equipped with an engine in the front box as is still the practice today.

Work on the assembly line

In the first 20 years, the production process was still dominated by highly trained craftsmen, who assembled each car as if it were a puzzle of some kind; the individual parts were machined until they made a perfect fit (the British occupational term for this type of work – fitter – had to be taken quite literally). As a result, no one car was precisely identical to another. These production methods made it next to impossible to produce mass quantities of automobiles. The automobile continued to be a luxury item and remained so in Europe for a considerable length of time. In the United States, however, attention had long been paid to the possibility of producing components in such a manner that they could conform to the required fit without the necessity of further adjustments and be completely interchangeable (the so-called American system; Hounshell, 1984). Manufacturing equipment which could provide the necessary precision to achieve this goal became available only at the beginning of this century. Automobile manufacturer Henry Ford, who had made it a practice to always procure the most recent and advanced machinery, recognized early on the possibilities of segregating the production of components from final assembly of vehicles. If all parts fit readily, the work of final assembly could be accomplished without highly trained workers. Ford experienced other problems, however. Assembly work was not particularly interesting and had to be executed at an accelerated pace. Turnover of personnel was high. To increase productivity, Ford introduced the principle of assembly line production, setting the organization of manufacturing work completely on its head. Workers no longer walked from one assembly location to another; the work now came to them – and at a continuous (and intense) rate. These developments were accompanied by a dramatic expansion of task differentiation, so that each worker executed only a few manual procedures. As a result of these production and work organization measures, labour productivity soared to unheard of levels. The same, however, also occurred with respect to turnover and sickness-related absenteeism. The solution to these problems came in the form of a considerable wage increase (the so-called 'five dollar day') paid to gain a loyal and dependable workforce. Ford, in effect, passed on a share of the productivity gains to his employees in the form of higher wages. The foregoing describes the most significant elements of what is called 'Fordism' as a production scheme: assembly line manufacturing with extensive task differentiation and high wages (Lichtenstein and Meyer, 1989). This system proved extremely well suited to production of mass quantities of standardized goods. Ford commenced production of his famous Model T in 1908. He produced 19,000 units that year. Production levels reached 180,000 in 1912 and 308,000 by 1914! During the same period, the price of a Model T plummeted from $850.00 in 1908 to $360.00 in 1916.

Fordism

Mass production requires mass consumption. More consumers can be reached through reduced prices. However, gains from increases in productivity clearly cannot be passed on twice: increasing wages while simultaneously decreasing prices can only succeed if there is a sizeable gross to apportion. Over time, Ford also had to contend with competition. The profit margin at Ford narrowed and before long wages at Ford ceased to be significantly different from those at other companies. In the 1920s, General Motors (GM) evolved into the most threatening rival. This company experimented with a different approach to reaching consumers: greater product differentiation. While Ford supplied only *one* model in *one* colour, GM introduced a variety of models in assorted colours and price categories. As a result of these marketing tactics, GM soon outpaced Ford, which has never recovered its lead. Thus, the 1920s saw changes in both the nature of competition and the structure of the industry. By the mid-1930s, only a handful of automobile manufacturers remained extant in the United States. The economic crisis of 1929, with the collapse in stock prices on Wall Street, may be seen as a logical consequence of economic structures such as those which had evolved in, for example, the automobile industry. Automobile manufacturers engaged in mass production, but the competitive pressure to pass on productivity gains in the form of lower prices declined, and there was no mechanism to ensure a corresponding rise in wages. The result was mass production without mass consumption. The attendant economic stagnation persisted until well into and after the Second World War.

The foundation for the eventual recovery, however, was laid in the 1930s. Both intentionally and to some degree unintentionally, the social and political infrastructure reacted to the economic crisis by forging various mechanisms to strengthen purchasing power and thereby sustain demand: on the one hand providing compensation for unemployment, illness and old age, while recognizing and protecting the status of labour unions on the other. The labour movement also began to assume a role in maintaining stable economic growth. These developments did not proceed uniformly across all countries, and recognition of labour unions did not occur with equal swiftness everywhere, particularly in the United States and certainly not at Ford. Nevertheless, in the post-war period, labour organizations became a significant constituent of the institutional system which undertook to ensure a reasonable equilibrium between mass production and mass consumption. As a result, an unprecedented period of growth and progress ensued. The institutional paradigm upon which this rested may appropriately be denoted as 'Fordism'. Consistent with the practices at Henry Ford's factories, Fordism involves a combination of increased productivity and augmented purchasing power (Piore and Sabel, 1984; Tolliday and Zeitlin, 1986).

Fordism in Europe

Following the Second World War, Fordism evolved into a universal model for the industrialized West with respect to both the method of production (the assembly line) and social policies and practices (wages rising along with productivity, emergence and recognition of industrial trade unions, rise of the welfare state). Although the manner in which Fordism was effectuated in various West European countries was marked by considerable differences, the similarities were even greater. Consistent features found everywhere included an enhanced role for the labour movement and the growing significance of the government as dispenser of social security and guardian over macro-economic development (by preserving purchasing power and thus sustaining consumer demand). In the context of the automobile industry, this meant, among other things, widespread adoption of 'American' methods and consolidation of the status of strong labour organizations.

The introduction of Fordist methods of production in European automobile factories commenced as early as the 1920s, stimulated by Ford's enormous success and bolstered by the openness practised by Ford with respect to his methods: he provided detailed information and access to his factories to interested competitors as well as the press. French and Italian automobile manufacturers such as Citroen, Renault, Berliet and Agnelli were fascinated by the Fordist model. Compared to the North American market, however, European automobile markets remained much smaller and more segmented, with the result that the pure Ford model could only be applied on a circumscribed basis. Production levels were insufficient to warrant implementation of more extensive automation or strict supervision, let alone higher wages. Instead of across-the-board salary improvements, European manufacturers remained committed to various variants of piece-rate. As a consequence, the rate, volume and methods of work were neither strictly prescribed or regulated, nor dictated by technological means (that is, the assembly line). Workers retained a measure of control over their work pace and methods.

The emergence of industrial labour unions is undoubtedly directly related to the advent of mass production and the diminished relevance of the skilled trades to the production process. The growth and recognition of these unions have necessarily been strongly influenced by the political environment at the national level. In countries such as France, the United States before the Second World War, and in post-war Germany, the configuration of political power was such that their governments brought pressure to bear on employers to accept unions and further affirmed organized labour's rights through legislation. In contrast, the British government in the 1930s was considerably less predisposed to support new prerogatives for employees and modern industrial unions failed to emerge there. Even after the war, British automobile workers remained organized in various craft unions. In post-war Italy, the national government advanced the establishment of a type of works council in which workers constituted half of the voting membership. The objective of these councils was to increase productivity by means of cooperation between management and workers. Their significance was diminished when the balance of political power shifted to the Christian Democrats in the 1950s. The leverage of the industrial labour movement was further circumscribed by its susceptibility to the influence of the communists, who were permanently entrenched in the political opposition.

On the eve of the first oil crisis (1973), clearly divergent variants of the Fordist model could be discerned in European automobile factories both in the organization of work and with respect to the role of the labour movement. Workers in Great Britain, through their representatives (shop stewards), exercised a considerable hold over their work ('job control'), while the craft unions enforced a precise demarcation of tasks for the members of various trades and thereby maintained their job security. While this was often viewed as evidence of the immense power of the British workers' movement, it should be noted that 'job control' was also the result of the manner in which British management, in a departure from the Fordist model, adhered to the practice of performance-based pay (piece-rates). A governmental investigatory commission (the Donovan Commission) reported in 1968 that these unique features of British industrial relations played an important role in the lurking crisis of the British automobile industry. Management in France and Italy had emulated the Fordist production model more closely. Automobile factories in both countries were increasingly populated with numerous unskilled and often uprooted foreign workers (in France) and migrant labour (from the south of Italy). The latent tensions occasioned by these developments erupted suddenly in the late 1960s. In Italy, works councils arose outside the existing organizational framework which were highly radicalized and which sought direct confrontation with management. In France, labour unions affiliated with the CGT encountered great difficulty in exercising any control over the rebellion in 1968. Germany was confronted with a general strike movement of some magnitude around 1970, although this was less directly aimed at the established unions than the movements in France and Italy. In post-war Germany, the Fordist production model also left its mark on the organization of work in the automobile industry, but without diminishing the traditional role of the skilled trades to the same extent as in the United States. The German skilled trades, however, are not organized in craft unions such as those in Great Britain. German industrial relations are largely determined by the existence of a powerful union organization which encompasses all metal workers (including those outside the automobile industry), and through legislation governing the establishment of joint works councils (*Betriebsräte*). These councils exercise significant authority, and management is required to reach agreement with the *Betriebsrat* before effectuating changes in the organization of work.

4   Challenges to Fordism

The labour unrest of the late 1960s was generally regarded as a signal that changes were necessary in the organization of production, as well as society generally. Fordism began to lose some of its lustre, but the direction of future developments remained unclear. No one foresaw the turmoil awaiting the automobile industry, which constituted the mainstay of Fordism.

While consolidation had indeed taken place within the European automobile industry after the war, this was almost exclusively confined within national borders. By approximately 1970, one could find within every large European country at least one mass producer of passenger vehicles: Fiat in Italy, Renault and Peugeot (PSA) in France, Volkswagen in Germany and British Leyland in Great Britain. The latter currently operates under the name Rover and has meanwhile down-sized to such a degree that the designation 'mass producer' is no longer appropriate. Rover is no longer an autonomous enterprise. For several years it was a subdivision of British Aerospace, which sold its shares to BMW in 1993. In Spain, SEAT was created as a state enterprise in the 1950s and taken over by Volkswagen in the 1980s. In addition to these national companies, American automobile manufacturers Ford and General Motors have historically had a presence as mass producers in Europe, notably in Great Britain and Germany.

The European automobile industry is also characterized by the fact that so-called specialists are active in the passenger vehicle market alongside the mass producers. These are the companies which concentrate exclusively at the top end of the market. Not counting extremely small companies, they include such manufacturers as Alfa Romeo, Audi, Jaguar, Saab, Volvo, BMW and Mercedes–Benz. The number of independent specialists has dwindled sharply in recent years and it is questionable whether there is any meaningful distinction left to be made between mass producers and specialists. Alfa has become a division of Fiat, Audi has been a subsidiary of Volkswagen for some time, Jaguar has been taken over by Ford, Saab is half owned by GM. An attempt to merge Volvo and Renault failed unexpectedly in the autumn of 1993. The reasons for the specialists' loss of independence are complex. While the mergers of the 1950s and 1960s may be attributed to gains achievable through large scale production, the current focus is on drastic increases in research and development costs of new models as well as the mass producers' augmented capacity to offer technologically advanced and high-quality models, and at lower prices than those asked by the 'true' specialists.

The recent escalation in takeovers and collaborative alliances is a reflection of the sharpened competition within the European automobile industry. The automobile industry world-wide has been in transition since the beginning of the 1970s (Altshuler et al., 1984). This may be explained in terms of three phenomena.

- The sharply higher standards generally set by governments with respect to safety, economy and toxic emissions.
- Countless new technical options for improving both the production process and the automobile made available particularly through developments in micro-electronics and sensor technology.

- The appearance of a formidable contingent of new entrants into the world market: the Japanese and, in their wake, the Koreans.

This threefold challenge has confronted Western automobile producers with well-nigh insurmountable obstacles.

Since the 1970s, Japanese automobile manufacturers have engaged in an unprecedented export offensive. This has yielded them a market share of approximately 29 per cent of the North American automobile market, while their share of the West European automobile market amounts to approximately 12 per cent. The smaller incursion into West European markets is apparently attributable less to the strength of the European manufacturers than to the protectionist policies of some European countries (particularly France and Italy), and the resolve on the part of the Japanese to direct themselves primarily at the North American market. The success of Japanese manufacturers was long described in the same terms applied to analyses of competition from the Third World: low wages and low prices. It is currently undisputed that Japanese success is based on high productivity combined with superior quality. In addition to possessing the most advanced technologies, Japanese manufacturers appeared capable of reacting swiftly to new standards placed on the automobile with regard to safety, economy and pollution. On the basis of varying interpretations of the nature of the challenges facing them, automobile manufacturers fashioned diverse strategies, which were not without impact on industrial relations. Automobile manufacturers were confronted in each country with manifestly distinct labour relations, which in turn influenced the methods and tactics of the manufacturers. The organization of work and the structure of industrial relations are cardinal elements to be addressed in the process of transformation. After two decades of adaptation and change, it is now acknowledged that the automobile industry faces 'the end of Fordism'.

5   New strategies and models

Over time, diverse strategies were cultivated by automobile manufacturers to enable them to cope with the multiple challenges which arose in the 1970s and 1980s. These included the following distinct approaches.

1   Relocation of production to low wage regions.
2   Automation of production.
3   Increased outsourcing of production components to suppliers.
4   Transformation of work organization in production.
5   Comprehensive reorganization of all components of the enterprise, from product development through marketing.

It should be noted at the outset that these strategies largely gained adherence in the sequence set out above. Each strategy can also be described as a response to experiences with, and the improvement of, each preceding strategy. The truth is obviously more complex: even now, different strategies are combined in specific ways by enterprises.

Relocation

In the mid-1970s, the conviction grew among many observers of the automobile industry that this business sector was 'mature' and would, like the textile industry, resettle in countries and regions with lower labour costs. Particularly in Latin American countries, the automobile industry had already achieved a substantial presence as a result of the protectionist development policies of certain governments (especially those of Brazil and Mexico). The concurrent phenomenon of American consumers turning to the purchase of smaller cars led to a blurring of differences with the European market. American manufacturers launched the notion of a 'world car' which might be sold world-wide and would be comprised of parts which could consistently be produced in the most economical locations. The realization of this vision came up against numerous technical and political impediments. Automobiles are, after all, considerably more complicated than textiles. The large-scale relocation of production to low wage countries has not yet materialized, and the development of a 'world car' proved more difficult than originally estimated. There is, nevertheless, an increased flow of parts imported from developing countries. In addition to a definite level of 'globalization' of production, a politically and commercially motivated regionalization of both production and research and development activity is visibly under way. Both the threat of protectionist measures as well as the logic of just-in-time delivery (discussed below) has forced automobile manufacturers to localize a great degree of their productive capacity within those regions of the world where their products are sold: North America, Europe and Southeast Asia (Dankbaar, 1984).

Automation

The expectations surrounding the world car initiative were essentially still premised on a Fordist mass production paradigm of higher production levels and correspondingly lower costs. The same could be said about the strategy of automation. Mass production is conducive to extensive automation, the most prominent European example of which is the Volkswagen Beetle, which came off the assembly line in much the same design year after year. In the second half of the 1970s, the impulse toward automation received yet another stimulus, not from an escalation of mass production, but from the introduction of programmable automatons and robots. They made possible the evolution toward flexible instead of fixed automation. As a result, machines were no longer discarded upon changes in product design, but were simply reprogrammed. Moreover, the same assembly line could now accommodate concurrent production of various models. Particularly in automobile body construction, numerous welding robots quickly appeared, which effected a fundamental transformation in the nature of work in this department. Robots also appeared in the paint shops and, with great dexterity, assumed the work of human painters. In this manner, robots eliminated scores of jobs including a considerable number of unpleasant and unhealthy ones. The work in automobile body construction and the paint shops now consists primarily of control operations conducted at a video terminal, as well as relatively elaborate maintenance functions and a succession of residual activities which robots have not (to date) been capable of appropriating.

There is a wide range of opinions as to the degree to which actual improvements in productivity and cost effectiveness have been realized. What quickly became clear, however, was that the proposition that Japanese competitive capacity was based on an intensive utilization of robotics was as illusory as the notion that they prevailed on the basis of extremely low wages. Even after Western factories had overcome their perceived handicap in robotics and even gained the advantage in some areas of automation, Japanese manufacturers still retained their edge with respect to costs. Attention was then focused on another discovery: the absence of stockpiled components in Japanese automobile factories. These inventories represent idle capital not being applied to production. Production without stockpiling is therefore always more economical.

Just-in-time

The magnitude of inventories appears a relatively negligible detail, but in reality goes to the heart of the Fordist method. Mass production seeks to profit from economies of scale. Higher levels of production make possible a greater degree of task differentiation with commensurately lower training requirements and qualifications for workers. Higher levels of production also make it more attractive to produce parts in-house instead of depending on external suppliers. There is, however, a downside to this approach. Lower levels of training of workers also invites greater opportunities for human error. The complexity of the production process increases as more items are manufactured in-house. To prevent errors from paralysing the entire operation, extra reserves are stockpiled which function as buffers between the various departments. Similarly, parts from outside suppliers are stored to ensure a consistently available inventory of suitable quality.

The Japanese automobile industry has long known a lower degree of vertical integration than most North American and European manufacturers. The relationship between automobile manufacturer and outside supplier has also developed differently. While the Western model typically exhibits complete dominance by the manufacturer, Japanese producer–supplier relationships are frequently more balanced. In light of the Japanese experience, the West is now beginning to realize that while squeezing outside suppliers may result in lower prices, it also leads to deficiencies in quality and both a disinclination and lack of opportunity on the part of suppliers to assist in product development. In emulation of the Japanese model, Western manufacturers are now striving towards a reformulation of their relationship with their suppliers. To begin with, a growing number of parts are now being outsourced. After all, why should a worker be paid to upholster seats at metalworkers' wages when the work can just as well be accomplished by a supplier enterprise at the much lower salary of a textile worker? Production is thus displaced from the Fordist automobile complexes to the more manageable factories of the much smaller supplier. Automobile manufacturers now show a willingness to enter into long-term contracts with a stringently selected cadre of suppliers. In exchange, the manufacturers demand high quality and prompt delivery timed as nearly as possible to the moment that the designated parts are actually needed in production: just-in-time. In some cases suppliers are given more responsibility for the design and development of entire components. As a result of all this, the industry is slowly evolving in the direction of more separate production entities with greater diversity in working conditions and labour–management relations.

The strategy of increased contracting out of production components and the just-in-time delivery of parts obviates to a great extent the need for stockpiled inventories in the final assembly plants. From an organizational perspective, however, the elimination of the buffers between the various production segments is even more significant. This calls for a thorough fine tuning of all phases of production and, above all, the elimination of all error. The Fordist method opted for task differentiation, not only between the various production functions, but also between production and quality control. The worker was not charged with determining whether the task had been correctly executed: that was ascertained by an inspector. Mistakes were corrected rather than prevented. Surprised North American and European managers were forced to concede that the Japanese were able to combine high productivity with high quality and with a lower degree of task differentiation (Cusumano, 1985). Various production tasks were less definitively apportioned among individual workers. Workers were charged with assisting one another when their tasks were completed. Moreover, there were no quality inspectors; everyone was accountable for the quality of their own work. And, although seldom occurring in practice, Japanese workers even had the authority to stop the assembly line if they encountered a problem – such as an ill-fitting part – which they could not resolve. The minimization of all external and internal inventories was coupled with the implementation of numerous measures intended to secure consistently high quality.

Teamwork

In recent years, Western manufacturers have sought to imitate many of these measures and effectuate more or less fundamental changes in the organization of work. These attempts can be broadly delineated as a blurring of the task differentiation which was a hallmark of the Fordist model (Kern and Schumann, 1984; Roth and Kohl, 1988). The task cycle on the assembly line was extended; rotation among different tasks was encouraged; diverse forms of teamwork were developed; primary and ancillary tasks were combined into new functions, with particular attention being paid to 'self-inspection' (the worker inspects his own work and confirms by means of a sticker or note that all is well, or, alternatively, that a problem exists); the lines of demarcation between production and maintenance work were redrawn so as to also assign maintenance duties (routine, preventative) to production workers.

In addition to the above, Japanese innovations such as 'quality circles' were also introduced. With quality circles, employees could make suggestions for improvements in the production process or the product both during and outside of working hours and could also participate in effectuating their proposals. This was obviously a considerable departure from the Fordist conceptual model, which was premised on the unique capacity of engineers to design the optimal organization of the production process, to which workers were to give strict adherence.

Comprehensive transformation

To change the organization of work in the production process in this manner proved to be a complicated endeavour. It reached deep into the existing role patterns and power relationships in the factory. The organization of work in Western automobile factories remains in flux even now. At the same time, however, it has been observed that Japanese competitors have developed divergent forms of organization for the enterprise as a whole in other respects; these have resulted in dramatically improved results in, for example, product development. While the life span of a model produced by European and American manufacturers may amount to as much as six to ten years, that of the Japanese is scarcely four to five years. A specialist such as Mercedes–Benz will produce more units over the total lifetime of a model than a Japanese mass producer. It may justifiably be questioned as to which is the true 'specialist': Mercedes, which can spread the fixed costs of an expensive car over a large number of units, or the Japanese manufacturer, which can budget comparable costs over a smaller number of cheaper automobiles and still make a profit. The strategy of comprehensive organizational transformation has only taken visible shape in the past few years: this approach flows from the insight that the organization of the enterprise as a whole, from research to product development up to and including marketing, can be structured in more effective ways. This involves in the first instance a different organization and linkage of the various stages of the product development process and the necessarily related redesign of the methods of production. Secondly, it also encompasses an improved harmonization of development functions and actual production, as well as research and development, production and marketing. An influential study of the automobile industry by the Massachusetts Institute of Technology (MIT) has introuced the expressions 'lean production' and 'lean enterprise' to characterize this comprehensive strategy. It is called 'lean' because it uses less of every input to produce the same output (Womack et al., 1990).

As outlined above, the influence of the 'Japanese model' has become ever more apparent among the various strategies adopted by Western automobile producers in the past two decades. The question arises whether there is now an evolutionary process at work comparable to that of the early years of the automobile industry. Will the success of the Japanese manufacturers lead to a world-wide displacement of Fordism in favour of 'Toyotism' (Dohse et al., 1985)? And what are the implications of this for employment relations? Both the organization of work and the labour market are structured differently in Japan from those of Western countries. A significant proportion of the personnel in large enterprises enjoys a guarantee of permanent, life-long employment and rarely moves from one employer to another. Salary is to a great degree linked to years of employment (seniority) rather than the actual job content of the position. These employees are largely organized in company unions which maintain only minimal ties with the peak organizations. There is a greater tendency to identify the interests of the workers with those of the company than is found in most Western countries. With the introduction of Japanese forms of work organization the question naturally arises as to whether employment and labour–management relations conceivably could – or should – also be modified along Japanese lines.

6   Employment relations, labour–management relations and the organization of work

All the strategies mentioned above exercise an influence on labour relations: they alter the prospects and opportunities of employers as well as employees to affect employment conditions and work content. Globalization allows employers to exert pressure on the unions to choose between job security or higher wages. Automation similarly leads to loss of jobs, in addition to a demand for a more skilled workforce. Outsourcing threatens to place the interests of various segments of the workforce and their labour unions in conflict. Reorganization of work processes may provide some advantages to workers, but not necessarily to the labour organizations that represent them. Full-scale reorganization of the enterprise strains the relationships between managerial/supervisory staff and line workers, with complex repercussions on employment conditions. The consequences outlined here ensue when the enterprise succeeds in implementing its strategies. The result is a shift in the power balance between employers and employees, which necessarily affects the terms and conditions of employment.

Precisely because these consequences are more or less predictable, there is a great likelihood that employees and their organizations will attempt to obstruct the enterprise in effectuating its strategies, or at least redirect them. In so doing, employees utilize the various means of leverage available to them: numerical and organizational strength, legal and contractual procedures, customs and practices. Execution of the enterprise's strategy may end up paralysed by the existing 'system' or scheme of industrial relations. Unless the enterprise is unable to devise some other strategic solution, an impasse may occur in which the call for changes in the industrial relations framework will sound ever louder. Proposals for new work rules, new contracts and new forms of organization will often emanate from management. The government will also frequently play an important role because numerous aspects of labour–management relations are often grounded in legislative regulation or judicial decisions.

This section will specifically address the interplay between attempts by employers to alter the organization of work on the one hand, and stability or change in the industrial relations system on the other hand (Dankbaar, 1989; Dankbaar et al., 1988; Jürgens et al., 1989). In connection with this, it should be recalled that while industrial relations everywhere were indeed transformed during and after the spread of Fordism, they were marked by considerable heterogeneity of form and practice in various Western countries. The political power relationships in these countries necessarily played a significant role in sustaining these variants. With the introduction of new Japanese forms of work organization, a distinction can similarly be made between the adaptive capacity of the prevailing industrial relations system and the influence of the broader power relationships in the affected countries. Automobile producers were confronted with divergent constellations of factors influencing the attainability and implementation of strategies for change in each nation. These impacted on both their choice of strategy and potentially on their willingness fundamentally to challenge the existing labour–management relations paradigm.

Great Britain

By the end of the 1960s, it was generally concluded in many circles in Great Britain, and particularly among employer groups, that existing industrial relations stood in the way of improvements in productivity and flexibility in the British automobile industry (particularly at British Leyland). Decentralized collective bargaining and all manner of unwritten agreements ('custom and practice') made it difficult to manage the production process in a decisive manner. Undermining the power of the workers' unions was considered a necessary component of any policy for restructuring in the automobile industry by the Thatcher government and certain sectors of management. A difference of opinion exists even today as to whether labour organizations were strong or management simply weak. In any case, after the power of the labour movement was sharply curtailed with the support of the government, the market position of the British automobile industry eroded even further (Marsden et al., 1985). This was particularly the case for what remained of the British-owned enterprise which, as indicated, is now part of BMW.

The situation was somewhat different for the Ford factories in Great Britain. Labour–management relations at Ford had always been relatively centralized by British standards. Notwithstanding its independent European product development and partially British management, Ford always remained an American company with a distinctive highly centralized organizational structure. In the United States, Ford, General Motors and Chrysler had reacted to the heightened competition by moving in the direction of attempting to involve employees and the UAW labour union in determining adaptive strategies (after attempts to by-pass the union failed). This led not only to considerable concessions on the part of the labour union, but also to innovative collective bargaining agreements wherein the automobile manufacturers undertook to guarantee employment in exchange for elimination of the closely defined boundaries between various tasks (job demarcation); the unions had previously used these to secure guaranteed employment opportunities and job progression for their membership. It was thus apparently possible in the United States to achieve through negotiations such changes in labour–management relations schemes as gave the enterprise the latitude to effectuate innovations in the organization of work with the concurrence and sometimes even active support of the labour unions (Katz, 1985). Attempts to introduce new, Japanese-inspired work practices in a comparable manner were met with solid resistance at the Ford factories in Great Britain. The blurring of job demarcations and job descriptions constituted a direct threat to the craft unions and the established rights and privileges of the trades they represented. Although the strength of the workers' resistance declined during the 1980s, and the productivity of British factories improved considerably, they nevertheless continued to compare negatively with Belgian and German Ford facilities. Although the active opposition of labour unions could be neutralized, they could not be constrained to cooperate actively. The result was that more and more work was transferred to the European mainland (Belgium and Germany). Compared to 20 years ago, Ford Europe has become significantly less British.

The revitalization of the UK automobile industry now appears to depend largely on ventures by Japanese manufacturers. In addition to Honda, which was brought to Great Britain to salvage British Leyland, Nissan also demands close consideration (Wickens, 1987). With the backing of the British government, this company opened a factory in a region where the automobile industry had previously been unrepresented. Remarkably, Nissan was able to negotiate an exclusive collective bargaining agreement with a single labour union barring participation by all other craft unions. Other companies have followed Nissan's example. While this development is nothing less than revolutionary for British industrial relations, it amounts to little more than a catch-up manoeuvre when seen from an international perspective. It would be a very different matter if the union truly operated as a company union in a manner consistent with the Japanese example and placed a greater priority on the interests of its Nissan membership than on those members employed in other enterprises.

The British automobile industry was not defeated by the Japanese so much as by the overwhelming competition from Europe which ensued after the UK embraced membership in the European Community. While Japanese automobile manufacturers are regarded as a threat in other European countries, they offered the British the hope of sustaining their automobile industry as a national endeavour. Now that Rover has been taken over by BMW, this national option no longer exists.

Germany

The German automobile industry is positioned on the other end of the European spectrum. Volkswagen survived after experiencing considerable difficulties in the 1970s in moving from the 'Beetle monoculture' to a modern assembly line with an array of models. The company reacted to the heightened competitive environment primarily by investing in new technologies. As a result of its experience with production of the Beetle, Volkswagen commanded extensive expertise with respect to automation. In contrast to the United States, where a comparable automation strategy undertaken by General Motors led to enormous losses, Volkswagen was able to apply new production techniques without encountering insurmountable problems. The enterprise even produced its own robotics systems. The introduction of highly automated operations in body construction, the paint shop and in sections of final assembly (where the majority of tasks remain manual in nature) obviously entailed a complete overhaul of the organization of work. New job descriptions had to be developed, and correspondingly new salary structures and forms of organization had to be devised. It was possible to achieve these changes in Germany within the framework of existing labour–management relations (Streeck, 1988). That does not mean that management was easily able to obtain all that it wished. The new organizational forms, job descriptions and salary structures were the result of rigorous bargaining with workers' representatives. Of particular importance was the fact that the metalworkers' union (IG Metall) was extensively represented in the works councils (*Betriebsräte*) at all Volkswagen factories. This meant that workers' representatives were always in a position to exploit their legislatively established right to participation. This may possibly have made it easier for them than for their counterparts in Great Britain and the United States to give up existing work configurations and associated prerogatives in exchange for new structures which, in addition to placing employment opportunities at risk, also offered the potential for improvement in the quality of work.

Another factor which must be taken into account is that German automobile factories historically counted among their employees a much greater proportion of well-educated skilled trade workers than those of the other car-manufacturing countries. The German adaptation of the Fordist model was strongly influenced by the tradition of in-house training of skilled labour. The British and German models constitute two extremes. This also applies to workers' rights which emanate from collective bargaining between employers and employees (the so-called *contractual rights*), as well as those rights of workers or their representatives which are grounded in law (the so-called *legal rights*). In Great Britain, contractual rights are derived from largely unwritten understandings and practices. There are almost no legally established rights for workers. Contractual rights in Germany are founded in elaborately detailed collective bargaining agreements, in addition to which workers also enjoy extensive legal rights. British management in the automobile industry had good reason to assume that the organization of work in that industry could not be transformed without changes in the industrial relations system. The sought-after modifications could be brought about only after undertaking an offensive against the unions and shop stewards. This led to the rather ludicrous scenario of unions first being subjected to an 'old-fashioned' all-out assault, and subsequently invited to provide constructive input into new forms of work organization incorporating greater responsibility on the part of workers and a higher quality of work. Germany immediately commenced with transformation of the organization of work which inspired observers to declare in the early 1980s that the demise of Fordist task differentiation was at hand. Automation and robotization came to have different implications in these two countries. In Great Britain, automation was regarded as an avenue toward workforce reduction and suppression of the labour movement, while the Germans saw it as a means of modernizing the production process. One outcome of Germany's approach is that its automobile industry employs a much greater number of workers than its foreign competition: a rationalization phase appears to have been skipped. Germany's success with respect to automation and flexibility was purchased with relatively high labour costs, although this applies more to Volkswagen than to Ford and Opel (GM), the other two German mass producers. The latter two, and particularly Ford, acted on mandates from their US parent companies in implementing policies to reduce substantially personnel levels throughout the 1980s. Thus, as with Ford in the UK, the international strategy options and orientation of the parent company have repercussions for the management policies of its foreign subsidiaries. When subjected to the influence of the industrial relations of various countries, however, these global strategies nevertheless translate into clearly distinct local managerial approaches, with divergent results for both the organization of work and productivity in a given factory.

France and Italy

The development of the automobile industries of France and Italy demonstrates a number of parallels as well as differences. Japanese competition has been kept largely at bay in both countries by means of protectionist measures, and automobile manufacturers have historically followed the Fordist model to a great extent. The labour movement in each is or was dominated by communists to a significant degree. One difference lies in the fact that government policy in recent years has been set by socialists under Mitterand in France, while the Christian-Democrats have held sway in Italy until recently. Another difference is that Italy has long had but a single major manufacturer, Fiat, while France has both Renault and Peugeot (PSA). Moreover, the latter two are quite distinct. Renault was nationalized after the Second World War and remained a pure state enterprise until recently. This meant among other things that Renault was required to operate as a model of social policy and was able to do so because losses were picked up by the state. In contrast, PSA is wholly privately owned, and evolved out of the takeover of Citroen and the European venture of Chrysler (Talbot) by Peugeot. The enterprise has in the recent past undergone a trying process of reorganization and integration in the course of which competition by Renault was often regarded as 'unfair'.

Both the French and Italian automobile industries have endured profound employment contraction over recent decades which constituted a serious setback for the labour movement in each country. The political settings for these realignments differ greatly, however. After the turmoil of the late 1960s, labour relations at Fiat had initially improved to a considerable degree, but began to deteriorate again in the latter half of the 1970s (Contini, 1986). Extremist factions – which did not shy away from terrorist activity – controlled the workers' councils in the factory. Union leadership was unable to offer clear alternatives and ended up on the defensive. The majority of workers were ultimately without any organization with which they could identify. During the 1979 slump in the automobile market, Fiat management took the initiative and laid off 24,000 employees, including a large number of activists. The labour movement was incapable of responding to these reductions and lost much of its influence and stature. Fiat had early on begun to introduce robots and other programmable automatons. Given the troublesome industrial relations context, it was hardly surprising that it aggressively pursued such rationalizing, labour reducing technologies. However, Fiat (like General Motors in the United States) has been consistently reported as struggling to make effective use of these technologies. The combination of highly antagonistic labour relations and the continuous emphasis over many decades on Fordist work organization with minimally qualified workers would hardly appear to be a plausible starting point for the introduction of advanced technology.

In France the focus was from inception more intensely concentrated on the need for new forms of work and the training of 'polyvalent' workers. The French government undertook a number of initiatives in the area of industrial relations and education in the 1980s which were crucial to this approach and no doubt account for the fact that developments in France were less turbulent than those in Italy. Minister of Labour Auroux introduced a series of laws in the area of industrial relations in 1982 which provided for participatory mechanisms for worker representatives (*droit d'expression*). The legislation appeared to be particularly inspired by the German model, but did not go as far. The same may be said of subsequent attempts to reform the French system of vocational training. While its highly selective, elitist character does indeed produce a respectable number of highly qualified engineers, the French educational system also spawns numerous drop-outs who never attain their degrees.

7　Convergence?

Does the foregoing provide grounds for concluding that labour relations in the automobile industry of the countries under discussion are converging into a new model? They certainly all appear to be moving in the same direction in terms of the organization of work. This dynamic typically involves merging production tasks (multiskilling, polyvalence), often in combination with rotation among several workplaces. Secondly, we can observe everywhere a blending of primary and ancillary functions. A third general trend is the proliferation of all manner of worker participation schemes, such as quality circles, but also through legally constituted mechanisms such as works councils. In addition, there is a discernible shift in the labour relations arena from collective bargaining on a national scale to negotiating agreements at the level of the enterprise or even the individual production unit. With the exception of those in Germany, the importance of national labour organizations has clearly diminished as a result of membership attrition. From this vantage point, the widely held notion of a 'Japanization' of the organization of work and labour relations in the automobile industry appears to be a plausible one. There are, however, distinct limits to any convergence toward the Japanese model of labour–management relations. Not only are many aspects of Japanese labour relations more or less unacceptable to European workers (and employers), but a complete convergence is not really necessary. This becomes clear if one considers the mechanisms by which convergence may take shape. Fundamental to this process is the pressure on enterprises to improve performance generated by competition. The pressure of economic rivalry impels enterprises to compare their methods and accomplishments with those of others and to imitate those practices which lead to improved performance. Adoption of other methods can lead to changes in the industrial relations system, as noted above. It is clear that any resulting tendencies toward convergence will be invigorated with increased competition. As other circumstances relieve competitive pressure, the need to engage in burdensome and conflicting adaptations in labour relations will be correspondingly diminished. In this regard, protectionism has undoubtedly benefited the French and Italian automobile industries with respect to existing labour relations. It should be noted, however, that protectionist leanings did not preclude the French government from taking (convergent) initiatives.

Even if competitive pressures were equally apportioned among countries and enterprises, this would not automatically lead to convergence in industrial relations. The fact remains that the enterprises involved seek to continue to compete and to that end must achieve a certain level of performance (in terms of quality and productivity). The precise manner in which these performance levels are reached is of secondary importance, even though there will be intense pressure to imitate the methods of the more successful enterprises.

A number of competitive strategies have been reviewed above. Each enterprise opts for a particular combination of measures on the basis of its own traditions and analyses, as well as an assessment of its strengths and weaknesses. While the direction may be the same, the individual routes will vary. Labour–management relations in various countries will have pivotal implications for the specification and execution of strategic options. Whether they change as a result is not really crucial to the manufacturer. The paramount goal of the enterprise is not to transform its labour relations, but to remain competitive. If that goal can be achieved within the parameters of existing institutions, they will likely not be altered. This is to date the case with respect to German industrial relations, which have been sufficiently malleable as to be able to absorb necessary changes in work organization. Industrial relations therefore need not be identical, so long as the result in terms of the competitive position of the enterprise is roughly comparable.

What are the implications for a possible convergence in Europe? To the extent that European internal borders disappear, the French and Italian industries will experience increased competition from the Japanese. (The EU Commission and the Japanese government have agreed that limitations on the import of cars from Japan will be gradually lifted and eliminated completely by the year 2000. Japanese organizational concepts will be put into practice to a greater degree than is presently the case. Within the framework of European unification the German model of industrial relations is also being advanced more insistently. It should be recalled, however, that the German approach includes a significant legislative component in the area of works councils. As these rights are adopted or rejected by European nations via Brussels, an evolutionary dynamic will unfold which will necessarily diverge from the Japanese model in essential respects. Does this signify convergence toward a European model? It goes without saying that industrial relations in

European countries will tend toward harmonization as a result of increased regulation emanating from the EC. For the time being, however, it would appear improbable that national distinctions will entirely disappear. As with the emergence of Fordist labour–management relations, the political context will also play a significant role in this period of adaptation and transformation.

13 Service work in European countries: organization, technology and industrial relations in banking and retailing

Albert Mok and Kea Tijdens

1 The service sector in post-industrial society

Industrial societies are becoming more and more complex and diversified. Some 25 years ago Daniel Bell (1973) launched the concept of the post-industrial society, the core of which is the service sector. Although there has been, and still is much discussion about this concept (for example, Gershuny, 1979), it cannot be denied that most European countries have become service societies. For these countries the term 'industrial society' hardly applies. The service sector is very important for employment. In 1991 in the 12 countries of the European Union (excluding the former German Democratic Republic), 62 per cent of the workforce was employed in the service sector, 31.8 per cent in industry and 6.2 per cent in agriculture. Moreover, some segments of the service sector are seeing the rapid introduction of information technology, making service work an interesting object of study.

The service sector is culturally embedded like no other human activity; it is a true reflection of the life styles and the need structure of a society. The service relationship consists of interactions between people, often within the context of a network, that is, a regular set of contacts or connections between people or groups (Granovetter and Swedberg, 1992: 10). Even when a machine mediates between the server and its client, for example the automated teller machine in banking, the service relationship is still expressed in interactions within a network. The service transaction involves a large element of trust, shared beliefs and moral obligations. In this way it resembles a collective transaction more than a market transaction.

The institutional and legal arrangements governing labour relations, employment contracts and the labour market differ greatly across Europe (Hartog and Theeuwes, 1993), as does the extent of the informal sector within which so many of the services rendered are transacted. These differences influence rather than determine the different contents and modes of service work in the countries studied. All this makes the service sector an important object of international comparative studies.

At the same time such a comparison is fraught with methodological difficulties. The larger the service sector, the less adequately the concept of a 'service sector' describes the economic activity. Service activities are heterogeneous, ranging from private services to public services, from the transportation of people from the home to the transmission of information into the home, and from work aids to leisure activities. Therefore, this chapter does not deal with the service sector as a whole. Two branches within the sector are analysed, namely, retailing and banking. For the same reason only five European countries are compared: the United Kingdom, Belgium, Sweden, the Netherlands and Germany. These northern European countries have been chosen because they have more or less comparable structures in banking and retailing services. This chapter is based on a review of literature, including our own research in retailing and banking (Mok and Geldof, 1994; Tijdens, 1993). Four issues are addressed. First we will discuss organizational characteristics, products and ownership in the banking industry and retail trade in the five countries mentioned (section 2). Starting in the 1980s, the service sector has been subject to a far-reaching technological transformation. The second issue, then, is how information technology (IT) has influenced workflows in banking and the retail trade, and how IT is used to support concepts of service in retailing and banking (section 3). Not all work in the service sector is service work. It is therefore important to know how we define service work and moreover which strategies firms develop to provide their service to customers. In our next section we focus on the underlying concepts of service, for instance what type of service is provided and what are the characteristics of the socio-economic groups to which the clients of banks and retailing firms belong (section 4). Finally we will explore the impact of service work on industrial relations in a wider sense (section 5) referring to sector-related industrial relations as well as to the relationship between employer and employee.

2   Retailing and banking

The service sector as a whole, and banking and retailing in particular, are affected by five major societal trends (Kruse et al., 1994).

- The overall ageing of the population.
- More sophisticated consumer demands.
- Increasing competition between firms.
- Internationalization.
- Extensive use of information technology.

These developments in society and in the community, together with the increasing feminization of the workforce, are having an important impact on the service relationship as well as on industrial relations. We hope to make this clear later in this chapter.

Banking

After the Second World War, industry in Europe was in great need of investment capital. The money to finance industrial expansion came from the savings of citizens. By opening deposit and salary accounts for a far larger group of private clients, banks found new methods of financial expansion. The number of bank accounts quickly grew and there was a consequent rapid increase in the number of payments done by giro. Banks were forced to set up workflows for payment transfers. The traditional way of banking, serving an elite clientele and for business purposes only, was abandoned in favour of banking services for everyone: retail banking. Retail banking emerged in the 1960s and changed the bank organization and its business processes completely. For example, in nearly every country the number of local branches increased. To finance and manage the large networks of branches and to manage the capital generated by retail banking, many banks merged. In all five countries the process of bank mergers has continued during the past two or three decades, and today only a few banks dominate the national banking sector. The majority of the largest banks in the world are retail banks, whereas only a few savings banks belong to this group.

In the 1980s and 1990s four major trends predominated (Boonstra and De Jong, 1993). In North as well as West European countries these trends are threatening the new forms of banking which arose in the 1960s and 1970s. First, the market for mass banking products for households and companies appears to be more or less saturated. Secondly, companies are increasingly entering the financial markets through economic agents, by-passing the banking system. Thirdly, competition in the financial markets has increased, partly in response to a huge wave of innovations. Some of these innovations were technical in nature and others financial, but all were made possible by information technology. Finally, customers have become more aware of performance. It is therefore increasingly difficult for banks to cross-subsidize loss-incurring products. For example, many German banks have used high-income customers to subsidize banking services for mass market segments (Boonstra and De Jong, 1993).

Payment transfer is one of the products incurring the biggest losses. It was subsidized by interest income from call deposits (Fassbender and Wuffi, 1990). On the one hand, these policies leave banks very vulnerable to competitors aiming directly at the upper market segment; on the other hand maximizing profits from mass market segments requires different branch and workflow strategies, for example a direct writing approach versus marketing through a branch network.

Many European banks are in the process of shifting their strategies from a customer-based approach to a product-based approach. Dutch banking firms introduced price policies for payment transfers. Moreover, a substantial drive for cost reduction can be expected in European banking. Boonstra and De Jong (1993) have observed this tendency in the United Kingdom, but continental banks are said to be handicapped because national public opinion is less tolerant of mass redundancies. There is a relationship between union density and these employment policies in the respective countries: the stronger the unions, the less likely are large-scale redundancies.

In the countries we studied, a wide variety of banks can be distinguished with regard to ownership and products. There are three main types of ownership: privately owned banks, publicly owned banks, and cooperative societies incorporating farmers, catholics (the Raiffeisen banks in Germany and the Netherlands) or workers. Three main products can also be distinguished: financing (sometimes subdivided into mortgages, long-term financing and short-term financing), savings and payment transfers. So-called general banks deal with all of these types of products, whereas specialized banks offer only one type. Of course, each type can be divided into specific product areas. For example, payment transfers have to be subdivided into cash, cheque and giro transfers. In some countries post office systems have become important competitors in retail banking. The banking sector in the five countries can be briefly described on the basis of these five criteria (see Box 13.1).

Retailing

The retail trade is a telling example of the embeddedness of service work in society. For centuries the small shop, privately owned by independent artisans and entrepreneurs, dominated the scene. The shopkeeper was the

Box 13.1 *The (retail) banking sector in the United Kingdom, Belgium, Germany, the Netherlands and Sweden*

Retail banking in the **United Kingdom** is less important than in other countries, because financial products are overwhelmingly provided by financing and building societies. In the UK hardly any publicly owned or cooperative banks can be found, nor has the privatized National Girobank captured a large market share. Payment transfers in the United Kingdom are based on cheques. Hence only 60 per cent of the adult population has a bank account, whereas this is almost 100 per cent in the other countries.

In **Belgium** four large banks account for over 80 per cent of the balance sheet, whereas over 50 mostly specialized banks account for less than 20 per cent. The large banks have many branches, making Belgium one of the European countries with a very high branch density. Three of these large banks are privately owned general banks, the fourth is a partly private, partly public savings bank, one of the largest and oldest in the world. Many credit banks are also publicly owned, and a minority of the savings banks and credit banks are cooperative societies. In Belgium about 20 per cent of the balance sheet is served by publicly owned banks, whereas the cooperative banks serve about 5 per cent. The Postal Giro System has never been very strong in Belgium.

For **Germany** we focus on the banking sector in the former FRG. Three large general banks dominate the banking sector. Branch density is even higher than in Belgium. Savings banks are publicly owned banks which underwrite local governments' financial needs. Cooperative societies can be found in the agricultural sector as well as in the sector for medium-sized and small firms. Germany has the largest share of public ownership (50 per cent), if taken as the percentage of the balance sheet total for the national banking sector. Cooperative banking – *Raiffeisen- und Volksbanken* – accounts for 26 per cent of the balance sheet. The Federal Post Office Authorities have expanded rapidly since the early 1970s.

In **the Netherlands** there are also three large general banks dominating the banking industry. The number of branches grew rapidly in the 1960s and 1970s due to competition for savings accounts. The former state-owned Postbank addressed large groups of clients with low incomes, whereas the privately owned ABN-AMRO addressed firms and well-to-do clients. The cooperative Rabo addressed the agricultural sector. Their market share is 25 per cent, whereas 20 per cent of the Dutch balance sheet is served by publicly owned banks. The three large banks have about 2500 branches in all.

In **Sweden** the state-owned Postgiro began to expand its services in the 1960s and now dominates the retail banking sector. Cooperative banking is not well developed, covering a market share of less than 10 per cent. Commercial banks mainly target industrial and trade financing.

Table 13.1 *Contrasting structures in the retail trade in some European countries*

	No. of enterprises ('000)	No. of employed ('000)	Turnover per person (bn Ecu)
Belgium	127.8	274.7	35
Germany	439	2,353	322
Netherlands	95	637.5	45
UK	348.2	3,030	280

Source: Kruse et al., 1994: tables 1 and 2

focal point in the local network and an important source of information about life in the community, although his status was low compared to manufacturing. Napoleon described the English as 'a nation of shop-keepers', and that was not intended as a compliment (Child and Loveridge, 1990: 166). However, the nineteenth century saw the start of important changes in retailing, with the coming of the department store (the first were Zion Cooperative Mercantile Institute [ZCMI] in Salt Lake City, Utah, 1849, and Le Bon Marché, Paris, 1852). The department store offered the rising middle classes more luxurious goods and even provided them with a leisure pursuit. Later, in the nineteenth century in the UK, and after the turn of the century in the rest of Europe, the newly emancipated 'Fordist' workers became mass consumers who bought mass-produced goods in large quantities and more cheaply at multiple retail outlets (chain stores), cooperatives and later, after the Second World War, in the emerging self-service stores and supermarkets. As a result, the retail sector has gradually come to be regarded as a mature industry (!) and its status has risen accordingly. Now, nearing the end of the twentieth century, we see the further development of structures, products and commercial strategies, with more specialization by product and customer segment and a new emphasis on the quality of service (Kruse et al., 1994: 146).

There is a trend towards greater concentration of firms in the retailing sector all across Europe. That means a decreasing number of food outlets and increased productivity, although in some countries the number of non-food retail outlets has risen (1994: 17).

All figures in Table 13.1 are for retailing in 1990. Per 10,000 inhabitants there are 128 retail outlets in Belgium, 70 in Germany, 64 in the Netherlands and 61 in the United Kingdom. In the countries of Southern Europe these figures are much higher, for instance 175 for Portugal and 174 for Greece. In the latter countries (as well as in Spain and Ireland) retail stores are mostly owned by sole proprietors (between 80 and 90 per cent), while in northern countries the larger firms dominate the retailing scene, with no more than 60 per cent being sole proprietors. These figures reflect differences in culture, in buying habits, and in the place of the shop in the community. One cultural factor worth mentioning is that Greek employees who take early retirement, especially women, tend to invest their capital after retiring in setting up a shop, thus contributing to the large number of traditional stores in that country (Kruse et al., 1994: 20).

Many of the larger firms in Western Europe are in the process of internationalizing. They are opening outlets in foreign countries, entering into mergers, acquiring foreign firms, undertaking joint ventures and engaging in cross-border trade.

3   Technological developments

To achieve competitive advantages by means of information technology, Sager (1988) divided the strategies of banks into three groups: strategies to improve price and performance, strategies to influence market access, and strategies to develop products. The same strategies apply to the retailing industry. It is no easy task to categorize a strategy, however. For example, a cash dispenser is both a product innovation and a price and performance innovation. In this section we will explore to what degree banks and retailers use information systems to compete for market access in order to attract new clients.

Information technology in retailing

Consumption has become a much more important, or even dominant aspect of European life style since the Second World War, and the significance of retailing has increased accordingly. Much of the post-war expansion in retail employment has been accompanied by a feminization of the workforce and by an increase in part-time work.

An international comparative research venture into the impact of IT in the service sector, known as the MESS project (see Child and Loveridge, 1990), identified eight modes of retailing: home shopping, discount warehouses, department stores, service multiples, hypermarkets/superstores, supermarkets, specialist traders and convenience stores. The classification was based on three contingent features: the product range, the range of transactional locations and the perishability or durability of the goods sold (Child and Loveridge, 1990: 168–169). Nowadays the different types of retail stores often belong to the same national or multinational groups.

The most important technological development was the use of EPOS (electronic point of sale) cash registers in the 1980s, with the introduction of laser scanners to read bar codes or Universal Product Codes. This technological breakthrough came much later in Europe than in the United States and Japan.

The EPOS terminals potentially – and in an increasing number of places effectively – constitute the front end of totally integrated computer-based retailing systems. Not only does the terminal generate the bill for the customer, but the computer system initiates stock-keeping as well as book-keeping, and it automatically produces orders for delivery of products to the stores.

Another change is the decreasing importance of cash. Cash is being replaced by Electronic Fund Transfer at the Point of Sale (EFT/POS) and by the use of credit and chip cards. Here too, information technology is becoming more and more important.

Information technology in banking

While retail banking was in the process of expanding, the transfer of payments became the source of one of the largest workflows in the sector and therefore one of the earliest objectives of automation. The introduction of information technology in banking can be divided into four phases, more or less parallel to the four decades (Tijdens, 1993).

In the first phase, during the 1960s, investment in centrally located mainframe computers permitted the centralization of deposit accounts, which made the automation of interest calculations and electronic fund transfer (EFT) possible. The centralization of accounts, due to the use of mainframe computers, was followed by a partial centralization of the workflows. In this first technological phase, banks in all five countries were forced to reconsider their production processes as well as the division of decision-making between branches and headquarters.

The second technological phase took place in the 1970s as data communication networks were set up. Banks wanted to centralize the administration of accounts and decentralize contacts with clients and encoding. To achieve these goals, four technical conditions had to be met:

- a mainframe with enormous capacity and real-time facilities;
- memories with integrated databases for client data;
- networks for online communication;
- terminals and local computers at the branches.

In the five countries under study, banks made different choices as far as the sequence of meeting these conditions was concerned. Moreover, retail banking presupposes cooperation between banks as a condition for a smooth giro payment circuit, mainly by standardizing account numbers and coding handwritten payment orders, and by standardizing clearing procedures. Clearing houses were established in all five countries, though the degree to which banks cooperate differs, the Dutch having the most centralized system with only one clearing house for all banks and the German banks establishing clearing houses in each *Bundesland*.

The third phase of retail banking automation took place in the 1980s. The purpose of introducing automation in banking was generally to prepare transactions for booking as near to the source of input as possible. Bank management wanted to see data typed in at the counters, at the branches or by the clients themselves in their homes, and to have those data entered directly into the central payments files. At this stage customer-operated automated teller machines (ATMs) were introduced (for example in the UK and Belgium) – the 24-hour 'through the wall' cash dispensers. All this presupposed not only the existence of a data communication network between the branches and the computer centre, but also a change in parts of the administrative production from batch to real-time processes, as well as integrated databases for client data. Again, the five countries differed, this time in their decision to implement either front-office or back-office automation, the UK and Belgium focusing on front-office automation, and the Netherlands on back-office automation. A major factor in explaining these differences is the impact of centralized agreements to standardize payment circuits.

The fourth phase of retail banking automation emerged in the 1990s and involved the introduction of electronic fund transfer at the point of sale (EFT/POS) and the promotion of home banking. ATMs presently allow more complex transactions and orders than only the dispensing of cash (so-called self-banking). EFT/POS allows retail store customers to pay for goods at the point of sale through electronic transfer of funds from their bank account to the store's bank account. Countries leading the way in the introduction and generalization of EFT/POS were Belgium, Germany and the UK. Home banking (sometimes called phone banking) allows customers to obtain information and carry out transactions from terminals (or simple telephones) located in their homes, which are connected to the bank's computer via the telecommunications network.

There are several reasons for introducing information technology. IT makes it possible to handle masses of data. Banks tend to exploit this possibility for purposes of managing internal workflows and databases rather than to use in direct contact with clients. In all five countries, banks started using IT in the 1960s, whereas clients first became aware of IT in the 1980s; IT was used to handle the increase in the number of clients as well as in the amount of savings, to improve pricing and performance. Information technology hence played a role in indirect competition. ATMs and cash dispensers are the only information technology used to compete for clients.

4   Concepts of service work

Despite its increased importance, the 'service sector' is still not an operational concept. It is usually defined *per negativum*. Littek complains that there is actually no satisfactory definition of what 'services' and 'service work' mean. Negative characteristics prevail, merely indicating that service 'differs from' industrial production modes (Littek, 1992: 745). But in what respect? In order to identify the key differentiators within the service sector, three dimensions of service activities are distinguished based on Child and Loveridge (1990: 35–37).

The first is the service relationship: whether the service is provided to the public directly or indirectly. Loveridge (1984) distinguishes between personal services, rooted in pre-industrial domestic or gentlemanly service to property owners, and impersonal services, an outgrowth of the bureaucratic division of labour and the creation of clerical tasks and modern professions.

The second dimension arises from the function that is attached to the service work: is the service provided on a commercial or a public service basis? Since the arrival of the welfare state, more and more services have been provided on a non-commercial, public service basis. With the gradual erosion of the welfare state as a result of budget deficits in most of the countries of the European Union, public services are increasingly being privatized. Not only is the public being made to pay individually for services which used to be collective and free of charge, but what are essentially collective goods, such as provisions for the elderly, those unable to work and the chronically ill, are being shifted back from communal provision to private care (Berghman and Cantillon, 1993).

The third dimension of service activity concerns the codification and diffusion of knowledge bearing upon the service transaction – the extent to which such information and knowledge are available to the consumer or confined to service-providing staff. If the client is to play his or her part in the rendering of services, the relevant technology will have to be adapted to accommodate this participation and the division of labour will have to be altered accordingly.

The differentiation in service activities results in a differentiation of service work. In industry the process of introducing information technology has had varying outcomes: in some cases the substitution of labour by machines, diminished worker control and deskilling, in others the creation of new jobs, enhancement of worker control and reskilling (Francis, 1986). But can the industrial scheme be applied to the service sector? The picture as a whole is mixed, complex and difficult to predict without detailed knowledge of the particular situation. Information technology is a malleable, adaptable technology, open to many uses. It is far more flexible than the so-called flexible manufacturing systems (Child and Loveridge, 1990: 44–45).

Our theoretical perspective is therefore concerned with the reciprocal nature of relationships involving the use of technology within and between service organizations. This avoids a simple technological determinism, which neglects the differences between people, sectors, organizations and countries. Ours is not a culture-free perspective on technology which stresses convergence (Kerr et al., 1960), but a culturally specific perspective which has an anthropological point of departure (Clegg, 1990; Crozier, 1963).

In service work information technology brings with it a shift in the role of the worker as well as of the client: from the tool and its use and guidance, to the system and its maintenance, regulation and control (see Figure 13.1). In answering the MESS research question as to why so many service organizations have so readily adopted information technology, most of the

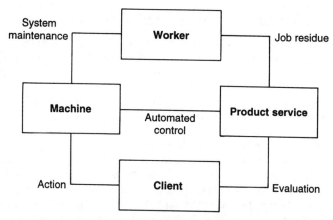

Figure 13.1   *Technology and the changing relationship between worker and customer (after Davis and Taylor, 1990: xiii)*

managers of these organizations replied that investment in IT is the only way to survive in an ever more competitive consumer market. The changes in work structures, staff qualifications and work organization, including the new worker–client relationship which this entails, have to be dealt with in the context of the internal and external labour markets and of the industrial relations system. The more sophisticated the machine–service relationship, the more limited the contribution of the worker (Davis and Taylor, 1990: xiii), and the more important the quality of the service being rendered becomes for the relationship between service organization and client. For the new service relationship a change in 'work habitude' is needed, that is a change in the way service workers deal with the instruments and modes of their work situation (Baethge and Oberbeck, 1986: 33). This point is illustrated in Box 13.2 by an example familiar to anyone who uses a bank or credit card regularly.

Concepts of service and technological developments have led to dilemmas in banking in every country. Most frequently customers visit a branch to take out cash. In the 1970s, the concept of cross-selling was based on the conviction that clients could be sold bank products even if they did not intend to buy them. Bank clients would act the way shop clients do and buy products impulsively. Cross-selling policies therefore focused mainly on clients coming in for cash. However, from a labour cost point of view cashiers were expensive, and for safety reasons banks had to avoid having cash money at the counters. This dilemma was partly solved by splitting up cashier jobs between those handling small amounts of cash and those handling larger amounts, so that it was possible to reduce the amount of money kept at the counter. Moreover, information technology made it easy to avoid contact with clients wanting cash by introducing 'money through the wall'. Cross-selling did not take off in the 1980s, however: a bank branch was something other than a shop. This insight

---

Box 13.2   *The automated teller machine in banking*

A good example of the new machine–service relationship in the banking
sector is the automated teller machine (ATM). This is a machine located
outside or in the hall of the bank premises which dispenses cash, provides
information on the client's accounts and deals with other monetary matters.
Most of the transactions are conducted on-line and in real time, so that
overdrafts may be refused for instance. The main job of the bank employee
(the teller) as regards the ATM is to maintain the system by putting
banknotes into the machine. The rest of his or her job, the administrative
processing of the monetary transactions, has become residual. The machine
automatically controls the provision of the service. In order to get the
service rendered (for instance cashing a certain sum of money), the client
must himself follow specific instructions described on the screen. After
following the instructions, the client receives the money and/or the printed
documents dispensed. All that remains for the client is to evaluate the
quality of the service provided. Was my transaction accepted? Did I get the
right sum of money? Did I get the information asked for? Did the machine
work well and with enough speed? And there is no teller present to hear
the client's complaints!

In our example the cashier or teller never sees the client, and service is
provided indirectly. The intermediary between service organization and
customer is no longer the worker, but automated control. If customers have
the necessary information, they can serve themselves. This is a distinct
change from the traditional situation in service provision, because the very
notion of service carries with it the direct contact between service worker
and service receiver, without any intermediary. In that sense 'self-service' is
a contradiction in terms.

---

enabled banks to minimize contacts with clients wanting small amounts of
money by further developing information technology for cash dispensers
and ATMs. At the same time they were also able to introduce a policy of
not cross-subsidizing bank products, as we saw in section 2.

The client policies of banks have become more aggressive in the 1990s.
Marketing policies concentrate more on commercial activities, like savings
accounts, insurance-related products, loans etc., for well-defined market
segments. More than ever before, this involves aggressive market strategies.
This change has resulted in a modified front-office work organization,
made possible by the use of information technology. Counter employees
nowadays are no longer cashiers but skilled sellers of a variety of bank
products which may include mortgages, insurance policies and travel
arrangements. In general the two main functions in the structure of work in
retail banks have become polarized, at least at the local level. On the one
hand there is the old cashier function (tellers and administrative employees
combined) and on the other hand the newer commercial function, stressing
the recruitment of new clients and the marketing of (new) services

(Stroeke, 1990: 116). Even the job of the local bank manager has undergone a change, in the sense that his external activities (like deciding on client credit lines) have increased and his internal functions (like managing the bank branch's personnel) have become less important. Internal checks on employee performance can easily be done with the help of the computer data. This also applies to the retailing sector.

5 Industrial relations

Industrial relations is a broad concept, encompassing labour relations at industry level as well as relations between employer and employees. In this section we focus first on employment relations, then deal with co-determination through unions and works councils (as related to introduction of information technology and service concepts) and finally discuss vocational training systems.

Industrial relations are influenced by many factors, among them information technology and service concepts, but supply and demand factors on the labour market, personnel characteristics and union density are very important factors as well. We will not discuss whether there is a causal relationship between these factors and industrial relations. Instead, we want to explore how service concepts and technological developments are dealt with in industrial relations. Union density in retailing and banking differs considerably from one country to the next. Whereas levels of membership in the banking sector in the Netherlands do not exceed 10 per cent, this is about 72 per cent in Sweden.

Share in employment

Employment in the service sector has grown for some decades. While annual growth rates from 1973 onwards have been largely negative for agriculture and for industry, they varied between 0.3 per cent and 3.6 per cent in the service sector for all five countries from 1973 to 1988 (OECD, *Employment Outlook*, July 1989). Employment in the wholesale and retail trade appears to be more vulnerable to recession than in the financial and business services sector. During the two most recent recessions, the largest increases in unemployment occurred in the retail and wholesale trade, and smaller rises have occurred in the services sector (OECD, 1992).

Considering the importance of white-collar employment, there are major differences between the five countries. From the Second World War onwards the greatest increase in the white-collar sector took place in the United Kingdom, Sweden and Belgium. For instance, in Belgium the percentage of white-collar workers in the active working population increased from 21 per cent in 1950 to 42 per cent in 1970 and to almost 60 per cent in 1990 (De Witte, 1994: 13). In 1970 the figure for Sweden was 42 per cent, in 1990 58 per cent. It goes without saying that this enormous change in the composition of the workforce was greatly stimulated by the increased participation of women in the labour market, especially in the service sector. In the Netherlands and Germany there were substantial increases too, but they were less spectacular and they came later than in the three other countries mentioned (OECD, 1992). Employment figures for retailing and banking are given in Table 13.2. Female employment in banking, insurance and business services rose from 40.9 per cent in 1970 to 43.9 per cent in 1990.

As the table shows, retailing is much more important for national employment than banking. The percentage of women working in retailing is higher than in banking in all five countries, though in general differences are less than 10 percentage points. Banking and retailing are female-dominated industries, except for banking in Belgium and the Netherlands. Detailed figures for the UK are not available.

The impact of information technology on employment is not quite clear. Redundancies due to labour-saving technologies might be counterbalanced by employment-generating effects of information technology due to product growth and new products or new markets. Moreover, predicted savings in labour costs appear to be realized only to a limited extent.

However, it would not do to count 'heads' alone. We have to take into account the number of part-time workers (mostly women), which in the service sector as a whole, and in retailing in particular, is on the increase. The Netherlands is the champion, with 47.3 per cent of retailing employees working part-time (32 hours per week or less), then the UK with 40.7 per cent, Germany 37.3 per cent and Belgium with 17.4 per cent (Kruse et al., 1994: table 5), while the duration of part-time work tends to decrease to less than 20 hours per week. The figure for Belgium seems low, but retail workers there already have a statutory working week which is shorter than that of the other countries. There are many flexible employment contracts in retailing in Belgium, where only 44 per cent of employees work fixed daily working hours (Kruse et al., 1994: 38). Precise figures for Sweden are not available, but there an estimated 40 per cent of employees in retailing work part-time.

Employee relations and co-determination

In several countries bank employers resist negotiating about information technology, according to a FIET (International Federation of Commerical, Clerical, Professional and Technical Employees) report (FIET, Geneva). The widespread proliferation of information technology in banking has added a new dimension to collective bargaining which has cut across some traditional negotiating areas. However, the unions in the various countries have taken differing approaches in attempting to enforce their policy of demanding to negotiate the introduction of information technology. In Belgium, Germany and Sweden statutory machinery has been established ensuring that employees and trade unionists have the opportunity to sit on either works councils or boards of directors and therefore have the chance

Table 13.2 *Number of persons employed in the banking and retailing sectors*

	1970[1]	1980[2]	1990[3]
Belgium			
Banking sector	n.a.	n.a.	95,000
% of total labour force	n.a.	n.a.	3.0
% female workers in banking	n.a.	n.a.	42.1
Retailing sector	n.a.	n.a.	274,700
% of total labour force	n.a.	n.a.	8.3
% female workers in retailing	n.a.	n.a.	52.8
Germany			
Banking sector	411,000	555,000	678,000
% of total labour force	1.6	2.1	2.4
% female workers in banking	n.a.	n.a.	53.2
Retailing sector	1,978,000	2,163,000	2,353,000
% of total labour force	7.5	8.0	8.3
% female workers in retailing	n.a.	n.a.	62.2
Netherlands			
Banking sector	78,500	116,900	145,000
% of total labour force	2.0	2.3	2.3
% female workers in banking	41.2	45.2	44.8
Retailing sector	241,771	435,000	559,000
% of total labour force	6.3	8.5	8.8
% female workers in retailing	54.1	52.9	57.4
Sweden			
Banking sector	46,900	51,900	77,300
% of total labour force	1.2	1.5	1.7
% female workers in banking	57.8	63.6	60.3
Retailing sector	324,000	318,000	314,200
% of total labour force	8.6	9.1	7.0
% female workers in retailing	64.8	63.7	60.1
United Kingdom			
Banking sector	587,000	491,000	631,000
% of total labour force	2.5	2.1	2.8
% female workers in banking	n.a.	n.a.	n.a.
Retailing sector	1,943,000	1,967,000	2,353,000
% of total labour force	8.3	8.6	10.3
% female workers in retailing	n.a.	n.a.	n.a.

[1]The Netherlands, 1973.
[2]Sweden and the Netherlands, 1981.
[3]Belgium, 1991.
n.a. = not available.

Sources:
Belgium: Nationaal Instituut voor de Statistiek, *Sociale Statistieken*, Brussels, 1993 and Kruse et al., 1994: table 5
Germany: *Statistisches Jahrbuch*, 1992, including self-employed, excluding unemployed
Netherlands: *Enquête Beroepsbevolking*, 1990, *Arbeidskrachtentelling*, 1981, *Statistiek werkzame personen*, 1973
Sweden: AKU *Arsmedetal*, 1970, 1981, 1990
UK: *Annual Abstracts of Statistics*, London, Central Statistical Office, 1970, 1980, 1990

Table 13.3 *Technological innovation and industrial democracy*

	Negotiation rights	Information about planned changes	Participation in working groups with employers	Participation in legal industrial democracy structures
Belgium	Yes	Yes	Yes	Yes
Germany	Yes	Yes	Yes	Yes
Netherlands	Yes	Yes	Yes	Yes
Sweden	Yes	Yes	Yes	Yes
UK	Generally consultative	Yes generally	No generally	No

Source: FIET, 1980, for Germany, Sweden and the UK; Van Ruysseveldt and Visser, 1996

to influence policy. In Sweden a central agreement on information technology was negotiated in 1979, including separate agreements for each bank which allow discussions about information technology to take place. Belgium has had a central collective agreement (since 1983) on union and workers' involvement in the introduction of new IT, although the managements of service establishments generally regard technology as part of their 'management prerogative'. Besides, the definition of what is 'new' in technology is often very unclear. As a result of this not many technology agreements have been concluded so far in Belgium. In the Dutch banking industry works councils negotiate about large IT projects, whereas the unions make collective bargaining agreements about vocational training and employment numbers in the banking sector (DCA, 1989). In the UK, union density in banks is high compared to that in the other countries. Terms and conditions are negotiated nationally for clerical staff and at company level for appointed staff. Table 13.3 provides a summary of the position in the five countries.

Human resources strategies

In banking, technological innovations, intensified competition, reduced market segments and increasingly older personnel – part of the general ageing of the population – have forced employers to alter human resources policies, mostly to accommodate more flexibility in the use of labour and to reduce labour costs. In general the workforce in banking is highly stratified by grade and hierarchical in structure. Tasks are described in detail (Cressey and Williams, 1990). The staff of all European banks is growing older (Kirchner, 1984), and the inflow and turnover rates are not adequate enough to meet the planned staffing levels, so that management is being forced to look for other tools such as the introduction of cost savings, the extension of part-time work or the stimulation of the internal labour market.

New human resources policies are most likely to focus on employee training or on recruitment strategies. In Germany, due to the 'Kaufmann-system', vocational training programmes can be influenced more easily than in other countries, where this type of system does not exist. In the Netherlands for example there are no training programmes preparing students for a job in the banking industry (Hove and Tijdens, 1990). Employees obtain their firm-specific training on the job and by attending courses given at an institute set up by the employers' association. In the 1980s the training policy of the Dutch employers changed, as a result of a changing surplus in the labour market. They tried to establish vocational training for bank jobs within the existing educational system. This policy concerned training at the secondary school level as well as at the tertiary and university level. Opportunities to acquire the necessary credentials are being pushed back from the employment period to the pre-employment period. This system resembles the German 'Kaufmann-system'.

In retailing the trends referred to above lead to new skill requirements and to a polarization of the workforce as a whole into two groups. The first consists of a small number of highly trained sales personnel and specialists (like systems and marketing analysts and computer programmers) and the second of a large number of low-skilled stock-room and check-out point personnel (Kruse et al., 1994: 41). This is closely related to the increase in the number of large self-service stores and to the automated handling of stocks and points of sale. Many of the lower-level staff members are women who work part time, and they have fewer opportunities to rise to managerial positions than do male employees. It is estimated that in the countries under investigation, with the notable exception of Sweden, the percentage of women in higher managerial positions in retailing does not exceed 15 per cent and is generally even lower (Kruse et al., 1994: 39; Mok, 1985: 95). The report by Kruse et al. mentions the fact that skills and therefore training requirements within the retailing sector differ widely, depending on the type of trade, the category of personnel and the strategy of the company. For career advancement in retailing, firm-specific technical, behavioural and sales skills are needed, as well as general managerial skills and a broad understanding of the economic context and basic constraints facing the retailing trade. In the end, much if not everything depends on the employment strategies of the managements of the individual firms. The question is whether firms are prepared to spend time and money on the advancement prospects of their staff, and whether they are aware of the connection between quality of staff and quality of the service rendered.

References

Aglietta, M. (1976) *Régulation et crises du capitalisme*. Paris: Calman-Lévy.

Akerlof, G. (1982) 'Labor contracts as a partial gift exchange', *Quarterly Journal of Economics*, 97:4, pp. 543–569.

Akerlof, G. and Yellen J. (eds) (1986) *Efficiency Wage Models of the Labor Market*. Cambridge: Cambridge University Press.

Altshuler, A. et al. (1984) *The Future of the Automobile: the Report of MIT's International Automobile Program*. Cambridge, MA: MIT Press.

Anon (1988) 'Arbeitszeit zu kurz und unflexibel', *Der Arbeitgeber*, 40, p. 8.

Atkinson, J. and Meager, N. (1986) *Changing Working Practices: How Companies Achieve Flexibility to Meet New Needs*. London: National Economic Development Office.

Azariadis, C. and Stiglitz, J. (1983) 'Implicit contracts and fixed price equilibria', *Quarterly Journal of Economics*, 98: Suppl., pp. 1–22.

Badie, B. and Birnbaum, P. (1983) *The Sociology of the State*. University of Chicago Press.

Baethge, M. and Oberbeck, H. (1986) *Zukunft der Angestellten: neue Technologien und berufliche Perspektiven in Büro und Verwaltung*. Frankfurt/New York: Campus.

Baethge, M. and Oberbeck, H. (eds) (1992) *Personalentwicklung im Handel: zwischen Stagnation und neuen Perspektiven*. Frankfurt/New York: Campus.

Baglioni, G. (1990) 'Industrial relations in Europe in the 1980s', in G. Baglioni and C.J. Crouch (eds), *European Industrial Relations: the Challenge of Flexibility*. London: Sage.

Baglioni, G. and Crouch, C. (eds) (1990) *European Industrial Relations: the Challenge of Flexibility*. London: Sage.

Baglioni, M., Chiesi, A. and Maraffi, M. (eds) (1972) 'First comments on sectors: construction, chemicals, machinetools'. Manuscript. Milan: Istituto Superiore di Sociologia.

Baldamus, W. (1961) *Efficiency and Effort*. London: Tavistock.

Bamber, G. (1988) 'Technological change and unions', in R. Hyman and W. Streeck (eds), *New Technology and Industrial Relations*. Oxford: Basil Blackwell, pp. 204–219.

Bamberger, M. (1989) 'Collectieve onderhandelingen in Frankrijk: de opkomst van het bedrijfsniveau', in M.J. Huiskamp (ed.), *Decentraal onderhandelen: Westeuropese ervaringen*. Deventer: Kluwer, pp. 49–65 (in series *Praktisch Personeelbeleid, Capita Selecta*).

Barbash, J. (1984) *The Elements of Industrial Relations*. Madison: University of Wisconsin Press.

Bean, C., Layard, R. and Nickell, S. (1987) *The Rise in Unemployment*. Oxford: Basil Blackwell.

Bell, D. (1973) *The Coming of Post-industrial Society*. New York: Basic Books.

Benveniste, C. (1987) 'Pour la première fois, une hausse du SMIC induite par la croissance des salaires ouvriers', *Economie et Statistique*, 199–200, May–June, pp. 7–11.

Berber, M. (1976) 'Strategic factors in industrial relations systems: the metalworking industry', *Labour and Society*, 2, pp. 18–24.

Berghman, J. and Cantillon, B. (eds) (1993) *The European Face of Social Security*. Aldershot: Avebury.

Bilderbeek, R. and Buitelaar, W. 'Bank computerization and organizational innovations: the long winding road to the bank of the future', *New Technology, Work and Employment*, 7:1, pp. 54–60.

Blanchflower, D.G. and Freeman, R.B. (1990) 'Going different ways: unionism in the US and other advanced OECD countries'. London: LSE, Centre for Economic Performance, discussion paper no. 5.

Blyton, P. (1994) 'Working hours', in K. Sisson (ed.), *Personnel Management, a Comprehensive Guide to Theory and Practice in Britain*. Oxford: Blackwell.

Boonstra, W.W. and De Jong, H. (1993) 'The future of European banking', in S.C.W. Eijffinger and J.L. Gerards (eds), *European Monetary Integration and the Financial Sector*. Amsterdam: NIBE.

Bosch, G. (1988/1989) 'Duration, structure, reduction and flexibilisation of the working week in the FRG', in *Papers Presented at the International Symposium on Working Time (ISWT)*. Paris and Vienna.

Bosch, G. (1989) *Wettlauf rund um die Uhr? Betriebs- und Arbeitszeiten in Europa*. Düsseldorf: Verlag JHW Dietz Nachf.

Bosch, G. (1994) 'Schluß mit dem Mythos des "kollektiven Freizeitparks" ', in *Das Magazin*, 5:1.

Bosch, G., Dawkins, P. and Michon, F. (1988/1989) 'Structure, duration, flexibility and reduction of working time in industrialized countries', in *Papers Presented at the International Symposium on Working Time (ISWT)*. Paris and Vienna.

Boulin, J-Y. (1988/1989) 'Durée et organisation du temps de travail en Europe: tendances institutionelles et réalisations à l'echelon des entreprises', in *Papers preseneted at the International Symposium on Working Time (ISWT)*. Paris and Vienna.

Boyer, R. and Mistral, J. (1983) *Accumulation, inflation et crises du capitalisme*. Paris: Presses Universitaires de France.

Bresky, T., Scherman. J. and Schmid, I. (1981) *Med SAF vid rodret: Granskning av en kamporganisation*. Stockholm: Liber Forlag.

Brody, D. (1980) *Workers in Industrial America: Essays on the 20th Century Struggle*. New York/Oxford: Oxford University Press.

Brown, W. and Terry, M. (1978) 'The changing nature of national wage agreements', *Scottish Journal of Political Economy*, 25, pp. 119–133.

Bruin, T. de (1979) 'Eins, zwei, drei, vier, die Arbeitszeit verkürzen wir!', *ESB*, 64 (3188).

Brumlop, E. (1986) *Arbeitsbewertung bei flexibelen Personaleinsatz*. Frankfurt.

Butera, F. (1974) 'Mutamento dell'organizzazione del lavoro ed egemonia', *Economia e Lavoro*.

Carew, A. (1976) *Democracy and Government in European Trade Unions*. London, Allen & Unwin.

CERC (1988) *Les structures des salaires dans la Communauté Economique Européenne*. Paris: Documentation Française.

CERC (1989) *Les français et leurs revenus*. Paris: Documentation Française.

Child, J. and Loveridge, R. (1990) *Information Technology in European Services: towards a Microelectronic Future*. Oxford: Basil Blackwell.

Child, J., Loveridge, R. and Warner, M. (1972) 'Towards an organizational study of trade unions', *Sociology*, 7:1, pp. 71–91.

Clegg, H.A. (1970) *The System of Industrial Relations in Great Britain*. Oxford: Basil Blackwell.

Clegg, H.A. (1976) *Trade Unionism under Collective Bargaining: a Theory Based on Comparisons of Six Countries*. Oxford: Basil Blackwell.

Clegg, S.R. (1990) *Modern Organizations: Organization Studies in the Postmodern World*. London: Sage.

Commons, J.R. (1909) 'American shoemakers, 1648–1895: a sketch of industrial evolution', *Quarterly Journal of Economics*, 19, pp. 1–32.

Contini, G. (1986) 'The rise and fall of shop-floor bargaining at Fiat 1945–1980', in S. Tolliday and J. Zeitlin (eds), *The Automobile Industry and Its Workers*. Cambridge: Polity Press, pp. 144–167.

Cook, A.H., Lorwin, V.R. and Kaplan Daniels, A. (eds) (1983) *Women and Trade Unions in Eleven Industrialized Countries*. Philadelphia: Temple University Press.

Cressey, P. and Williams, R. (1990) *Participation and New Technology*. Dublin: European Foundation for Improvement of Working Conditions.

Crouch, C. (1982) *Trade Unions: The Logic of Collective Action*. London: Fontana.

Crouch, C.J. (1986) 'Sharing public space: states and organized interests in Western Europe', in J.P. Hall (ed.), *States in History*. Oxford: Basil Blackwell, pp. 177–210.

Crouch, C.J. (1990a) 'Trade unions in the exposed sector: their influence on neo-corporatist behaviour', in R. Brunetta and C. Dell'Aringa (eds), *Labour Relations and Economic Performance*. Basingstoke: Macmillan, pp. 68–91.

Crouch, C.J. (1990b) 'United Kingdom: the rejection of compromise', in G. Baglioni and C.J. Crouch (eds), *European Industrial Relations: the Challenge of Flexibility*. London: Sage, pp. 326–355.

Crouch, C. (1991) 'Comparative occupational training systems: the role of employers' associations and trade unions', Paper for the EGOS Colloquium (Session I 'Employers' associations and trade unions in changing industrial relations'), Vienna, July.

Crouch, C. (1993a) 'Ambiguities of decentralisation', in *Economic and Political Changes in Europe*, International Industrial Relations Association, 3rd European Regional Congress, Bari/Naples, 23–26 September 1991, pp. 881–893.

Crouch, C.J. (1993b) *Industrial Relations and European State Traditions*. Oxford: Clarendon Press.

Crouch, C. and Pizzorno, A. (1978) *The Resurgence of Class Conflict in Western Europe since 1968*. London: Macmillan.

Crozier, M. (1963) *Le phénomène bureaucratique*. Paris: Seuil.

Cusumano, M.A. (1985) *The Japanese Automobile Industry: Technology and Management at Nissan and Toyota*. Cambridge, MA: Harvard University Press.

Dankbaar, B. (1984) 'Maturity and relocation in the car industry', *Development and Change*, 15, pp. 223–250.

Dankbaar, B. (1989) 'Technical change and industrial relations: theoretical reflections on changes in the automobile industry', *Economic and Industrial Democracy*, 10, pp. 99–121.

Dankbaar, B., Jürgens, U. and Malsch T. (eds) (1988) *Die Zukunft der Arbeit in der Automobilindustrie*. Berlin: Sigma.

Davis, L.E. and Taylor, J.C. (eds) (1990) *The Design of Jobs*. Harmondsworth: Penguin.

DCA [Dienst Collectieve Arbeidsbetrekkingen] (1989) *CAO-afspraken 1988: een onderzoek naar de resultaten van de CAO–onderhandelingen voor het jaar 1988*. The Hague: VUGA.

Dell'Aringa, C. and Lucifora, C. (1990) 'Wage determination and union behaviour in Italy: an efficiency wage interpretation', in C. Dell'Aringa and R. Brunetta (eds), *Labour Relation and Economic Performance*. London: Macmillan.

De Witte, H. (ed.) (1994) *Op zoek naar de arbeidersklasse: een verkenning van de verschillen in opvattingen en leefstijl tussen arbeiders en bedienden in Vlaanderen, Nederland en Europa*. Leuven/Amersfoort: Acco.

Dickens, W.T. and Lang, K. (eds) (1987) *A Goodness of Fit Test of Dual Labor Market Theory*. Cambridge MA: National Bureau of Economic Research.

Dohse, K., Jürgens, U. and Malsch, T. (1985) 'From 'Fordism' to 'Toyotism'? The social organization of the labor process in the Japanese automobile industry', *Politics and Society*, 14:2, pp. 115–146.

Ebbinghaus, B.O. (1993) 'Labour unity in union diversity: trade unions and social cleavages in Western Europe 1890–1989'. Florence, PhD thesis (unpublished).

Ebbinghaus, B.O. and Visser, J. (1994) 'Barrieren und Wege 'grenzenloser' Solidarität. Gewerkschaften und Europäische Integration', in W. Streeck (ed.), *Politisches Viertel-jahresschrift*. Special issue on 'Staat und Verbände'.

Edelstein, J.D. and Warner, M. (1978) *Comparative Union Democracy: Organisation and Opposition in British and American Unions*. New Brunswick, NJ: Transaction Books.

Elchardus, M. (1990) 'De modernisering van de tijd: mogelijkheden en grenzen', in J. von Grumbkow (ed.), *Tijd in arbeid en organisatie*. Deventer/Heerlen: Kluwer/Open Universiteit.

European Commission (1979) *Consultation in the member states of the Community: problems and perspectives*. Social Policy Series No. 40. Brussels: European Commission.

European Industrial Relations Review (1993) 'Single union deals examined', *European Industrial Relations Review*, 235, pp. 22–27.

European Trade Union Institute (1985) *Technology and Collective Bargaining: a Review of 10 Years of European Experience*. Brussels: ETUI.

Eurostat (1978) *Structure of Earnings Survey*. Luxembourg: Office of CEC.

Eurostat (1988) *Labour Cost Survey*. Luxembourg: Office of CEC.

Eurostat (1993) *ACP Basic Statistics: Comparison with some European Countries, Canada, USA, Japan and USSR*. 30th edn. Luxembourg: Office of CEC. (See also previous years.)

Farnham, D. and Pimlott, J. (1979) *Understanding Industrial Relations*. London: Cassell.

Fassbender, H. and Wuffi, P. (1990) 'European banking after 1992', *McKinsey Quarterly*, Spring, pp. 131–141.

FIET (International Federation of Commercial, Clerical, Professional and Technical Employees) (1980) *Bank Workers and New Technology*. Geneva: FIET.

Fitzroy, F. (1991) 'Wage structures, employment problems, and economic policy', in Marsden, D. (ed.), *Pay and Employment in the New Europe*. Cheltenham: Edward Elgar.

Flanders, A. (1954) 'Collective bargaining', in H.A. Clegg and A. Flanders (eds), *The System of Industrial Relations in Great Britain: its History, Law and Institutions*. Oxford: Basil Blackwell, pp. 252–321.

Flanders, A. (1970) *Management and Unions: the Theory and Reform of Industrial Relations*. London: Faber.

Fox, A. (1974) *Beyond Contract: Work, Power and Trust Relations*. London: Faber.

Francis, A. (1986) *New Technology at Work*. Oxford: Clarendon Press.

Freeman, R.B. and Medoff, J.F. (1984) *What Do Unions Do?* New York: Basic Books.

Gallie, D. (1978) *In Search of the New Working Class*. Cambridge: Cambridge University Press.

Garnsey, E. and Roberts, C. (1988/1989) 'Duration, structure, reduction and flexibilization of working time in Great Britain', in *Papers Presented at the International Symposium on Working Time (ISWT)*. Paris (1988) and Vienna (1989).

Garonna, P. and Reboani, P. (1989) *Les politiques d'aménagement du temps de travail et les relations industrielles en Italie*. Rome.

Garraty, J. (1978) *A History of Unemployment*. New York: Praeger.

Gasparini, G. (1988/1989) 'Les horaires atypiques de travail, quelques réflexions sur le cas d'Italie et de la France', in *Papers Presented at the International Symposium on Working Time (ISWT)*. Paris (1988) and Vienna (1989).

Gershuny, J. (1979) *After Industrial Society: the Emerging Selfservice Economy*. London: Macmillan.

Giddens, A. (1974) *The Class Structure of the Advanced Societies*. London: Hutchinson.

Gill, C. and Krieger, H. (1992) 'The diffusion of participation in new information technology in Europe: survey results', *Economic and Industrial Democracy, an International Journal*, 13:3, pp. 331–358.

Glaude, M. and Hernu, P. (1986) 'Les salaires en 1985', *Economie et Statistique*, 184, pp. 3–22.

Goldfield, M., (1987) *The Decline of Organized Labor in the United States*. Chicago/London: University of Chicago Press.

Gourevitch, P., Martin, A., Ross, G., Bornstein, P., Markovits, A. and Allen, C. (1984) *Unions and Economic Crisis: Britain, West Germany, and Sweden*. London: Allen & Unwin.

Granovetter, M. and Swedberg R. (eds) (1992) *The Sociology of Economic Life*. Boulder, CO: Westview Press.

Grant, W. (1983) 'The organization of business interests in the UK Construction industry', in *WZB-Discussion Papers IIM/LMP*, 83–25. Berlin.

Grant, W. and Marsh D. (1977) *The CBI*. London: Hodder & Stoughton.

Green, F. (1992) 'The distribution of union membership in Great Britain: an individual-based analysis.' Unpubl. PhD thesis, University of Leicester.

Gregory, M., Lobbar, P. and Thomson, A. (1985) 'Wage settlements in manufacturing 1979–1984: evidence from the CBI Pay Databank', *British Journal of Industrial Relations*, 3.

Gregory, M., Lobbar, P. and Thomson, A. (1986) 'Wage settlements in manufacturing 1979–1984: evidence from the CBI Pay Databank', *British Journal of Industrial Relations*, 2.

Hancké, B. (1993) 'Trade union membership in Europe, 1960–1990: rediscovering local unions', *British Journal of Industrial Relations*, 31:4.

Hardin, R. (1982) *Collective Action*. Baltimore, MD: Johns Hopkins University Press.

Hartog, J. and Theeuwes J. (eds) (1993) *Labour Market Contracts and Institutions: a Cross-national Comparison*. Amsterdam: North-Holland.

Hayek, F.A. von (1971) *Die Verfassung der Freiheit*. Tübingen: Mohr.

Hibbs, D.A. (1990), 'Wage compression under solidarity bargaining in Sweden', Economic Research Report No. 30. Stockholm: Trade Union Institute for Economic Research (FIEF).

Hicks, J.R. (1955) 'The economic foundations of wages policy', *Economic Journal*, 65:259, pp. 389–404.

Hicks, J.R. (1974) *The crisis in Keynesian economics*. Oxford: Basil Blackwell, 1974.

Hirschman, A.O. (1970) *Exit, Voice, and Loyalty: Responses to Decline in Firms, Organizations and States*. Cambridge, MA: Harvard University Press.

Hobsbawm, E.J. (1964) *Labouring Men: Studies in the History of Labour*. London: Weidenfeld & Nicolson.

Hounshell, D.A. (1984) *From the American System to Mass Production: the Development of Manufacturing Technology in the United States, 1800–1932*. Baltimore, MD: Johns Hopkins University Press, Ch. 6.

Hove, T. van den and Tijdens, K. (1990) 'Opleiden binnen het gezichtsveld van de banken', *Vernieuwing, Tijdschrift voor Onderwijs en Opvoeding*, 49:10, pp. 15–18.

Huiskamp, M.J. (1983a) 'De cao-structuur in de Nederlandse industrie', part I. *Economisch-Statistische Berichten*, 68:3392, pp. 131–137.

Huiskamp, M.J. (1983b) 'De cao-structuur in de Nederlandse industrie', part II. *Economisch-Statistische Berichten*, 68:3393, pp. 154–158.

Huiskamp, M.J. (1983c) 'De cao-structuur in de Nederlandse industrie', part III. *Economisch-Statistische Berichten*, 68:3394, pp. 180–184.

Huiskamp, M.J. and Risseeuw, P. (1989) *Ondernemingsraad en arbeidsvoorwaarden*. Amsterdam: VU-Uitgeverij.

IDE International Research Group (1981) 'Industrial democracy in Europe: differences and similarities across countries and hierarchies', *Organisation Studies*, 2:2, pp. 113–129.

ILO (1989) *Working time issues in industrialised countries*. Geneva: International Labour Organization.

ILO (1991) *Yearbook of Labour Statistics*. Geneva: International Labour Organization.

ILO (1993) *World Labour Report 6*. Geneva: International Labour Organization.

d'Iribarne, A. and Fossati, H. (1986) *Diffusion des technologies informatisées de production, emploi et formation dans les petits et moyens établissements de la région PACA*. Aix-en-Provence: Laboratoire d'économie et de sociologie du travail, document LEST, pp. 86–102.

Joosse, D. et al. (1990) *Zelfstandig samenwerken in autonome taakgroepen*. The Hague: COB/SER.

Jürgens, U., Malsch, T. and Dohse, K. (1989) *Moderne Zeiten in der Automobilfabrik, Strategien der Produktionsmodernisierung im Länder- und Konzernvergleich*. Berlin: Springer.

Kahn-Freund, O. (1967) 'Legal framework', in Allan Flanders and Hugh A. Clegg (eds), *The System of Industrial Relations in Great Britain*. Oxford: Basil Blackwell.

Kahn-Freund, O. (1977) *Labour and the Law*. London: Stevens.

Kahneman, D., Knetsch, J. and Thaler, R. (1986) 'Fairness as a constraint on profit-seeking: entitlements in the market', *American Economic Review*, 76:4, pp. 728–741.

Karsten, L. (1990) *De achturendag: Arbeidstijdverkorting in historisch perspectief 1817–1919*. Amsterdam: Stichting Beheer IISG.

Kassalow, E.M. (1969) *Trade Unions and Industrial Relations: an International Comparison*. New York: Random House.

Katz, H. (1985) *Shifting Gears: Changing Labor Relations in the US Automobile Industry*. Cambridge, MA: MIT Press.

Katzenstein, P.J. (1985) *Small States in World Markets: Industrial Policy in Europe*. Ithaca, NY/London: Cornell University Press.

Kennedy, T. (1980) *European Labor Relations: Text and Cases*. Lexington, MA: Heath.

Kern, H. and Schumann, M. (1984) *Das Ende der Arbeitsteilung? Rationalisierung in der industriellen Produktion*. Munich: Beck.

Kerr, C. et al. (1960) *Industrialism and Industrial Man*. Cambridge, MA: Harvard University Press.

Kirchner, E.J. (1984) *Report on the Social Implications of Introducing New Technology in the Banking Sector*. Luxembourg: Commission of the European Communities.

Kjellberg, A. (1983) *Facklig organisiering i tolv länder*. Lund: Arkiv.

Kjellberg, A. (1992) 'Sweden: Can the Model Survive?' in A. Ferner and R. Hyman (eds), *Industrial Relations in the New Europe*. Oxford: Basil Blackwell.

Klandermans, B. (1984) 'Mobilization and participation in trade union action: a value expectancy approach', *Journal of Occupational Psychology*, 57, pp. 107–120.

Klandermans, B. and Visser, J. (1995) *De vakbeweging na de welvaartstaat*. Assen: Van Gorcum.

Knowles, K.G.J.C. and Robertson, D.J. (1951) 'Difference between the wages of skilled and unskilled workers 1880–1950', *Bulletin of the Oxford Institute of Statistics*, April, pp. 109–127.

Kochan, T.A. (1988) 'The future of worker representation: an American perspective', *Labour and Society*, 13:2, pp. 183–201.

Kochan, T.A., Katz, H.C. and MacKersie, R.B. (1989) *The Transformation of American Industrial Relations*. New York: Basic Books.

Kochan, T.A., MacKersie, R.B. and Capelli, P. (1984) 'Strategic choice and industrial relations theory', *Industrial Relations*, 23:1, pp. 16–39.

Koopman, P.L. and Drenth, P.J.D. (1993) 'Industriële democratie in Europa herzien: Vergelijkende replicatie studie tien jaar later', in J. van Doorn, P. Meurs and T. Mijs (eds), *Het organisatorisch labyrint*. Utrecht: Het Spectrum, pp. 214–233.

Kruse, W. et al. (1994) *Training in the Retail Sector: a Survey for the FORCE Programme*. Berlin: CEDEFOP.

Lallement, M. (1988/1989) 'Réglementation et détermination conventionnelle du temps de travail: éléments de comparaison entre la France et l'Allemagne', in *Papers Presented at the International Symposium on Working Time (ISWT)*. Paris (1988) and Vienna (1989).

Lamers, G., Sloot, B. and Veldt, O. (1989) *Arbeidstijdwetgeving in negen industriële landen, de vernieuwing van Nederlandse arbeidstijdwetgeving in een internationaal perspectief*. The Hague: Ministry of Social Affairs and Employment.

Lammers, C.J. (1981) 'Arbeidsverhoudingen vanuit een interorganisationeel perspectief', *M&O*, 35.

Lammers, C.J. (1989) *Organisaties vergelijkenderwijs: ontwikkeling en relevantie van het sociologisch denken over organisaties*. Utrecht: Het Spectrum.

Lane, C. (1989) *Management and Labour in Europe: The Industrial Enterprise in Germany, Britain and France*. Aldershot: Edward Elgar.

Lange, P. (1992) 'The politics of the social dimension', in A.M. Sbragia (ed.), *Europolitics: Institutions and Policymaking in the 'New' European Community*. Washington, DC: The Brookings Institution, pp. 225–256.

de Lange, W. (1989) *Configuratie van arbeid, vormgeven aan arbeidstijden, bedrijfstijden en arbeidstijdpatronen*. Zutphen: Thieme.

Leroy, R., Meulders, D. and Plasman, R. (1988/1989) 'Durée, structure, réduction et flexibilisation du temps de travail dans 11 pays industrialisés, le cas de la Belgique', in *Papers Presented at the International Symposium on Working Time (ISWT)*. Paris (1988) and Vienna (1989).

Levinson, K. (1991) 'Medbestämmande i strategiska beslutsprocesser: facklig medverkan och inflytande i koncerner.' Department of Business Studies, University of Uppsala.

Lichtenstein, N. and Meyer, S. (eds) (1989) *On the Line: Essays in the History of Auto Work*. Urbana/Chicago, IL: University of Illinois Press.

Lipset, S.M. and Rokkan, S. (1967) 'Cleavage structures, party systems and voter alignments: an introduction', in S.M. Lipset and S. Rokkan (eds), *Party Systems and Voter Alignments: Crossnational Perspectives*. New York: Free Press.

Lipset, S.M., Trow, M.A. and Coleman, J.S. (1956) *Union Democracy*. Glencoe, IL.: Free Press.

Littek, W. (1992) 'Service sector/service work', in G. Szell (ed.), *Concise Encyclopaedia of Participation and Co-management*. Berlin/New York: Walter de Gruyter, pp. 743–755.

Loveridge, R. (1983) 'Sources of diversity in internal labour markets', *Sociology*, 17, pp. 44–62.

Loveridge, R. (1984) 'Micro-electronics and the growing polarisation of service employment', in *Proceedings of the Labour Process Conference*. Birmingham: Aston Business School.

Loveridge, R. and Mok, A.L. (1979) *Theories of Labour Market Segmentation: a Critique*. The Hague/Boston/London: Martinus Nijhoff.

Madigan, K. (1990) *Further Education and Training and Collective Bargaining: the Experience of Five Countries*. Paris.

Marin, B. (1985) 'Austria: the paradigm case of liberal corporatism', in W. Grant (ed.), *The Political Economy of Corporatism*. London: Macmillan.

Marks, G. (1989) *Unions in Politics. Britain, Germany and the United States in the Nineteenth and Early Twentieth Centuries*. Princeton, NJ: Princeton University Press.

Marsden, D.W. (1981) 'Vive la différence: pay differentials in Britain, West Germany, France and Italy', *Employment Gazette*, 89:7, pp. 309–318.

Marsden, D.W. (1990a) 'Institutions and labour mobility: occupational and internal labour markets in Britain, France, Italy, and West Germany', in R. Brunetta and C. Dell'Aringa (eds), *Labour Relations and Economic Performance*. London: Macmillan.

Marsden, D.W. (1990b) 'Occupational pay and unemployment in Britain, France, Italy, and West Germany', in W. Molle, and A. Van Mourik (eds), *Wage Structure in the European Community*. Aldershot: Gower.

Marsden, D.W. (1990c) *The Flexibility of Wages and Changing Economic Conditions*. Geneva: International Labour Office.

Marsden, D.W. and Redlbacher, L. (1984) *Guide to Sources of Wages Statistics in the European Community*. Luxembourg: Statistical Office of the European Communities.

Marsden, D.W. and Ryan, P. (1991) 'Youth pay and training in industrial countries' (with Paul Ryan), in P. Ryan, P.F.P. Garonna and R.C. Edwards (eds), *The Problem of Youth*. London: Macmillan.

Marsden, D., Morris, T. and Willman, P. (1985) *The Car Industry: Labour Relations and Industrial Adjustment*. London/New York: Tavistock.

Martin, R. (1968) 'Union democracy: an explanatory framework', *Sociology*, 2.

Marwell, G. and Oliver, P. (1993) *The Critical Mass in Collective Action: a Microsocial Theory*. Cambridge: Cambridge University Press.

Maurice, M. and Sellier, F. (1979) 'Societal analysis of industrial relations: a comparison between France and Germany', *British Journal of Industrial Relations*, 17:3, pp. 322–336.

Maurice, M., Eyraud, F., d'Iribarne, A. and Rychener, F. (1986) *Des entreprises en mutation dans la crise: apprentissage des technologies flexibles et émergence de nouveaux acteurs*. Aix-en-Provence: Laboratoire d' économie et de sociologie du travail.

Maurice, M., Sellier, F. and Silvestre, J.J. (1982) *Politique d'éducation et organisation industrielle en France et en Allemagne: essai d'analyse sociétale*. Paris, Presses Universitaires de France. (Published in English as: *The Social Foundation of Industrial Power: a Comparison of France and Germany*. Cambridge, MA: MIT Press, 1986.)

Maurice, M., Sorge, A. and Warner, M. (1978) 'Societal differences in organising manufacturing units: a comparison of France, West Germany, and Great Britain'. International Institute of Management Discussion paper 79–15. Berlin: Wissenschaftszentrum.

Maurice, M., Sorge, A. and Warner, M. (1980) 'Societal differences in organizing manufacturing units. A comparison of France, West Germany and Great Britain', *Organization Studies*, 1, pp. 59–86.

Michels, R. (1925 [1911]) *Zur Soziologie des Parteiwesens in den modernen Demokratie.* Stuttgart: Alfred Kröner.

Michon, F. (1987) 'Time and flexibility: working time in the debate on flexibility', *Labour and Society*, 12, p. 1.

Millward, N. and Stevens, M. (1986) *British Workplace Industrial Relations, 1980–1984.* Aldershot: Gower.

Millward, N. and Stevens, M. (1987) 'Symposium British Workplace Industrial Relations 1980–1984', *British Journal of Industrial Relations*, 2, July, pp. 273–294.

Millward, N. and Stevens, M. (1992) *British Workplace Industrial Relations, 1990.* Aldershot: Gower.

Millward, N., Stevens, M., Smart, D. and Hawes, W.R. (1992) *Workplace Industrial Relations in Transition.* Aldershot: Gower.

Ministry of Social Affairs and Employment (Ministerie van Sociale Zaken en Werkgelegenheid) (1994) *Notitie over arbeidsduurverkorting.* The Hague.

Mintzberg, H. (1983) *Structure in Fives: Designing Effective Organizations.* Englewood Cliffs, NJ: Prentice Hall.

Mok, A.L. (1985) 'Le banche in Belgio: conseguenze dell'automatione sullo sviluppo dei ruoli lavorativi', in E. Invernizzi (ed.), *Organizzazione del lavoro in banca e automazione.* Milan: Angeli, pp. 83–100.

Mok, A. (1990) *In het zweet uws aanschijns.* Leiden/Antwerp: Stenfert Kroese.

Mok, A.L. and Geldof, D. (1994) 'The changing face of service work in European countries', in W. Littek and T. Charles (eds), *The New Division of Labour.* Berlin/New York: De Gruyter.

Myrdal, H.-G. (1990) 'The hard way from a centralized to a decentralized industrial relations system. The case of Sweden and SAF'. Paper prepared by the director of SAF for the Conference 'Employers' Associations in Europe: Policy and Organization', Trier, September 1990.

North, D.C. (1991) 'Institutions', *Journal of Economic Perspective*, pp. 97–112.

OECD (1965) *Wages and Labour Mobility.* Paris: Organization for Economic Co-operation and Development.

OECD (1979) *Collective Bargaining and Government policies in Ten OECD Countries.* Paris: Organization for Economic Co-operation and Development.

OECD (1987) *Employment Outlook.* Paris: Organization for Economic Co-operation and Development.

OECD (1989) *Employment Outlook.* Paris: Organization for Economic Co-operation and Development.

OECD (1991) *Labour Force Statistics 1969–1989.* Paris: Organization for Economic Co-operation and Development.

OECD (1992) *Employment Outlook.* Paris: Organization for Economic Co-operation and Development.

OECD (1993) *Employment Outlook.* Paris: Organization for Economic Co-operation and Development.

OECD (1994) *Employment Outlook.* Paris: Organization for Economic Co-operation and Development.

Offe, C. (1981) 'The attribution of public status to interest groups: observations on the West German case', in S. Berger (ed.), *Organizing Interests in Western Europe: Pluralism, Corporatism, and the Transformation of Politics.* Cambridge, Cambridge University Press, pp. 123–154.

Offe, C. (1985) *Disorganized Capitalism: Contemporary Transformations of Works and Politics.* Cambridge: Polity Press.

Offe, C. and Wiesenthal, H. (1979) 'Two logics of collective action: Theoretical notes on social class and organizational form', in M. Zeitlin (ed.), *Political Power and Social Theory*, vol. I, Greenwich, CT.

Oi, W. (1962) 'Labor as a quasi-fixed factor', *Journal of Political Economy*, 70.

Olson, M. (1965) *The Logic of Collective Action: Public Goods and the Theory of Groups.* Cambridge, MA: Harvard University Press.

Olson, M. (1982) *The Rise and Decline of Nations: Economic Growth, Stagflation and Social Rigidities.* New Haven, CT: Yale University Press.

Paci, M. (1973) *Mercato del lavoro e classi sociale in Italia.* Bologna University Press: Il Mulino.

Pestoff, V. (1983) 'The associative action of Swedish business' interests: the organization of business' interests in the Swedish chemical and drug industry', Research Report No. 1983–9, Department of Political Science, Stockholm University.

Pestoff, V. (1984) 'The organization of business' interests in the Swedish building and construction industry', Research Report No. 1984–12, Department of Political Science, Stockholm University.

Pestoff, V. (1991) 'The demise of the Swedish model and the rise of organized business as a major political actor'. Paper prepared for the Conference of the Society for the Advancement of Socio-Economics, Stockholm.

Petterson, L. (1988/1989) 'Structure of the working hours in Sweden', in *Papers Presented at the International Symposium on Working Time (ISWT).* Paris (1988) and Vienna (1989).

Pfeffer, J. and Salancik, G.R. (1978) *The External Control of Organizations: a Resource Dependence Perspective.* New York.

Phelps Brown, E.H. and Hopkins, S. (1955) 'Seven centuries of building wages', *Economica,* 22:87, August, pp. 195–206.

Piore, M and Sabel, C. (1984) *The Second Industrial Divide.* New York: Basic Books.

Pollard, S. (1969) 'Trade unions' reactions to the economic crisis', *Journal of Contemporary History,* 4:4, pp. 101–115.

Poole, M. (1986) *Industrial Relations: Origins and Patterns of National Diversity.* London/ New York: Routledge and Kegan Paul.

Pot, F. (1988) 'Technologie, vakbekwaamheid en beleid', in J. Van Ruysseveldt and J. von Grumbkow (eds), *Arbeid in verandering: de strategische rol van vakmanschap en management.* Deventer/Heerlen: Kluwer/Open Universiteit, pp. 60–68.

Purcell, J. and Ahlstrand, B. (1989) 'Corporate strategy and the management of employee relations in the multi-divisional company', *British Journal of Industrial Relations,* 27:3, pp. 396–417.

Reder, M.W. (1955) 'A theory of occupational wage differentials', *American Economic Review,* 5, pp. 833–852.

Reynaud, B. (1989) 'Les systèmes de rémunération ouvriers dans la crise: quels choix stratégiques?', *Economie et Prévision,* 90.

Richardson, R. and Nejad, A. (1986) 'Employee share ownership schemes in the UK: an evaluation', *British Journal of Industrial Relations,* 24:2, pp. 233–250.

Rogers, J. and Streeck, W. (eds) (1994) *Works Councils: Consultation, Representation, Cooperation.* Chicago, IL: University of Chicago Press.

Rosanvallon, P. (1988) *La question syndicale: histoire et avenir d'une forme sociale.* Paris: Calman-Lévy.

Roth, S. and Kohl, H. (eds) (1988) *Perspektive: Gruppenarbeit.* Cologne: Bund.

Rothstein, B. (1991) 'Labour market institutions and working class strength', in S. Steinmo, K. Thelen and F. Lonstreth (eds), *The New Institutionalism: State, Society and Economy.* Cambridge: Cambridge University Press.

Routh, G. (1980) *Occupation and Pay in Great Britain 1906–79.* London: Macmillan.

Rowe, J.W.E. (1928) *Wages in Practice and Theory.* London: Routledge and Kegan Paul.

Rubery, J., Deakin, S. and Horrell, S. (1990) *Change and Continuity in Working Time Patterns in Britain.* Cambridge.

Sager, M.T. (1988) 'Competitive information systems in Australian banking', *Information and Management,* 15.

Santi, P. (1981) 'I differenziali retributivi occupazionali nell'industria italiana e la politica sindacale negli anni "70" ', *Rivista Internazionale di Scienze Sociale.*

Saunders, C.T. and Marsden, D.W. (1981) *Pay Inequalities in the European Communities*. London: Butterworths.

Scharpf, F.W. (1987) *Crisis and Choice in European Social Democracy*. Ithaca, NY: Cornell University Press.

Scheuer, S. (1992) 'Denmark: return to decentralization', in A. Ferner and R. Hyman (eds), *Industrial Relations in the New Europe*, Oxford: Basil Blackwell, p. 168.

Schmitter, P. and Streeck, W. (1981) 'The organization of business interests. A research design to study the associative action of business in the advanced industrial societies of Western Europe' (revised and extended version), IIM Discussion Papers IIM/LMP 81–31, Wissenschaftszentrum, Berlin.

Segrestin, D. (1990) 'Recent changes in France', in G. Baglioni and C. Crouch (eds), *European Industrial Relations: the Challenge of Flexibility*. London: Sage, pp. 97–126.

Seyfarth, Shaw, Fairweather and Geraldson [law firm] (1972) *Labour Relations and the Law in France and the United States*. Ann Arbor, MI: University of Michigan Press.

Shalev, M. (1992) 'The resurgence of labour quiescence', in M. Regini (ed.), *The Future of Labour Movements*. London: Sage, pp. 102–132.

Shimada, H. (1988) 'Japanese trade unionism: post-war evolution and future prospects', *Labour and Society*, 13:2, pp. 183–201.

Shutt, J. and Whittington, R. (1991) 'Fragmentation strategies and the size of small units: cases from the North West', *Regional Studies*, 21, pp. 13–23.

Sitter, L.U. de (1981) *Op weg naar nieuwe fabrieken en kantoren*. Deventer: Kluwer.

Skogh, G. (1984) 'Employers' associations in Sweden', in John P. Windmuller and Alan Gladstone (eds), *Employers' Associations and Industrial Relations: a Comparative Study*. Oxford: Clarendon Press.

Slomp, H. (1990) *Labor Relations in Europe: a History of Issues and Developments*. Westport, CT: Greenwood Press.

Sorge, A. (1991) 'Strategic fit and the societal effect: interpreting cross-national comparisons of technology, organization and human resources', *Organization Studies*, 12:2, pp. 161–190.

Sorge, A. and Streeck, W. (1988) 'Industrial relations and technical change: the case for an extended perspective', in R. Hyman and W. Streeck (eds), *New Technology and Industrial Relations*. Oxford: Basil Blackwell, pp. 19–47.

Sorge, A. and Warner, M. (1986) *Comparative Factory Organisation: an Anglo-German Comparison of Manufacturing, Management and Manpower*. Aldershot: Gower.

Sorge, A., Hartman, G., Warner, M. and Nicholas, I. (1983) *Microelectronics and Manpower in Manufacturing: Applications of Computer Numerical Control in Great Britain and West Germany*. Aldershot: Gower.

Stinchcombe, A.L. (1964) 'Social structure and the founding of organizations', in J.G. March (ed.), *Handbook of Organizations*. Skokie, IL: Rand McNally.

Storey, J. (1992) *Management of Human Resources*. Oxford: Basil Blackwell.

Streeck, W. (1982) 'Organizational consequences of corporatist cooperation in West German labour unions', in G. Lehmbruch and P.C. Schmitter (eds), *Patterns of Corporatist Policy-Making*. London/Beverly Hills: Sage, pp. 29–81.

Streeck, W. (1984) *Industrial relations in West-Germany: a Case Study of the Car Industry*. London: Heinemann.

Streeck, W. (1987) 'The uncertainties of management in the management of uncertainty', in P. Hall (ed.), *European Labor in the 1980s*. Special issue of *International Journal of Political Economy*, 17:3, pp. 57–87.

Streeck, W. (1988) *Kollektive Arbeitsbeziehungen und industrieller Wandel: das Beispiel der Automobilindustrie*. Wissenschaftszentrum: Berlin.

Streeck, W. (1989) 'The territorial organization of interests and the logics of associative action: the case of Handwerk organization in West Germany', in William D. Coleman and Henry J. Jacek (eds), *Regionalism, Business Interests and Public Policy*. London: Sage, pp. 59–94.

Streeck, W. (1991) 'Interest heterogeneity and organizing capacity: two class logics of collective action?', in R. Czada and A. Windshoff–Héritier (eds), *Political Choice, Institutions, Rules and the Limits of Rationality*. Frankfurt/Boulder, CO: Campus.

Streeck, W. (1992a) 'Interest heterogeneity and organizing capacity: two class logics of collective action?', in *Social Institutions and Economic Performance: Studies of Industrial Relations in Advanced Capitalist Economies*. London: Sage, pp. 76–104.

Streeck, W. (1992b) 'Productive constraints: on the institutional conditions of diversified quality production', in *Social Institutions and Economic Performance: Studies of Industrial Relations in Advanced Capitalist Economies*. London: Sage, pp. 1–40.

Streeck, W. (1992c) 'Revisiting status and contract: pluralism, corporatism and flexibility', in *Social Institutions and Economic Performance: Studies of Industrial Relations in Advanced Capitalist Economies*. London: Sage, pp. 41–75.

Streeck, W. (1993) 'The rise and decline of neocorporatism', in L. Ulman, B. Eichengreen and W.T. Dickens (eds), *Labor and an Integrated Europe*. Washington, DC: The Brookings Institution, pp. 80–101.

Streeck, W. and Schmitter, P.C. (1985) 'Community, market, state – and associations?' in W. Streeck and P.C. Schmitter (eds), *Private Interest Government: Beyond Market and State*. London: Sage, pp. 1–29.

Stroeke, J.H.M. (1990) 'Informatietechnologie bij banken', in L.A. ten Horn and F.R.H. Zijstra, *Informatietechnologie in de maatschappij: toepassing, beleid, perspectief*. Leiden/ Antwerp: Stenfert Kroese, pp. 99–117.

Sturmthal, A. (1953) *Unity and Diversity in European Labor*. Ithaca, NY: Cornell University Press.

Swaan, A. de (1989) *Zorg en de staat*. Amsterdam: Bert Bakker.

Swenson, P. (1989) *Fair Shares: Unions, Pay, and Politics in Sweden and West Germany*. Ithaca, NY: Cornell University Press.

Taddei, D. (1988/1989) 'Réorganisation, réduction du temps de travail et emploi en France dans la CEE', in *Papers Presented at the International Symposium on Working Time (ISWT)*. Paris (1988) and Vienna (1989).

Tallard, M. (1988) 'Bargaining over new technology: a comparison of France and West Germany', in R. Hyman and W. Streeck (eds), *New Technology and Industrial Relations*. Oxford: Basil Blackwell, pp. 284–296.

Taylor, A.J. (1989) *Trade Unions and Politics: a Comparative Introduction*. London.

Teychiné Stakenburg, A.J.T. (1957) *SVZ, Stand van zaken: Vijftig jaar arbeidsverhoudingen in Rotterdam*. Rotterdam.

Thelen, K.A. (1991) *Union of Parts: Labour Politics in Postwar Germany*. Ithaca, NY/ London: Cornell University Press.

Tijdens, K. (1993) '25 jaar produkt- en procesinnovaties in het binnenlandse girale betalingsverkeer in het bankwezen', *Tijdschrift voor Politieke Economie*, 15:3, pp. 67–89.

Toffler, A. (1980) *The Third Wave*. New York: Morrow.

Tolliday, S. and Zeitlin, J. (eds) (1986) *The Automobile Industry and its Workers*. Cambridge: Polity Press, 1986.

Traxler, F. (1991) 'The logic of employers' collective action', in D. Sadowski and O. Jacobi (eds), *Employers' Associations in Europe: Policy and Organisation*. Baden-Baden: Nomos.

Traxler, F. (1994) 'Collective bargaining: levels and coverage', in *OECD, Employment Outlook 1994*. Paris: OECD, pp. 167–194.

Traxler, F. (1995) 'Gewerkschaften und Arbeitgeberverbände: ein internationaler Vergleich', in W. Müller-Jentsch (ed.), *Kontinuität und Wandel: Zwischenbilanz der industriellen Beziehungen*. München-Mering: Hampp (in press).

Traxler, F., and Unger, B. (1990) 'Institutionelle Erfolgsbedingungen wirtschaftlichen Strukturwandels', in *Wirtschaft und Gesellschaft*, Part 2. Vienna, pp. 189–225.

Treu, T. and Martinelli, A. (1984) 'Employers' associations in Italy', in J.P. Windmuller and A. Gladstone (eds), *Employers' Associations and Industrial Relations: a Comparative Study*. Oxford: Clarendon Press, pp. 264–293.

Turner, H.A. (1962) *Trade Union Growth, Structure and Policy*. London: Allen & Unwin.

Turner, L. (1991) *Democracy at Work: Changing World Markets and the Future of Labor Unions*. Ithaca, NY: Cornell University Press.

Tzannatos, Z. and Zabalza, A. (1984) 'The autonomy of the rise of British female relative wages in the 1970s: evidence from the New Earnings Survey', *British Journal of Industrial Relations*, 22:2, pp. 177–194.

Ulman, L. (1955) *The Rise of the National Union*. Cambridge, MA: Cambridge University Press.

Ulman, L., Eichengreen, B. and Dickens, W.T. (eds) (1993) *Labor and an Integrated Europe*. Washington, DC: The Brookings Institution.

Van Ruysseveldt, J. (1991) 'Arbeidsverhoudingen, arbeidsruilrelaties en technologische innovatie: gezichtspunten vanuit cross-nationale en inter-sectorale vergelijkingen', in SISWO, *Informatietechnologie en arbeidsorganisatie in de dienstensector*. Amsterdam: SISWO, pp. 71–103.

Van Ruysseveldt, J. and Janssens, F. (1989) 'Werkstructurering en automobielassemblage 1 en 2', in J. Van Ruysseveldt and J. von Grumbkow, *Kwaliteit van de arbeid: hedendaagse stromingen*. Assen/Heerlen: Van Gorcum/Open Universiteit, pp. 95–128.

Van Ruysseveldt, J. and Visser, J. (1996) 'Weak corporations going different ways: industrial relations in the Netherlands and Belgium', in J. Van Ruysseveldt and J. Visser (eds), *Industrial Relations in Europe*. London: Sage.

van Waarden, F. (1987a) *Het geheim van Twente: fabrikantenverenigingen in de oudste grootindustrie van Nederland 1800–1940*. Amersfoort/Leuven: Acco.

van Waarden, F. (1987b) 'Machtsvorming in een werkgeversorganisatie: de beginjaren van de Algemene Werkgevers Vereniging (1919–1925) als voorbeeld', *Tijdschrift voor Arbeidsvraagstukken*, 3:4, pp. 16–27.

van Waarden, F. (1989a) *Organisatiemacht van belangenverenigingen: de ondernemersorganisaties in de bouwnijverheid als voorbeeld*. Amersfoort/Leuven: Acco.

van Waarden, F. (1989b) 'Territorial differentiation of markets, states and business interest associations: a comparison of regional business associability in 9 countries and 7 economic sectors', in William D. Coleman and Henry J. Jacek (eds), *Regionalism, Business Interests and Public Policy: a Comparative Analysis*. London/Beverly Hills: Sage.

van Waarden, F. (1991) 'Ontstaan van ondernemersorganisaties in Nederland', *Beleid en Maatschappij*, 3, pp. 132–144.

van Zuthem, H.J. (1973) *Inleiding in de economische sociologie: mensen en machten in het economisch leven*. Amsterdam: De Bussy.

Vilrokx, J. and van Leemput, J. (1992) 'Belgium: a new stability in industrial relations?', in A. Ferner and R. Hyman (eds), *Industrial Relations in the New Europe*. Oxford: Basil Blackwell, pp. 357–392.

Visser, J. (1986) 'Die Mitgliederentwicklung der westeuropäischen Gewerkschaften. Trends und Konjunkturen 1920–1983', *Journal für Sozialforschung*, 26:1, pp. 3–34.

Visser, J. (1987) 'In search of inclusive unionism: a comparative analysis'. Thesis, University of Amsterdam (unpublished).

Visser, J. (1989) *European Trade Unions in Figures: 1913–1985*. Deventer/Boston: Kluwer.

Visser, J. (1990) *In Search of Inclusive Unionism*. Deventer/Boston: Kluwer.

Visser, J. (1991) 'Trends in union membership', in OECD, *Employment Outlook 1991*. Paris: Organization for Economic Co-operation and Development, pp. 97–134.

Visser, J. (1992) 'The strength of union movements in advanced capitalist democracies: social and organizational variations', in M. Regini (ed.), *The Future of Labour Movements*. London: Sage, pp. 17–52.

Visser, J. (1993) 'Why countries differ: explaining cross-national variation in union organization', *International Journal of Comparative Industrial Relations and Labour Law*, 9:3, pp. 206–226.

Walsh, J. (1993) 'Internalisation versus decentralisation: an analysis of recent developments in pay bargaining', *British Journal of Industrial Relations*, 31:3, pp. 409–432.

Watson, T. (1987) *Sociology, Work and Industry*. London: Routledge and Kegan Paul.

Webb, S. and Webb, B. (1913 [1897]) *Industrial Democracy*. London: Longmans.

Webb, S. and Webb, B. (1920 [1894]) *The History of Trade Unions.* London: Longmans, Green and Co.

Weber, M. (1925) *Wirtschaft und Gesellschaft,* part III. Tübingen: J.C.B. Mohr (Paul Siebeck).

Western, B. (1993) 'Postwar unionization in eighteen advanced capitalist countries', *American Sociological Review,* 58.

Wickens, P. (1987) *The Road to Nissan.* Basingstoke: Macmillan.

Williamson, O.E. (1985) *The Economic Institutions of Capitalism: Firms, Markets, Relational Contracting.* New York: Free Press.

Wolter, H. (1979) 'Aussperrung und Verhältnismäßigkeit – Kritik des "obersten Gebots" des Arbeitskampfrechts', in K.J. Bieback et al., *Streikfreiheit und Aussperrungsverbot: zur Diskussion einer gewerkschaftlichen Forderung.* Neuwied/Darmstadt: Luchterhand, pp. 224–252.

Womack, J.P., Jones, D.T. and Roos, D. (1990) *The Machine that Changed the World.* New York: Rawson.

Wood, A. (1978) *A Theory of Pay.* Cambridge: Cambridge University Press.

Woodward, J. (1965) *Industrial Organization: Theory and Practice.* Oxford: Oxford University Press.

Wootton, B. (1955) *The Social Foundations of Wage Policy.* London: Unwin University Books.

Index